THE COLUMBUS CENTRE SERIES

THE ARYAN MYTH

THE COLUMBUS CENTRE SERIES

STUDIES IN THE DYNAMICS OF PERSECUTION AND
EXTERMINATION

General Editor: Norman Cohn

ANTHONY STORR
Human Destructiveness

HENRY V. DICKS
Licensed Mass Murder

DONALD KENRICK & GRATTAN PUXON
The Destiny of Europe's Gypsies

LÉON POLIAKOV
The Aryan Myth

STUDIES IN RACE RELATIONS
ALBIE SACHS
Justice in South Africa

The Aryan Myth

A HISTORY OF RACIST AND NATIONALIST IDEAS IN EUROPE

by

LÉON POLIAKOV

Translated by

EDMUND HOWARD

1974

CHATTO · HEINEMANN
for
SUSSEX UNIVERSITY PRESS

Published by
Sussex University Press
in association with
Heinemann Educational Books
48 Charles Street
London W.1

ISBN 0 435 82215 2

© Léon Poliakov 1971

English translation © Sussex University Press
and Heinemann Educational Books 1974

Printed in Great Britain by
T. & A. Constable Ltd
Hopetoun Street
Edinburgh

To My Wife

Man is an incorrigible genealogist, who
spends his whole life in the search of a
father.

(Don Cameron Allen,
The legend of Noah, Urbana, Ill., 1949.)

ARYAN (Sanskrit). Name of the Persians,
later of the Indo-Germanic peoples, who
settled in Iran and in north-west India. . . .
The designation "Aryan" in the sense "not
of Jewish descent" is problematic.

(Trans. from *Universal-Lexikon*, Cologne, 1968.)

CONTENTS

CONTENTS

EDITORIAL FOREWORD

Following a proposal originally advanced by Mr David Astor, a research centre was set up in the University of Sussex in 1966 to investigate how persecutions and exterminations come about; how the impulse to persecute or exterminate is generated, how it spreads, and under what conditions it is likely to express itself in action. The Centre was originally called the Centre for Research in Collective Psychopathology, but later adopted the more neutral name of the Columbus Centre, after the Trust which finances it.

The Centre's work has now resulted in a series of books and monographs on subjects ranging from the roots of European nationalism and racism to the fate of the Gypsies as a minority, from the causes of the persecution of "witches" to the causes of the exterminations carried out under the Third Reich, and from the biological to the psychological roots of the very urge to persecute or to exterminate.

From the beginning, the Centre's work was designed on a multi-disciplinary basis. The disciplines represented in the present series include history, sociology, anthropology, dynamic psychology and ethology. Moreover, while the research was being done and the books written, the various authors constantly exchanged ideas and information with one another. As a result, while each book in the series belongs to a single discipline and is the work of a single author, who alone carries responsibility for it, the series as a whole is coloured by the experience of inter-disciplinary discussion and debate.

The enterprise was also designed on an international scale. Although this has been a British project in the sense that it was sponsored by a British university and that 95 per cent of its finance was also British, the people who did the research and wrote the books came from several different countries. Indeed, one of them was a Frenchman who worked in Paris throughout, another a German who worked in Berlin. Everything possible was done to exclude national bias from a study which might all too easily have been distorted by it.

The work was financed throughout by the Columbus Trust. It was originally made possible by massive donations to the Trust from

Mr David Astor, the late Lord Sieff of Brimpton and Sir Marcus Sieff, and the Wolfson Foundation, promptly followed by further most generous contributions from Mr Raymond Burton, the Rt. Hon. Harold Lever, Mr I. J. Lyons, Mr Hyam Morrison, Mr Jack Morrison, Sir Harold Samuel, the American Jewish Committee, the J. M. Kaplan Fund, Inc., and the William Waldorf Astor Foundation. His Grace the Archbishop of Canterbury, Sir Leon Bagrit, Lord Evans of Hungershall, and Messrs Myers & Company, also showed their goodwill to the enterprise by giving it financial assistance.

Since the Centre came into existence many people have devoted a great deal of time and energy to one or other of the various financial and advisory committees associated with it. They include the chairman of the Columbus Trust, the Rt. Hon. the Lord Butler of Saffron Walden; two successive Vice-Chancellors of the University of Sussex, Lord Fulton of Falmer and Professor Asa Briggs; Mr David Astor, Professor Max Beloff, Professor Sir Robert Birley, Professor Patrick Corbett, Professor Meyer Fortes, Dr Robert Gosling, Mr Ronald Grierson, Professor Marie Jahoda, Dr Martin James, Professor James Joll, the Rt. Hon. Harold Lever, Professor Barry Supple, Dr John D. Sutherland, Professor Eric Trist, Professor A. T. M. Wilson, Mr Leonard Wolfson, and the Registrar and Secretary of the University, Mr A. E. Shields, who has acted as the secretary of the Centre's Management Committee. It is a pleasure to acknowledge the support and counsel they have so willingly given.

The series also owes a great deal to the devoted service of the late Miss Ursula Boehm, who was the administrative secretary to the Centre from its inception until her death in 1970.

NORMAN COHN

AUTHOR'S PREFACE

During the team meetings of the Columbus Centre I profited greatly from the suggestions and ideas of all my colleagues, and particularly from those of the psychiatrist Henry Dicks and the historian and political scientist Wolfgang Scheffler, whose fields of study lay closest to my own. The Director of the Centre, my friend Norman Cohn, read and criticized the manuscript chapter by chapter, and many of the improvements that I made are due to his suggestions.

Gavin Langmuir, of the University of Stanford, Alexis Philonenko, of the University of Caen, Rita Thalmann, of the University of Tours, and Alain Besançon, Jean-Pierre Peter and Alberto Tenenti, all of the Sixth Section of the Ecole pratique des hautes études, have also helped greatly by their criticism. Two other friends, Roger Errera and Pierre Nora, very nobly read the entire manuscript and gave most valuable advice. The few pages of the Conclusion were written after consultation with the biologist Jacques Nunez, the anthropologist Daniel de Coppet, the Hellenist Pierre Vidal-Naquet, the exegetes Jean Zaklad and Charles Touati, the psychoanalysts Janine Chasseguet-Smirgel and Béla Grunberger.

Whatever the imperfections of this book, especially where it deals with disciplines other than my own, they would have been much greater but for the friendly assistance I received from all these sources.

ACKNOWLEDGEMENTS

The extract from Ernest Harms, *Origins of Modern Psychiatry*, 1967, is reproduced by courtesy of Charles C. Thomas, Publisher, Springfield, Illinois, U.S.A.

The extract from *The Five Nations* by Rudyard Kipling is reprinted by permission of Mrs George Bambridge, Eyre Methuen Ltd, Macmillan Co. of Canada and Doubleday & Co. Inc, New York, U.S.A.

INTRODUCTION

From about 1940 to 1944, the most important differentiation between the inhabitants of Europe was that between Aryans and Semites: the former were permitted to live, the latter were condemned to die. In most cases the sentence was actually carried out during the course of those four years. The reasoning behind this has been the subject of many books. It will be enough to quote the most influential author of the period, Adolf Hitler:

> . . . The Jew completely lacks the most essential prerequisite of a cultural people, namely the idealistic spirit. . . . He is and remains a parasite, a sponger who, like a pernicious bacillus, spreads over wider and wider areas according as some favourable area attracts him. . . . Wherever he establishes himself the people who grant him hospitality are bound to be bled to death sooner or later. . . . He poisons the blood of others but preserves his own blood un-adulterated. . . . To mask his tactics and fool his victims, he talks of the equality of all men, no matter what their race or colour may be. . . . To all external appearances, [he] strives to ameliorate the conditions under which the workers live; but in reality his aim is to enslave and thereby annihilate the non-Jewish races. . . . The black-haired Jewish youth lies in wait for hours on end, satanically glaring at and spying on the unsuspicious girl whom he plans to seduce, adulterating her blood and removing her from the bosom of her own people. The Jew uses every possible means to undermine the racial foundations of a subjugated people. . . . The Jews were responsible for bringing negroes into the Rhine-land, with the ultimate idea of bastardizing the white race which they hate and thus lowering its cultural and political level so that the Jew might dominate.[1]

The allusion to the Negro in the Rhineland, who is only slightly less obnoxious than the Jew, may be noted. In fact, for Hitler, three major groups made up the whole of mankind, of which only the Aryan was a true representative, the real master of the Universe:

... [the Aryan] is the Prometheus of mankind, from whose shining brow the divine spark of genius has at all times flashed forth, always kindling anew that fire which, in the form of knowledge, illuminated the dark night. . . . As a conqueror, he subjugated inferior races and turned their physical powers into organized channels under his own leadership, forcing them to follow his will and purpose. By imposing on them a useful, though hard, manner of employing their powers he not only spared the lives of those whom he had conquered but probably made their lives easier than these had been in the former state of so-called "freedom". . . . While he ruthlessly maintained his position as their master, he not only remained master but he also maintained and advanced civilization. . . . If we divide mankind into three categories—founders of culture, bearers of culture, and destroyers of culture—the Aryan alone can be considered as representing the first category. . . . Should he be forced to disappear, a profound darkness will descend on the earth; within a few thousand years human culture will vanish and the world will become a desert.[2]

Such was the historical philosophy of National-Socialism's leader. If it did not hinder him from becoming the master of the Third Reich —it seems on the contrary to have helped him—the reason was that similar views, sometimes with a different emphasis, had been held for two or three centuries by numerous thinkers in Germany and elsewhere.

It is well known that the division of the European population into Aryans and Semites was originally based on a confusion about the nature of men (races) and their culture (languages). This confusion was pushed so far that, at the end of the nineteenth century, the Aryan theory had achieved pride of place among men of learning alongside the theory of spatial ether. In its various forms, the Aryan theory nearly always involved a value-judgement in favour of the Aryans, and the ideologists of the Third Reich did no more than stress this bias out of all proportion. We are therefore dealing in the first place with an episode in the history of anthropology, badly warped by European ethnical egotism. The latter has very ancient pre-scientific origins. As a matter of fact, it is the simple expression of an urge which is universal among human groups or cultures; namely that of claiming a distinctive origin, an ancestry which is both high-born and glorious. In order, therefore, to understand why nineteenth-century European thought about the nature of man took this direction rather than some other, we must study the underlying emotions, and to do that we must reach into the remote past.

Let us establish one truth right away: history, geography, comparative religion and ethnography, each shows that every society claims a genealogy, a point of origin. There is no culture, however old, which has not in this manner provided itself with a spontaneous anthropology. "Looked at in this light, the pre-history of anthropology is very old, as old as the history of humanity itself."[3] Thus the members of a human group descend from a god, or a hero or an animal. The genealogical myth is therefore the first type of historical thinking and, at least in this respect, it is true to say that there are "no societies without history". Indeed, human history must have started with the quest for origins.[4]

These etiologies (= histories) were usually associated with cosmologies (= philosophies). We believe that they represent two kinds of reply to the oldest of all questions, which can also be expressed in two ways—where do I come from, and who am I? Psychoanalytic theory suggests that the first of these, the question which so obsesses all children, must have preceded and led up to the second, which is so persistent and so worrying to adults. Now, it is from the same maternal womb as my blood brothers and sisters that I receive my life and obtain my nourishment. Before we can even lay claim to common ancestors, perhaps before we emerge as individuals (if it is indeed true that the idea of "Thou" is more ancient than that of "I"), we find ourselves in the presence of the same parents. It is on this primordial foundation that all our adult loves and hatreds, the rivalries and bonds between persons of equal birth, the unions or conflicts among families, are developed in all their ambivalence.* This explains why references to a common ancestor, or to *myths of origin*, are universal and what their function is. It is to make explicit those obscure emotional forces which determine the hostilities or alliances between clans and tribes. Under a medley of ideological disguises, these forces are still operative in our industrial society, and the Nazis attempted to appropriate them when they invoked "primeval intuitions of blood and soil" (*Urahnungen von Blut und Boden*). In doing this they wanted to appeal to pre-Christian times and thus contest the belief in a common descent of all mankind which was affirmed by the Old Testament and

---

* *Das Du ist älter als das Ich* (Nietzsche). According to psychoanalysis, and to certain Hegelian insights, it is the existence of others, and in the first place of one's father, which makes one self-conscious as a separate individual.

by the Christian view of man. It is significant that even among modern
authors some, like C. G. Jung with his "Archetypes" or G. Le Bon
with his "racial soul", have devised concepts to take account of this
well-nigh indestructible psychological reality which continues to attract
our attention, even more perhaps in the atomic than in the steam age.

However, the concepts which have been advanced so far are not
really sufficient because, once the stage of those early cultures which we
call primitive has been superseded, reality becomes immensely complicated. Events which happen during the development and differentiation of societies, when states and empires arise and when social
organization and general knowledge are growing, appear to indicate
that the archaic drives, which find expression in the myths of origin,
have been either repressed or else diverted for the benefit of political
passions which draw their sustenance from quite different mythologies
or ideologies. These are tremendous problems and we shall not ourselves tackle them by proposing other concepts or elaborating another
anthropology. Our method will be historical. As we proceed we shall
try cautiously and as far as possible undogmatically, to throw light
upon the history of western society by means of depth psychology;
for the instrument which was forged by Freud, though far from
perfect, enables us to explore better than any other means, the unconscious foundations of collective beliefs.

We are bound to admit, in considering the remote European past,
that we know nothing about the myths of origin which the authors
of the rock paintings believed in, and that we are only slightly more
informed about those of the Celts and Iberians. It is quite another
matter with the Romans and the Germans. What is more their speech,
in contrast with that of other legendary ancestors, gave rise (sometimes
by mutual integration) to great cultural languages. It is with this
evident truth that we shall take up the burden of our historical enquiry.
It may be worth while to relate this contrast to the course of European
history in the first half of the twentieth century.

At first sight, it might seem strange to credit the myths of the
Eternal City or of the German forests with any part in the rise of
Mussolini or Hitler. Such a suggestion, which has the appearance of
short-circuiting fifteen centuries of history, is contrary to usual historical methods and ideas. The fact remains that the Fascists invoked
the former myth, and the Nazis the latter. If they were able to do
this with such astonishing repercussions, it was because the genealogies
corresponding to these myths have never ceased to be cultivated

throughout European history, as we shall see further on. Their influence can be discerned in the Salic Law, in the Divine Comedy, in the exegesis of Luther, in the diatribes of the philosophers of the Enlightenment, and they were to become the basis of popular mythologies in the nineteenth century before being embodied in the swastika and the lictors' fasces.

This vast subject has obviously been studied in a great number of historical works (the last of which is the admirable book by Arno Borst[5]) but no author has considered it from the point of view which we propose to adopt. Though the subject has been studied both with a sincere desire for impartiality and with a view to justifying political passions and interests of every kind, no detailed demythologizing has yet been undertaken. Contemporary specialists who have investigated Fascist or racist ideologies display no inclination to look into the remote past when searching for origins. In seeking to connect the European convulsions of the twentieth century with known or unknown pre-Christian myths, we shall venture into territory which is practically unexplored. Exceptional caution is needed: all the more so because some of the subjects we propose to deal with have been guarded, particularly since 1945, by a taboo which will not make our task any easier.

There can be no doubt that if, at the beginning of this century, the West still entertained the flattering notion of its superior civilization, often thought of as an Aryan birthright, the Hitlerite catastrophe banished such ideas from political and public life so effectively that now a fresh confusion has arisen, between science and ethics. Anti-racism has been promoted to the rank of a dogmatic orthodoxy which the present state of anthropological knowledge is unable to corroborate, but which will brook no criticism, and which is an impediment to sober thinking. This has produced a self-censorship, to a great extent retroactive, by authors of all kinds, but particularly historians who, often without knowing it, try to reinterpret the history of modern thought under this influence. *It begins to look as if, through shame or fear of being racist, the West will not admit to having been so at any time*, and therefore assigns to minor characters only (like Gobineau, H. S. Chamberlain, etc.) the role of scapegoats. A vast chapter of western thought is thus made to disappear by sleight of hand, and this conjuring trick corresponds, on the psychological or psycho-historical level, to the collective suppression of troubling memories and embarrassing truths. The last fanatics or instigators of Aryanism here play the part of the king's fool. Another way of making these troublesome reminders vanish from the field of consciousness is to level the accusation exclusively at Germany. Hence the problem of the "unredeemed past" of Germany, which quite rightly upsets a minority of German intellectuals and, in other countries, has provided food for thought for a number of critics, must be considered as a problem for the entire Western World, which refuses to probe deeply into this old ideological sore.

Such are the roots of a form of censorship which falsifies contemporary scientific thought to the point that it becomes "a weathercock shifting with ideological winds", to use the words of the American anthropologist P. L. van den Berghe.[6] Nevertheless, these ideological winds reflect the uneasiness of a society which not so long ago, in thought if not in deed, was an accomplice of Hitler's racism: a society whose repressive taboos are therefore rooted in prohibited actions, "for performing which a strong inclination exists in the unconscious".[7] One might go so far as to believe that the rioting French students, who in May 1968, when we were writing these lines, demonstrated with cries of "we are all German Jews",[8] were likewise attempting, though without realizing it, to dispose of that taboo.

The complexities of our undertaking are therefore manifold. They derive from the vast field to be covered, from the relative novelty of the method, from habits of thought which are likely to be shocked at times and which might make common cause with authentic Freudian repressions. These difficulties have imposed the plan adopted for this work, especially in the choice of a restricted geographical area of study. To make our approach as clear as possible, we shall distinguish to some extent between the distant (emotive, implicit) sources of the Aryan myth and its closer (ideological, explicit) sources. It must always be understood, however, that the former have at all times brought their dynamism to the latter. In the second part of this book we shall study the more immediate sources, those which appeared after the intellectual revolution of the Enlightenment. Here we are helped by numerous precursors who have already laboured in the field from an historical point of view, and we can confidently progress. As to the first part of the book, it will be dedicated to an examination country by country, of the myths of origin of different European peoples in which we shall perceive the remote and the confluent sources of the Aryan ideology. This recital will necessarily be shorter, and it may be that many readers will consider its main argument as no more than a point of view. Nevertheless, we are in no doubt that the study of these old stories, of the movements, cross-currents, transformations and disappearances of legends born in Judaea, in Greece, in Scythia or in India, and preserved in Rome or in Iceland, will contribute to an understanding of the European convulsions of the twentieth century.

Before relating our contemporary era to the pre-Christian past of our continent, it will be useful to recall the myth of origin propagated in the intervening period by the Church. Christianity taught that all men descended from a common ancestor, Adam, through the patriarch Noah and his sons, whose progeny is described at length in the Bible (Genesis, x). Even before the Christian era, Jewish exegetes were busy identifying the branches of ancient races, and they were doubtless the first enquirers who tried in this way to extend their knowledge to the whole of the known world.[9] According to a Talmudic saying, the common ancestry of mankind should edify all its members, for none could say to another "My father is greater than thine".[10] The Fathers of the Church took up these genealogies again and combined them with local and regional traditions. Each people was thus endowed with a specific myth of origin, though all derived from Noah, thereby giving firm expression to the overriding concept of the universal brotherhood of man.

After Noah, the lines of descent passed through Japheth, Shem or Ham, to whom there was sometimes added a fourth brother, Jenithon or Manithon. The imagination of writers was given free rein and innumerable variants were proposed. The dominant tendency, however, which conformed to certain etymological hints contained in the Bible, was to attribute the paternity of Europeans to the children of Japheth, that of the Asians to those of Shem, and that of the Africans to those of Ham. It should be noted that the latter were the objects, according to the Bible, of a mysterious curse, for they were condemned to serve their cousins as slaves ("And Canaan shall be his servant . . .", Genesis ix, 27).* Following this passage, a widely adopted theory established the division of the three main medieval social orders with Ham as the ancestor of the serfs, Shem as that of the clerks, and Japheth as that of the nobles. Thus from the earliest times the Hamites

* According to the account in Genesis (x, 6), Ham had four sons, only one of whom, Canaan, was cursed by Noah. However, it was customary to regard all Ham's descendants as being burdened with the consequences of Ham's affront to Noah.

or Blacks were placed on the bottom rung of the human hierarchy. Adopting this line of thought, an apocryphal Arab Gospel of the sixth century, in which Jesus changes some Jewish children into goats, reveals a great deal in a few words when it makes Jesus address their mothers as follows: "The children of Israel have the same rank among the peoples as the Negroes."[11]

In the course of our story, which will take us through country after country from western Europe to Russia, we shall often have to refer to these basic genealogies.

Part One

EARLY MYTHS OF ORIGIN

CHAPTER ONE

SPAIN

The Gothic Myth

The most unusual feature of Spanish history, when it is contrasted with that of other great western nations, is its centuries-long domination by the Moslems. The invasion of 711, however, makes it easy to forget the invasion three centuries earlier when, in the wake of Swabian and Vandal tribes, the Visigoths conquered the country and made it their home. Yet this conquest left an equally powerful trace in the history and traditions of the Spaniards.

Earlier, the Roman domination had so far effaced indigenous culture that the wholly Latinized inhabitants of the peninsula had retained only the vaguest feeling of having other roots and of being descended from Iberian forefathers. (But we shall not consider the details of these tribal and regional memories nor tarry to expound the exceptional case of Basque language and culture.) Once they were converted to Christianity the Iberians became aware that, together with the rest of humanity, they had Adam and Noah for ancestors.

After the Germanic invasions, Archbishop Isidore of Seville, the most erudite and influential writer in pre-Carolingian Europe, undertook to relate the conquered Iberians more closely to their Visigoth conquerors by deriving the former from Tubal and the latter from Magog, both of them sons of Japheth. In his writings he did not hesitate to assign pre-eminence to the conquerors who had, not so long ago, enslaved the Eternal City and thereby gained a title to universal overlordship.[1] Nevertheless, he bestowed on the conquered the prestige of becoming their cousins. As a faithful supporter of the Visigothic dynasty, Isidore of Seville was probably inspired by the hope of peaceful co-existence. Examples are not wanting in anthropology and in history, beginning with the legends of Alba and of Rome, to illustrate the fusion of two myths of origin in order to achieve blood brotherhood. The union was, according to many Spanish historians, never successfully effected, and one of the most illustrious of these writers, Menendez y Pelayo, declared that the Visigoths were not

Spaniards. There was no lack of contrary views drawing the argument, like Isidore of Seville, towards the German camp. From 1780 onwards, Hertzberg, who was the first Prussian apostle of Germanism, stated that "the Spanish and Portuguese nations are descended first and foremost from the Visigoths, the Vandals and the Swabians, with some addition of indigenous elements from ancient Spain, of Romans and of Saracens . . . one can certainly justify their being described as Germans".[2] In 1868, the *Anthropological Review* of London assured its readers that "a Spanish family, which had remained completely blond and purely Gothic and had retained for centuries a position of official supremacy, had been discovered in Yucatan".[3] Again in 1944 the Swedish historian, J. Nordstrom, wrote that "the expansion of Christian Spain was an expansion of the Gothic race". The history of the Goths was the subject of much study in Sweden from which country they were traditionally held to have derived. When the perspicacious Americo Castro in turn criticized Nordstrom, he wrote that "the aspiration to be Goths shows that the Spaniards of the Middle Ages were nothing of the kind; nor was the country as yet Gothic which they reconquered and populated once again".[4] But these pacific disputes between scholars, even in a country so prone to internal divisions as modern Spain, never really convulsed the contestants. It was not always thus, however. If these erudite polemics appear to be completely isolated from the time when, according to Americo Castro, the Spaniards aspired to be Goths, it is because, in the newly unified Spain of Ferdinand and Isabella which claimed to be wholly descended from Tubal, genealogical rivalries had an altogether different meaning.

At this point Spain's Moslem or Judaeo-Moslem past intervenes. After the Christian *Reconquista*, the baptized descendants of Moslems and Jews found themselves branded with dishonour, and laws for maintaining purity of blood divided Spaniards into two castes, the pure-blooded Old Christians and New Christians whose blood was tarnished. The dividing line was not the Germanic or Iberian stock of the remote ancestor but his orthodoxy or his heterodoxy. Spanish theologians worked out a doctrine according to which the false beliefs of both the Moors and Jews had soiled their blood, and this stain or "nota" had been transmitted by heredity to their furthest descendants, who were set apart in the almost untouchable caste of the New Christians or *conversos*. Thus, in defiance of the dogma proclaiming the regenerative virtue of baptism, an institutional form of racism made its first appearance in European history. The theologians who invented this doctrine did not dispute that both categories of Christians were descended from the common father, Adam, but they did maintain that the rejection of Christ had corrupted the *conversos* biologically. Traditionally, the *conversos* were predominant in crafts and commerce, and economic rivalries were cloaked by sanctimonious hatred or became a pretext for it. This deep division, which was both economic and genealogical, has certainly weighed heavily on the Iberian peninsula, especially in turning the Old Christians away from productive work and in stimulating a frantic desire for ennoblement which even reached down to the labouring class; it also delayed the rise of a middle class. It seems clear that, in favourable circumstances, certain paratribal longings can get enough free rein to refashion ideologies at will and to bear incisively on the course of history.[5]

This singular chapter of Spanish history, a legacy of its Moslem past, has obscured the traces of a socio-racial cleavage which goes back to pre-Moslem times. It is none the less true that the Gothic myth has preserved some devotees even in modern Spain. In making a comparison between the Gothic and Frankish myths the French anthropologist Bory de Saint-Vincent wrote in 1827: "The Goths have acquired such a reputation that a Castilian does not consider himself a noble if he is not descended from a Gothic family. Such a misconception is similar to that of the minor nobility between the Rhine and the Pyrenees who don't want to be Gauls and declare that they are Franks."[6] The comparison was rather lame because in modern France the "controversy about the two races" developed, as we shall see, with quite a different degree of intensity. Nevertheless, in its article under the heading "Godo", the Dictionary of the Spanish Academy still defines: "*Hacerse de los godos*", to boast of being noble; "*Ser godo*", to be of noble family.* At the beginning of the twentieth century, the Latin-Americans called those Spaniards who were obsessed with ideas of nobility, *Godos*.[7] Here the term had taken on a mainly ironic quality, and this was already the case during Spain's Golden Age. Cervantes, for example, put this gloss on Don Quixote's character, *Godo Quijote, illustre y claro*.[8] The death-knell which was being tolled for Spanish chivalry was sounding also for the Gothic myth. But in the Middle Ages the knights and princes who prepared the way for the Reconquest, took their Visigothic past as seriously as their feudal status.

* These details were kindly furnished by M. Marcel Bataillon.

On this subject, the Spanish historian, José Maravall, recently wrote:

> The illusion of the Gothic legacy has certainly had the quality of
> a myth. To begin with there was in all probability no question
> of explaining an actual fact, but there was a tradition designed to
> give a meaning to a course of conduct and to a series of warlike
> encounters. Finally, in the course of our medieval history, this
> tradition acquired the force of a collective belief. In fact, if a
> number of kings and princes behaved as they did it was because
> they heard on all sides that they were heirs to the Goths. This was
> the cause of the strikingly dynamic character of our medieval
> history which, more than any other, is like an arrow shot at
> random across the centuries. . . .

He adds later on:

> The tradition of the Gothic heredity, which eventually spread
> across the whole of Spain, obviously cannot be regarded as a true
> account of the events in Spain during the Middle Ages. But if we
> are going to study the concept of Spain at that time, we must
> recognize in that tradition one of the most vital factors in this
> concept and in the political action deriving from it.[9]

The influence exercised by "Gothic heredity", as described to us so
perspicaciously by Sr Maravall (though searching, so it seems, for the
right words), would be called in Freudian terminology a psychic
reality. In other words, everything happened as though the Christian
princes of medieval Spain, inspired by the conviction that they were
Goths, made every effort to behave like the offspring of a conquering
race. This clarifies Americo Castro's analysis of the Spaniards, who
wanted to be Goths though they knew they were not, and therefore
attempted to identify themselves with kings who based their claims
to pre-eminence on their unmatched descent. In 1436, eight centuries
after the Visigoths invaded Spain, the delegate of John I of Castile still
claimed at the Council of Basle that his king was a Visigoth by blood,
so as to obtain precedence over the envoys of other princes, including
those descended from the "northern Goths".[10]

It is important to note that the name Goth enjoyed great prestige
throughout Europe. From earliest times the Fathers of the Church and
the chroniclers had endowed it with a glamour which indicated the
fear and awe inspired in them by the conquerors and new masters
of Rome—the Gothic barbarians whom they alternatively flattered
and cursed. Saint Ambrose, for example, compared them to the fearful

giants, Gog and Magog, mentioned in the Bible, while Saint Augustin saw in them an instrument of Divine Providence, and Salvian contrasted their innocent, youthful behaviour with that of the decadent Romans. Such examples could be multiplied and they all show what a tremendous impression was produced on contemporaries by the fall of Rome.[11]

It is from these writings that the new and versatile fortunes of the word Gothic were originally derived. After the Renaissance it was used to designate all that was outworn and discredited (Gothic barbarism) or, conversely, all that was sublime and eternally young (Gothic freedom). Aesthetic appreciation (Gothic cathedrals) became the final arbiter in this debate. Meanwhile, in England, "Gothicism" enjoyed a spell of popularity as a synonym for "Germanism"; and it fared still better in Sweden, the legendary home of the Goths, where they were also identified with the Germanic people.[12] The Emperor Charles V is reputed to have held that almost the entire nobility of Europe was descended from the Scandinavian Goths.[13] It is well known that in Germany "Gothic script" is still used to designate an obsolete lettering considered the national form of writing. In all countries, these strongly evocative terms revived memories of half-legendary events. These events, known in Romanic languages by the name of barbarian invasions, are described in German—and the distinction is not without significance—as migrations of peoples (*Völkerwanderungen*). In this wise, different epochs, cultures and languages spoke, each in a distinctive manner, of a past which was to become the age of reference for the patriotic mythologies of the principal European nations.

In conclusion, we may note the old tendency in Spain to over-value Germanic blood and to give preference to descent from Magog over the indigenous posterity of Tubal. We shall find similar trends in other countries. These were manifested to begin with by the establishment of descent from other Biblical characters. Thereafter, once the Church's influence had waned and the universal first parent, Adam, was relegated to the lumber-room of discarded ideas, those same tendencies reappeared under the guise of the nationalist or racist ideologies of modern times, which also spoke of common (historical or biological) origins. In Spain, where the Gothic myth went into an early decline, it was succeeded by a form of racism which was elaborated and expressed in theological terms. The originality of Spanish history, from our point of view, could be highly instructive. For it was anxiety about the purity of faith, at a time when the country was reaching unity, that led to the establishment of the Spanish Inquisition. The myth of purity of blood and lineage, however, soon made a mockery of the religious ideal. The real confrontation was thereafter between a pure caste, derived from the line of Japheth, and an impure stock which was later characterized as semitic. This contest was carried on in the course of a history filled with internecine struggles which, muted in the Baroque period, though ferocious in the twentieth century, were caused by a great number of factors about which historians differ widely. What is certainly true—and it is well to be clear about this from the start—is that the aggressive drives of the people in Spain were mostly so directed as to produce internal upheavals.

CHAPTER TWO

FRANCE

The Controversy about the Two Races

If fortune has endowed any name with a more glorious history than that of Goth, it must surely be that of Frank. No German word has pushed out more roots into the soil of Europe, from the Franche-Comté to Franconia, from Frankfurt to Villefranche. The concepts of freedom, integrity and power are associated with it in all western languages. *Gesta Dei per Francos* was the name once given to the Crusades. The East also adopted this appellation where, even to this day, a Westerner is called a "Frank" or a "Frenk" which may be regarded as evidence of the wide range of French influence. A slave who received his freedom was "enfranchised" and, in this sense, the emancipation of Negroes and of Jews by the French Revolution was a true enfranchisement. An apologist of the *ancien régime* was quite right when he wrote in 1815: "Etymology is related to what is most noble and glorious in human feelings."[1] "Qui estoit franc est devenu esclave" was the translation into the vernacular of the Bible passage in Maccabees I, 2.[2] This antonym may be expressed in another way as well—the Frank, a Germanic man and a free man, may equally be contrasted with the serf (= servus) as with the slave (= Slav). Thus the key-words in French political history slyly hint at the superiority of the German stock over the Latins and over the Slavs. This was a superiority both of race and of class, because the two notions of upper and lower classes and of superior and inferior races, which are quite distinct today, were not so easy to disentangle when it was a question of contrasting conquering peoples with those they had conquered.

In this way, while the invading Germans and the Gallo-Romans became inevitably integrated on the soil of France, the former lost their tribal or racial characteristics and became the core of a privileged class of free men, who were the future nobles. Nevertheless these Franks, or enfranchised men, went on insisting on their congenital or hereditary superiority for several generations after they had been converted. It was in the eighth century that a rousing prologue was added to the Salic Law, as follows: "Illustrious race, founded by God Himself, strong in arms, steadfast in alliance, wise in counsel, of singular beauty and fairness, noble and sound in body, daring, swift, awesome, converted to the Catholic faith. . . ."

Faced with such a judgement passed upon itself by the ruling class, the entire people aspired to the prestige of Germanism. It is enough to quote as evidence the disappearance, from the seventh century onwards, of the old, Latin Christian names to make way for names of Germanic origin. Of the same origin are the words describing the institution of the French monarchy or the terms relating to war and armaments.[3] This prestige, imagined as inherent in the blood and transmitted by heredity, has continued to operate in France, as we shall see, up to modern times.

In fact, the cultural and biological fusion between Franks and Gallo-Romans was completed at the end of the first millennium. This was certainly not achieved without difficulties and it was to smooth these away that some anonymous clerics* in the seventh century suggested a common genealogy to relate the two lines of descent, as had been done in Spain by Isidore of Seville. This linking-up by blood relationship enables us to distinguish more clearly the rules by which the national myths of origin were elaborated.

The Roman conquerors, during the second century B.C., faced by the cultural superiority of the Greeks, were most anxious to claim a line of descent which was both similar to and distinct from the Grecian, so they related themselves to the fugitive Trojans (through the myth of Aeneas, the founder of Troy whom Virgil extolled in the Aeneid). A millennium later, the Merovingian genealogists resumed and completed the process: since the Gallo-Romans were reputed to be of Trojan origin, the Franks could also claim the same ancestry though by a different line, namely, through such legendary characters as Frankon, the son of Hector, and his great-grandson Pharamund, who were the ancestors of the future French nobility and of the "French". Inevitably, the Trojan myth developed a number of different versions. Under the Carolingian mayors of the palace, for instance, several chroniclers, inspired no doubt by the legend of Romulus and Remus, affiliated the Romans and the Franks to the hostile brothers Vassus and Francus respectively, with a view to relating the vassals to their sovereign lords.[4] It goes without saying that in all these versions the

* Thus the so-called chronicle of Fredegar. Gregory of Tours was still ignorant of the Trojan genealogy.

Franks and the Trojans were descended from the Biblical Patriarchs and from Adam, the common father of all mankind. Where an intervening link was called for it was supplied by a grandson of Japheth, Kittim. At the end of the Middle Ages, however, further speculation about the relationship between "Celts", "Gauls" and "Galatians" suggested another line of descent which led from the Trojans to Gomer, Japheth's first-born. Thus the uncertain genealogy of the French people already appeared in outline as a confrontation between the Gallic land and its Germanic conqueror, between Gaul and the "sang troyen et germain" of which Ronsard sang. A great medievalist, Marc Bloch, wrote: "The realization that our name of Frenchmen was the name of conquerors and invaders seems to have given rise early on, among the more reflective of our thinkers, to feelings of almost tragic anxiety."⁵ This anxiety, as it became intensified with the passing of the generations, may well have played a traumatic role in French history.

Under the Carolingian Empire, the name of Frank acquired fresh prestige, even on a European scale. Then the Frankish kings became masters of the Continent, where henceforth a distinction was made between "Western France" and "Eastern France". In Otto Freising's well-known chronicle, the Germans are mentioned as a branch of the Frankish people.⁶ Again, in the twelfth century, Frederick Barbarossa, who had Charlemagne canonized, called himself "Emperor of the Franks and the Teutons".⁷ So great was the power of the Frankish myth under the Carolingians that in the Slav languages a king is "korol" or "krol", derived from the German name, Karl. Hence while the Slav is a "slave" in western languages, the western emperor is the "king" in the Slav languages. Napoleon, the better to establish his First Empire, posed as the successor of Charlemagne. (Some of his decrees began with the preamble "Forasmuch as Charlemagne, our predecessor . . .".) Richard Wagner wrote in praise of the Frankish myth that 'its profound meaning was in the primitive conscience of the Frankish people, in the soul of this royal race . . . which commanded respect and was everywhere considered to be of a superior nature".⁸ Was it not this idea of royal dynastic greatness that, in our day, prompted Charles de Gaulle, in Germany, to invoke the myth of Charlemagne, the giant, for the purposes of his policy of French *grandeur*?*

If, however, popular French annalists of the Middle Ages placed

---

* One may wonder what influence the combination of such a Christian name with such a surname had on the dreams and destiny of General de Gaulle.

Charlemagne at the apex of French history by naturalizing him and if both the writers and the nobility cultivated the Trojan legend and the memory of Pharamund, the predominant tendency of the period was to emphasize what united, and not what divided, Christians. Rather than the lateral or national branches of the collective genealogical tree, it was the central trunk, common to all men, which served to edify the masses. The portals and the stained-glass windows of the churches showed Adam or Noah; Charlemagne rarely, and never Frankon or Pharamund. The French bothered little about whether they were descended from Japheth or the Trojans. They were Christians. Moreover, it was generally understood, at least among the learned, that the human race had once spoken a universal language which was current before the dispersion of Babel, and that this language was Hebrew. There was general agreement as to the place where humanity was cradled. It was in Judaea, on the confines of the Holy Land.

In the sixteenth century, at the threshold of modern times, the problem of national origins or of the lateral genealogical branches became prominent. During the Renaissance the influence of classical antiquity began to rival that of the sacred scriptures; and scholars, while still claiming descent from Adam, went to school with their great Greek and Latin ancestors. The medieval genealogies now began to be called in question. The doubts of the humanists were directed first of all to the Trojan myth, but though Ronsard expounded it in his *Franciade* (1572) without believing in it very fervenlty[9], it proved so resistant that scholars in the nineteenth century were still affirming its truth in order to bolster up their theory about the Asian origin of Europeans.[10] The Biblical myth, integrated with revealed religion, seemed even more unshakeable. However, by instigating a relentless investigation of Biblical texts which brought to light contradictions and improbabilities, the Reformation sowed the first seeds of doubt.[11] And there was another reason why attention was focussed on national origins. Beyond the Rhine, German humanists were already beginning to advance their claims to universal dominion. The *Germania* of Tacitus, discovered shortly before, as well as the annals describing the German invasions, supplied them with an arsenal of simple and powerful arguments which were well adapted to the reasoning of the age. In order to refute them, new theories began to spring up in France, each one more ingenious and unexpected than the last, but the diversity of opinions shows how difficult it was to put up a case when confronted with the title-deeds invoked by the Holy Germanic Empire.

Some writers, especially Calvinists such as Jean du Tillet or François Hotman, who were hostile to royal prerogatives, accepted the idea of Germanic origins and supremacy. Thus du Tillet wrote:

> Those who described the French as being truly of German origin did them more honour than those who believed they were descended from the Trojans, since honour is due only to virtue. For no nation has suffered so little corruption of its morality, nor striven so mightily and for so long to maintain its freedom by arms, as the German nation. . . .[12]

Still greater was the number of historians who, as good supporters of the dynasty, relied on the equation Franks = French in order to "francize" Charlemagne. To this end they appealed to the old chronicles according to which Charlemagne spoke and dressed in the Frankish fashion (*more francorum*). Nevertheless, there likewise appeared at this time, in the writings of François de Belleforest (d. 1583), the phrase "our ancestors the Gauls". This forgotten author actually justified the "usurpation" of Hugh Capet on grounds of "divine providence, which purposed to restore to the native Gauls authority over their country and take it away from German and Frankish foreigners who had usurped it until that time".[13] The learned orientalist Guillaume Postel (d. 1581), who introduced the study of Hebrew into France, also assigned priority to the Gauls and considered them genealogically more eminent than the Germans.[14] After making this first appearance, those Gaulish ancestors vanished and did not emerge again until the end of the *ancien régime*.

Indeed, the most popular theory and the most ingenious, against which Leibniz was still inveighing at the beginning of the eighteenth century, was that of re-migration propounded by Jean Bodin. This famous humanist maintained that in the Gallic language ("though not in Latin, Greek and even less Hebrew") *frank* meant free or independent. Moreover, relying on a passage in Caesar,[15] he concluded that a number of Gauls, weary of the Roman yoke, had emigrated beyond the Rhine to regain their freedom, thus becoming Franks, and that when the Roman Empire began to disintegrate they returned under their new name to the mother-country to liberate their brothers. The honour of the Gauls was thus saved.[16]

Etymological speculation and childish word games of this kind have been rife in western history ever since the Fathers of the Church, but it was the humanists of the Renaissance who first utilized them in

B

the service of a new-born chauvinism. It may be remarked, further-more, that Bodin's theory attributes to the Frankish Gauls certain virtues which were unknown to the enslaved Gauls. A century later one of his followers, Audigier, wrote: "It will therefore be found, unexpectedly though undeniably, that our nation had the same origin as that race, the most awesome, the most daring and the most illustrious which the world has ever seen."[17]

Thus during the reign of Louis XIV, historians were at one in reserving their praises for the Franks to the exclusion of all other races. We can cite the example of two well-known writers. In the words of Loyseau: "The victorious Franks were of noble birth; the vanquished Gauls were of common stock. The conquering Franks claimed for themselves the profession of arms, the administration of public offices, the enjoyment of their fiefs."[18] And Mézéray described them as follows: "They were a proud people, tough, aggressive but without any hint of cruelty and far more humane than the other northern races. Nevertheless, they were jealous to the last degree as to their honour and their freedom and, as they were unable to endure a moment's tranquillity, they were constantly engaged in raids against the other provinces of Germany and against the Gauls."[19] Moreover, in Mézéray's view, the Franks entered Gaul as liberators and found the country "well disposed to yield them homage". This view hence-forth became the official truth, and respect for the genealogical tree of Frankish descent had to be observed. A royal historian, the Abbé Daniel, ran into a certain amount of trouble for excluding Pharamund, Chlodio and Meroveus from the list of Louis XIV's ancestors.[20]

After this period, moreover, historians did not as a rule look back beyond the Germanic origins of the French nation. The detailed genealogies, which traced all the peoples of the world through each generation back to Adam, were a thing of the past in the century of Cartesian logic. It was then that the idea of the nation became separated from the notion of humanity at large. As for the theologians and philosophers, they deemed it sufficient to make only a passing bow to Japheth, the common ancestor of Europe. Thus Bossuet wrote: "Japheth, from whom most of the people of the West are descended, has remained famous among us", while Pascal declared: "The science of genealogy starts with Japheth". There is no further mention of the subject even by Pascal.[21] The unbroken line and succession of the Patriarchs could not hold together against the rational spirit of the age, and it was through the gap thus created that the speculations of the Age of Enlightenment as to the origin of Man would sweep, to give rise in due course to the Aryan myth. Biblical pedigrees still commanded the attention of certain clerics, but only of the few who insisted on a literal interpretation of the Book of Genesis and who, inspired by this fundamentalist approach, kept up an interest in pre-Roman times.

One of these, a Benedictine monk from Brittany called Dom Pezron, while seeking around 1700 to "show France her cradle", became the first Celtomaniac in the country. In a century when, as he put it, "more attention was devoted to reason than to authority", Dom Pezron did not hesitate to assert that "a couple of words of Scripture will throw more light on the subject than all the writings and histories" of the rationalists. As for himself, he would "defend the true Faith". In the course of commenting on the ninth and tenth chapters of Genesis—"which are often studied all too superficially"—and supported by the Fathers of the Church, he re-established the claims of Gomer to be an ancestor of the Gauls, whom he identified as the Titans of Greek mythology. Pursuing his research into the family tree, he also quoted the Jewish chronicler Josippon:

> According to this author, the descendants of Gomer are the French who inhabit the country round the Seine. *Filii Gomer sunt Franci qui habitant in terra Franciae ad flumen Seinae.* Thus speaks this circumcised man. It is clear that when he says sons of Gomer he means the Gauls whom he calls Franks, or Frenchmen who live on the Seine, to distinguish them from the Franks who inhabit Germany.

We recognize here the semantic confusions of the Carolingian age.

Dom Pezron placed the original homeland of the Titans "in the Asiatic provinces . . . and not in those of Gaul which are in the far West and which were not peopled until a long time afterwards". He even pinpointed this homeland in upper Asia, in the fabulous region of Bactriana between Media and Tartary. "We are descended", wrote Dom Pezron, "from this renowned race for we were born in the territory of the Gauls."[22] During the following century, the Romantic Celtomaniac, Henri Martin, hailed Dom Pezron as a great precursor who was endowed with powers of divination.[23] His contemporaries, with a few exceptions,* had nothing but contempt for such antiquated fables. The stage was now set, in the quest for origins of the French people, for the *Controversy about the Two Races*.

* The most notable of these was Pierre-Daniel Huet, Tutor to the Dauphin and Bishop of Avranches (see p. 140).

The battle was launched by the champions of the nobility, the powers and privileges of which were being eroded by royal absolutism. To start with, this disgruntled class secretly circulated political propaganda including subversive pamphlets. In the name of freedom and equality, which they claimed for their own exclusive benefit, they made use of the old argument about race. It was for this reason that they decried the name of Gaul. The first example of this kind of pamphlet, published in London in 1740, is attributed to Abbé Jean le Laboureur (d. 1675). In this he writes: "The French were all equal and it was only merit which distinguished one from another." The Gauls, "after losing their territories by the laws of war, submitted to conquerors and remained subjugated. . . .[24]" The point was emphasized by Comte Henri de Boulainvilliers (d. 1722):

> To begin with, the French were all free and completely equal and independent . . . and they fought so long against the Romans only to be sure of preserving their treasured freedom. . . . After the conquest of the Gauls, they were the only recognized nobles, the only people recognized as lords and masters. . . .

This quality was restricted to them alone since it was innate and "the favours of monarchs can offer only titles and privileges; they cannot make any other blood flow in the veins than that which is inherited".[25] The argument is directed as much against royal power as against the ennobled commoner.

These ideas are to be found in the *Mémoires* of Saint-Simon. He too justified the privileges of his caste by right of conquest, as in the following passage:

> From this fact is derived the nobility, a unique body in the State whose members were at first called men at arms and then nobles in contrast with the vanquished who, by reason of their total servitude, were called serfs.

We can also quote the learned Nicolas Fréret whose dissertation on the origin of the French, though not written with any polemical intent, was followed for no apparent reason by a period of imprisonment in the Bastille in 1714.* After the death of Louis XIV there was no lack of refutation of these arguments, but even the conciliatory and widely accepted theories of the Abbé Dubos[26] merely rehabilitated the Romans, while leaving the Gauls to cut a rather sorry figure. The

---

* According to Marc Bloch (*Sur les grandes invasions*, etc., *op. cit.*) Fréret was imprisoned in 1714 on the pretext of having attacked the Trojan theory.

popular opinion favoured Frankish supremacy, and the views which are to be found scattered throughout the *Esprit des Lois* may be regarded as typical.

In a number of passages in that book Montesquieu describes the ancient Germans as being the forebears of the French. He praises the "admirable simplicity" of these ancestors as well as their tradition of liberty and independence. He ascribes to them a delicate sense of honour. "The German peoples were no less sensitive in matters of honour than we ourselves; they were even more so. . . . For these ancestors of ours were exceedingly susceptible to an affront." As to their courage, "it would seem, if Tacitus is to be believed, that they acknowledged two capital offences only; they hanged their traitors and they drowned their cowards". Finally, borrowing an opinion which was commonly held on the other side of the Channel, Montesquieu attributed English parliamentary institutions, which he recommended as a model for France, to these Germanic virtues.[27]

These views drew a slashing retort from Voltaire. "Who were these Franks", he asked, "whom Montesquieu of Bordeaux calls our forebears? They were, like the other northern barbarians, ferocious beasts in search of pasture, of shelter and of some protection against the snow. . . . Are the Houses of Lords and of the Commons or the Court of Equity to be found in the forest? One would scarcely have thought so. No doubt the English have to thank German customs for their fleets and commerce. Perhaps also they owe their fine manufactured goods to the admirable habits of the Germans who preferred living on the fruits of rapine to working."[28]

With equal zest Voltaire scourged other upholders of the Germanic pedigree. "Who were", he wrote, "these Franks? Where did these people come from who, though few in number, in a very short time conquered the whole of Gaul, which Caesar was unable entirely to subdue in less than ten years? I have just read an author who begins with these words: the Franks from whom we descend. One moment, my friend! Who tells you that you are descended in a direct line from the Franks? Hildvic or Clodvic, whom we now call Clovis, probably had no more than twenty thousand men, ill clad and poorly armed, when he conquered eight or ten million *Welsche** or Gauls who were held in servitude by three or four Roman legions. There is not a

* The *Welsche* (or *Welsches* in French) were a Gallic tribe who were neighbours of the Germans to the south. The name came to be applied by the Germans as a term of contempt for Latins in general whether Italian or French.

single great family in France which can produce, I will not say the least proof, but the least presumption of being descended from a Frankish founder."[29]

This reprimand was addressed, it seems, to the Abbé Velly who was the author of a popular *History of France* (1768). It might equally have been directed to Joseph Barre, who in his *History of Germany* (1748), stated that he had every right to consider Germany his country because it was the cradle of his ancestors; or to the Comte de Buat who began his *Histoire ancienne des peuples de l'Europe* (1722) with the assertion: "The ancient peoples of Europe, whom we describe as barbarians, were our ancestors." Those ancestors still had partisans under the Second Empire like, for example, Ozanam in his *Études Germaniques* or Moet de la Forte-Maison in *Les Francs*, while the classic translations of Burnouf have perpetuated them in our own times.[30] In the event, Voltaire, that exploder of myths, was an isolated figure. He was perhaps the only man who could have expressed himself so trenchantly in his own time. The subject was indeed still a sensitive one since it affected the origins of the aristocracy. "The pride of our great families might be understandably wounded", wrote the Abbé Mably, "were they told that they were part of the common people, at a time when aristocratic rank already existed. But that they should be offended at not being noble when there was as yet no nobility would be a kind of madness. If this mortifies them, I must ask forgiveness. . . ."[31]

One can discern the passions, or even the taboos, already prevailing. The old feudal nobility of the sword claimed a different descent from that of the commonalty who were of Gallo-Roman ancestry. While unable to compete with them, other social classes, in default of blue blood derived from the Crusaders, were able to invoke their Germanic ancestors, thus identifying themselves with the same legendary forebears. This was done by the bourgeois Barre and Velly and by Montesquieu, a nobleman of the gown. These men were able, in spite of their exclusion from the upper caste, to participate in its lineage, which was that of the king, the father of all Frenchmen. Besides which, their appeal was to a traditional belief, to a solidly established myth of descent. When, between 1755 and 1759, the Parliament of Paris came into conflict with the power of the Crown, it likewise invoked the precedent of the Frankish assemblies.[32]

It was in these circumstances that the myth of Germanic supremacy, now coloured in favour of one theory and now of another, continued to command the support of the majority in France during the Enlightenment. One widely held view was that, at the time of Dagobert or of Charlemagne, the Gallo-Romans were allowed to become Franks or Frenchmen and by this means were able to infiltrate into the ranks of the nobility. This was what the Abbé Mably tried to prove in his *Observations on the History of France* (1765) which was for a long time considered authoritative. In substance, what he maintained was that the Franks were tolerant barbarians who admitted the natives into their ranks, while the latter, accustomed to servitude, preferred to go on in their previous condition.

> The long despotism of the Emperors debased their spirit so that while some of them did not wish to become free others, through ill-considered vanity, retained the closest attachment to the laws and customs of their nation. Habit forges chains which it is difficult to break.[33]

Diderot's *Encyclopaedia* made a distinction between three kinds of nobles:

> Three kinds of nobles existed at the beginning of the monarchy: those descended from the Gaulish chivalry who followed the profession of arms; others who derived from the Roman magistrature and who combined the exercise of arms with the administration of justice, civil government or finance; and the third were the Franks, all dedicated to the practice of arms, who were exempt from all personal servitudes and taxes. For this they were called *Franks*, as opposed to the rest of the population which consisted almost entirely of serfs. This franchise was understood as the hallmark of *nobility* itself so that *Frank*, *Freeman* or *Nobleman* were normally synonymous expressions.[34]

Whether through tradition or verbal association, the Franks continued to be considered as superior beings, descendants of a superior nobility. Under the Restoration, the Comte de Montlosier made a distinction between the "old Franks who exercised the noble professions exclusively" and the "new Franks who were specially dedicated to the lucrative professions".[35] This distinction reminds one of the Spanish division between the Old and the New Christians. Perhaps the Comte de Montlosier was inspired by this example.

To be sure, the writers of the Enlightenment, who described both the Franks and the Gauls as barbarians, tried to be impartial to each. The Abbé Mably exclaimed: "To what excesses did not the French surrender themselves, combining the ferocious vices inherited from the Germans with the cowardly vices derived from the Gauls?" But it is human nature to admit more readily to being fierce than to being afraid. In 1787, the Abbé Brizard summarized Mably's book in a panegyric after his death. "In it one observes freedom emerging with them (the Franks) from the forests of Germany to snatch the Gauls from the oppression and yoke of the Romans."[36] It is interesting to note that, on the eve of the Revolution, the Controversy about the Two Races became a triangular dispute involving the Roman conquerors, the enslaved Gauls and the Frankish liberators.

Immediately after the summoning of the States General, the same kind of argument could be found in Sieyès's famous pamphlet, *Qu'est-ce que le Tiers Etat?* It was precisely because he wanted an end to the ancient abuses that Sieyès declared: "The Third Estate must not be afraid to look back to the past . . . it will once more become noble by taking its turn as conqueror." For this advocate of the *bourgeoisie*, the question was one of abolishing the privileges of the nobility, even of carrying out a purge on the body of the nation if that should prove necessary.

> Why should [the Third Estate] not relegate to the forests of Franconia all those families which persist in the foolhardy pretence of being descended from the race of the conquerors and of having succeeded to the rights of conquest? The Nation, thus purged, would, I believe, be able to console itself by the thought that it was constituted of the descendants of the Gauls and the Romans only. In truth, if one insists on distinguishing one manner of birth from another, might we not persuade our luckless fellow-citizens that the descent which they derive from the Gauls or the Romans is at least as worthy as that which they might have received from the Cimbri, the *Welsche** and other savages who emerged from the swamps and forests of ancient Germany?

Once Germany had been thus dismissed as the cradle of the nation, two other possibilities remained, Gaul or Rome. It is scarcely necessary to recall how the leaders of the French Revolution, following in the wake of Rousseau and the Encyclopaedists, were apt to appeal to republican Rome as their guide and chose Cato or Brutus rather than Brennus or Vercingetorix as their ancestors. The customs, the arts, the political vocabulary (*dictatorship*, *consulate*) of that time were inspired by classical Antiquity. Nevertheless, the Gauls were not without their supporters. The "first grenadier of the French Republic" La Tour

* *Sic!*

d'Auvergne, for instance, was enthusiastic about Gallic origins[37] and wanted "at last to restore the Gauls to the list of the nations since they were an illustrious race which seemed to have been cancelled from it", even though "from their earliest beginnings they had vied with Rome". La Tour d'Auvergne even attempted to prove that the Gallic tongue was the original language of the human species. A certain Ducalle pushed this kind of reasoning to its limits when writing to the administrators of the department of Paris as follows:

> How long will you endure that we bear the infamous name of French . . . now that we have at last thrown off our shackles? While they repudiate the offer of brotherhood, we make a show of extravagant servility in calling ourselves by their name. Are we really the offspring of their impure blood? God forbid, citizens! We are descended from the pure-blooded Gauls. . . .[38]

This appeal, however, had no sequel—any more than the efforts of certain intellectuals under the Empire, who created a Celtic Academy and proposed to publish a "kind of Celtic Bible, where everything which Antiquity has handed down to us about our earliest ancestors will be gathered together".[39] The Frankish cause, however, was supported by far more illustrious champions. The greatest of these was Catherine II of Russia who wrote to Grimm in April 1793.

> Do you not see what is happening in France? The Gauls are driving out the Franks. But you will see the Franks return and then the ferocious beasts thirsting for human blood will either be exterminated or forced to hide wherever they can.[40]

The dispute was renewed during the Bourbon restoration when revolutionary thought began systematically to lay the myth of the Germanic Franks with the help of the new myth about the Gauls. No doubt the overwhelming changes between 1789 and 1815 should have taken full effect rather earlier: loyalty to the mother-country replacing filial devotion to the king; the cult of progress or of the *future* replacing sacred traditions or the cult of the *past*, and inaugurating a new scientific age; the legitimacy of the Right being gradually eclipsed by the rising claims of the Left—all these examples of affective transference and inversions of time and space showed how deep the changes had been. Now, love of one's native land seeks material ties; it presupposes a symbolic motherhood and cannot be satisfied with the legendary ideals of Sparta or of Rome. That is why the children of the Revolution, while they proclaimed their attachment to the methods of scientific thought, whether naturalistic or materialistic, turned their eyes from antiquity to the soil of the motherland. Michelet, who was the bard of republican France, laid great stress on geography as well as on physiology, physics, botany and mineralogy as aids in explaining history.[41]

The successors of the Comte de Boulainvilliers, in seeking to regain the privileges of their caste, were also compelled to invoke the new racial arguments. "We are not of your community," cried the Comte de Montlosier. "We are of ourselves one whole. Your origin is clear and so is ours. . . . The Franks were as the salt of a people who were themselves the salt of the earth." To prove his point, he referred to the *Germania* of Tacitus, "that gospel of honour and of all the human virtues" which was comparable to the New Testament, "the gospel of all the religious virtues".[42] Without going to these extremes, other titled writers, notably Chateaubriand—"the man", wrote Tocqueville, "who perhaps better than any other has preserved the remembrance of the ancient races"[43]—thought that Germano-Frankish superiority was beyond dispute.[44]

It was at this stage that the romantic historian Augustin Thierry unleashed his counter-attack. He accepted the choice of ground of his adversaries but unlike them he justified it not by tradition but by the advance of physiology. "Recent studies in physiology," he wrote, "like thoroughgoing research into the great events which have changed the state of society in different nations, show that the physical and moral constitution of nations depends far more on their descent from certain primitive ancestors than on the influence of climate."[45] Here we see racial characteristics promoted to the rank of a great explanatory principle, allegedly based on science, and already beginning to fan political passions. "Heaven is our witness", cried Thierry, "that we were not the first to discern, nor were we the first to proclaim that sombre and terrible truth, that there are two enemy camps on the soil of France. This has to be stated since history makes it plain: whatever may have been the mixture of the two primitive races, their spirit of unending contradiction has survived to this day in the two parts of the combined population, which have always remained distinct. . . . Legitimate descent and political lineage are obvious facts. Let us grant them to those who claim them and let us boast a quite different descent. We are the sons of the men of the Third Estate. This Third Estate issued from the communes which were the sanctuary of the serfs. The serfs were those who were vanquished in the conquest . . .

so we are led to the extreme conclusion of a conquest which has to be erased."[46] However, some of Thierry's polemical methods suggest that he himself retained the mentality of the conquered. He even went as far as to assign the victory of the Revolution to its aristocratic leaders—"those deserters to a better cause were its most gallant supporters and we, sons of the vanquished, still see such leaders at our head".[47]

The other great instigator of historical research in the period after 1789-1815 was François Guizot who divided France into two races of peoples even more sharply than Thierry.

> The Revolution was a war, a real war, such as the world recognises when it is waged between nations. For over thirteen centuries France contained two nations, a people of conquerors and a people of the conquered. . . . Franks and Gauls, lords and peasants, nobles and commoners, all these, long before the Revolution, were all alike called Frenchmen and were equally entitled to claim France as their country. But time, which nourishes all things, will not destroy anything that is. . . . The struggle continued throughout all the ages, in every possible manner, with all kinds of arms. When in 1789 the representatives of all France met together in a single assembly, the two peoples hastened to resume their ancient quarrel. The day had at last arrived for bringing it to a close. . . .[48]

Guizot also used the idea of a *conquered race* in his argument. Doubtless these polemics (which French historians of the second half of the twentieth century practically never refer to, owing perhaps to the tacit taboos which we mentioned above) made an important contribution to the diffusion of the idea of race. They even revealed, quite openly, attitudes which we should today qualify as racist. In 1912, when these matters could be more freely discussed, Camille Jullian recalled in the following terms the final chapter in the Controversy about the Two Races when he gave his opening lecture at the Collège de France:

> This tremendous duel turned France's past history into an epic which was moving and miraculous, and comparable to those battles between gods and giants of which the Greek poets sang. The narration of this epic roused the poetic and grandiloquent minds of men in the Romantic era. When the bright days burned in the furnace of a hot summer in 1830, enthusiasts asked themselves if that July sunshine was not casting its light upon the final rout of the ancient conquerors and on the triumph, marked by Providence, of the immortal race of the Gauls.[49]

There can be little doubt that Camille Jullian was right. If the July Revolution marked a political consummation, in that it established the *bourgeoisie*, once and for all, as the ruling class in France, it also marked the starting-point for the triumphant career of the Gallic view of France. It was in 1830 that Balzac depicted the dying Marquis of Esgrignon, "a proud and noble Frank", crying out as he expired: "The Gauls have triumphed."[50] And this triumph was heralded as early as 1823 by Saint-Simon in terms no less emphatic:

> The descendants of the Gauls, that is to say the industrialists, have constituted the money power, the dominating force. . . . But government remained in the hands of the Franks . . . so that our society now presents the extraordinary phenomenon of a nation which is essentially industrial and of which the government is substantially feudal. . . .[51]

Beyond the Rhine, by contrast, some theoretical writers of the same period saw in the triumph of Gallicism over Germanism the major cause of the decline of France.[52] A different view was expressed by Jules Michelet when, towards the end of his life, he was writing about his *History of France*:

> This laborious work, which lasted about forty years, was conceived in a moment, in the lightning of July. During those memorable days, a great light flashed and I perceived France. . . . On that bright July morning, her tremendous promise, her dynamic power, this more than human enterprise did not strike fear in a young heart,

and he ended:

> I was the first to represent France as a person.[53]

How did young Michelet envisage her? In 1831 he announced the plan of his work.

> As to the general order [of the book] the first volume will deal with the race. . . . Race follows race, one population after another —the Gauls, Cimbri, Boii, and, on the other hand, the Iberians, Greeks, Romans. The Germans come last. . . . These races formed layers one above the other and enriched French soil with their deposits. Above the Celts were the Romans; finally the Germans.[54]

Thus the Germans were last in order of time. Michelet attributed to them an inborn respect for rank which was due to their tranquil and malleable disposition ("the German aristocratic principle") to which

he opposed his own ideal—"equality, the equity of modern times";
". . . it was a glorious achievement of our Celts to have introduced
the idea of equality into the West". Elsewhere he inveighed against
the writers of the past who had handed down an image of the Germans
as young and heroic barbarians. He considered this a kind of optical
illusion which, because of the accidental combination of events which
caused the barbarian invasions, had produced the impression of the
"unchanging genius of this race".

Despite this critical attitude, however, a careful reading of Michelet
discloses a certain fascination for the Germans, though perhaps this
was no more than the tribute which the new bourgeois society continued to pay to families of noble birth. When, for example, he undertook in his second volume to paint a complete picture of France,
province by province, he halted abruptly in Lorraine. "I restrain myself
from crossing the mountain barrier and from entering Alsace. The
Germanic world is a dangerous one for me. I find there a lotus-land
which makes me forget my own country. . . ." What lay behind this
attraction; to what can this ambivalence be ascribed? The answer is to
be found, we think, in his *Introduction* of 1831 where he contrasts
France, a nation, with Germany, a race, and describes them as follows:

> Germany gave her Swabians to Switzerland and to Sweden;
> her Goths to Spain, her Lombards to Lombardy, her Anglo-
> Saxons to England, her Franks to France. She gave both a name
> and renewal to all the peoples of Europe. Language and people
> were a fertile element which flowed and penetrated all around.
> Even today, when the age of the great migrations is long past,
> Germans are happy to travel and they welcome the foreigner in
> their own country. They are the most hospitable of people. . . .
> The character of this race, which was to mingle with so many
> others, was marked by a docile self-denial. The vassal yielded
> willingly to his lord, the students and artisans to their corpora-
> tions. In these groups the end to be pursued was of secondary
> interest; the essential elements were friendly meetings, mutual
> service and all those rites, initiations, ceremonies and symbols
> which provided their members with the religion of their choice.
> The communal table served as an altar on which the German
> sacrificed self-interest. . . . It is not surprising that we see in
> Germany, for the first time, one man becoming the liegeman of
> another, shaking hands and swearing fealty to him until death.
> This kind of dedication, which makes the Southerner laugh, has
> nevertheless been a cause of greatness in the German race. It was

by this means that the tribes which conquered the Empire, each grouped around its chief, were able to lay the foundations of the modern monarchies. To those chieftains, whom they themselves had chosen, they dedicated their lives and their power. In the old Germanic sagas, all the exploits of the nation are linked with some hero. The honour of the people is centred upon its leader who emerges as its all-embracing exemplar. . . .

This account, which would have appeared fanciful, not to say fantastic, to historians of earlier generations, ends on a note which to us must seem prophetic. For a Germany described in this fashion was just what its younger élites, formed as they were by the history of Tacitus, wanted to revive. This was the Germany which was evoked by the pen of Jacob Grimm in a work which Michelet had studied and translated "with incredible passion".[56] Nevertheless, the fact remains that even in his moments of greatest exaltation Michelet, unlike Thierry, kept a sense of proportion and never used the racial element as a main principle of historical explanation. His friend, Henri Martin, by contrast "showed this Gallic race as getting the better of its Germanic conquerors in the end, thanks to Descartes, Voltaire and the men of the Revolution".[57]

In the eyes of Henri Martin, it was the greatness of Gaul which, thanks to an unchanging purity of blood, constituted the greatness of France. It was the Druids who had taught the world the immortality of the soul. The Greeks had "lighted their torch at the great hearth of the Celtic people", and Gallic laws had found their latest expression in the Revolution. "It was from the souls of our fathers that we heard this ringing cry across the centuries! Its protest was taken up by the new Gaul, the France of the Revolution." As to Gallic courage, "the essential characteristic which dominates everything we have said, this hall-mark of the Gallic race, consists in facing up to death in a way no other race has done"; and it was for this reason "that an ideal of Celtic chivalry, in no manner derived from German origins" had been able to develop.

These were immortal virtues and they were imprinted in the flesh and limbs of the Gauls, in their rounded heads, and even, one might say, in their very entrails. Thus the same Henri Martin, in the guise of physical anthropologist, detected a more pronounced development of the respiratory organs and a lesser volume of space for the intestines among the French than among the Germans.[58] If we are to render justice to Henri Martin, we must admit that he fathered a Celtic myth which, in the manuals of the Third Republic, found popular expression in the phrase "our Celtic ancestors" though nowadays it only reveals itself in the adventures of Asterix and Obelix.*

Asterix is certainly a character to be reckoned with. Much could be said about his pranks. They certainly reveal an aspect of Gallic humour. Yet beneath this cloak he touches a deep chord in young and old alike, the same feeling which not so long ago motivated great collective drives and was a connecting link between mass killings and political doctrines.

However, we have now reached a point when we must pause awhile, because by 1837 a writer like Henri Martin was already thinking in terms of "the great Indo-European family of Japheth of which *Ariya*, that *Holy Land* of the earliest ages, appears to have been the cradle" and of "the primogenital right which is claimed in these days by the mysterious *Ariya* of Central Asia".[59] As a matter of fact, Central Asia never claimed anything of the kind. It was the Europe of the scientific age which was forging for itself a new genealogy and a new Holy Land. Thus we can discern, long before Gobineau, the direct and explicit origins of the Aryan myth. That myth exhibits the peculiar quality of being totally Manichean, in contrast with those which have been discussed so far; for, whatever the bias of different authors, all showed the same tendency to alternate Light and Darkness in their portrayals. In the case of such writers as Taine and Renan there was, too, an attraction for the youth and virility of the so-called Germanic races. Renan, for instance, in September 1870, regarded the defeat of Sedan as a proof of the racial superiority of the Germans.[60]

One final observation must be made on the last great protagonists of the Controversy about the Two Races. All agree that France is the product of a mingling of races. "It was not without protracted convulsions that the ten nations, of which we are the heirs, were able to combine into one", wrote Thierry; while Guizot asked, "Who told you that you are Germans and that we are French?" But this uncertainty about origins and lineages, which were thought to imply different blood-strains, was balanced by the belief in their harmonious fusion. Michelet, in the language of his time, compares this fusion with a process of organic chemistry.

Having said this, is the result France? No; a great deal more still remains to be said. France fashioned herself out of elements which

* Comic strip heroes in a popular series by Goscinny, published by Dargaud, Paris. (Tr. Note)

might have produced an altogether different mixture. The same chemical components yield either oil or sugar. But, if these facts are established, not everything is thereby explained. There remains the mystery of a special, intrinsic existence. How much more account should we not take of this principle when a living and active mingling, like that of a nation, is in question.

A little further on, Michelet entitles another section of his book *Destinées malheureuses des races restées pures* and cites as an example the dramatic fate of the Jews. No doubt he was making a virtue of necessity; he was adapting his anthropology to a political and moral ideal embodying the beliefs of his age, just as scholars have done in all periods. One need only recall such instances as Isidore of Seville or Fredegar, and the innumerable nineteenth-century variants which we shall have occasion to mention in due course.

But cannot these contradictory ideas which modern Frenchmen have contrived about themselves—all these myths about Franks and Celts and Latins, which cancel one another out—be related to the universalism of France, the spread of her influence, the fertility of her culture? And might they not, on the other hand, have a bearing on her history in the course of which collective hatreds have so often been put at the service of internal quarrels? Michelet, the visionary, condensed these two questions in a single formula: "In the eyes of Europe you must know that France will never have any other but a single immutable name, which is her true, eternal name; the Revolution!" To ask these questions is not to suggest the answers, and it seems to me that in the present state of our knowledge of collective psychology, we lack the conceptual instruments to pursue such enquiries in a useful manner. I do not believe that the following chapters will supply the elements of an answer, but I do feel that, in other forms, these questions are bound to present themselves to us again.

CHAPTER THREE

ENGLAND

THE LINEAGE OF SHEM AND THE NORMAN YOKE

For obvious reasons, islands retain traces of the past, whether of extinct animal species or of customs and traditions, which have disappeared on the mainland.

In the Mediterranean, the last representatives of the accursed race of Spanish *conversos* linger on in Palma, Majorca.[1] Jewish troglodytes still exist on the island of Djerba. The Sicilian *mafia* or the Corsican *vendetta* are even more famous survivals. In the Atlantic ocean, it was in Iceland that the songs and forgotten legends of the Germanic *Edda* were recorded. We owe our knowledge of the Celtic myths of origin to traditions preserved in Ireland. In Britain, the pre-Christian system of Scottish clans was only abolished officially during the eighteenth century. And of all the Germanic tribes only the Angles and the Saxons have maintained intact their primitive genealogies, which go back to the great god Odin or Woden.[2]

The British Isles, it is true, had a great deal to remember, for, though they have not been invaded since 1066, they were frequently colonized during the two preceding millennia. Iberians, Celts, Romans, Germans and Scandinavians contributed to their population, and finally the Normans. The sequence, up to and including the Germans, was the same as in France or in Spain, but the Celts retained their culture after the Roman withdrawal because romanization had never been completed. The Germans, in consequence, remained German, since assimilation can only take place with a higher form of civilization. As a result the cultural situation was very complex, and became more so with partial francization which followed.

At the time when Christianity was spreading in the British Isles and when monks, who were trained to write, performed the role of keepers of the collective memory, co-existence between Celts and Germans, Britons and Anglo-Saxons was extremely turbulent. But little by little it brought about a near identity of the terms "British" and "English". From the very beginning the kaleidoscopic population of the islands had to learn the art of compromise, of which the greatest achievement without any doubt was the fusion of tongues which produced the English language. English humour, that interior compromise of the self with oneself, no less than the notion of *fairness*, may well derive from this primal source. During the Middle Ages, King Arthur, that legendary conqueror of the English, became their national hero, and Richard Cœur de Lion, whose favourite oath was "Do you take me for an Englishman?" was only slightly less popular.[3] In a period of nationalist fervour, an English author was comforted by the thought that Arthur and Richard were, after all, British heroes (though perhaps that touch of humour was involuntary.[4])

The English had four great mythologies with which to construct their own myth of origin—the Greco-Roman, the Celtic, the Germanic and the Hebrew. It is well known that the two latter were the mainstay of their traditions and were carried across the Atlantic. Thus Thomas Jefferson suggested marking the seal of the United States with portrayals of the two great ancestral crossings, that of the sea by Hengist and Horsa, the Saxon chiefs, and that of the desert by the children of Israel.[5] This reminiscence of a crossing supplies us with a first line of enquiry.

The Celts, as a matter of fact, had forgotten their first crossing. They became Christians before the Anglo-Saxons, and adopted a genealogy similar to that of the continentals, that is to say, one derived from Japheth. They also invented, on the authority of Isidore of Seville, an eponymous ancestor called Brut or Brutus.[6] They made no attempt to claim a blood relationship with their conquerors, no doubt because they remained rebellious and lived under the sovereignty of their minor kings. On the other hand, the defeats and the exiles, which the earliest chronicles of British history record in the annals of Gildas and of Nennius, could easily be interpreted as divine punishments, comparable to those already inflicted on the obdurate people of Israel. In the writings of Gildas, the Celts become the real Israel "praesens Israel".[7]

It is possible that the Venerable Bede (died 735), the "father of English history" who drew largely on the Celtic chronicles for his history, may have borrowed this theme from them. Or perhaps this too was due to the fact of living in an island; for the prophets of the old Testament mention "the isles of the sea" which wait for the Eternal God. Now the old chroniclers read the prophets assiduously and gave them the most literal interpretation. An example is the imprecation which Hosea hurled against the Jews—"Ye are not my people and I will not be your God."[8] Who then were the new Elect, the "praesens Israel" of Gildas? Edmond Faral has written: "At the root of Bede's thinking was the idea that the Anglo-Saxon people was a predestined race. It was through them that a new political authority was to be established in Britain which should lay the true foundations for the Church. God had chosen it for his purpose and therein lay its special worth."[9] Bede approved of the massacre of the Celtic monks of Bangor by the pagan king Ethelfrid because the kingdom was promised to the Anglo-Saxons. And he did not forget that "the powerful nations of the Jutes, the Angles and the Saxons" came from Germany so that he was concerned also with the evangelization of the "Old Saxons" who stayed behind on the Continent.[10]

Other monks, during this period, were transcribing genealogies which went back to Woden, and relating this national ancestor, through the lists of patriarchs, to the universal ancestor Adam, just as their continental brethren were doing. But among the former, the recollection of a sea-crossing was incorporated into the story of a child asleep in a ship who landed on an island of which he became king. This theme reminds one of the infant Moses and one cannot exclude the possibility of some obscure connexion. It was certainly true that the Anglo-Saxon child king Sceaf was transformed in the writings of the copyists into Seth and later Shem, and the consequence of this, from the early Middle Ages onwards, was that the English repudiated Japheth, the ancestor of the Europeans, and claimed filiation from the eldest of Noah's sons. From henceforth, it may be said, England was no longer part of Europe.

Towards 1900, the strict followers of the Lord's Day Observance Society regarded King Alfred as the founder of the English custom of the Sabbath-day's rest, while some British socialists invoked his wise laws in making their claim for an eight-hour workday,[11] and the royal family practised circumcision on the heirs to the throne. Can British customs and traditions be related to the "semitism" ascribed to the ancient Anglo-Saxon dynasties? And if so, in what way?

Immediately after the Norman conquest, in his *History of the Kings of Britain*, Geoffrey of Monmouth, who was a Welsh bishop, threw a ray of light on the workings of the medieval imagination which, in turn, has been a source of inspiration for modern fantasies.

His history, which was highly fanciful, was from a literary point of view one of the most influential of the Middle Ages and gave rise to the cycles of stories about *Brut* and about the Round Table. Under the Norman kings, the author was free to glorify his Breton ancestors. To this end he drew deeply on all the mythologies. This explains how his Brutus, alleged to be the grandson of the Trojan Aeneas and the founder of the royal race of Bretons, has a destiny similar to that of Oedipus,* while the divine promises made to the last sprig of this race, Cadwallader, are of Biblical inspiration. Another glorious and imaginary Breton King, Ebraucus, seems to have been none other than the Hebrew king David, barely disguised as "David Hebraicus".† This Ebraucus was soon included in the Anglo-Saxon genealogies, either between Adam and Woden, in the capacity of a counterpart of Sceaf or Shem, or lower down in the scale, between Woden and King Alfred.[12] In this way the royal English line was becoming more and more hebraized at a time when the name David shone conspicuously in Scotland and in Wales, which explains why several of the Princes of Wales have had this Christian name in modern times. On the other hand, thanks to the influence of Geoffrey of Monmouth and his followers, Brutus joined David-Ebraucus in some genealogical lists where the Anglo-Saxons thus became related to the Bretons and Trojans and, in their wake, became descendants of Japheth.[13]

We will not go into the details of these complicated legends and genealogies through which even the specialists can scarcely thread their way. Some of them believe that the gradual transformation of Sceaf into Seth and Shem was due to mistakes made by the copyists.[14] But even if there were such mistakes, the fact that they were committed, and even more, that they were repeated, cannot be attributed to mere chance. This is a question, therefore, which deserves to be investigated further.

What exactly did the clerical scholars of the Middle Ages understand by a royal lineage derived from David and from Shem? It certainly did not signify a "semitic race" in the modern sense of the term. The attempt to situate man within natural history, so common today, was utterly foreign to the thinking of the Middle Ages. Medieval

---

* It may be said that Geoffrey of Monmouth's King Brutus is a Christian conception of Oedipus. In his case the augurs predict, before his birth, that he will kill his father and mother. The latter dies in child-birth and when he is fifteen he kills his father, accidentally, in a hunt. He is banished from Italy, his country, and after many wanderings he conquers Britain.

† Ebraucus, "a man of remarkable strength", reigned for forty years (like David) and had twenty sons (we know the names of seventeen of David's sons). Geoffrey of Monmouth actually stated: "At that time, David was reigning in Judaea."

anthropology was based on the Scriptures; it was a chapter of Theology. Thus the English clerks, in affiliating their royal dynasty to the ancestor of the Hebrews, sought to emphasize its chosen and sacred character; for had not Noah conferred upon his first-born, Shem, a special blessing? The only chronicler who commented on the royal genealogy when copying it, Ælred of Rievaulx (d. 1166), refers to this blessing, and his commentary is revealing:

> ... [from Enoch] Noah was descended who alone was found worthy, with his wife and his children, to escape from the destruction of the world. His first-born, Shem, was blessed by his father. The Jews say that Shem was the High Priest of God and that, later on, he was called Melchizedek, who offered bread and wine as a symbol of our priesthood and, because of this, Christ was told "Thou art a priest forever after the order of Melchizedek" (Ps. cx, 4). Thus it was from Shem that the genealogy descended to Woden, whose authority was so great among his people that the fourth day of the week, which the Roman pagans called the day of Mercury, was dedicated to him, a custom which the English follow to this day.[15]

In this way Ælred of Rievaulx, mindful of the claims and ambitions of his king, Henry II, and the better to magnify his ancestors, linked the views of the rabbis, who identified Shem with Melchizedek, to the tradition of the Church, according to which this mysterious priest-king, who had blessed Abraham, was a pre-figuration of Christ if not indeed the Christ himself. It was undoubtedly because of views such as these that Shem was often considered during the Middle Ages the ancestor of the clerical estate. Now, if all Christian kings were "anointed of the Lord" and thereby partakers of priestly dignity, this aspect of their office was especially pronounced in the case of English kings, whom their subjects revered as "the Christ of the Lord"[16] from the time of their conversion in the eighth century right up to the twentieth century. Continental churchmen also described the barbarian kings, once they were converted, as belonging to the sacred lineages of Shem-Melchizedek and David. Thus, at the time of Chilperic, Venantius Fortunatus declared: "Our Melchizedek, whom we justly call king and lay priest, has consummated the work of religion", while Charlemagne, at least among his friends, was called by the Christian name of David.[17] On the Continent, however, the rites and the Old Testament atmosphere which surrounded the royal families were progressively abandoned under Roman influence, while in the British Isles, thanks to the persistence of tradition, they survived with little change down to our own times. The kings of England went on being crowned after the fashion of Solomon, under the auspices of the prophet Nathan and the priest Zadok, and their enthronement was completed to the words of the psalmist: "Once have I sworn by my holiness that I will not lie unto David" (Ps. lxxxix, 35).

To be descended from Shem was to belong to a royal, sacerdotal and divine lineage and was a certain way of guaranteeing, and of translating into Christian terms of reference, the divine ancestry claimed by English kings—something which Woden, a downgraded pagan deity, could no longer ensure. For this reason an orthodox and Christian warranty, Shem-Melchizedek, was borrowed from the Old Testament. Throughout English history, the priestly, near-divine character of the monarchy was asserted with special tenacity, both by the servants and propagandists of the Crown and by heretics. Wycliffe, for example, wrote in *De Officio Regis*: "The dignity of the king is greater than that of the priest, for the king reflects the goodness of Christ and the priest only his humanity." The ease with which Henry VIII of England was able to break away from the See of Rome and to establish in his country the most absolute form of Caesaro-Papism is thus readily comprehensible. As a man of the Renaissance, he did not avail himself of Biblical genealogies but relied on quite different reasoning such as the need to provide a male heir for the nation, or arguments from the Scriptures. National and dynastic traditions, however, provide the key to a situation in which he was able to assert himself as Supreme Head of the Church and claim to be "king, emperor and pope",[18] thus opening the way for the Reformation in England.

In this respect, the century which separates this Reformation from the English Revolution is the one when the priestly pre-eminence of its kings was snatched from them by a people resolved to take its destiny into its own hands. In Europe everywhere, the study of the Scriptures and popular unrest brought about new heresies and sects which the Church of Rome called judaistic; but it was only the English who identified themselves wholeheartedly with the people of Moses. The leaders of Puritanism, like Cromwell and Milton, thought of this affiliation in an allegorical Christian manner. They did not pretend that Jews were flesh and blood ancestors of the English. They merely substituted the English for the Jews so that the former became, in their turn, the people chosen by the Almighty for a special and at the same time a universal mission. Cromwell quoted Isaiah in Parliament: "This people have I formed for myself; they shall shew forth my praise" (xliii, 21), and he announced that the English were God's people. He explicitly likened the circumstances of their election to that of the Jews—"the only parallel of God's dealing with us I know in the world is Israel's bringing-out of Egypt . . .".[19] Milton, too, rendered thanks to the Almighty for the special favours which He bestowed upon the English. "Why else", he asked, "was this nation chosen before any other, that out of her as out of Sion should be proclaimed and sounded forth the first tidings and trumpet of Reformation to all Europe . . .?" His fellow-countrymen had also hearkened to the plea of Moses: "For now the time seems come, wherein Moses the great Prophet may sit in heaven rejoicing to see that memorable and glorious wish of his fulfilled, when not only our seventy Elders, but all the Lord's people are become Prophets."[20]

In 1804, during another period of unrest, William Blake, in his poem *Jerusalem*, expressed the same idea even more clearly:

> *And thus the Voice Divine went forth upon the rocks of Albion:*
> *I elected Albion for my glory: I gave to him the Nations,*
> *Of the whole Earth; He was the angel of my Presence, and all*
> *The sons of God were Albion's sons, and Jerusalem was my joy.*[21]

This messianic atmosphere was favourable to the return of the Jews to England under Cromwell, and to their settlement on the western shores of the Atlantic. Some of the Puritans, however, who considered the Jews in real life as rivals, were against admitting them for they did not wish to be confused with them. Such was the case of the pamphleteer, William Prynne, who was the author of *A short demurrer to the Jewes remitter in England* (1656), or of the hypocritical "Rabbi Busy", a Puritan of course, portrayed by Ben Jonson, who ate pork in public to demonstrate his execration and hatred of the Jews.[22] Many other sectaries interpreted the Old Testament literally and set off to find the promised land or had themselves circumcised. The extent to which circumcision is still practised in Anglo-Saxon countries is well known. Yet others, like Cromwell's friend John Sadler, tried to show that Anglo-Saxon laws were derived from Talmudic law and wondered whether the British Isles were not first populated by Phoenicians and if the Druids were not indeed Canaanites.[23]

This debate is not wholly ended. The belief in a carnal descent from the Jews was sufficiently rooted in Great Britain for such an enlightened writer as the deist, John Toland, to use it as his prime argument in his

Reasons for Naturalizing the Jews in Great Britain and Ireland (1714) when, addressing himself particularly to the clergy in England, he wrote:

> You know how considerable a part of the British inhabitants are the undoubted offspring of the Jews and how many worthy prelates of this same stock, not to speak of Lords and commoners, may at this time make an illustrious figure among us. . . . A great number of 'em fled to Scotland which is the reason so many in that part of the Island have such a remarkable aversion to pork and black puddings to this day, not to insist on some other resemblances easily observable.*

It should be noted that Toland, as a man of the Enlightenment, sought to sustain his thesis by historical and positivist, rather than legendary, arguments; but the fact remains that no other country nurtured such fables and hence no author elsewhere attempted to support them on historical grounds. Similar views still find currency in our times and are expressed in a variety of ways, beginning with the widely held belief that many Englishmen are descended from Jews, and leading on to the erudite studies of Werner Sombart who maintained that from every point of view the United States was a Jewish nation.[24]

Many aspects of English history, such as the relative mildness of anti-semitism, pro-Zionist feelings, the amazing career of Disraeli, are thereby explained. The belief in a physical link with the Jews, which is the hard core of the idea of a spiritual descent from them, was responsible, in the course of time, for the birth of a movement, that of the British Israelites, which numbered hundreds of thousands of followers and which claimed the ten Lost Tribes of Israel as its ancestors. They relied on scriptural arguments, a kind of proof which has become discredited in our time and of which it is enough to quote one sample: was not the meaning of *Ish Brit* in Hebrew, the man of the Alliance? The British Israelites have prospered in all the English-speaking countries, though principally in Britain itself, since the beginning of the nineteenth century. Queen Victoria and King Edward VII were patrons of the movement[25] which has published many books and pamphlets and produces its own newspaper, *The National Message*. In their own view, the British Israelites are of purer Hebraic race than the real Jews themselves so that, at a time when

---

* Toland held the opinion that when the Jews were expelled from England in 1290, some of them remained in the island either by becoming converts or by taking refuge in Scotland.

many of the latter began to regret their semitic origin, some Englishmen vaunted their exclusive claim to this stock. In 1970, a major
interest of the British Israelites was to prevent Britain's entry into the
European Common Market, so as to avoid the Queen being subjected
to continental politicians and to spare her subjects, who are bene-
ficiaries of "the Common Law of England going back to the Ten
Commandments of Moses", from submitting to the "Byzantine
Roman Law going back to the Emperor Justinian". With reference
to the Treaty of Rome they spoke of "Gestapo-like regulations".[26]
Moreover, some British Israelites (in a personal capacity) attribute all
the ills of this world to the "Elders of Zion", while some others prefer
this accusation against the Jesuit order.

In the eyes of these latter-day guardians of British traditions, their
Hebrew ancestry in no way runs counter to their Germanic or
Germano-Celtic heredity, their *Celto-Anglo-Saxondom*. Both are successive shoots of a genealogy corresponding to medieval ideas. Thus
the beliefs and questionings of the British Israelites are the last vestiges
of those of the Fathers of the Church, such as Jerome or Isidore of
Seville. In one essential respect, however, they are moved by the spirit
of the modern age. If they affiliate Queen Elizabeth to King David
and his subjects, as far back as the Lost Tribes, through King Alfred
and his ancestor Woden-Odin, they do not look beyond Moses. The
patriarchs from Shem to Adam have no place in their genealogies.
They may have definite ideas about the origin of the English but this
does not seem to apply to that of the ancient Hebrews, and they do
not ask how the human race made its appearance on this earth.

Is this a sign of the times? Generally speaking, the curiosity of the
English was restricted, from the beginning of the modern age, to the
more recent genealogical offshoot, namely, to the question of their
own national origin. From the point of view of descent, the Norman
conquest was a mere parenthesis because in 1154 the throne was occupied by Henry II, regarded as a collateral descendant of King Alfred
and thus a "semite". William the Conqueror is still the most contro-
versial figure in English history, and the bitterness of the antagonism
between his Frankish knights and the indigenous population is very
differently interpreted. What is beyond dispute is that for three
centuries a nobility and clergy who were French and Latin in culture
were set against an English-speaking people and that the latter, for
the most part illiterate, were badly equipped to enlighten posterity as
to their feelings or resentments. The silence of the documents is no

proof one way or the other. Anyway, it is broken in the sixteenth century when anti-French feelings came out into the open. These were supported, to begin with, by the religious reformers who looked for the purity of the primitive English Church in the pre-Norman past. The nature of these polemics was revealed in 1558 by John Aylmer, a future Bishop of London, who denounced:

> effeminate Frenchmen: Stoute in bragge but nothing in dede. . . .
> We have a few hunting termes and pedlars French in the lousye
> law brought in by the Normanes, yet remayning: But the lan-
> guage and customs bee Englishe and Saxonysche.[27]

That was how the campaign against the Norman yoke began. It was fed by concepts which derived in part from ideas and arguments brought over from the Continent, from "mother Germany"; and which seemed to revive millennial memories. The popular traveller Thomas Coryat, who had visited Germany, declared:

> To detayne thee long with preambles of praises of this imperial
> and renowned Region out of my little experience of the same,
> were a matter very superfluous. . . . Only the better to encourage
> thee to see her glorious beauty, whereof I myself have to my un-
> speakable joy perceived a little glimpse, I say with Kircherius
> that Germany is the Queene of all other provinces, the Eagle of
> all Kingdoms and the Mother of all Nations.[28]

And the Englishman, Thomas Coryat, concluded with the words of the German, Hermann Kircher:

> Whither dost thou bend thy course? to what end dost thou travell
> with the swallow, leaving thy nest? doth not Germany in respect
> of the plenty and commodity of those things, by many degrees
> excell all other nations? . . .[28]

  Better and more effective ammunition was afforded by the study of ancient authors, especially Tacitus, whose *Germania* was at that time exciting the imagination of scholars throughout Europe, especially in those countries where the idea of liberty could be described, with some semblance of truth, as of Germanic origin. Richard Verstegen, whose *Restitution of Decayed Intelligence* ran to five editions between 1605 and 1670, asserted on the authority of Tacitus that the Germans were able to lay claim to three unequalled titles—they had always been masters in their own country; they were invincible; they were a pure race. Whatever anyone might say, the English were also, in Verstegen's opinion, a pure race:

> And whereas some do call us a mixed nation by reason of these Danes and Normannes coming in among us, I answer (as formerly I have noted) that the Danes and the Normannes were one and the same people with the Germans, as were also the Saxons: & wee not to bee accompted mixed by having only some such ioyned, unto us again, as sometime had one same language and one same originall with us.[29]

As befits a peaceful antiquarian, Verstegen related all the English, as distinct from the Celts, to one another. This method was to be adopted again in the nineteenth century by the Oxford historians. Under Cromwell, however, other English writers attempted to arrange their past history in a different way in order to reach more militant conclusions.

The Puritan Revolution was indeed one of those special moments when the disinherited make their voices heard and when, thanks to a political upheaval, aspirations of which little is heard at other times suddenly emerge into daylight. In this case the poorer classes gave expression to their feelings through popular movements such as the *Levellers* and *Diggers*. Christopher Hill has pointed out that the signatories of their manifestos all bear Saxon names, as did the working-class characters in Shakespeare's plays.[30] Thus class was coupled with "race", that is to say, with a culture; or, to put it more exactly, at the root of this class confrontation there was a cultural confrontation which was perceived as a conflict between different bloods. Moreover, what we have observed about French history in the second half of the first millennium can be applied, in a general way, to English history in the first half of the second millennium—but the roles are reversed, since the role of the Germanic Franks, as the governing class who were in the long run culturally assimilated, devolved in England upon the Norman French. As in the case of France, one can detect a tendency to mistake the part for the whole. In the eyes of King James I the majority of English gentlemen were of Norman descent and Bishop Goodman, the king's historian, considered that this was true of the English in general,[31] because the aristocracy was England. But, as in the case of France, the counter-attack by the people was not long in coming.

The *Levellers* and *Diggers* pressed for equality or a primitive form of communism, a golden age which looked to the Golden Age of the past. They found their inspiration not only in the Scriptures but in an idealized concept of the Anglo-Saxon past. They also claimed to speak for all Englishmen when they rose up against an oppression which they said had begun in 1066, with tyrants and robbers coming over from France—the first of whom was William the Bastard who had the laws written in French so that "the poor miserable people might be gulled and cheated, undone and destroyed".[32] Evil was thus shown to be embodied in an aristocracy and a royal power which were not, or at least were no longer, English but were imported from abroad. Innumerable anonymous pamphlets fulminated against "that outlandish Norman Bastard" and the leader of the Levellers, Lilburne, taunted the judges during his trial by crying out: "You that call yourselves Judges of the Law, are no more but Norman intruders."[33] John Hare, in his pamphlet *St Edward's Ghost or Anti-Normanism* (1647), wanted to cast out the carcasses and bones of the Norman dukes from English soil. To this end, he proposed depriving William of his title "the Conqueror", abolishing his laws and expurgating the English language of all words of French origin.[34] Among the misdeeds with which he reproached the Conqueror was that of allowing the Jews to enter England, whereas the Anglo-Saxon monarchs would have been careful to exclude them. This view was upheld with a great display of erudition by William Prynne in his *Short Demurrer* in 1656. Other examples of the anti-Norman campaign may be found in Christopher Hill's study, *The Norman Yoke*.[35]

Nathaniel Bacon, a nephew of Francis Bacon, was a more moderate Puritan and a figure of greater importance. He developed a theory about the origins of the English people which is worthy of attention. Referring to Gildas the Wise, he wrote that God, "surveying the forsaken condition of other Nations", had set apart the British Isles, "long before the Son of God was inwombed, and whiles as yet Providence seemed to close only with the Jewish Nation". God's plan was "that in one Isle the glory of God's bounty might shine forth to all the barbarism of *Europe* in making a beautiful Church out of the refuse of the nations". This refuse might be the Britons or Saxons or Scandinavians or Normans, it did not matter which. In his puritan humility, Bacon even thought that "this island hath from time to time been no other than as a Sewer to empty the superfluity of the German Nations". On this premise it is, however, clear that all the nations which contributed to the amalgam of Great Britain were of Germanic origin. Even the Britons came from Germany in contrast to their neighbours the Gauls, who were "strangers in blood unto the Britons, however nigh they were in habitation". Bacon particularly stressed the fact that the Britons were able to resist the yoke of the Romans better than the other nations, "and they were the last of the Churches of Europe to give their power to the Roman beast; and Henry the Eighth . . . the first that took away that power again." After resisting the Anglo-Saxons for a long time the Britons merged with them. "In all of which, God (taming the Britons' pride by the Saxons' power and discovering the Saxons' darkness by the Britons' light) made himself Lord over both people in the conclusion."[36] It was typical of the outlook of his period, that Bacon attributed the divine election of the English to the inscrutable designs of Providence as well as to a fortunate mixture of races all of which, including the Normans, were considered by him to be Germanic.

If the French Revolution gave birth to the Gallic myth, the Glorious Revolution convinced the English people of their Germanic origin. After 1688, most writers regarded the constitutional system in Great Britain as the embodiment of liberties derived from Germanic or Gothic sources. Thus in dealing with the origin of parliament Swift wrote:

> . . . for great councils were convoked . . . from time immemorial by the Saxon princes, who first introduced them into this island from the same original with the other Gothic forms of government in most parts of Europe . . . and the Germans of old fell upon the same model, from whence the Goths their neighbours, with the rest of those northern people, did perhaps borrow it (1719).[37]

Bolingbroke put forward a more original doctrine. He too considered the Council, composed of the King, the lords and the free Saxons, as the first model of the English Parliament, though English freedoms were even more ancient since they existed in pre-Roman times.

> I feel a secret pride in thinking that I was born a Briton when I consider that the Romans, those masters of the world, maintained their liberty little more than seven centuries and that Britain which was a free nation above 1700 years ago, is so at that hour. . . . Their long resistance against the Saxons shows their love of civil liberty (1730).[38]

Without any doubt, however, the view expressed by David Hume in his well-known *History of England*, when he contrasted the "degenerate" and "abject" Britons with the valiant Anglo-Saxons, was more typical of the general opinion of Englishmen.

According to Hume, when the Anglo-Saxons subjugated the Britons "their manners and customs were wholly German and the same picture of a fierce and bold liberty, which is drawn by the masterly pencil of Tacitus, will apply to these founders of the English government". The Celts, in fact, were so utterly incapable of enjoying freedom that when, on leaving, the Romans enfranchized them "the abject Britons regarded this present of liberty as fatal to them". In the same vein Hume depicts William the Conqueror in the blackest colours as the tyrant who put an end to the liberties of the English by "seizing their possessions and reducing them to the most abject slavery". Thus began "all the calamities which the English endured during this and subsequent reigns and gave rise to those mutual jealousies and animosities between them and the Normans which were never appeased till a long tract of time had gradually united the two nations and made them one people". Following the custom of his time, Hume attributed to the Nordic and Germanic peoples "sentiments of liberty, honour, equity, and valour, superior to the rest of mankind". These were the sentiments that had made Europe great.[39]

Other writers spread similar ideas in the United States. Tom Paine, for example, wrote as follows: "A French bastard landing with an armed banditti and establishing himself King of England against the consent of the natives is, in plain terms a very paltry, rascally original".[40] But it was Walter Scott, above all, who gave a dynamic impetus to these ideas at a very favourable time, namely in the aftermath of the Napoleonic wars when all Europe was beginning to think in terms of race. In *Waverley*, *Rob Roy* and *Ivanhoe*, the struggles of English history were portrayed by his pen as clashes between hostile races— Scots against English, English against French—in a Britain composed of many different peoples. A typical example is Athelstane's reply to De Bracy in *Ivanhoe*: "My lineage, proud Norman, is drawn from a source more pure and ancient than that of a beggarly Frenchman whose living is won by selling the blood of thieves whom he assembles under his paltry standard. Kings were my ancestors, strong in war and wise in council. . . .[41]" Conversations and scenes of this kind, accompanied by Walter Scott's personal reflections, made the new philosophy of history popular throughout Europe. In France, Augustin Thierry praised him as "the first writer to have undertaken to present history in a way which is both real and poetical . . . to portray the true aspect

of events which have been so deformed by modern phraseology".[42]
The influence of Walter Scott on historiography was well known in
his own time. In faraway Russia, Pushkin observed: "The new school
of French historians has been formed under the influence of the
Scottish novelist. He has acquainted them with entirely new sources."[43]

In England this tendency reached its apotheosis in a wave of
Teutonism in the 1840's exemplified by the names of the Celt-hating
Dr Arnold of Rugby, Carlyle (who glorified Cromwell's "old Teutsch
fathers"), Bulwer Lytton, and many other thinkers and novelists.[44] As
on the Continent, it was the historians who were the most extreme
and active propagators of these views. Edward Freeman, though he
described the Normans as "disguised kinsmen" of the English, compared the invasion of England by William the Conqueror to that of
Germany by Napoleon. He even went so far as to indict the old
chronicler Laweman, who had translated into English the *Historia
Brittonum* of Geoffrey of Monmouth, when he wrote: "It was treason
against the tongue and the history of his race for Layamon to translate
that Brut into English."[45] His emulator, Charles Kingsley, put the
following speech into the mouth of an imaginary ancestor who was
addressing a Slav:

> The golden-haired hero said to his brown-haired bondsman, "I
> am a gentleman who have a 'gens', a stamm, a pedigree, and know
> from whom I sprung. I am a Garding, an Amalung, a Scylding,
> an Osing, and what not. I am a son of the Gods. The blood of
> the Asas is in my veins. Do you not see it? Am I not wiser,
> stronger, more virtuous, more beautiful than you? You must obey
> me and be my man, and follow me to the death. Then, if you
> prove a worthy thane, I will give you horse, weapons, bracelets,
> land; and marry you, it may be, to my daughter or my niece. And
> if not, you must remain a son of the earth, grubbing the dust of
> which you were made."[46]

Nevertheless, the affiliation of the English gentleman to the Aesir
lasted only a short time. At the end of the nineteenth century it had
ceased to be fashionable while at the same time a counter-offensive
by the real or imaginary descendants of the Normans on the one hand,
or by the Celtomaniacs of Scotland and of Wales on the other, had
begun to make some headway. This new climate is well illustrated
by the remarks of the anthropologist, John Beddoe, in 1885: "It is
not very long since educated opinion considered the English and Low-
land Scots an almost purely Teutonic people. Now the current runs

so much the other way that I have had to take up the attitude of an apologist of the 'Saxon' view."[47] The English were returning to the traditional view that their nation was formed of a cross between several different races. Sir Arthur Keith, another anthropologist, declared at the beginning of the twentieth century: "It is often said, that we British are a mixed and mongrel collection of types and breeds",[48] which is what Geoffrey of Monmouth had already proclaimed in the twelfth century when he wrote:

> Britain is inhabited by five races of people, the Norman-French, the Britons, the Saxons, the Picts and the Scots. Of these, the Britons once occupied the land from sea to sea before the others came.[49]

Such a variety of myths and memories was ill-suited to any form of Teutonic mania which, anyway, became politically suspect after the unification of Germany in 1871. From then on, the new and powerful German Empire set itself up as the main heir and keeper of the German inheritance, and the English suddenly found themselves beginning to look like poor relations.

In fact they felt themselves to be, in their own way, just as multi-racial as the French, if not more so. But in the complex tangle of emotions which constitutes the almost indefinable substance of national character, might not the ancient Old Testament ancestry have played its part, restraining extremism and maintaining a certain ironic detachment? Perhaps that is why the young Disraeli was able, during the full tide of the Teutonic mania, to exalt the semitic race and decry the ancestors of the English as "flat-nosed Franks" or "Baltic pirates" without these extravagances preventing him from becoming Prime Minister and Lord Beaconsfield.[50] And it was for this reason also that Kipling, even while talking of the White Man's Burden, was able to exhort his fellow-countrymen to preserve humble and contrite hearts, to remember the chastisement of Nineveh and Tyre, and to arm themselves against the temptation of pagan frenzies. He put them on their guard by calling on Jehovah, the Lord of Hosts:

> *If, drunk with sight of power, we loose*
> *Wild tongues that have not Thee in awe,*
> *Such boastings as the Gentiles use,*
> *Or lesser breeds without the Law—*
> *Lord God of Hosts be with us yet,*
> *Lest we forget—lest we forget!*

For heathen heart that puts her trust,
In reeking tube and iron shard,
All valiant dust that builds on dust,
And, guarding, calls not Thee to guard—
For frantic boast and foolish word—
Thy Mercy on Thy People, Lord![51]

In spite of this, it was characteristic of the British families who could do so to point with pride to a family tree which reached back to William the Conqueror or earlier. Nine hundred years after Hastings, "it is a good thing in England to bear the name of Harcourt, or Talbot or Courtney".[52] Even after the Second World War, when no French or Spanish snob any longer boasted of being descended from a family which arrived with the Franks or the Visigoths, some Englishmen were proud to claim ancestors who had "come over" with the Conqueror.[53] England still feels itself an island.

CHAPTER FOUR

ITALY

The Seed of Aeneas

Italy likewise, in the course of a history more prolonged than that of other nations, was the home of different peoples and civilizations— Greeks and Gauls, Lombards, Byzantines and Normans, the French, the Germans and the Spaniards. But she never integrated them into the heart of her tradition. To put it another way, her memories of the past never crystallized in the formation of an *Italianism* to match the *Latinism* of her greatest age. This was because Italian history was always dominated by the heritage of Roman Antiquity. The grandiose myth of the Eternal City, the mistress of the world, overshadowed all other forms of genealogical kinship. And though the imperial myth was constantly appropriated from the Italians by their neighbours and pupils and finally became part of the common patrimony of Europe, it never ceased to be the special attribute of the Italian people. In the eyes of French and German scholars the culture of Antiquity, that repository of wisdom and of the arts, remained a foreign culture, the obsolete culture of dead languages. For the Italians, on the other hand, this culture was inscribed in their buildings and in their landscape. It was their birthright and retained the freshness of its very beginnings.

The pre-eminent position of Italy in European culture had an influence, throughout the centuries and in a variety of ways, on the ideas which the Italians, not to speak of other nations, had formed of themselves. Thus it was primarily from Latin sources that the myth of Germanic origins was created. The Germans, as we shall see, in order to propagate their claims to universal hegemony, began by drawing their arguments from Tacitus and the writings of the Latin Fathers. The Russians, in their own way, did likewise. When the Muscovite Grand Dukes began to build their empire, Ivan the Terrible invoked the political myth of the Third Rome and called himself Czar, that is to say, Caesar. Rome, in the eyes of the newly converted pagans, seemed as old as human history and destined to endure until the Last Judgement. *Quando cadet Roma*, wrote Bede, *cadet mundus*.

Trojan ancestry, which was claimed by Frankish and German kings, was that of Aeneas, son of Venus, the great forebear of the Romans. Elsewhere, obscure tutelary gods gave birth to the cult of certain local saints. Italy alone could proudly claim a universal prophet, Virgil, who was thought to be a harbinger of Christ, of equal standing with David and Isaiah.* However much, therefore, the Italians may have declined politically—and their decadence contrasted at each stage with the omnipotence of Imperial Rome—they were able, in their capacity as sole legitimate heirs to the Roman heritage, to look down on other Europeans.

It is, therefore, scarcely surprising that, in spite of analogies in historical development, no sign of a Lombard myth comparable to the Frankish or Gothic myths ever appeared in Italy. Germans in modern times have spared no effort to emphasize the dynastic role of the Lombards and have even gone so far as to attribute the masterpieces of Italian culture to Germanic blood. But if Lombardy recalls the fact of an invasion, the term "Lombard" is only small change in the context of European culture, a pawnshop in Slav languages and nearer in its meaning to "Jew" than to "Frank" or "Goth". So that modern Italy has not experienced anything like the Germanic blood-cult or the imaginary racial conflicts which marked so profoundly the history of the other western nations. The Roman myth, moreover, in its ancient splendour, could aspire to equality with the Biblical myth, since the legends of the Eternal City were as old and imperishable as those of the "Eternal People". This may have been one of the reasons why the country in which the Vicar of Christ chose to establish his residence remained throughout history, as has often been said, "the most pagan country in Europe". This consideration deserves further study.

In 258, long before Constantine and before the Empire officially became Christian, Rome celebrated a first triumph over Jerusalem when the feast of Saint Peter was fixed for the 29th of June, a date traditionally reserved for the cult of Romulus-Quirinus, the legendary founder of the city.[1] So the metropolitan church may be said to have

---

* The commentators refer especially to Virgil's fourth *Eclogue*: "The last age foretold by Cumae's seer has come. The great march of generations begins once more. Now too the Virgin returns and Saturn's reign returns. Now a new generation descends from heaven. Do thou, chaste Lucina, look with favour on the birth of the child with whom the iron age will pass away and a golden age appear in all the world" (Verses 4 to 10).

become Roman before it became Catholic, and, if this tribute to the Caesars ensured its imperial pre-eminence, it could only be in exchange for the divinization of Peter who took the place of the god of the Curiae, Quirinus. It is tempting to suggest a case of syncretism, namely, the Christianizing of Venus's grandson, henceforth sanctified as the Prince of the Apostles. The Roman glory of Peter grew from century to century. Pope Damasus naturalized both Saint Peter and Saint Paul as Romans. Leo the Great considered them the true founders of the Eternal City and in that capacity their relics were soon objects of veneration, material and tangible symbols, though this veneration became restricted to the bones of Saint Peter only[2] (the search for his mortal remains has been renewed in the twentieth century, in 1915 and then in 1939). The exclusiveness of this veneration is understandable; it was reserved for the keeper of the Keys of the Kingdom, the guardian of the world beyond, the blessings of which mortal men sought in this world of ours by means of offerings and of gifts. It was thanks to these early gifts that the patrimony of Peter was founded and that the papacy became by degrees the centre of finance in the Middle Ages. For this reason too, in the dark and difficult periods of the Church's history, she adored the Prince of the Apostles to the point of considering him as God on Earth (Gregory II), or as Caesar and Consul (the Archbishop of Salerno). This legendary figure of the first Pope was regarded as the founder of a dynasty like the god Wotan of the royal German lineages. And that, no doubt, was why the hurriedly baptized barbarians of the Gothic hordes, who fought for possession of Italian territory, held him in such awe.

This protective, almost eponymous role became very noticeable in the eighth century when the papacy, which was abandoned by a weakening Byzantium, stood alone to face the ambitions of the Lombard kings. The earlier domination of the Goths had been ephemeral and their disappearance was proof, in a way, of the assimilating power of Italy which was exercised above all through the influence of the urban civilization of the Romans. The Lombards, who invaded Italy in 570, were far more redoubtable. They had preserved their Germanic customs and traditions intact. They remembered their legendary mother, Gambara, their gods Wotan and Freya and the long line of their kings. Their tribal name of "Long Beards" called to mind a remote pre-Indo-European matriarchy.* To begin

* According to Lombard tradition, their tribal name was given them by Wotan and, in order to impress the enemy tribe of the Vandals, the Lombard

with, they kept apart from the Romans and followed their ancient customs and laws. The papal epistles of that time give us some idea of the anti-German prejudices at the Roman court. The Lombards were perjurors, lepers, afflicted by a disgusting smell—a non-people in short.[3] Their chieftains, nevertheless, had seized Italian lands for themselves, and their kings, installed at Pavia, held the better part of the country. Because of this, the social evolution which marked the history of other western nations also began to develop in Italy. Personal names, in particular, were becoming purely Germanic just as they were in Merovingian Gaul, and the vocabulary began to follow suit (even in our day Italian retains about 300 words of Lombard origin). In neighbouring regions, the peninsula was called *regnum Langobardum*, the kindgom of the Lombards.[4]

Nevertheless, the peninsula did not become a Germanic kingdom, for the Lombards never gained possession of the Eternal City though they gathered round it on all sides. Several times they reached its gates without ever entering. In 739, when their pressure was most menacing, Pope Gregory III begged for help from Charles Martel, king of the Franks, appealing for the protection due to the "special people of the Church".[5] He sent the king presents, relics, the chains of Saint Peter and the keys of the Apostle's tomb. Thus began the special relationship between the Frankish dynasty and the successors to the Prince of the Apostles which was to weigh for more than a thousand years on the destinies of Europe. In 754, Pope Stephen II formed strong personal ties with Pepin the Short whom he crowned king in the church of Saint-Denis. It was probably during his stay in Paris that the idea of the Donation of Constantine was born, by which the first Christian emperor was reputed to have made over to the popes "all provinces, palaces and districts of the city of Rome and Italy and of the regions of the West". Thanks to this forgery, the Pontifical State was supplied with a birth certificate in due and proper form and was able to set itself up as heir to the Roman Empire of the West.

Pope Stephen fashioned other links with the Franks. From his tomb, Saint Peter was made to send them a message of woe which became threatening as it reached its conclusion: "Ego apostolus Dei Petrus, qui vos adoptivos habeo filios. . . . Currite, currite. . . . Coniuro vos, coniuro . . . sic non vos dispergat et proiat Dominus, sicut Israheliticus populus dispersus."[6] Stephen, moreover, started a cult for an

women, counselled thereto by Freya, were able to disguise themselves, with the help of their hair, as a host of bearded warriors, thus putting the enemy to flight.

imaginary daughter of the apostle, Saint Petronella, through whom he claimed a relationship with his "friend" Pepin. In the reign of his successor Pope Hadrian I, Charlemagne, after finally defeating the Lombards, went to Rome and at Easter, 774, pledged himself in writing to uphold the Donation of Constantine. He signed "over the body of Saint Peter and on the Gospels which were kissed".[7] Later, there occurred the famous ceremony of Christmas 800 when Charlemagne was crowned Emperor (against his will, it seems, and quite unexpectedly), and Pope Leo III granted him the whole Roman Empire in gift, transferring it "from the Greeks to the Germans" and by this gratuitous investiture giving rise to the theory of pontifical supremacy. It was in this way that some of the least admirable of the popes, whose names are now forgotten, were able, in spite of their weaknesses and their betrayal of many hopes,* to install in the Eternal City the most stable and at times the most vigorous government in the Christian West. This was the measure of Rome's magic, but it also rested henceforth on a relic more renowned than any other.

The above digression was necessary to explain how a theocracy, which felt itself to be Roman, was impelled into the centre of European history, and it leads to other questions. Dante, who contributed more than anyone to the formation of the Italian myth of origin, reproached the Emperor Constantine with having settled in Constantinople, thus tearing the seamless robe of the Roman Empire, and with "becoming Greek to make place for the Apostle [Peter] with good intention bearing evil fruit".[8] This evil fruit was the Papal States. Another great patriot, Machiavelli, was equally critical of papacy, whose "antinational" power impeded the formation of a national Italian monarchy. The theocratic State, which divided Italy in two and was enthroned on the sacred hills of Rome, did in fact prevent the unification of the country both in a geographical and in an emotional sense. Moreover, the popes drew off a part of the spiritual energies, elsewhere released for the benefit of kings or States, while another great part of these energies was devoted to fighting against the temporal power of the popes. The conflict took shape in the Middle Ages during the struggles between the feudal families and the merchant class, the first tending to support the imperial or Ghibelline camp while the second sided with the Guelf or papal party. These loyalties were revived and redefined in the nineteenth century during the polemics between the

---

* The ninth and tenth centuries of papal history have been referred to as "the age of pornocracy".

neo-Ghibelline and neo-Guelf ideologues. Both sides aspired to the unity of the Italian nation and both regarded themselves as Roman; but this affiliation was directed by one side to establishing direct descent from ancient and pagan Rome, while on the other the relationship was sought with Christian and pontifical Rome which, as has been shown, itself laid claim to being the universal legatee of classical Antiquity. These two tendencies, which came into conflict at the time of the *Risorgimento*, never fell back on the racial arguments already current beyond the Alps. Italy never witnessed anything similar to the Controversy about the Two Races but she did experience what one might call two kinds of dedication, either catholic or secular, to that particularly Italian form of ancestor worship which is Romanism (*Romanità*). These different attitudes do not seem to have disappeared as a result of the unification of the country since Italians, according to whether they belong to the Left or to the Right, tend to be in favour of or opposed to the papacy which itself remains Italian. In this con-nexion, the *Enciclopedia Italiana* during the Fascist period, in its article on Italy, wrote of "the interior troubles, the disagreements between the civil and religious powers, which became a specifically Italian phenomenon and made all the problems of Italian life more turbulent and more difficult to solve".[9] And, instead of the column in which the German encyclopaedias of that time dealt with the racial idea (*Rassengedanke*), the Fascist encyclopaedia devotes its space to a study of the Idea of Rome (*Idea di Roma*) throughout the ages. This brings us to the very heart of our subject.

*   *   *

Without an indigenous royal race of their own, it was not until the twelfth century that the Italians, at the time when the Communes were first being established, pushed back the classical genealogy of the Romans, that of Aeneas, to the first ancestor, Adam. As is usual in these cases, a political motive was involved. Rights of precedence, which in Italy were not dynastic but communal or municipal, had to be explained and justified and claims to antiquity which were at the same time titles of nobility were therefore asserted. A first example of this was when the people of Rome, soon after 1140, at the instigation of the reformer Arnold of Brescia, rose up against the papal govern-ment and its feudal system. The popes were driven from the town, the Senate was reconstituted and the glorious insignia of *S.P.Q.R.* reappeared among the ruins of the Capitol. The *populus romanus* displayed the old titles which it believed had been usurped by the mighty of this world. "Rome is sovereign; she created the Empire; she is the mother of kingdoms, the world's capital, an example of all virtues, the mirror of all cities. . . ."[10] A contemporary description of the "golden city of Rome", the *Graphia auree urbis Roma*, listed the generations which go back from Aeneas to Noah.[11] But the method employed for this purpose was different from that in use beyond the Alps, for it established a direct link between the Eternal City and the patriarch without the intermediary of his offspring and, what is more, it transferred the survivors of the Flood to Rome. Immediately after the Deluge, or perhaps just before it, Noah and his three sons, carried on a raft, arrived in Italy and built a town on the same site where Rome was to be founded. There followed the identifications or family trees fashionable at the time. Japheth was said to have sired Janus so that this Roman god became the grandson of Noah. A popular variant of this story was to unite Noah and Janus in the same person. Among the genealogical speculations which were worked out in Europe, that of the Romans was unique of its kind. It was only the Eternal City which, on an almost equal footing with Genesis, could claim to have been founded by Noah, the regenerator of the human race, *che si puo dire un altro Adamo*, as one of the texts in the vernacular had it.[12]

The genealogical tree of the *Graphia auree urbis Roma* resuscitated a number of mythological figures, both classical and Biblical, such as Hercules, Saturn, Nimrod and Ham. Those who continued or adapted this tree in other Italian cities added new characters amongst whom was Antenor, the Trojan counsellor of Priam, and the giant Atlas, son of the Titan Japet (identified with Japheth)—adopted as founders by Venice and by Florence respectively—while the Biblical patriarchs were less favoured so that quite a number of ancestral lists did not go back further than the pagan gods and heroes. Thus at the very beginning of their existence, Italian towns furnished themselves with pedigrees, one more glorious and luxuriant than the other, all of which went back, through Rome, to the mythological pantheon of the Ancients.

Florence can serve as an example. Her great chronicler, Villani, records, in passing, the arrival of Noah in Italy, but he attributes much more importance to the coming of Atlas, the founder of Fiesole, Florence's old rival. Moving on to historic times, he shows Julius Caesar to have been the founder of Florence and if, as a patriotic Florentine, Villani affects not to be interested in Roman history except in so far as it relates to the foundation of his own city, his parish-pump patriotism becomes Italian patriotism as soon as he deals with the "barbarians" beyond the Alps. Villani's chronicle is typical of the state of mind of the Florentines. When addressing the Romans in 1391, they even boasted of having once been Romans themselves, and Dante described his native city as *bellissima e famosissima figlia di Roma*.[13]

It was not only men of letters who were fascinated by the prestige of Roman Antiquity. Italian folklore also acquired mythological heroes, whose memory was perpetuated by their ruined temples which harmonized with the landscape.[14] This tradition is still alive today, as can be seen from the popularity of films on classical subjects made by Italians for Italians, or by the sensationalism of the Italian press and television when announcing, early in 1972, the discovery of the remains of a small temple alleged to have contained the mortal remains of Aeneas.[15]

The obsession with Antiquity may be observed in other fields. It is enough to remember the role reserved to Rome by Italian theologians. For Thomas Aquinas, Rome had been destined from her foundation to be the centre of Christianity. His successor, Tolomeo da Lucca, and other Italian canonists, thought that this pre-ordained destiny justified papal omnipotence, since God became man immediately after the universal empire had been founded by Augustus and had delegated to His Vicars on Earth *omnes potestates in coelo et terra*.[16] It was part of this theocratic conception that Rome succeeded Jerusalem at the moment of the Nativity. The Eternal City was, however, the mainstay of everything and papal theocracy only an accessory. Arguments of this kind could as well be made to serve the cause of the emperors or even to bolster heretical movements. It needed only a simple change of badge to substitute hatred of the popes for idolatry of them. It was the converse attitude which the Divine Comedy was to propagate.

Virgil, Dante's guide, speaks to him, from the second Canto of the *Inferno* onwards, about the glorious mission of Aeneas whom God chose "to be the father of life-giving Rome and of her empire both of which, verily, were established for the holy place where sits the successor of Saint Peter".[17] The papacy, however, had transformed this holy place into a "sewer of blood and stench"[18] as a result of the tragic error of Constantine who is treated as the cause of all Christianity's ills.[19] It is the Roman eagle, a pagan bird, which Dante continues to regard as the living symbol of Divine Justice. "Because I was just and holy", it says, "I have reached a height of glory beyond the yearning of all human desire."[20] Elsewhere, Christ is seen by the poet as the guarantor of Roman justice since the Romans are the true people chosen by God. Because of this, Brutus and Cassius, the assassins of Caesar, are placed beside Judas in the ninth circle of Hell.[21] The cult of Rome reveals its true character when we see Dante weeping over the misfortunes of Italy and imploring aid from "sovereign Jove who upon earth for us was crucified".[22] Only a little less pagan is Beatrice who before conducting Dante into Paradise exhorts him in these terms: "And with me thou shalt be forever a citizen of that Rome whereof Christ is a Roman."[23]

Christ, the Roman citizen for all time! One can understand why Dante, the most Italian among Italians, should have shown little interest in patriarchal genealogies since those in the *Aeneid* were the only real and living ones in his eyes.[24] This preference for pagan rather than Bible myths is reflected also in the relative indifference he shows toward the Jews. And here again Dante is a witness for posterity. There is little trace in the *Divine Comedy* of the contemporary degradation of the Jews and none whatever of their past election by God, for this has been appropriated entirely by the Romans.

Roman glory, however, and universal domination by Rome of which the poet awaits an imminent re-establishment, is in palpable contrast with the present condition of Italy "the slave, hostel of woe, ship without pilot",[25] ancestral soil which is fought over by usurping popes and foreign tyrants.

A similar outlook is to be found among the great Italian humanists who claimed descent from the Romans and dreamed of a different world, as their invention of the name Renaissance vividly suggests. It is immediately apparent that, with regard to their myth of origin, the Italians were in a privileged and exceptional situation, for not only were they the first creators of their genealogy but this was related to ancestors who were born on the same soil as themselves. If humanism stimulated the birth of nationalist feeling everywhere, this again was due to the example of the Italians who alone could unquestionably claim direct descent from the Romans without collateral links or even without contradicting themselves. Moreover, the reverence felt by other nations for this legacy; the spread of an ancient mythology which was to become popular through the fine Arts; the diffusion of Roman Law from which all the legislators of Europe derived inspiration, and of a liturgical language which alone was thought worthy to contribute to the cult of religion; all these advantages of Latinity could not but render such a heritage even more valuable in the eyes of its legitimate heirs, despoiled by the barbarians who had made Italy the battlefield of Europe. All the Italian humanists dreamed of the grandeur that was Rome and paid homage to their ancestors; and Petrarch's *De viris illustribus*, a pantheon of illustrious men in which neither Greek nor Biblical names are admitted, makes a pair with Boccaccio's *De genealogia deorum*, a theogony in which the earth god Demogorgon is portrayed as a pagan Adam.

Let us consider for one moment the case of Petrarch, who has been called "the first modern man" and whose writings seem everywhere to reflect the ancient dream. If this renovator of antique learning sang the glories of Rome in Latin and his love for Italy in the vulgar tongue, both sentiments were united in his mind. Rome, in his view, was pre-destined by Jupiter to become the sacred city of the Christians, and he made the greatest god of the Romans declare: "I will put on a clothing of flesh, I will accept the burden of humanity, I shall suffer a shameful death. . . ." Elsewhere, in his *Italia mia* the poet bewailed, as Dante did, the sorrows of his motherland, polluted by the blood of barbarians. "O noble Italian stock, free yourself from the burden and the superstition of Germanic invincibility!"

> Vertù contra furore
> Prenderà l'arme e fia 'l combatter corto;
> Chè l'antico valore
> Ne l'italici cor non è ancor morto.

A century and a half later, at the end of his *Principe*, Machiavelli was inspired by these lines in *Italia mia*, and he was followed in this, at the end of the eighteenth century, by Alfieri. These sentiments still have a familiar ring in Italian ears.

The name of Petrarch is also connected with the adventure of Rienzi who, encouraged by him, undertook to restore the Roman Empire.

The popes were then residing at Avignon while certain feudal families were in charge of the government at Rome. In 1347 Cola di Rienzi, a young enthusiast nourished on old books and the prophecies of Joachim of Flora, was carried to power by the Roman populace. In him the imperial dream was to combine with the expectation of the Holy Spirit, and with the eschatology of a paradise on earth, the Third Reign. Once he had made himself master of Rome, Rienzi called together the representatives of the Italian towns to discuss the unification of the whole country. In order to mark the beginning of a new era, he dated his decrees from *the first year of the liberated Roman Republic*, thus giving the first example of a symbolic break in time. At least his rule, which only lasted one year, was not stained with blood. He called himself, *liberator Urbis; zelator Italiae, Spiritus Sancti miles*, and conferred upon all Italians the citizenship of Rome. His enterprise foundered and the Roman lords got the better of him. But so long as he was in power, the homage of Italian cities and of foreign kings was not wanting and, to judge by the testimony of Petrarch, the papal court at Avignon considered his success assured.[26]

On returning to Rome after the Great Schism, the popes themselves became adherents of the new humanist religion. Aeneas Silvius Piccolomini, the most cultivated among the popes of the Renaissance, chose the name Pius II, not in remembrance of the first Pope Pius about whom nothing is known, but as a tribute to the "pious Aeneas" of Virgil, since, according to a Piccolomini tradition, their family was descended directly from Romulus. Pius II was utterly contemptuous of the pedigrees which went back to Noah. Arno Borst said of him that in propagating the myths of antiquity he had destroyed the medieval conception of genealogies. In fact, he ridiculed the old wives' tales, the *anilia deliramenta*, of the ignorant who thought they could trace back their genealogies to the Flood. Why not push back into the womb of Eve, he asked?[27] It may be that the novels and erotic poetry of so cultivated a man of letters as Aeneas Silvius Piccolomini were not less instrumental than the dissolute life of Alexander Borgia or the thirst for pleasure of Leo X in directing the hatred and contempt of Italian public opinion against the papacy.[28] Machiavelli reproached the papal court at Rome with having destroyed all feelings of piety and religion in Italy, and Guicciardini was even more explicit. Confronted with popes of such dubious faith, these patriots rediscovered in themselves the sentiments of good Christians.[29]

An attempt was made, however, during the pontificate of Alexander Borgia, to re-establish the position of the Noachian genealogy and to reconcile it with classical mythology. About 1498, the Dominican friar, Giovanni di Viterbo, claimed to have discovered a chronicle of the Babylonian historian, Berossus, which furnished detailed evidence of the political consequences of the Flood. According to this account, Noah divided up the earth among his sons, the real number of whom was nearly twenty (though Moses had not considered it necessary to list them all). Each of these sons, bearing a pagan name, became the founder of a Christian nation. As for Noah himself, he settled in Italy under the name of Janus, as had been foretold three centuries earlier in a "golden legend of Rome".[30] This story was to dominate Italian genealogical studies throughout the Counter-Reformation and well beyond it, as is shown by such writings as De primis Italianis colonis (1606) and De Noe in Italia adventu (1655) and a great number of "Origini" of one town after another.[31] This chronicle of the pseudo-Berossus had an even greater popularity among the Germans because it supplied them with an ancestor in the person of Noah's son Tuiscon (called Tuisto by Tacitus), who thus began his great patriotic career. It was not till 1726 that Johann Mascov, one of the first modern historians of Germany, proclaimed the demise of this legend.[32]

The Age of Enlightenment, in Italy as elsewhere, discredited the old oriental genealogies. In order to replace them, scholars attempted to relate the Romans to the Etruscans. The latter had always been vaguely discernible behind Romulus and Aeneas just as, in France, the Gauls lurked in the shadows behind the Frankish dynasty. South of the Alps, however, it was not a question of new-born bourgeois ambitions seeking an outlet, but of national pride attempting to restore to Italy a cultural primacy which by then was universally accorded to Greece in her capacity as the birthplace of the Arts and of Philosophy. It was, therefore, a temptation for Italian scholars to put the Greeks to school with the mysterious Etruscans. Vico, himself, while deriding the "vanity of nations which all regard themselves as ancient as the world itself" (Scienza nuova seconda), gave way to this temptation when he fixed the birth of Pythagoras and of geometry in Etruria (De antiquissima Italorum sapientia). An Etruscan Academy was founded in 1726; tombs were dug up; Piranesi's famous prints made the general public acquainted with the ruins; in 1767, an enthusiastic prelate, Mario Guarnacci, published a Historico-Etruscan memoir on the most ancient Kingdom of Italy in which, relying on the pseudo-Berossus, he introduced the Etruscans into Italy from Egypt, thus short-circuiting the Greeks, and accused the Romans of having destroyed a wise and ancient people.[33]

Etruscomania, or etruscheria, reached its apogee in the period of the Napoleonic wars through the enthusiasm of Vincenzo Cuoco, a follower of Vico. His essay, Platone in Italia, was a landmark in Italian scholarship. A new age called for new ancestors. In place of Noah, this patriot summoned Plato to Italy there to be restored to the bosom of his ancestors; it was the Etruscans and not the Greeks who were originally "the inventors of nearly all forms of knowledge which adorn the human spirit". Aristotle and Plato himself were no more than usurpers, "mere copyists".[34] Napoleon's short-lived Kingdom of Etruria, which he founded in 1801, owed its origin to this passion for Italian high antiquity which, in the nineteenth century, led to even more bizarre speculation. With the progress of archaeology, the Etruscans seemed scarcely to meet the required standards of age so that one historian, Mazzoldi, discovered Italy as the site of legendary Atlantis, while another, Ianelli, linked the Romans with the Egyptians.[35]

The Italy of the *Risorgimento*, the young Italy of the nation's rebirth, was decidedly anxious to be the oldest nation on earth. Let us look at Abbate Gioberti's famous *Primato morale e civile degli Italiani*. The better to strengthen a belief in universal Italian *primacy*, this writer referred to the ancient wisdom of the Pelasgians, "the race most richly endowed, capable of uniting and accommodating within itself all ethnographic differences and contradictions, thanks to its harmonious temper, in the same way that ideas which are opposite in appearance are made to agree in the Supreme Being". As an apostle of Italian superiority who was also an orthodox believer, Gioberti tried to reconcile the tradition of the church with mythology and at the same time with science, and he justified the inequality among human races by reference to the confusion of Babel which had shattered the unity of mankind.[36] But it would be impossible to quote, let alone to read, all that has been written on this subject. Mazzini, for his part, seems to have adhered to the Etruscan theory.[37]

All these claims, though not devoid of meaning, were scarcely more than an amusement for intellectuals. Nobody would have died for the Etruscans but the pick of the Italian *bourgeoisie* were ready to sacrifice their lives for Rome. This cult of the Eternal City, as the historian Prezzolini has pointed out recently, shows the true extent of the Italians' originality:

> The real difference between the Italian and other civilizations lies in the fact that Italian intellectuals believed that the Italian people were not merely the natural and authentic descendants, but the only legitimate heirs of Rome. They hoped for the resurrection in Italy of the ancient power of Rome. . . . This belief took such a hold of the cultivated classes in Italy that it influenced their thought for centuries. It contributed in no little measure to the struggle to achieve a greatness which was completely out of reach of the political strength of the Nation.[38]

There are few Italian writers, whether in modern or in ancient times, who have not subscribed to this cult, and, often enough, it is that aspect of their work which posterity has fastened upon, as with Foscolo's *I Sepolcri* or Leopardi's *Sopra il monumento di Dante*. Manzoni became an historian in order to show how *romanità* had been preserved and saved by the popes of the early Middle Ages.[39] The tenor of these professions of faith and of these disputes does not differ much from that which can be observed in the times of Arnold of Brescia and Cola di Rienzi. Towards the end of his life Mazzini wrote:

> Rome was the dream of my youthful years, the creative force of my spiritual ideals, the religion of my soul. I entered it on foot one evening in the first days of March, trembling and almost in adoration. Rome was for me the temple of humanity and so it remains even now in spite of the humiliation of present times. . . . Within its walls there was fashioned the Unity of the World. There, while other nations, after accomplishing a brief mission, had disappeared forever without serving more than once as leaders, life continued eternally and death was unknown.[40]

Mazzini recalled the glories of the past, those of pagan Rome and those of Christian Rome, and projected them into the future. He dreamt of establishing a *Third Rome* which was to be the centre of a universal religion. He wanted to "mould for Italy a crown of re-generated peoples; to make Rome the head of the world, the word of God among the races of mankind".[41] Thus Rome was to be restored as a universal temple at the service of all mankind from which this faithful heir of Dante and Machiavelli wished to exclude the temporal power of the Holy See.

The other great ideologist of the unification of Italy, Gioberti, suggested federating all the nations of the earth under the pontifical and Roman aegis. The Romans, he declared, had been a priestly people chosen by Providence for the establishment of Catholicism, and he compared the Italians of his time to the tribe of Levites. To bring this vision into sharper focus he employed concentric images; Rome was the soul of Italy; Italy of Europe and Europe of the world. Therefore, Rome was destined to become the capital of a universal republic pre-sided over by the popes.[42] It will be observed that Rome was equally desirable to both the contending parties in the *Risorgimento*. The anti-clerical side had, in fact, adopted Garibaldi's motto: *Rome or death*.

Carducci described Garibaldi as the new Romulus. The arts no less than science were imbued with patriotic passion. Since they were convinced of their descent from the Romans and stood by this lineage, the Italians showed little enthusiasm for those historico-philosophical speculations which attributed an Aryan origin to Europeans. Carlo Cattaneo, in about 1840, referred ironically to "the excellence and nobility of the North" and to "the magical peregrinations of the Aryans". A certain Carlo Troia enquired why international scientific circles had all of a sudden become inflamed with curiosity about India. He, personally, preferred to derive the population of Europe from the Middle East in the traditional way.[43] When, at the end of the nineteenth century, philology passed on the torch to anthropology, Italian scientists displayed the same restraint or lack of understanding. According to Lombroso's view, primitive humanity was black. It was later transformed or "converted", as he puts it rather oddly, into the yellow, Hamitic, Semitic and thereafter into the Aryan races, by mean of terrestrial cataclysms.[44] Thus the Aryans were definitely descended from the Negroes. International scientific opinion was sceptical and talked of Italian dilettantism, especially as Lombroso was not an isolated case. The anthropologist, Giuseppe Sergi, writing of the Aryans in Italy, praised the Etruscans for having repulsed the invasion attempted by these unlettered primitives, thereby saving Mediterranean civilization. The latter was the work of Italiots and Greeks. It was clear that, so far as Sergi was concerned, there was no question at all of the Aryans having partaken in the creation of classical culture or in the foundation of Rome.[45] Both Lombroso and Sergi did, nevertheless, believe in the Aryans after a fashion.

From 1903 onwards, however, another Italian scholar, Enrico de Michelis, launched a radical attack on this belief which he declared was founded on "a confusion between language, blood and life". He examined in great detail how, at the beginning of the nineteenth century, the myth had been created which derived the people of Europe from the plateaux of Asia in imitation of the Biblical narration about Paradise and the peopling of the earth. This great scholar was the first man to speak, in this context, of the genesis of scientific myths.[46]

There has been an unceasing dialogue about this question of descent between the scientific hypotheses of former times and collective beliefs. The Italians held the belief that they were descended from the Romans and that they therefore belonged to a single race. This feeling may have been diffuse but was nevertheless so real that without it Fascism could not have been what it was. It is debatable whether this feeling has altogether disappeared even in our own day.* However, the historian of Fascism, Renzo De Felice, recently observed that the *razza di Roma*, "glorified by Mussolini, had nothing to do with anthropology or biology since the Italian conception of race was 'creative' and 'spiritual' ".[47] This seems very vague and implies a contradiction in terms because the scientific age has known no races except those which are such by reason of their blood. Nevertheless, we are brought back to the contrast between the Italian concept (the idea of Rome) and the German concept (the idea of race). The Italians had one thing in common with the Germans, however. They thought they were descended from a single stock—in this case it was a Latin one—but they held this belief in a different way from the Germans. And this difference, undoubted though it is, appears at first sight to elude any attempt at historical explanation.

But let us see if it is possible to find a relationship between certain so-called national qualities which have influenced the fortunes of politics and war—the individualism and scepticism of the Italians, the herd instinct and fanaticism of the Germans—and the genealogies which were marked, in the one case as in the other, by collective representations of *age* and *youth*. We have seen how the leading Italian thinkers searched back ever further till they were burrowing into prehistory, and how Gioberti appealed, in support of Italian primacy, to a cultural priority largely based on age. By contrast, the doctrine of the transalpine Aryans was based on the superiority of a young race of conquerors whose purity and vigour were poles apart from the decadence of the races described as old. These theses were all the more striking because the opposition between them corresponded with the great break between the modern and ancient cultures, with the beginning of modern history in the West. From this point of view, all the nations North of the Alps, which were post-Christian or "child nations", were the antithesis of a nation which was reputedly pre-Christian—a "father nation"—and related by this fact to that other nation with a history of three thousand years, the Jews.

With this in mind, one cannot fail to observe that Italian history

* After the fall of Fascism and Hitlerism, the great historian G. P. Bognetti thought it useful to recall that Italian civilization was not, in its origin, purely Latin and emphasized the Germanic contribution to it ("the men of the North had an essential function in it"). Cf. Bognetti, *L'età lombarda*, Milan 1966, Vol. III, pp. 187 *et seq.*

shows only occasional evidence of anti-Jewish fury and of the campaigns against the Jews with which the annals of other European countries are filled, as though the descendants of Aeneas, confident of their primogeniture, would not bother to claim it against the sons of Moses. This beneficial detachment rested on a relationship of equality which, as we have seen, seemed to have found its reflection in the myth of origin, for it was Noah himself who came to fertilize the soil of Italy and to breed a nation. No other great tradition of the European Middle Ages has dared to claim such tribute from one of the Patriarchs. When, in 1934, Mussolini still spoke of the Jews in the Italian manner, it was like an echo of this naturalization of Noah. "The Jews", he said, "have been in Rome from the time of the kings. They may have supplied some garments after the Rape of the Sabines. They wept over the bier of Julius Caesar. There were fifty thousand of them in the time of Augustus. They were never molested."[48] At that time the Duce also dealt with the Führer's pretensions by invoking the prestige of antiquity. "Thirty centuries of history enable us to contemplate with contemptuous pity the doctrines that have been put forward beyond the Alps by the descendants of men who did not even know how to write when Rome had Caesar, Virgil and Augustus."[49] We shall return in the next chapter to this Italo-German conflict and see what can be made of it in terms of age and youth. We shall approach the problem by examining the meaning of the notion of purity which, allied to that of youth, was a characteristic of German obsessions.

At all events, the conflict is not a recent one. Dante, in order to emphasize the nobility of the race of Aeneas, recited, on Virgil's authority, a list of its august forebears: "Asia provides it with its closest ancestors like Assaracus. . . . Europe, on the other hand, gave it the oldest of its grand-parents, Dardanus . . . and Africa its most ancient grand-mother, Electra. . . ." He also listed its female ancestors the more to enoble it—Creusa of Troy, Dido of Carthage and the Italian Lavinia, and concluded: "Who would not recognize it as the sign of a divine destiny to see united in a single man the noblest blood from every part of the world."[50]

From the point of view of Germanic doctrine this sign was an infamous one, a sin against the purity of race, since it made Aeneas a half-caste three times over. On this point, however, Italians are still on the same ground as they were in Dante's time.

CHAPTER FIVE

GERMANY

LANGUAGE AND RACE

Every nation's history is unique, but the characteristics of German history differ greatly from those of other European countries. These differences are as real now as they have always been. Thus an English, Italian or Russian textbook of history starts off, and continues, by relating what has taken place on national soil. But a German textbook almost always begins by dealing with the expansion of the Germanic peoples, that is to say with events which took place fifteen or twenty centuries ago in Italy, France or Spain—anywhere except Germany. This is primarily a matter of historical sources, since we know a great deal more about the wanderings and wars of Goths, Franks and Lombards than about Frisians and Saxons (about whom, prior to their conversion, we know next to nothing). But as a consequence the Germans have been led, from their earliest days at school, to take an interest in the ancestors of other nations, even to cast a possessive glance over the whole of the European continent.

This special kind of internationalism, which formerly had its counterpart in the aristocratic prestige which "Germanism" enjoyed amongst other peoples, is still echoed today in the different names for the Germans that different languages have. One might describe this as a little kaleidoscope of Europe itself—"Germans" to the English; "Saxons" to the Swedes formerly, and still today to the Finns; "Niemcy" to the Russians and Poles (though the latter sometimes call them "Swabians"); and "Tedeschi" to the Italians. The Germans adopted the root of this last word (in what circumstances we shall see later on) to become "Deutsche". This dialogue between Germany and neighbouring countries has been going on since the Middle Ages, and the confused identity of the Germans in the eyes of Europe did not help them form any clear ideas about themselves.

Nietzsche was aware of this when he wrote that the Germans eluded definition.[1] Defying his compatriots, who were worshippers of "pure race", Nietzsche proclaimed racial cross-breeding as the origin of

the Germans; in other words, he declared them to be racially heterogeneous. But this was to commit, like many other intelligent people in
the nineteenth century though in a reverse sense, the mistake of a too
positivist or biological approach to man. It would be more pertinent
in this context to point to the persistence of the old clannish or tribal
divisions in the form of Stämme,[2] or Länder.

The singularity of German history may be shown in another way.
German historians are apt to refer to "Germanic beginnings" (germanische Frühzeit) followed by "German beginnings" (deutsche Frühzeit).
If the first were played out with all Europe as their stage, the second
were even more paradoxical in that they took place primarily in a
country which, if we are to believe extant sources, was not Germany
but France. Let us imagine for one moment that a detailed history
had been discovered, say in the sixteenth century, of the Frisians or of
the Thuringians. German historiography might have been completely
changed by this and—who knows?—European history might have
followed a different course. But one has to build with the materials
available. It was all the easier for Clovis and Chilperic to become great
ancestors for the Germans because the ruling class of their times, from
the Rhine to the Loire, does indeed seem to have spoken a Germanic
language. The dynasty of the Carolingian mayors of the palace was
likewise German. So too was Charlemagne who has a better claim to
be the mainspring of German history than of French, since the imperial
myth was to flourish in Germany and not in France. There is a
"portrait" of Charlemagne by Dürer but none by Foucquet.

Nevertheless, contrary to general belief, the feeling of a collective
German identity came fairly late. Moreover—and this is another
peculiarity of German history—it arose, as the etymology of the words
deutsch, Deutsche themselves shows, not from the idea of a common
descent but from the consciousness among the different Stämme of
sharing a common language. This consciousness emerged from a confrontation with the older Latin or Welsch language and culture, thus
illustrating on a grand scale the Hegelian theories of self-consciousness
or the aphorism of Nietzsche: "The Thou is older than the I." This
feeling of community among the Stämme, confronted with Latin
civilization, showed itself for instance, soon after the foundation of the
First Reich (962), in the person of Liutprand, Bishop of Cremona, who
was Emperor Otto's right-hand man. In him, the feeling of Germanic
unity is accompanied by hatred of the Welsche. "We Lombards,
Saxons, Franks, Lotharingians, Bavarians, Swabians, Burgundians", he

wrote, "have such utter contempt for the Romans that when we try to express our indignation we can find no term with which to insult our enemies more damaging than that of Romans. This single word means for us all that is ignoble, cowardly, sordid, obscene."[3] It is worth noting that, as late as the beginning of the twentieth century, some school textbooks in Germany contrasted *Welschland* with *Deutschland*, the former being a general term for foreign countries.[4]

In writing the history of the words *deutsch*, *Deutsche*, the philologist Leo Weisgerber, is at pains to show that, as a general rule, the names of European languages are derived, etymologically, from the names of countries or of peoples (thus *Franks→Francia-France→French* people →*French* language, etc.); but in the case of the Germans the reverse is true, because the name of the common language (*theodiscus, diutisk*), which appeared in the time of Charlemagne, ante-dated by a century or two the generic appellation of *tütsche* or *Deutsche* and only gave birth to *Deutschland* much later.[5] Thus it is not only by comparison with other European languages, as we have shown above, but also in the context of the internal etymological situation that the terms *Deutsche* and *Deutschland* are exceptional. The birth of a new word is a sign of a new awareness; but the feeling which elsewhere was formed round the symbol of something tangible, round the name of some specific thing (tribe or dynasty, province or national soil), in Germany alone was born from a linguistic or ideal notion. Weisgerber draws the conclusion that "German history from its very beginnings recognized a spiritual principle as the foundation of the status of nations",[6] a remark which follows strictly the tradition of German idealism.

His comments, which might give rise to some interesting insights into the principal currents in German philosophy and culture, would appear to contradict our main thesis on the role of myths of origin, namely, the affirmation of a common descent in the rise of national feeling. Indeed, it was not until the sixteenth century, at the time of the Reformation, that a common ancestor for the Germans was suggested in the form of the Biblical Ashkenaz, who had hitherto fulfilled this function only for the *Stamm* of the Saxons. It remains to be seen whether, in the final analysis, the "spiritual" concept of a community of language and the "carnal" concept of affiliation by race did not both reflect the same collective aspirations. From the Middle Ages onwards, we shall find that some writers, who at times glorified the German language and at other times the German race, would occasionally appeal to the same texts.

All these problems raise the question of how traditions and memories are transmitted. According to a widely held view, the cult of the Germanic race was related to and even nourished by pre-Christian memories rooted in the native soil from which Wotan and Thor were never wholly extirpated. Closer examination, however, reveals the Germanic pantheon as a laborious reconstruction after an eclipse of the Nordic gods which was almost as total as that of the Etruscan or Celtic. Indeed, German mythology was only preserved outside Germany in Scandinavian sagas or in the writings of Roman historians and the only myths of origin preserved by direct transmission are those of the expatriate, more or less de-Germanized, *Stämme*—the Goths, Lombards, Burgundians, Angles and Saxons.[7] This is another aspect of the uniqueness of German history.

The survival of these pre-Christian beliefs among the Germans scattered abroad makes it likely that their royal dynasties and feudal courts preserved them to retain a Germanic identity and to distinguish themselves from the natives. We have seen how the fusion of two cultures was accomplished by the adoption of a shared genealogy like the Trojan. The case was different in Germany where the idea of a common genealogy was preceded by that of a common tongue—the German language which the clerks opposed to other languages. Thus, at the beginning of the tenth century Notker the Stammerer, who was a monk of Saint-Gall, made a clear distinction between "we who speak the Teutonic tongue" and those who spoke the language of the Romans or Slavs.[8]

This peculiarly German mode of differentiation is all the more significant because we find it again, disguised as anthropological theory, a millennium later on. For German racism imposed two different lines of demarcation. One was *geographical* or *exterior*, and was thought of as marking off the territories inhabited by Germans from those inhabited by other "races" (whence the significance of the "anti-race" of Jews inside Germany); while the other was thought of as running *through* the other European countries, and dividing the "Germanic racial elements" from other, less valuable, elements. In essence, this division simply reproduced the great linguistic cleavage established in Carolingian times. Thus, after a thousand years, a community feeling which had been expressed originally in terms of language came to be formulated in terms of race as though these concepts, which became interchangeable, covered the same deep, psycho-historical reality.

On the other hand, there is no doubt that the Germans soon began to cultivate their own genealogical traditions and built them up, in Germany itself, with material taken exclusively from a Christian or classical past. But we should here distinguish between the imperial myth, which was derived from the legend of Troy, and the special traditions related to the *Stämme*.

As far as the princely line of the Franks was concerned, the terminological muddle, after the partition of the Carolingian Empire, was the same on both sides of the Rhine. Germany was the eastern kingdom of the Franks, the *Öst-Reich*, of which Austria (*Oesterreich*) has perpetuated the name. It was the *Francia* of the German chroniclers of the ninth and tenth centuries, or the *Regnum francorum et teutonorum* of Frederick Barbarossa in the twelfth century. This *Francia*, however, was sometimes called *Germania* by the early chroniclers of the *Öst-Reich* and it was contrasted with *Gallia* beyond the Rhine, long before French authors began to magnify the Gauls. The Franks were then the noblest race in Germany just as they were in France. It was thanks to their genealogy that the Germans could enjoy the honour of being descended from the Trojans and, through them, from Japheth and from Adam. It was thanks to them that the theorists of the imperial idea sought to validate the title deeds of the Holy Roman Empire "transferred from the Greeks to the Germans", that is to say, the Franks.

At the end of the thirteenth century, after the new dynasty of the Hapsburgs had come to power, Canon Alexander von Roes distinguished between *Francia major* (Germany) and *Francia minor* (France). Roes already knew of three great European nations, the Italian, the French and the German. To the Italians he attributed piety; to the French, wisdom; to the Germans, power. The latter were, indeed, the real Franks while the French were only of Frankish origin (*francigenae*). Roes went no further in explaining his thesis, but one of his late followers, Twinger von Königshofen (1346-1420) developed the idea as follows: the Franks having established themselves in German lands (*dütschen landen*) mixed with other *dütsche* and gave birth to Germans. The *francigenae* or French, on the other hand, were born of mixed Frankish and *Welsch* parentage. It would be wrong, however, to call Alexander von Roes, as Paul Joachimsen did, "the first German theorist of race", since he also compared the Romans, descended from the Trojans, to the root, the Germans to the trunk and the French to the branches.[9] Roes thought that Caesar had peopled Germany with Romans and that "German" came from *germen*. In other words, for

Roes as for the German Middle Ages in general, there was a direct line of descent between past and present, between classical Antiquity and Christianity. It was only in the fifteenth and sixteenth centuries, as we have seen, that German humanists cut off the trunk from the root (or the branches from the trunk) and thus prepared the ground for genealogical interpretations that were explicitly racist. For Roes, by contrast, the German Holy Roman Empire could not be hereditary because it was universal and Christian. It had to be elective. The Holy Spirit wished it so. There is an obviously paradoxical contrast between specific "royal lines" of Germanic origin, which in Spain, France and England formed the nucleus of a central genealogical myth, and the imperial dynasties, universal and elected, which, though attached doctrinally to the Roman soil, were not easily accommodated to this theory of origin.

As to the genealogies of individual *Stämme* it is worth while recalling an eleventh-century tradition, according to which the Bavarians originally came from Armenia, the place "where Noah emerged from the Ark" (though the legend does not state whether Noah spoke German). The Saxons claimed descent at one and the same time from Alexander the Great and (in memory of their Ascanian dynasty) from Ashkenaz, the first-born of Gomer, and the future common ancestor of all the Germans. The Swabians dated their arrival in Germany from the time of Julius Caesar, to whom the main German towns, such as Cologne and Ratisbon, also attributed their foundation. One finds here the usual mixture of Biblical traditions and memories of classical Antiquity. For further detail, the reader may be referred to the valuable work of Arno Borst.[10]

Borst draws attention to an isolated witness who, already in the twelfth century, attributed to the Teutonic language a unique position which the language of the *Welsche*, derived from Latin, could not aspire to. A female follower of one of the Rhenish religious teachers, Hildegard of Bingen (d. 1179), declared that Adam and Eve spoke German, and explained why: *Adam et Eva Teutonica lingua loquebantur, quae, in diversa non dividitur ut Romana.*[11] As against the Romance languages which branched out and multiplied, the German language, of totally different origin, was single and must therefore have been the original language of the human race. This reasoning so conjoins language and race that both converge towards Adam. Even bearing in mind the limited knowledge then available, one gets the impression that only believers in an original language, born before time began, would have dared to put forward such a claim. Their French, English and other rivals knew well enough that their languages were derived from other origins.

This impression is confirmed by the developments of this claim after the sixteenth century. The arguments put forward by the Alsatian doctor, Lorenz Fries, in 1518 to show the superiority of German over French are significant: "Is our language lesser? No, it is greater for it is an original language (*ursprünglich Sprach*); it was not, like French, collected together by begging (*zusammengebettelt*) from the Greeks and Latins, from the Goths and the Huns."[12] So began a cult of the purity of the German language which led to great extravagances at the time of the Thirty Years War. Later on, Fichte, the better to exalt German national feeling, would strike this chord above all others, while many of his contemporaries were already extolling the virtues of their national blood. It is therefore legitimate to consider the confusion between language and blood as a permanent feature of German history. Both are, however, a source of life and power, and all the evidence points to the fact that in the unconscious they have the same meaning.

Nevertheless, neither the anonymous follower of Hildegard of Bingen nor the numerous other authors who acclaimed the German language (without necessarily putting it into Adam's mouth) used it as a justification for political domination. They were content to glorify German speech at the expense of all others especially that of the *Welsche*. It was only in the fifteenth and sixteenth centuries, with the renewal of classical studies, that claims to universal hegemony were justified by arguments based on language (rather than by imperial titles, or affiliation to the Rome of the Caesars). Then, in a period of two or three generations, new myths of origin and a new vision of the world, were fabricated.

A book written in Alsace between 1490 and 1510 called *The Book of a Hundred Chapters* could now develop certain theses which, as Norman Cohn has pointed out, foreshadow in a peculiar way the ravings of the Hitlerites.[13] Its anonymous author ("the Revolutionary of the Upper Rhine") wanted to secure German hegemony by setting up a millennial Reich and he flourished title-deeds which went back to a legendary period of pre-history drawn mostly from the Old Testament. "Adam was a German", he declared.[14] Having established this fact, he announced the enslavement of non-Germanic peoples on the one hand and the massacre of the Roman Catholic clergy on the other. He placed his hopes in a supreme commander who was either real (the Emperor Maximilian I) or legendary (the Emperor Frederick) in order to "rule the whole world by the might of armies". He appealed to a national religion in which the Ten Commandments were to be replaced by the Seven Commandments of Trier and Sunday by Thursday, the day of Christ-Jupiter (for he seemed to be ignorant even of the name of the god Thor). His Christianity was obviously veering, well before the Reformation, in a specifically heretical and Germanic direction.

"We Germans", he wrote, "are free, we are all noble; we have ruled and taken possession of the whole earth by force and before long, with God's help, we shall bring the world into submission to the ancient order." German primacy was proved etymologically too. Was not German or Germanic (*allemand, alémanique*) the language of all men (alle-Mann)? After Adam, it was the "bold German man Seth" who had spoken this language, as was shown by the works of his son Enoch (whose original manuscript the author claimed to have consulted). When the Flood was over, Japheth settled in Germany and gave birth to an imperial line which produced all the great conquerors in history from Alexander the Great to Tamerlane.

The superiority of the Germans, their elect nature, was also revealed in another sphere. Here too the "Revolutionary of the Upper Rhine" anticipated certain tendencies of modern German thought when he made the Germanic Adam and his glorious progeny free from original sin, since Jesus came only to save the infidel Jews. It should be observed that the *Book of a Hundred Chapters* spends no time on the Jews, even in the passages attacking merchants and usurers. All the anger of this revolutionary author is reserved for the descendants of Ham—meaning the Slavs—and above all for the Romans. The enumeration of the misdeeds of these poisoners and born slaves, whom it was necessary to reduce to slavery once again, takes up a large part of his astonishing manuscript.

Other men, whose names are known to posterity and some of whom, as we shall see, attained a high degree of eminence, likewise maintained that German rather than Hebrew was the original language of mankind. Even if it is not possible to attribute any specific influence on his contemporaries or on future generations to the anonymous revolutionary (since *The Book of a Hundred Chapters* remained in manuscript form and was not brought to light until 1893), its pan-German eschatology was certainly not invented out of nothing. It was the statement in an extreme form of tendencies which were to develop during the fifteenth century in the countries of Germanic culture. We must now describe this new mental climate and try to analyse its cultural model or, more specifically, the fantasy of the "ideal Germanic man" as it crystallized, in its broad outline, at that time.

★   ★   ★

It seems to have been at the Council of Basle (1434), after the Great Schism in the West, that the historical arguments of pan-Germanism were systematically formulated for the first time.[15] The ambassador of the Swedish king, Bishop Ragvaldsson, claimed absolute precedence for his monarch whose kingdom, he declared, was more noble and ancient than any other, and whose people, unlike other peoples who had migrated into Europe after the confusion of Babel, was an autochthonous race. In support of his claims, Ragvaldsson referred to the sixth-century chronicle of Jordanes according to whom Scandinavia was the "forge of the human race and the matrix of the nations". So, with the help of an ancient authority, there began a Swedish imperialist tradition which was to last until the seventeenth century—that is to say, as long as Swedish kings were able to play a major part in European affairs.

It is worth remarking, in this connexion, that the Scandinavian countries—through the Goths and later the Vikings—held titles and were able to muster historico-genealogical arguments of unique persuasiveness. But in the nineteenth and twentieth centuries it was the Germans who invoked these arguments on behalf of the Germanic race. Nationalist megalomania can only appeal to ancestral legends under certain conditions, namely, when there is a degree of past and present plausibility.★ After the defeat of Charles XII these conditions no longer applied to Sweden. All that remained was the special interest in the Goths, though there is no evidence to show that they originated in the Scandinavian peninsula. It is not even certain that they ever inhabited it.

As far as Germany is concerned, it was also in the fifteenth century that the legends and prophecies about the triumphal reign of the

★ By past plausibility, we mean the credibility of the myth of origin in itself, as it strikes a modern man. By present plausibility we mean that the nation concerned has some real chance of imposing its domination as a Great Power. The one and the other served until quite recently, at a collective level, to constitute those fragments of reality round which megalomaniac fantasies and projections progressively form themselves into a pattern.

Emperor Frederick began to proliferate against a background of popular agitation and heresy. This is one of the themes of *The Book of a Hundred Chapters*. Such legends had their counterpart in similar stories then circulating in other European countries. And there is no reason to suppose that this excitement was particularly virulent in medieval Germany, where even the name of Wotan had been forgotten, while the migrations of the old tribes across Europe were equally unknown. It was thanks to German intellectuals that these memories were exhumed and that such arrogant inferences were drawn from them. Indeed, between 1450 and 1550, the glorification of Germany's pre-Christian past was above all the work of a youthful German humanism whose study of classical texts yielded very different conclusions from those of Petrarch and Machiavelli and the other Italian humanists. Disputes between the pupils and their masters were intensified after the rediscovery of the *Germania* of Tacitus. This text, which for Italian writers merely confirmed the inveterate barbarism of the Germans, highlighted for German authors the simple virtues and invincibility of their ancestors.* Two comments by Tacitus, though both were hypothetical, led the Germans to conclude that they were *autochthonous* and of *pure* race:

> As to the Germans themselves, I think it probable that they are indigenous and that very little foreign blood has been introduced either by invasions or by friendly dealings with neighbouring peoples. . . . For myself, I accept the view that the peoples of Germany have never contaminated themselves by intermarriage with foreigners but remain of pure blood, distinct and unlike any other nation.[16]

The German humanists, as we shall see, fastened first of all on to the myth of autochthony or of "soil". It was only with the gradual abandonment of Biblical genealogies that the accent was placed on race or on "blood". In the language of psychoanalysis one would say that the witness of Tacitus, being above suspicion as coming from a Roman, was the main "fragment of reality" around which the megalomaniac delirium of the Germans organized itself in modern times.

* We are summarizing a complex process of evolution. On looking closer, one becomes aware that some Italian scholars were the first to glorify the warlike qualities of the Germans on the authority of Tacitus and other ancient historians. But this was in order to rally the German princes to the Holy See's plans for a crusade against the Turks. This was especially the case with Aeneas Sylvius Piccolomini, the future Pope Pius II.

Many other arguments were advanced, from the second half of the fifteenth century, to uphold German superiority and to prove it by examples. Notable among these were the two great inventions of the time, artillery and printing. Side by side with Johannes Gutenberg, the fabulous Berthold Schwarz shared the first place as a symbol of national glory. The growth of towns and trade in southern Germany provided rich patrons and a public for the early patriotic books. What is more, this kind of special pleading was supported towards the end of the century by an ambitious and powerful client in the person of the Emperor Maximilian I, the founder of Austrian power.

In 1501, the poet laureate, Heinrich Bebel, addressed the Emperor on the historical foundations for the claims of the House of Austria, which had adopted the insignia A.E.I.O.U.* Had not the German race conquered the whole world in times gone by and had they not brought into subjection peoples, some of which later on did not even remember that they had been German? Were not the Germans moved by the highest aspirations, by those ideals of Christianity which the Romans, goaded solely by their lust for power and glory, had known absolutely nothing about? In this connexion, Bebel reproached the Latin writers —the very ones whose writings buttressed his thesis—with having suppressed, through hatred or jealousy, a number of glorious deeds which the German heroes of antiquity had performed.[17]

The theme of German greatness was developed by the German humanists each in his own way, and they vied with one another in the variety and novelty of their arguments. The Alsatian Wimpfeling was already stressing that the modern nations owed nothing to the ancient ones. "We have our Charlemagne, our Ottos and our Fredericks", he cried, "we do not grudge the Romans their heroes" (all the more so as Trier was founded 1250 years before Rome). Nevertheless, he was just as prepared to bestow adulation on those Roman emperors, like Diocletian and Valentinian, to whom he attributed a Germanic origin.[18] The Swabian, Johann Naukler, was the first to emphasize, in his chronicle, the *autochthony* of the ancient Germans whose paternity he ascribed, on the authority of Tacitus, to an ancestor called Tuisto or Tuisco, but without as yet denying the Japhetic genealogy.[19] The pious Bavarian, Aventin-Thurmair, resuscitated the Ascanian or Saxon myth of origin; integrated the account in Tacitus with that in Genesis, and put forward Ashkenaz,

---

* *Austria Est Imperare Orbis Universo*—It behoves Austria to rule the World.

son of Gomer and nephew of Tuisto, as the ancestor of all the Germans.[20] His young fellow-countryman Irenicus-Friedlieb, by contrast, broke away resolutely from Biblical genealogies, sang a paean of triumph over the fall of Rome, and announced, in the manner of the "Revolutionary of the Upper Rhine", that the Germanic kingdom was the oldest on earth.[21] The Alsatian, Beatus Rhenanus, acclaimed for his critical intelligence, showed a preference for flattering etymologies. In his view *German* meant *Gar-Mann*, or whole man, *totus seu robustus vir*, and he identified himself in a most expressive way with the great ancestors: "Ours are the triumphs of the Goths, the Vandals and the Franks! Ours is their glory in the provinces of the Roman Empire!"[22] The Franconian, Celtis-Pickel, a translator of Tacitus who had travelled much, fixed the frontiers of ancient "Germany" along the Sarmatian or Scythian plains.[23] Sebastian Franck did not mince his words in proclaiming the advantage of autochthony. He wrote that the Germans had had the privilege of not being swept in like filth (*Unflat*) out of some other country but of being generated on the spot by Tuisto, the grandson of Noah. In consequence, he regarded Germany, the country, and German origins as one and the same thing.[24]

No man, however, promoted the rising Germanomania more than Ulrich von Hutten, a renowned knight and the founder of the national cult of Hermann-Arminius; for him the free and noble German people were the natural lords of the universe (*weltherrschendes Volk*). Hutten contrasted the cardinal virtue of the Germans, that of *virility*, with the *femininity* of the *Romano-Welsche*: "A woman-race, a crowd of weaklings, without heart, without courage, without virtue. None of them has fought in battle, nor is any of them skilled in the art of war. These are the people who rule us! This mockery breaks my heart. . . ."[25] In this way the picture of an archetypal Germanic ancestor was built up, to which each author added his touch and of which the fantasms of the "Revolutionary of the Upper Rhine" are merely the most extreme form.

It was the achievement of Luther prodigiously to expand the groundswell of nationalism, which coincided with the Reformation and gave Lutheranism its specifically German quality. "I was born for the Germans and I desire to serve them."[26] To serve them as a Christian or as a German? Let us pause to consider the Reformer's major work, *To the Christian Nobility of the German nation . . .* (1520), "a work which is required reading if one wishes to understand the evolution of modern Germany."[27] This is, to begin with, the heartfelt cry of a

Christian. In the passage where Luther compared the pope to Anti-Christ he merely mentioned the contrast with the "German nation, the constancy, loyalty and noble nature of which is praised by all historians".[28] However, in a short chapter which Luther added later[29] (as though he felt the need to fill a gap) it is the German in him who "sounds off with the call to battle" and demands a settlement of accounts with Rome. Luther explains that a gang of Romans had in past times exploited the Germans,

> a valiant people of good repute, in order to bring into their hands the power of the Roman Empire and turn it into a fief of their own. And that is what happened. The Empire was taken over from the Emperor at Constantinople and the name and title thereof were bestowed on us Germans. By this action we became slaves of the Pope and now a second Roman Empire has been built by the Pope on the Germans . . . we have the name but they have the country and the towns, for they have always abused our good faith to satisfy their proud and tyrannical instincts and they dub us "those crazy Germans who let themselves be duped and fooled at will". . . . So here we are, we poor Germans, put upon as usual like the simpletons we have always been. When we thought to become masters, we became the slaves of the craftiest of tyrants.

An incipient form of paranoia—that of the noble German caught in the Latin snare—is here revealed; and it seems all the more like an echo of Ulrich von Hutten, when Luther, with a great marshalling of scriptural quotations, urges Germany to take advantage of the providential coincidence of "a disposition of God" and "the contrivance of malicious men", without paying too much attention to scruples of conscience:

> For that the Empire was bestowed upon us by a disposition of God and through the contrivance of malicious men without any fault of ours, I would not advise that we should abandon it. . . . All this is part of the divine dispensation. . . . [God wishes] that this Empire be governed by the Christian princes of Germany.

The same state of mind was displayed by the Reformer in later years as when, in 1532, he declared: "There is no nation so despised as the German. The Italians call us stupid; France and England mock us as do all the others!" As a German historian observed in 1931,

Luther stood squarely by his opinions and his accusations during the whole of his life. They are to be found in the *Christian Nobility* of 1520 as in the *Papacy at Rome, Founded by the Devil* of 1545. They demonstrate his inner loyalty to the Empire, with title-deeds of national ownership held by the German people which, as the result of a divine act of transfer, became the leading people of Christendom. This Empire envisaged by Luther was no longer an office assumed by one man but belonged to the whole nation.[30]

Otto Scheel, Luther's biographer, discloses the fact that his hero, towards the end of his life, dreamt of a unified Germany, endowed with a permanent and invincible army.[31]

From the time of his earliest struggles, Luther devotedly emphasized the value of the mother tongue: "I thank God that I am able to hear and to find my God in the German language, Whom neither I nor you could ever find in Latin or Greek or Hebrew" (1518). German was promoted to the status of a fourth holy language, more admirable than any other, to which only Hebrew, as spoken by Adam before the confusion of Babel, could be compared. Sometimes it was even raised to the rank of an "Adamic" language, as with Luther's contemporary, Paracelsus.[32]

As for the origin of the Germans, Luther naturally sought to explain it in the light of the Genesis story. In this setting, he chose the Japheth-Ashkenaz genealogy and from it he deduced a right of primogeniture for his people, since Ashkenaz was Gomer's first-born, who himself was the eldest son of Japheth. It is noteworthy that the Reformer who brought about the religious schism and at the same time unified the national language, gave Ashkenaz credit for having taught this language to the Germans: "*Assanas germanicam linguam docuit.* . . . *Assanas est noster singularis heros.*" It is not the least of Luther's achievements that he gave his compatriots both a common language and a common ancestor, who was derived from the special traditions of Saxony, Luther's native country.[33]

Finally, it may be said that Luther, who was above all concerned with the inner life and the salvation of the Germans, was more modest in his claims than were the humanists. But what he drew from the latter was to become thenceforth, and with a high degree of authority, a part of the national heritage.

One of the greatest authorities on German humanism, Paul Joachimsen (1867-1930), has summarized the great change that took place between 1450 and 1550:

We witness the birth, out of German humanism, of a national Romanticism with a well-defined image. Not unlike what happened [in Germany] around 1800, it rested on the concept of a German *Volkstum*, which tried to instill a new content into every form of existence. First of all there was the concept of the "nation" itself . . .. The essential thing was that this concept, because it sought to link up with Germanic beginnings (*germanische Urzeit*), led to the creation of a *type of ideal German*.[34] A certain "simplicity", which had been referred to before then with some embarrassment, became a national characteristic and, because it was an ancestral heritage, filled all hearts with pride. The German national character became an ethical imperative at the root of all the judgements which were made on the contemporary period, and out of it an attempt was made to create a German style of living. In the same way, the romantic vision of the past coloured the idea of the national German Empire. The legal title to this Empire no longer derived from some papal transfer, it was founded on a hereditary claim of German popular might (*germanische Volkskraft*) which, at the time of the great invasions, conquered the Roman colossus.[35]

We can now try to interpret the national "cultural model" sketched out above, and to show what is specific about it. We have seen that the new "ideal of the German man" made a break with medieval tradition. The inheritance of Antiquity was no longer reverently received by the heir with a blessing, it was snatched up by brute strength. The Germans, as seen by the humanists, were the heirs only of their own achievements. This attitude led to the emphasis on autochthony. Posterity was urged to identify itself with the invincible Germans who overthrew the Roman colossus. Nothing was owed to the Ancients (the "Fathers") who have been supplanted by the Germans, the conquerors of the world. This break with the true historical line of descent, or this refusal to identify with the real cultural forefathers (which might indicate a refusal to accept the parental function) is well exemplified in a work published during the Third Reich (the fact that the author—needless to say—was not concerned with psychoanalytical interpretation only increases the value of his observations for our purpose):

> The way in which the humanists presented the question of the origin of the peoples, and, following this, that of their position in the world order, gives birth to a new criterion side by side with that of age—that of descent out of one's own self (*Abstammung aus sich selbst*).[36]

D

The problem of the German myth of origin, with its new insistence on autochthony or (as we have just seen it defined) being derived from one's own self (like the creation of oneself by oneself) is not unique in Europe. Further East, Russian culture also elaborated, in the course of centuries, the *cultural model* of a youthful people of heroes, issuing from its own native soil and for this reason superior to the nations of the "Old West". The reader may be referred, in this connexion, to the excellent work of Alain Besançon who has influenced my thinking on this question.[37] His study reveals that the dominant model of Russian history and culture was inspired by the Suffering Christ, or, as dynastic history in particular appears to indicate, a son sacrificed by his father (the "immolated Tsarevitch"). Hence, no doubt, the truly Christian character of this model. But the historical speculations of the German humanists end up by suggesting a solution which is quite the reverse. In the guise of the Roman colossus, it is the father who is the evicted protagonist, if he is not altogether eliminated, while the son usurps his rights and his power which are those of world domination. Sometimes the soil symbolizes the mother, sometimes (as with Sebastian Franck) the combination of soil and origin suggests a pre-Oedipal, Narcissistic fusion—for the "ideal of the German man", like all ideals, could inspire its devotees in different ways and start up a variety of psychological mechanisms, depending on the constellation of each individual's ideas. In any case the whole world, according to the humanists, belonged to the German by right of conquest. Such an archetype, at once triumphant and barbaric, was clearly incompatible with the Christian ideal, however great its malleability and whatever historical transformations it might undergo. This incompatibility became apparent when the mental climate of the West was propitious. In the nineteenth century it was in Germany, and Germany alone, that German-Christian heresies increased and multiplied on the one hand, while on the other attempts were made to re-introduce pre-Christian paganism.

It is suggested that these theological or ideological speculations, implying mostly a rebellion against the Judaeo-Christian sense of sin, can be related to the salient feature of the German archetype or "ideal German man". This feature was an imperturbably clear conscience, or rather a conscience which would stop at nothing to remain unruffled, until it ended in the fantasy of a being totally without conscience—the "blond beast", who is a beast, not a man. But the price to be paid for achieving this end, in terms of defence mechanisms and projections (particularly the choice of foreign enemies as the target) was a heavy one, and the political consequences are known to us all.

Among other influences in German history, stress has often been laid on the geographical or geo-political situation of this "country in the middle"; Nietzsche and Max Weber could be quoted in this connexion. Much has been made also, especially after 1945, of the authoritarian nature of German education. Yet it seems likely that this education merely strengthened the fascination exercised by the "ideal of the German man", so that youthful revolt was poured out into nationalistic channels and was turned against the foreigner. We believe that the true relevance of German history to our times consists in the influence, which has grown cumulatively with the centuries, of a delusion of a quite specific kind. From time to time this has resulted in a wave of persecution mania, centering on a threat which by definition was felt to be non-German and foreign (the Romans, the *Welsche*, the Slavs, the Jews), and leading to a closing of the ranks.

This delusion engenders plans to attack and to destroy antagonists who are at the same time imagined and real, though the imagined part of the delusion is easily the strongest. The mere existence of such antagonists may be resented as a provocation: to return to the period we have been dealing with, it was enough that Rome still stood, that the *Welsche* were ever ready to proclaim their cultural superiority and their antique origins, that they even won victories on the battlefield. Hence the explosions, characteristic in their ferocity, of German patriotic fury; hence the belief, which began at that time but which became traditional, in "national humiliations" inflicted on Germany. As far as the French "hereditary enemy" was concerned, German humanism entered the lists at the time of the political and dynastic imbroglio which centred on the Duchess Anne of Brittany in 1488-1492, when she was espoused by proxy to Maximilian and then really married to Charles VIII of France. The humanists, from Wimpfeling in 1491 to Sebastian Brant in 1519, bestirred themselves to obtain a literary revenge for this outrage, while the "Revolutionary of the Upper Rhine" vied with them in his fury. And when Francis I was made prisoner at the Battle of Pavia a poet exclaimed: "It doth seem that she is well avenged this day, the Lady of Brittany."[38] When, during the second quarter of the nineteenth century, Germanomania spread into German literary circles, Heinrich Heine, after emigrating to France, referred to these implacable attitudes: "One day in a beer-hall at Göttingen, a young Germanophile proclaimed that Konradin von Staufen, whom you, the French, had beheaded in Naples, had to be revenged. You have certainly forgotten about it long ago. But we forget nothing, we don't. You see, if we want to pick a fight with you, we shall not want for good reasons."[39] This enduring touchiness, heavily exploited by nationalist propaganda after the collective trauma of the First World War, was perhaps even better expressed in the notorious outbursts of William II at the time when Germany was in the full flush of her strength.

Obviously, individual neuroses and paranoia are not, clinically speaking, more frequent in Germany than in other European countries, nor were they formerly so, even though an authoritarian education and national traditions of discipline tended to foster certain types of neurosis. It is nevertheless true that the "ideal of the German man", outlined by the humanists, exercised a decisive influence in the nineteenth and twentieth centuries, and this in two ways. Firstly, Germans of all types tried to mould themselves in increasing numbers on the model thus placed before them; life imitated historico-political art. The most typical period of this imitation was after the Napoleonic wars. Secondly, Germans with assertive or megalomaniac temperaments similar to that portrayed in their imaginary "ideal man" were selected by society and made their mark in public life in ever larger numbers. Proof of this is to be found in the history of the Second Reich, though above all in that of the Third Reich. We believe that any consideration of German history between 1871 and 1945 cannot fail to demonstrate almost tangibly the importance as well as the functioning of these sociological mechanisms, which acted on the one hand as a stimulant and on the other as a selective process. To be convincing, any explanation of social behaviour must take account of such mechanisms which, along with those conditioned by economic factors, help to fill the intellectual chasm between psychiatric evaluations and the tragedy of European politics.

*   *   *

Let us now resume our narrative and examine first of all a characteristic aspect of German history which, though it reached its full development in the nineteenth century, was already discernible in Luther's time. I refer to the specifically German form of innate religiosity which is strikingly expressed in the writings of Eberlin von Günzburg, the most popular Lutheran propagandist of the years 1520–1530.[40] According to this unfrocked Franciscan, the old Germanic tribes were "good and pious Germans" and "a Christian people" (*christliche Leut'*). They had been diverted from the path of righteousness by missionaries sent from Rome, who had preached a gospel to them which had been adulterated and "circumcised". Because of this "the German people had been fraudulently led astray from Christian law to papal law, from plenitude to poverty, from truth to lies, from virility to effeminacy". But Luther and von Hutten, who were messengers of God, had guided them back to the right way: "It now pleases God to spread the true Christian faith throughout the world by means of the German nation." The special qualities of the latter will enable it to carry out this task. In listing these qualities Eberlin followed the humanists; nor was the invention of "the new and useful art of printing" forgotten.

Other authors, Catholics as well as Lutherans, each after his own fashion elaborated their genealogical theories and corrected or supplemented the Bible by reference to Tacitus. According to the most popular view (which commanded support until the eighteenth century) the ancestor Ashkenaz, identified with the Tuisto of Tacitus, arrived in Europe from Asia and preached the faith of the Patriarchs in a single and invisible God. His posterity, which comprised both Germans and Celts (usually considered a Germanic tribe) were the original people of Europe, the *Urvolk*, and the original language of the European Continent was German.[41] Pamphlets and handbills reiterated and simplified these views for the benefit of the public at large and extended the genealogies down to Arminius-Hermann, Ariovistus-Ehrenvest and Charlemagne. The final conclusion was represented in pictures. Thus a "Description of the Ancient German Heroes" showed, beneath the legend *Germania domitrix gentium*, a winged woman holding a sceptre and imperial globe in her hands while she rested her foot on the world.[42] We recognize there "the Queen of all the provinces, the eagle of all kingdoms" of Coryat-Kircher (see p. 46 above). Music also came to be considered as German in origin. Orpheus sang in the German language, so we are told by the famous Johann Fischart, while the Lutheran musicologist, Wolfgang Spangenberg, declared that the Germans owed nothing to the Greeks or Romans in this field, as they learned the art of song directly from the patriarchs Noah and Japheth.[43]

A clear deduction was that the Patriarchs spoke German. This, indeed, was the gist of an erudite theory worked out in the Netherlands; which is a reminder that it was only rather late in the day, after the creation of the Second Reich, that Germanomania became a purely German affair. We have already spoken about Swedish pretensions, and some of the Swiss humanists could also be cited.[44] During the second half of the sixteenth century, however, it was the rich and independent Netherlands which became the main centre for the cult of the German language.

Soon after the uprising of the Low Countries against Spanish domination, a doctor from Antwerp, Goropius Becanus, undertook to prove that the Biblical Patriarchs, and Adam first of all, spoke in a Germanic language. To the historical or historico-genealogical proofs already quoted, he added others of a philological nature, emphasizing the monosyllabic character of many German words of which the sounds, so he claimed, expressed the very nature of things. He concluded that even Hebrew was derived from the universal mother language, German.

Goropius's theory was received with interest but not without reservations. Indeed, the priority of German over Hebrew stank of heresy. His compatriots, however, preserved those of his ideas relating to the antiquity and "authenticity" of the Germanic languages, to which they willingly subordinated Latin and Greek, while restoring to Hebrew its claim to be the language of Adam and of Eve.[45] The cult of the national language was a serious matter in the Netherlands at the time of their greatness. Thus we see Hugo Grotius, in a poem dedicated to the *lingua germanica*, praising the latter because it had not been imposed by a conqueror on defeated nations (like Latin) and had remained free from any foreign contamination (almost certainly an allusion to English). *Lingua imperare nata*, he called it.[46]

At the beginning of the seventeenth century, the University of Leyden became the intellectual capital of northern Europe. The Danziger, Philipp Clüver (1580-1622), was a student and later a teacher there. This pious Lutheran, who is now considered one of the founders of historical geography, offered the Germans a new genealogy, more glorious even than that of the humanists. Tacitus's Tuisto was no more to be identified with Ashkenaz. He became the one true God who had revealed Himself to the Germans. His son, the *Mannus* of Tacitus, became Adam, while the three sons of the latter, Inguo, Istvo and Hermin were identified with Shem, Ham and Japheth. It is in Clüver's writings also that we see for the first time the names of old German divinities, Woden, Freya and Ostara, for he was a great reader of ancient Scandinavian chronicles. However, his aim was to prove that the Germans had received the rudiments of the Christian faith.[47]

A number of other German authors of the seventeenth century— like the chemist Kirchmaier, the polymath Conring, the philologist Freinshaim— were already paying tribute to the purity of the Germanic *race* and suggesting that it was being undermined by Christian morality; they even proposed legal measures to restore it.[48] Their writings failed to command any long-term interest and their names, except for Conring, are completely forgotten. The times were not yet ripe perhaps. The drive for purity, which in a scientific age and, one might say, before our very eyes, concentrated entirely on *race*, was quickly directed, in an age which was still the Age of Faith, to the protection of the mother tongue.

It is true that, in a Germany ravaged by the Thirty Years War and overrun on all sides by foreign armies, the language itself seemed to have become invaded and colonized. French preponderance asserted itself in every sphere. The domination of the *Welsche* seemed even more odious in French than in Latin. Martin Opitz,[49] the "father of German poetry", protested: "It is as heavy a yoke to be dominated and tyrannized by a foreign language as by a foreign nation." The reaction was singularly violent, and its effects endure to this day. Only the Germans continue to create indigenous composite words to replace terms internationally adopted from Latin or Greek, such as geography or television.* Does not this phobia of *Fremdwörter* indicate the refusal of "German Man" to owe anything to classical Antiquity? Unlike the biological purists of the twentieth century, however, the linguistic purists of the seventeenth saw their efforts crowned with success, on the whole.

The great champions of the mother tongue were also the authors whom posterity has judged worthy to be remembered. They nearly all emphasized simultaneously the qualities of the German language and the virtues of their ancestors, like the satirist, Johann Michael Moscherosch, who lectured his Francophile contemporaries through the medium of the legendary King Ariovistus-Ehrenvest,[50] or the dramatist and writer of romances, Daniel Caspar von Lohenstein, for whom the Germans were the pedestal (*Postament*) of World History; he incarnated Adam and Eve in "Tuisto" and "Hertha".[51] But the

---

* Translated respectively by *Erdkunde* and *Fernsehen*. Among great European languages, Russian also displays the same tendency but to a far lesser degree and no doubt in imitation of the German example.

most interesting case of all without any doubt is that of Johann Jakob von Grimmelshausen, the leading name in seventeenth-century German literature.

His best known work, *Simplicius Simplicissimus*, is a picaresque novel which is also an authentic record of the Thirty Years War. Among the numerous characters who figure in this fresco there is one madman who thinks he is the god Jupiter and promises the Germans that he will inaugurate a period of universal peace. Here is what this "God of the Lice" prophesied:

> I will awaken a German hero who will consummate all this through the strength of his sword. . . . I will forswear the Greek language and speak only German. In one word I will show myself to be so good a German that I will grant them, as I did before to the Romans, domination over the whole world. . . . I asked Jupiter how the Christian Kings would act in this affair. He answered: "The kings of England, Sweden and Denmark, being of German blood and origin, and those in Spain, France and Portugal, because the old Germans once conquered and governed them, would receive their crowns, kingdoms and countries as fiefs of the German nation, and then there will be, as in the time of Augustus, an eternal peace among all the nations in the world."[52]

It matters little whether Grimmelshausen wanted to warn his fellow-countrymen against false messiahs,[53] as some commentators think, or whether, as others declare, he attributed to the madman of his creation his own aspirations and secret fantasies.[54] One recognizes in him the messianic quality of the "Revolutionary of the Upper Rhine", and, underlying the features of his "gentleman Jupiter", that prototype of the "Ideal of the German Man", Emperor Frederick. In one of Grimmelshausen's lesser works, the "German Michael" (*Teutscher Michel*), one finds most of the arguments dealt with above in the space of a few pages: the Germans are a pure race; they have been settled in Europe from time immemorial, before the confusion of Babel; they subjected the whole of the West after overpowering the Roman eagles and they founded royal dynasties and aristocracies. The circle is completed with a eulogy of the language, this also being pure, "a language of heroes existing for and by itself" (*in, an und für sich bestehende Heldensprache*), as distinct from the other "patched-up" (*zusammengeflickt*) languages which are like a "harlequin's coat" (*Flicksprachen*).[55]

Some writers like to talk of the "mendicity" of these languages as did Justus Georg Schottel, the chief grammarian of this period. He was a Lutheran, like most of the other writers mentioned above, and he produced a long eulogy of the German language which began with a genealogy:

> When the languages split up and mankind was dispersed across the world, Ashkenaz, the supreme head of the family (*Oberhausvater*), crossed Asia Minor and settled in Europe where he made the land fertile and divided it. . . . He was the ancestor of the Germans, and had brought from Babel the old Cimbric or German language. . . . Today we still observe, everywhere in Europe, the presence of root-words of the German language, though these differ from one another in consequence of all kinds of changes and confusions, having been deformed and damaged by the admixture of foreign words.[56]

Schottel discovered these roots in the place-names of Europe, the names of its mountains, rivers, countries and towns. He wrote:

> If one takes a look at European countries and reflects upon the changes which have overtaken them, and takes into account at the same time the state of the language, one realizes that only immemorial Germany has not been submerged by foreign languages. It follows, therefore, that the possession of a pure language is the most certain confirmation of what Tacitus wrote about the Germans 1500 years ago: *Ipsos Germanos indigenas crediderim*. On the other hand, when one considers Italy, Spain, France, England, Greece and even Asia Minor and Africa, one can see that the state of the language has changed. Our ancestors concentrated great efforts to preserve their mother-tongue pure and free; they taught it to their children; they did not beg it from their enemies. . . .[57]

Schottel's views were approved by Leibniz. Leibniz was more fascinated by the problem of language than any philosopher had been before him and he studied all the languages of the known world; in trying to discover their common roots he grew more and more convinced of "a common origin of nations and a radical primitive language". Going one step further than Schottel had dared to do, he related this radical language to the *tütsche Haupt-und Heldensprache*. He did not criticize the substance of what Goropius Becanus had written but only the method of his argumentation.

What was this root-language or mother-tongue? Leibniz thought it must have been lost but hinted that German was closer to it than

Hebrew: "Hebrew and Arabic are the nearest approach to this language but they have been greatly distorted and it would seem that the Teutonic language has retained more of its original quality (to use the words of Jakob Boehme) than the Adamitic language." Hence, whatever the extravagance of his arguments, Becanus "may not have been excessively wrong in claiming that the German language, which he calls Cimbric, has as many, yes, more marks of a primitive character than the Hebrew itself".[58]

One wonders whether Leibniz ever pushed his speculations about the greater antiquity of German as against Hebrew to their conclusion. Perhaps his prudence as a scholar was strengthened by the fear of ecclesiastical censure. In any case, as far as Europe was concerned, he asserted categorically that the origin of the European peoples was to be looked for in the "Germanic past". He carried on controversies with French scholars about the origin of the Franks, and with Swedish scholars about that of the Goths, and he devoted a special work to the beginnings of all the European nations in the light of the origin of their languages. In this way he came to consider Germany the cradle, if not of the entire human race, at least of white humanity:

> Just as Gaul and Italy owe their oldest inhabitants to Germany, the latter, in the course of time, also gave Scandinavia hers; for I consider it beyond dispute that the Germanic tribes from the shores of the Baltic first colonized the Danish islands and subsequently Scandinavia itself. . . . It is possible to prove that the Danish, Swedish and Norwegian languages are derived from German in the same way that it can be proved that Italian, French and Spanish are derived from Latin, even though these latter nations were subject to Roman influence only through their language and not through their origin, which belongs to the Germanic North. . . .[59]

In expressing such views, Leibniz was anticipating opinions which numerous German archaeologists and prehistorians were to support with enthusiasm under the reigns of the Emperors William I and II. However, he defended his thesis in Latin which, towards the end of his life, he tended to put aside, not in favour of the German *Haupt-und Heldensprache* but of French, so as to be better understood by the mighty of this world. In the eyes of the purists he was branded as "belonging to the camp of those fashionable scholars who may be regarded as the bastards of their first ancestors", to use the words of a certain pastor Gottfried Schütze who added: "These restrict their understanding to the study of Greek and Latin and thereby become strangers to their own country. Miserable creatures! Why do you sin against your ancestors whose blood flows in your veins?"[60]

Between 1746 and 1776, Pastor Schütze, who had edited Luther's correspondence, published a series of writings to defend the civilization of the ancient Germans; he tried to show that their religious ethics were superior to those of the ancient Romans and that, unlike the latter, they did not carry out human sacrifice.[61] A glance at the index of his pamphlets gives some idea of the subjects dealt with:

> The *Polytheism* of the Romans hated by the Germans.
>
> *Caesar*, Roman Emperor, became emperor through the help of the Germans whom he wrongfully accused of atheism and treachery.
>
> *Romans*, a name hated by the Germans.
>
> *Barbarians*, a name erroneously given to the ancient Germans.

This artless apology shows us that the patriotic struggle in which the German humanists engaged at that time, in the fields of language and of race, was beginning to spread to a third front, that of mythology. In France and England too, men of the Enlightenment were beginning at this time to have doubts, on rational and scientific grounds, about Adam as a universal ancestor. But in Germany the Biblical myth was shaken first by the so-called rationalist theology of the eighteenth century, and this criticism coincided with attempts to rehabilitate the German gods.

The ingenuous pastor Schütze is a minor figure. It was the poet Klopstock who was to become the great popularizer of the ancestral mythology. The first centre of the new cult was Denmark, where a translation of the Icelandic *Edda*, and a *History of Denmark* by Paul Mallet, had just appeared.

Friedrich Gottlieb Klopstock, recognized after the publication in 1750 of his *Messiah* as a great poet, at first confined himself to subjects taken from the Bible or the Classics. His conversion to German mythology took place between 1766 and 1768 during a stay in Copenhagen. "I've turned Greek mythology out of doors", he cried.[62] In his odes he now substituted Wotan for Jupiter, Freya for Aphrodite, the Norns for the Fates. However, it was not merely a substitution: for the first great German poet of modern times was also the first German author to put forward a new world vision "composed entirely in the light of northern mists".[63] The result was that the Greek muses gave way to

Germanic war gods, and the blood shed in the lyrical or epic works of Klopstock flowed with increasing abundance. A recent critic went so far as to speak of "a tendency to a kind of blood drunkenness: on every page of the Hermann trilogy we come across this word *Blut*".[64]

It is hardly necessary to add that Klopstock pushed the cult of the German language to its furthest limits and regarded the use of foreign languages as high treason. In the ode to the mother-tongue (*Unsere Sprache*), there was the usual reference to Tacitus; it indicated that the German language was still as pure as the race had once been:

> *This [language] is what we were once ourselves,*
> *In those immemorial times when Tacitus described us:*
> *Unique, free of all taint, like only unto itself.*

In his "Republic of the Wise" (*Gelehrtenrepublik*), a kind of blueprint for organizing the intellectual life, Klopstock distinguished, in an aside, between two kinds of foreigners—the "Ausländer" of *Welsch* extraction and the "Altfranken" of Germanic stock. For himself he rejoiced at the idea that the "blood of the old Cherusci" flowed in his veins. He was liberal in scattering this Germanic blood around, for he found it "everywhere, now in the districts through which the Rhone flows along, now on the banks of the Thames . . . the Gauls called themselves Franks and the Britons, English" (in the Ode *Mein Vaterland*). A circle of young poets formed itself round Klopstock and was called the *Hainbund*. They considered themselves an association of those persons "in Germany who thought and felt themselves to be most German", and they strove to surpass the patriotic enthusiasm of their old master. Their mediocre output, though piously exhumed by a few scholars of the Nazi era, has left little trace in German literary tradition.

The torch was taken up by Herder, an infinitely more discriminating, more subtle and influential mythologist. We shall have a great deal to say about him as the precursor of the Aryan myth in the second part of this work. His interests extended to all mythologies—Biblical, Classical and Indian, as well as Nordic (about which he merely remarked "It is closer to ours than to any other")[65]—and he was, as is well known, an awakener of national traditions and feelings throughout central and southern Europe. Before long, however, his pupil Friedrich Gräter (1768-1830), the founder of the Nordic revue *Bragur*, began to emphasize certain special, "authentically German", virtues of the heroes in the *Edda* and the *Nibelungen*.[66] So at first only some rather feeble voices were raised, in the wake of Klopstock and in his manner, to celebrate the ancestral beliefs and to claim descent from Valhalla. Far from being "turned out of doors", classical mythology retained its devotees like Goethe and Winckelmann. But when those other, now forgotten, writers joined forces with the eulogists of the national language and race, even they helped to prepare the way for a quest for a "Germanic religion".

In 1780, the budding Germanomania obtained political consecration of an almost official kind. The Prussian statesman, Friedrich-Ewald von Hertzberg, read a paper to the Berlin Academy of Sciences on the "Causes of the Superiority of the Germans over the Romans" in which he took up again and modernized the old thesis of the German humanists, so as to prove that "the Prussian monarchy was the original home of those heroic nations . . . which founded and peopled the principal monarchies of Europe". Count Hertzberg therefore fixed the birthplace of the Germanic tribes in Brandenburg, a *new Macedonia*, which enabled him to compare Frederick II with some advantage to Alexander the Great.[67]

This learned paper did not go unnoticed. As late as 1808, the peace-loving Jean-Paul (Johann-Paul Richter) referred to it, and drew the conclusion that European wars were simply wars between Germans or, in other words, civil wars. "Nowadays", he wrote, soon after Prussia's defeat, "we willingly share the name of Franks and we remind ourselves through history that the majority of Frenchmen are not Gauls but transplanted Germans."[68]

In the aftermath of Jena and of Austerlitz, such a reminder was perhaps useful as a consolation and, at the moment of Germany's impotence and disintegration, it may have stimulated dreams of greatness more than at any other time.

To what extent were such expressions of opinion widespread at that period? The writings of the great generation of "poets and thinkers" suggest that they were common among men of letters, but more so among the poets than among the thinkers, and that it was easy to draw conclusions from these views which were flattering to German self-esteem. Here, once again, it is worth citing Herder who, in a characteristically equivocal passage, warned his fellow-countrymen against the idea of the Germans as a chosen race.

> The historian of mankind, however, must take care, that he chooses no tribe exclusively as his favourite, and exalt it at the expense of others, whose situation and circumstances denied them

fame and fortune. . . . We may rejoice, that people of such strong,
handsome and noble form, chaste manners, generosity and probity,
as the Germans, possessed the Roman world . . . but on this account
to esteem them God's chosen people in Europe . . . would be to
display the base pride of a barbarian.[69]

The way this warning was worded is most revealing, and it shows
that it was all too easy for the Germans, whom Napoleon constrained
to become patriots, to fall headlong into the trap. Herder's admonition
shows that the images and value-judgements for this patriotism already
existed; but now a new note appeared whose militant conclusions
were based on a pride which tended to barbarism. Only a few great
men escaped this tendency. They were, it is true, the really great ones:
Goethe and Wilhelm von Humboldt; and one might add Hegel, who
in those days saw Napoleon as the incarnation of the universal spirit—
"on horseback".

But already before the Napoleonic cataclysm the young Romantics,
conscious of their genius, had begun to celebrate Germany's universal
mission, an "election" which obviously implied the consciousness of
a common origin but which remained at first fundamentally peaceful.
In 1801, Schiller defined the German people as "the kernel of mankind
—elected by the universal spirit to strive eternally for the education
of the human race"; and he hoped that the German language might
prevail throughout the whole world.[70] With greater mystical enthusiasm, Heinrich von Kleist spoke of "a community in which the
gods have preserved the original image of the human species with
greater purity than in any other".[71] Even more typical was the politico-
moral treatise of Novalis, *Europe or Christianity*, which appeared in
1799.[72] The key idea of this book, which was inspired by the spectacle
of the political and moral confusion in France at the time of the
Revolution, was that Germany had a mission to restore a religion
which should reconcile all nations and re-establish Christianity in all
its ancient splendour. Novalis wrote:

> Europe will be healed thanks to the German character. . . . It is
> possible, without any doubt, to discern in Germany the omens
> of a new world. Germany leads the other European peoples with
> slow but confident step. While the latter are busy with war,
> speculation and the spirit of faction, Germany rises by her own
> efforts to a new level of culture, and with time this advance will
> gain for her an undisputed superiority.

Because of her moral pre-eminence Germany was entrusted with a religious mission of universal scope, though Novalis did not indicate by what means she was to carry out that mission.

The Christian vision is absent from the work of another great poet, Hölderlin. In *Burg Tübingen* (about 1790) the paltriness of Germany at that time led him to reflect on the greatness of Germany's past, and to seek in the ruins of old towers a means to "strengthen heroic hearts and conjure up through liberty and manly courage the souls of the ancestors": he evoked "the blood of Tuisco" and hoped to find peace in "the bosom of Valhalla". The same inspiration urged him in his *Song of the Germans* (about 1890) to reproach his "country, the heart of the peoples", for allowing itself to be pillaged and exploited by foreigners and for "betraying its own soul so stupidly". Here, in the guise of poetry, but already completely paganized, we can observe a renewal of the great claims made in his time by Martin Luther.

Military and political events, particularly between 1805 and 1810, naturally led men to draw practical conclusions from such reflections, and to draft practical plans for action. It may be convenient henceforth to distinguish between the "hawks" and the "doves" of the new German nationalism. In examining this contrast the comparison between the "dove" Jean-Paul, and the "hawk" Fichte, is very rewarding.

Soon after the collapse of Prussia, Fichte galvanized young Germans with his *Reden an die deutsche Nation* (Talks to the German Nation) of which Jean-Paul hastened to provide a major review. He praised the work highly and wished it a glorious career. Seemingly he disagreed with it only on details or, as he put it, "on the more or the less". It needed all Jean-Paul's subtlety to convey to his readers, while he covered Fichte with praise, that the latter was claiming for the "elected" German people nothing short of world domination and that he had perhaps lost his reason "following the example of those madmen who, according to Pinel and Röschlaub, act instinctively and unwittingly as if they were demented".[73]

Fichte, indeed, ascribed all the peoples of Europe, excepting the Slavs, to Germanic stock; but he drew a distinction among them between an "original race" (*Urvolk*), namely the Germans, and the "neo-Latin peoples" who were deficient, de-Germanized and sterilized through the loss of the "original language" (*Ursprache*). If this was madness it had already become a less agreeable form of madness than that of "gentleman Jupiter". Now it was full of menacing visions, and Fichte warned the Germans: "There is no way out: if you collapse, the whole of humanity will collapse with you and there will be no hope of recuperation." New and apocalyptic colours were being added to the picture of the ideal of German manhood. Hitler was to produce a paraphrase: "Should he (the Aryan) be forced to disappear, a profound darkness will descend on the earth, within a few thousand years human culture will vanish and the world will become a desert."[74]

In much the same way, at the beginning of the nineteenth century the principal builder of the Aryan myth, Friedrich Schlegel, who must nevertheless be counted among the "doves", described the Latin languages as "partially dead languages"[75] and therefore deficient in creative elements.

One notes how little distinction these writers made between the criteria of *language* and of *race*. Already in the camp of the "hawks" the fanatics of the Germano-Christian "election" theory, such as Ernst Moritz Arndt or Freidrich Ludwig Jahn, were pointedly and systematically glorifying Germanic "blood" and putting forward arguments which were derived both from the Old Testament, and from the new materialist anthropology of the Enlightenment, without fear of contradiction. "I do not think that I err", wrote Arndt, "in declaring that the powerful and vigorous wildstock called German was the right stock on which to graft the divine shoot, so as to produce the most noble fruit. The Germans . . . alone enabled the divine germ to mature, thanks to philosophy and theology; and they alone, like masters, animate and direct . . . the neighbouring peoples of foreign blood."[76] Jahn, for whom the Greeks and the Germans were the two "holy peoples", expressed himself more crudely: "Hybrid animals do not reproduce; and in the same way half-caste peoples lose their national power of reproduction."[77] When seeking to throw some light on the various currents of this veterinarian philosophy, Ernst Weymar recently came to this conclusion:

> Among the believers in the idea of a Christian and Germanic mission, the concepts of people and nation were most often objectively determined by the characteristics of origin and language. Each of these characteristics was in turn more or less strongly emphasized. The election of a people was determined by strength of blood or of spirit between which there appeared to be a link, though it was never established quite what this was.[78]

Perhaps this unidentifiable link consisted in the common attribute of *purity*. As a matter of fact, the national characteristics described as pure—whether blood or spirit, origin or stock or people, race or religion—tended to become interchangeable even in the writings of an idealist philosopher like Fichte, who invoked the concept of "nature" to justify the maintenance of barriers between people of different "origin" or "language".[79] He thus lent the weight of his metaphysical authority to the Germanophile mania of student youth. This bore its first political fruits in the revolutionary parliament of Frankfurt in 1848, where these passions reached such a pitch that an orator was able to say without fear of ridicule: "Do we not know that, as a result of the Treaty of Verdun, German nationality was definitely subjugated in France and in England by the Latin nationalities!"[80] That was how German patriots in the nineteenth century interpreted the history of Carolingian times.

In many respects Fichte was an astonishing forerunner. It was he, once again, who was the first to question the ethnic origin of Jesus of Nazareth and to conclude that he was not perhaps of Jewish stock,* thus sweeping aside the greatest obstacle in the quest for an authentically German religion. As a result, even the genealogies of the New Testament came to be doubted. Those of the Old Testament had already been discredited by the rationalist Lutheran theologians of the eighteenth century and nobody in Germany gave any further thought to Ashkenaz as a national ancestor.

With the Patriarchs, led by Adam, fallen into disfavour, their place was quickly taken over by the legendary Aryans, and it was in this new perspective that the privileged position of the Germans among the nations of the human race was to be asserted henceforth.

We shall examine the hierarchies and classifications of this new outlook in the second part of this book. There we shall see how the Germans, whose anthropological unity was accepted as self-evident, came to be considered as the quintessence of the European or White race, notably in those various examples of more or less Manichean anthropologies which contrasted a beautiful race with an ugly race (Meiners), an active with a passive race (Klemm), a diurnal with a nocturnal race (Carus), a virile with an effeminate race (Menzel), a human with a simian race (Oken) or a "nature" incarnated for the most part in the Negroes with a "spirit" embodied mostly in the Germans (Hegel).

The opposition between *youth* and *age* is another question which

---

* Fichte based this view on the Gospel of Saint John, which is the only one not to give a genealogy of Jesus derived from David; cf. L. Poliakov, *Histoire de l'antisémitisme, op. cit.*, Vol. III, p. 199.

requires examination. Admittedly, none of the different anthropological systems which we propose to look into adopted this kind of classification explicitly. The superiority conferred on the Germans as a young race was either implicit or was mentioned marginally. No doubt chronological difficulties were responsible (we shall return to this later). Moreover, in a Europe which was supposed to have been populated by Aryans migrating from India in successive waves, might not the palm of youth be more properly attributable to the Slavs who were generally thought to have come last?

Still, the main difficulty probably lay elsewhere, and the real answer is to be found in an altogether wider field of enquiry. The general phenomenon of the youth cult, which is essentially modern, deserves our attention for its own sake. In the West, the cult first made its appearance in Germany. It lay at the root of the romantic protest movement known as *Sturm und Drang* through which German letters, with Herder, Goethe and Schiller, first entered the arena of world literature, which they were to dominate for almost half a century. No doubt the specific "ideal of the German Man" had some relationship to the youth aspect of romantic ideologies—those ideologies which always flourished best in Germany and which some historians think originated there. This suspicion is reinforced when one considers another rebellion of the present against the past, the quarrel of the "Ancients" and the "Moderns", which was pursued in France and England during the seventeenth century and from which the idea of human progress emerged. Then, the rivalry was about being "old", not about being "young". The "Moderns" gave vent to their indignation, they refused to remain the "children" of the "Ancients". Their earliest spokesmen, however, when putting the case for present times, disclose a fundamental ambiguity in the ideas which were current up to their own age. "The opinion which men have of Antiquity", observed Francis Bacon, "is negligently formed and is no wise in agreement with the writings of Antiquity itself." And he added: "The oldness of the world is in our own time and not in that wherein the Ancients lived, for that was its youth."[81]

Pascal formulated the same idea in the following terms: "Those whom we call the Ancients, were truly young in all things and were the childhood of mankind properly speaking. . . . It is among ourselves that we may find this antiquity which we wish to dream of in others."[82]

Those great heralds of reason and science first pointed out the incongruities and lack of precision in the ahistorical, indeed timeless, view bequeathed by the Middle Ages; and it was in this mental climate that "modern man came of age"—though without repudiating the past, since he continued to value Antiquity. In psychoanalytical terms it could be said that the West generally identified itself with its ancient "Fathers" while seeking to surpass them, whereas Germany, on the contrary, tended in various ways to reject them and to deny their paternity.

The revolutionary views suggested by Bacon and Pascal teach us something else about the seemingly contradictory aspects of Age and Youth. Their arguments anticipate the change of attitude in time and space in the modern age to which we have already referred (see p. 29). If we consider the use of language as it reflects our intuitive experience of time, which is profoundly ambivalent since it is an experience both of birth and of decay, of construction and destruction, we find that the collective expression of this experience represented the opposite of its individual expression; indeed, it often still does, even today. This collective mode of expressing time looked to the "good old days" of the past as being older the further removed they were, while the future became ever younger as it approached its termination, the "youngest day" (in German *der jüngste Tag*) of the Last Judgement. In this vision of the world, language expressed the opposition between a past which was the time of the old ones and a future which was the time of the young. This way of experiencing collective time, enshrined in linguistic usage, exists to this day, alongside the modern view of time (where, to quote Pascal once again, the modern age began to consider "the whole succession of mankind . . . as a single man").[83] The resulting contradictions and confusions persist in our own day. Their roots lie deep not only in the immemorial past but also in the profound timelessness of unconscious psychic processes.

The above digression has prepared the way for fresh insights into the contrast between the "old Latin race" and the "young Germanic race" which we sketched out in the last chapter. From the cultural point of view, the age of a civilization has a precise meaning since it can be related to chronological points of reference. The undeniable antiquity of Latin culture inspired Italian patriots of all epochs to avail themselves of this traditional form of superiority; no doubt it was for this reason that emphasis was placed, even during the Fascist period, on the spiritual or cultural aspect of the *razza di Roma*. It is none the less true that the characteristic vagueness of the concept of "collective age" made it possible in modern times to simulate a rejuvenation of Italy by invoking the notion of rebirth, or rather of regeneration. This notion, too, lends itself to interesting psychoanalytical interpretations. It should be remembered that "youth" was one of the key-words of Fascism of which the anthem was *Giovinezza*.*

There was all the more reason, then, why an imagined physiological age of races (which we now know to be a nonsense) should leave the door wide open for every kind of speculation, in the absence of any well-founded and universally accepted standard of judgement. The ambiguity was clearly revealed when the extollers of the Germanic race—especially in the Nazi period—began to exploit both versions simultaneously. The Germanic race was original and had always existed ("blood" being identified with "soil") but it was also eternally young. This contradiction was reflected, from about 1870 onwards, in polemics between upholders of the "Aryan immigration" theory and the partisans of a new theory of "autochthonism". In 1925, a zealot of the latter theory declared that "it has to be admitted that the new doctrine, which implies an awareness of living from time immemorial on our native soil, ought to inspire each of us with a heightened sense of our strength and this entails special obligations. . .". As one would expect, there followed a reference to Antaeus and "our Mother Earth".[84]

Having said all that, we have to admit that we are not altogether satisfied by the above analysis. For one thing, the special obsession with "purity" which characterized the growth of German racism in the nineteenth century was influenced without doubt by social and cultural factors, especially by the authoritarian tradition of German education. It has not been possible to deal at length with all these factors in the present work. To have done so we would have had to clear many more paths, leading in their turn to other relevant perspectives, political or economic, each of which contributed in its own way to mould the future of Germany and Europe. Moreover, in our endeavour to highlight the powerful imprint made on German history by the cultural model of the "German Man", we seem barely to have touched on the disconcerting phenomenon of German neo-Paganism, which was sometimes cultivated openly but more often

* This kind of analysis can obviously be applied to other countries. In our own time, propaganda in Israel often describes the country as the youngest as well as —"miraculously" or "paradoxically"—the oldest country. This in itself is an example of a confused awareness of the problem of collective time.

claimed, paradoxically, to be a "German Christianity". But we shall return to these questions later.

Finally, it is worth remembering that, in the second half of the nineteenth century, the supreme prophet of these theosophies and heresies was Richard Wagner; that their principal rites and ceremonies were celebrated annually at Bayreuth, and that their redeemer was Parsifal, the Germanic Christ-Knight, described as "the third Adam of History" by one of the devotees of "the cult celebrated on the altars of the god Wagner".[85] But it should also be remembered that Germany produced, during the same period, some clear-sighted and patriotic critics. Among the latter was Mommsen, whose dry comments are more to the point than the anti-Wagnerian fulminations of Nietzsche. Mommsen stressed the "essentially aggressive character of German missionary nationalism" and warned against "the nationalist madmen who want to replace the universal Adam by a Germanic Adam, containing in himself all the splendours of the human spirit".[86]

CHAPTER SIX

RUSSIA

THE EURASIAN MELTING-POT

In the Soviet Union the myth of national origin is a matter for State control. About 1965 the young historian Andrey Amalrik (later deported to Siberia) was dismissed from his university because he criticized the official "anti-Norman" theory about the origins of Russia.[1] This theory was the cause of an historical controversy which may well have been the most protracted and bitter of all time, as it began more than two centuries ago. At the start, German scholars commissioned by the Court to study national history were ranged against Russian intellectuals with a European education, amongst whom Michael Lomonosov was outstanding. The dispute continued into the nineteenth century, when a genuinely Russian scholarship was developing. At that time the polemics between Normanists and anti-Normanists reached their height—though even then nobody, on either side, was imprisoned for his views.

The main cause of the dispute was a chronicle of Kiev known as the chronicle "of Nestor". This definitely suggested that from the ninth to the twelfth century Russia or "Rus" was governed by the Varangians, or Scandinavians, the term Rus itself originating in Sweden. The impression was confirmed by the undoubtedly Scandinavian names of the first princes of Kiev, and it was further supported by Icelandic sagas which tell how Vikings were drawn into the Russian plains by their appetite for plunder and their thirst for glory. Some became princes like the Swede Rurik, whose dynasty governed Russia up to the sixteenth century. Others were employed as mercenaries; until the end of the eleventh century, Rurik's successors were surrounded by a Swedish guard and waged war with their support.

A famous passage in the chronicle of Kiev was especially wounding to national and racial pride for in it the Slav tribes were reported to have appealed to the Vikings, to Rurik and his brothers, in the following terms: "Our land is great and rich, but there is no order in it. Come and rule over us." One can imagine how this appeal could be used by anyone wishing to argue the political inferiority of the Russians, especially as Russia only escaped from domination by western rulers to fall under that of an eastern people, the Mongols. Until about 1935, when Stalin introduced strict discipline into the teaching of history, all Russian schoolboys were familiar with the above passage. But of course there was much else in Nestor's account to arouse interest.

While stressing the part played by the Germanic dynasty of Varangians, this Christian monk divided the native population of the Russian plain into Slavs and non-Slavs, both of whom were affiliated to Japheth and were therefore totally different from the nomadic peoples of the Orient, the descendants of Shem. This observation is striking in the first place because the non-Slavic peoples, which Nestor enumerated, still exist in U.S.S.R. to this day, in the Federal Republics or Autonomous Territories. Secondly, while insisting on the primacy of Slav stock, Nestor mentioned the Finnish and Baltic neighbours—who were *inozemtsi* (men of another land) rather than *chuzhezemtsi* (foreigners) — without any of the animosity which characterized the German attitude towards the non-Germanic *Welsche*. Nevertheless, the identification of the people with their language was more complete among the Slavs than among the Germans, for the same word, *yazyk*, was used for both until the sixteenth century (and in popular speech until the nineteenth). The difference between Slav and Germanic usage is also apparent in the word *Nemtsy*, signifying "the mute", which is the antonym of the root *slov* or *slav* meaning "word" and "glory" and "the Slavs". Before being applied to the Germans only, *Nemtsy* was used to describe all the *chuzhezemtsi*, though not the *inozemtzi*. Of the latter Nestor wrote as follows:

> Other peoples [languages] pay tribute to "Rus" [namely to the Varangians]. These are the Chud, Merya, Ves, Muroma, Cheremiss, Mordva, Perm, Pechora, Yem, Litva, Zemgola, Kors and Livy. All these speak their own languages. They are descended from Japheth and live in northern climes. They all observe the usages, traditions, and laws of their forefathers, and they follow their own customs. . . .

According to the chronicler, the famous appeal to Rurik and his brothers was made by the Slavs, the Chud, and the Ves. It never occurs to him to criticize the customs of these idolaters, any more than those of the pagan princes of Kiev, whom he describes with respect and sympathy.

Admittedly, the chronicle does not stint its praise for Vladimir the Saint who, like a "new Constantine", had indoctrinated his subjects in the spirit of the Gospels; yet it is certain that Christianity took some time, perhaps centuries, to gain a solid foothold in Russia. In describing how the saintly Prince Vladimir taught the new faith concurrently with the alphabet to the sons of "his best vassals", Nestor faithfully recorded that "The mothers wept for these children. Being as yet not confirmed in their faith, they wept for them as if they had died." Numerous conflicts in the eleventh and twelfth centuries show the survival of paganism especially among country people, and the practice of two beliefs (*droyeverye*) was also not uncommon among the leaders. The cult of the great Earth-Goddess persisted under the guise of devotion to the "holy soil of Russia", later "Holy Russia", or in the custom of a "confession to the earth", traces of which are still met with in Dostoevsky's works.² The blasphemous obscenity attaching to the word for mother in the "maternal swear-words" is further evidence.* Vladimir the Saint, moreover, was identified with the sun-god Dajdbog since his surname meant "red sun" or "glorious sun". Nestor himself asserted that the pagans claimed the sky as their father and the earth as their mother. In the most celebrated Russian epic, the *Song of Igor* (c. 1200), there is no reference to Japheth or Adam. The Russians still worshipped their divine pagan ancestors; they remained "grand-sons of Dajdbog".

This may explain a peculiar feature of the first Christian genealogies of Russia. Unlike those in the West, the Russian chronicles never attempted to bridge the gap between Japheth and Rurik, by affiliating the latter to Biblical patriarchs or to the heroes of Antiquity. An unbroken genealogy of this kind was only worked out, as we shall see, under Ivan the Terrible in the sixteenth century. Until then, all that can be discovered is an attempt in the fourteenth century to "naturalize" King Solomon. An obscure legend and a famous heroic poem both declared that Solomon had once upon a time reigned in Russia.³ It should be remembered that the Russians were familiar with the Old Testament at that time because it had been translated into the Slav language by the first Christian missionaries who evangelized the country. One result of this was that educated Russians

---

* These *po matushke* swear-words are described in a medieval Russian collection of sermons as being thrice proscribed—because they insulted the Mother of God, the speaker's own mother and the universal Mother Earth. Cf. Alain Besançon, *Le tsarévitch immolé*, Paris 1967, pp. 43-4.

spared themselves the intellectual effort of studying the languages and cultures of Antiquity, which was doubtless the main reason why there was no Slav Renaissance. As late as the beginning of the sixteenth century it was impossible to find a good scholar of Greek in Moscow and a certain Maxim the Greek, a humanist, had to be sent for from Italy.[4]

Nevertheless, although it may have been baptized rather late and not too well, Kievan Russia in the eleventh century entered wholeheartedly into the concert of feudal European nations. A daughter of Yaroslav the Wise (Russia's Charlemagne, the son and husband of Scandinavian princesses and possibly no more "russified" than Pepin the Short was "francized") became the Queen of France,* while other marriages were contracted in the Germanic countries and in England.

Trade was flourishing at that time and, according to Henri Pirenne, Russian towns were more active and crowded than those of western Europe.[5] Among the Scandinavians Russia was known as *Gardarikki*, "the kingdom of cities". It was, however, with Byzantium that the Russians were to form the closest ties. The new religion and culture had come from there. The Russian Church was hierarchically dependent on Byzantium, and in the eyes of nearly all Slavs the Byzantine emperor was the legitimate heir to the universal Roman Empire or "Tsar" who resided in his capital or Tsargrad.† That, at any rate, was the situation up to 1240 when Russia was subjugated (with the exception of the free towns of Novgorod and Pskov on the confines of the Baltic) by a foreign power and ruled, for two and a half centuries, by the most terrible "Tsar" whom any Christian people had known.

★　　★　　★

The dream of a world empire never came so near to fulfilment as in the middle of the thirteenth century, when the power of the Mongols stretched from Vietnam to the Adriatic Sea. Gengis Khan and his successors had a plan of action and a code of values. By virtue of a divine decree, which was also binding on the Khans, the Mongols had been charged with the mission of bringing peace and order to the whole world. Their claims were based not only on a right but on a duty.[6] They were skilled politicians and ruled as colonizers, leaving

* This was Queen Anne, married to Henry I of France in 1051, who became regent after his death during the minority of her son Philip I.

† This name for Constantinople was current in Russia till the twentieth century.

the local princes where they found them. It was the task of the latter to exploit the local populations, to collect taxes and conscript auxiliary militia (thousands of Russian recruits went into battle and to their deaths in China).[7]

Feudal bonds were weak in Russia, and in 1240 it was overrun in the space of a few months; one after another the *Rurikovichi* submitted and became vassals, constrained to seek investiture at the hands of the Great Khan and to go to his capital in Asia to do homage or to settle their disputes. It was the Khan, therefore, who became the first real Tsar of All the Russias and who is so designated in the earliest writings.

In this situation, the Christian princes, among whom those of Moscow excelled as collaborators, were mere intermediaries or intercessors. It was the remote pagan Tsars who really wielded power, and they were linked to the Christian and national community of Russia by no other bond than that of violence and oppression. This tragic relationship with the supreme holders of a power which was exercised with cold cruelty and deceit is hinted at in the epics or *byliny* which refer to a "dog tsar" who has "caused much suffering to the land of Russia". Nevertheless before rebelling against him, the popular hero, Ilya Muromets, goes to render homage to him as though this "dog" were indeed a legitimate ruler:

> *Ilya betook himself to the dog tsar Kalin,*
> *He bowed before him and greeted him;*
> *"Peace and good health to you, tsar Kalin".*
> *Tsar Kalin then commanded him:*
> *"Serve me faithfully and sincerely".*[8]

In a different kind of source, a hagiography of Saint Stephen (the Apostle of the Finnish tribe of Zyrians), there is a reference to a "false tsar" whose legitimacy, nevertheless, is not questioned; his usurpation and faithlessness are accepted as a matter of course.[9] This ambiguity perhaps lies at the root of the distrust of political authority which the Russian people have shown throughout the course of their history; they have always regarded it as foreign and hostile.

The clergy too recognized the legitimacy of the Mongol tsars who granted them numerous and excessive privileges.* Thus the national

---

* Exemption from tribute, taxes and charges of all kinds; exclusive legal jurisdiction over church members, the right to inflict the death penalty for offences

Russian Saint Sergey of Radonezh, whose advice Prince Dimitry Donskoy sought on the eve of the Battle of Kulikovo (1380), reminded him of his duties as a vassal:

> Your duty, Sire, is to defend your people. Be prepared to offer up your soul and shed your blood. But first go before the Khan Mamai as a vassal and seek to stop him by your submission and by telling him the truth. Holy Scripture instructs us that if our enemies demand our glory, if they require our gold or our silver we can give them up. But let us only sacrifice our lives and shed our blood for the faith in the name of Christ. Listen, O prince, If you yield your glory and your riches to them God will not allow you to be defeated. He will raise you up because of your humility and he will put down their ungovernable pride. . . .[10]

The Metropolitan of Moscow, Cyprian, gave the same advice to Dimitry and stressed the legitimacy of Mongol power.[11] This shows a very different spirit from that of the western Crusades, and it is superfluous to add that the Russian Church never witnessed anything like the military orders of the Knights Templars or the Teutonic Knights or, more generally, like the opposition in the West of popes against emperors, bishops against princes and priesthood against laity. Obedience to the temporal power was praised by the clergy as the cardinal virtue. Moreover, this attitude was extended to the sphere of family and private morality, as is clear from manuals of general knowledge like the *Ismaragd* or the famous *Domostroy* which advised parents to save their children by terror.[12]

We must now examine how Russia, enslaved by the Mongols, was able during the fifteenth and sixteenth centuries to become a great European power and affiliate itself to ancient Rome without changing the style of life and political behaviour which, it would seem, have marked it for all eternity.

*   *   *

The victory of Kulikovo had no sequel, and historians believe that it must have been due to temporary discord in the Mongol camp. Moscow was recaptured two years later and put to fire and the sword by Tsar Toktamish, and the rule of his successors, though progressively weakened, lasted another hundred years. It was only in 1480 that the

---

against the Christian faith, etc. The higher clergy in Russia consequently formed part of the "Mongol faction". Cf. G. P. Fedotov, *The Russian Religious Mind*, Vol. II, Harvard 1966, p. 185.

Metropolitan Gerontius and Archbishop Vassian freed the grand-prince Ivan from his oath. On this occasion their language sounds a new note: ". . . we give you our blessing to go and fight Akhmed not as tsar but as a brigand and God's enemy. It is better to break an oath and save your life than to keep faith and perish, leaving the Tatars to wipe out Christianity."[13] After forcing the Golden Horde to retreat, Ivan III never again paid tribute to it. He adopted the title of *samoderzhets* or autocrat and called himself tsar to mark his independence.

The clergy were all the more prepared to advocate resistance because their own spiritual autonomy had preceded by a short period the political independence of Muscovite Russia. Great consternation was felt throughout Christendom when the Turks seized Byzantium in 1453. What was even more serious in Russian eyes was the acceptance by the Greek Church, in the hope of escaping *in extremis* from Muslim domination, of union with Rome and subordination to the hated Latin papacy. Moscow was now faced with the fact that, alone in the world, it stood for the true Orthodox belief. The fall of Byzantium, aggravated by the attempted union with sinful Rome, proved the decadence of the Greeks. The capital of religion had shifted by the sheer force of events from Constantinople to Moscow. The metropolitans now depended entirely on Russian princes who, following the example of the Greek emperors, were soon to be endowed with quasi-divine powers well expressed in the Byzantine saying: "The emperor resembles all men, but by his power he resembles Almighty God." In 1472, Ivan III of Moscow married the Greek Princess Zoë Palaeologus, thus establishing an initial, if somewhat remote, title of succession to the Byzantine Empire. During the years that followed, a number of genealogies and legends were circulated with a view to strengthening the claim. These foretold that Moscow's future glory was to be in no sense inferior to that of Byzantium, and they were at pains to erase as rapidly as possible all traces of the Mongol or Asiatic past.

The process began with the adoption of the two-headed eagle of Byzantium as a national emblem, and this was followed by the attribution to Byzantium of the dynastic symbols which in reality had been granted by the Mongol tsars to their faithful Muscovite vassals (in particular the famous crown called the "hat of Monomakh").*

---

* It seems probable that this crown was offered by the "tsar" Uzbeg to Prince Ivan I at the beginning of the fourteenth century. Cf. Vernadsky, *A History of Russia, op. cit.*, Vol. III, p. 386. But according to a Muscovite tradition it was

Later there appeared the popular legend of the "white tiara" of which 250 manuscripts exist. According to this, the legendary tiara of Pope Sylvester, who was supposed to have converted Constantine, had been brought to Byzantium and thence to Novgorod and to Moscow.[14] There was also a "Legend of the Empire of Babylon"; this reproduced an imperial genealogy in which Moscow was affiliated through Byzantium to ancient Babylon. The West which had looked no further back than Troy was suddenly outclassed.[15] Another version of the story, which was transmitted in the chronicles as well as by legends, advanced a more modern type of argument, based on a persistent mistranslation of the Bible, and proclaimed that the future Emperor of the Universe would come from a blond nation which could only be Russian.†

Finally the idea emerged of Moscow as the Third Rome. It started in Pskov, soon after the annexation in 1510 of this last of the free Russian cities. Its author was the learned Abbot Philotheus. He hoped by flattering the grand-prince to improve the fate of his fellow-citizens who were being deported and oppressed. So he wrote:

> . . . If you govern your empire with justice you will be a Son of Light and a Citizen of the New Jerusalem as I have already written. Now I say to you—Listen with care, pious Tsar. All Christian empires are united within yours, for two Romes have fallen, but the third stands and there will be no fourth. As the great prophet [Daniel] has foretold, your empire will never pass into the hands of others. . . .[16]

Moscow's claims to imperial power could, however, be asserted genealogically with greater effect by the affiliation of her princes to the Romans. In that case their claims would yield nothing to the

---

given by the Byzantine Emperor Constantine Monomachus to Prince Vladimir Monomakh in the twelfth century.

† This error, which is still current, goes back to the Greek translation of the Old Testament known as the Septuagint and is derived from the "Prophecy against Gog" in Ezekiel xxxviii, 1-2. "Son of Man, set thy face against Gog, the land of Magog, the chief prince of Meshech and Tubal, and prophesy against him." In the Greek translation the Hebrew word "rosh" (= head, principal, chief) became a name, that of an eighth son of Japheth, in whom the Byzantines were anxious to discern the ancestor of the Russians, *Ross* or *Russ*. The Russians for their part were able to make use of another paronym because *russyi* means "blond" in Russian.

western bearers of the imperial title, the "Roman and Germanic" emperors. No doubt that was why Basil III, the father of Ivan the Terrible, told Maximilian's ambassador that his great ancestor Rurik was of Roman stock.[17]

It did not take long for this idea to be formulated with greater precision and to be further developed, though it never commanded the same degree of popular support as similar claims in Italy and Germany in quite recent times. The reason for this lack of success in Russia is to be found in the way the idea was exploited.

When Basil III died Ivan was only three years old. After an unhappy childhood, when the future tsar saw rival cliques of boyars fighting for power and slaughtering each other before his eyes, he chose as his counsellor the Metropolitan Macarius who became "his father and mediator".[18] In 1547, when he attained his majority, he had himself crowned with every solemnity by his mentor who placed the Monomakh crown on his head and blessed him with a relic of the True Cross. But Macarius was not content merely to bestow the supreme title upon the young prince. In order to enhance the glory of his office, he provided him with an imperial genealogy going back, through Rurik, the Emperor Augustus and a number of fabled characters, to Aeneas and Noah. No other European monarch, not even Charles V, could boast of such titles.

In this way a genealogical fable which had been current for a number of years under the name of "the legend of the Princes of Vladimir" received official sanction.[19] In order to further the operation Arpacshad, described in Genesis as one of the sons of Shem and an ancestor of Abraham, was promoted to the status of being Noah's fourth son; while the Roman emperor acquired six brothers, Patricius, Augustalis, Evlagerod, Ilirik, Pion and Pruss among whom, before dying, he divided the world. Pruss, the youngest, inherited the land situated around the River Niemen, namely Prussia, and Rurik, forty generations later, was held to be his descendant in the direct line. Thus the Swedish Rurik became a Prussian or German but this did not did not disturb Macarius or Ivan. On the contrary, the official chronicle of this reign, called the chronicle of Nikon, expressly stated that "Rurik and his brothers were descended from the Germans".[20] This Germano-Roman genealogy was henceforth invoked in diplomatic correspondence to justify every kind of precedence and was even incorporated in the menology or calendar of the saints of the Orthodox Church.[21] In private, Ivan went so far as to declare that generally speaking the

Russian nobility was "descended from the Germans"—did not the
boyars come from *Bavaria*?[22] Even more astonishing was his reply to
the British ambassador, Giles Fletcher, to whom he declared that all
Russians were thieves. When the ambassador expressed polite surprise
Ivan the Terrible retorted: "I am not Russian. My ancestors were
Germans."[23] Genealogists tell us that through his mother Ivan was
descended from the Khan Mamai, but for this Tsar or Caesar the
Mongol yoke had never existed. "We are not Muscovites", he told
the Roman envoy, a Jesuit called Possevino. "Moscow was founded
nearly a century after the establishment of our empire in the Russian
state, though by God's will this age-old empire has been consolidated
in that city."[24] Though this pitiless monarch did so much to make
Russia great, and always insisted that his subjects abide by their ancient
customs, he was emphatic in distinguishing his lineage from theirs.
What is more, he offered the common people of Russia no genealogy
of their own.

It was only in the West that a few authors tried to find an ancestor
for the Muscovites among the lists of Biblical Patriarchs, or forged
such fables as that of the three brothers Czech, Lech and Rus.[25] In
Moscow itself nobody seemed concerned about the lineage of the
Russians; they were treated as disinherited bastards or, as Chaadaev
was to write in the nineteenth century, "illegitimate children, without
a heritage and with no links to bind them to their predecessors on
earth.* When, at the end of the interregnum of the "troubled times",
the Romanovs succeeded the dynasty of Rurik they too appropriated
the imperial Roman lineage for their own use. At the coronation of
Alexis in 1645, the Patriarch Joseph reminded him that his remote
ancestors had been masters of the world, and a mural in the Kremlin,
commissioned for the occasion, showed the division of the earth between
Pruss and his brothers.[26] Soon afterwards, "the first Slavophile of
Russian history", the Croat George Krizhanich, attributed all the
catastrophes of Russia to this *xenomania* (a word coined by him). "Ivan
the Terrible", he wrote, "wanted to be a Varangian, a German or a
Roman, anything except a Russian or Slav. . . . Our people have had
ineluctably to submit to this universal execration and shame as a
punishment for their sins. If the Varangian fable is true our Russian
soil has only produced four princes in a thousand years. . . . I firmly

* P. Tchaadaev, *Lettres philosophiques*, Paris 1970, p. 51. The "westernizer"
Chaadaev wanted thereby to emphasize the cultural sterility of Russia but it
strikes one as curious that he should have recourse to these genealogical similes.

believe and I declare without hesitation that this vainglorious pride of Tsar Ivan was not the least nor the latest cause of the devastation of Moscow and of the calamities which our people have suffered since that period."[27]

This was, in fact, a much debated problem of Russian history and has continued to be so. The theory that the Romanovs were of German origin, which had been internationally accepted,[28] was still current in Russia at the end of the nineteenth century.[29] In the West, and particularly in Germany, it was quite common formerly to distinguish between the *élites* or ruling class in Russia, thought to be of Aryan or Germanic origin, and the people who were of mixed or Mongol blood. Karl Marx, as we shall see, was a supporter of this view.[30] The problem extended far beyond the ruling dynasties.

At the time of Ivan the Terrible there were indeed dozens of families which rightly or wrongly claimed to be descended from Rurik, and were thus more or less automatically classed as Germanic. Following their example, other boyars also claimed western ancestry. Apart from any question of imitation or prestige, this allowed the feudal nobility of a people, which compared to others was young, to acquire a greater age, prolonging its genealogies by several generations or centuries or even millennia. Such was the case with the bailiff (*namestnik*) Eremeyev who not only declared that his grandfather had come from Italy at the time of Alexander Nevsky but quoted the Roman historian Suetonius in support of the antiquity of his lineage.[31] Somewhat less ambitious were the Bestuzhevs; they only claimed descent from the English family of the Bests whose ancestors had been crusaders.[32] A play on words might also be of use: the typical Muscovite name of Kozodavlev was considered to have been derived from Koss von Dahlen; the Russian Razumovskys discovered an affinity with the Polish Roginskys.[33] In listing the boyars who were massacred by Ivan the Terrible his accuser Prince Kurbsky (who was himself a *Rurikovich*) attributed German origin to the Vorontsov, Morozov, Sheremetyev, Kolychev and Sheyn families.[34] Other families continued to cherish the memory of their Tartar or Caucasian ancestry (many honours were bestowed upon oriental princes who became converts, and an extreme example of this was the farcical performance of Ivan the Terrible in 1575, when he pretended to cede his throne to a newly converted Tartar prince).[35] In addition, Russian expansion eastward to Siberia brought new pagan *inozemtsy* under the domination of Moscow and thus gave birth once more to a situation like that described by the monk Nestor; once more geographical or geo-political influences played a part.

The result of all these naturalizations or denaturalizations—it is hard to know which term fits best—was that the "race" of the Russian nobility seemed in modern times to be as heterogeneous as it possibly could be. In the nineteenth century, genealogists agreed that 90 per cent of the titled families were of non-Slav origin, mostly western and the rest from the East.[36]

To begin with the phenomenon which we have described above was a portent of the later separation between the upper classes, which even before Peter the Great had been open to western influence, and the people, for whom time seemed to have stood still ever since the glorious institution of the Orthodox Muscovite Empire. Before long a religious schism, the *Raskol*, was to show that the people were even prepared to be massacred to keep intact their rites, beliefs and customs. Russian epic or historical poetry confirms the split. It knows of only two great princely figures: one was the remote Kievan Vladimir the Saint surrounded by his circle of *bogatyrs*, who evoked memories of the Mongol yoke.[37] The other, much closer and more real, and much admired in spite of, or perhaps because of, all the blood he shed, was Ivan the Terrible, who became the leading figure of Muscovite or Great-Russian history. After this the epic vein is silent or concentrates on quite different personalities like the brigand Stenka Razin. It ignores Peter the Great, but we know from other sources that this king, who trampled underfoot all the traditions of the Russians and mocked their Church, came to be regarded by his people as a false Tsar; a German, perhaps even a Jew. Popular sympathy was entirely with the heir to the throne, Prince Alexis, who supported traditional Russia and whom his father tried and executed.*

There is little information to indicate the feelings of the illiterate peasant serfs in succeeding reigns, least of all their ideas about their own origins. Those which Russian intellectuals elaborated in the

---

* Cf. E. Schuyler, *Peter the Great*, London 1884, Vol. II, pp. 149 *et seq.* An eloquent witness to this popular sympathy is also to be found in the farce called *The Comedy of Tsar Maximilian and his disobedient son Adolf* of which some two hundred versions are extant. This shows how Maximilian (obviously a disguise for Peter the Great) puts his son to death for refusing to bow to Mahometan gods or Cimmerian idols, and who therefore represents orthodoxy or the people of Russia. Cf. M. M. Evreinov, *History of the Russian Theatre*, New York 1955, pp. 117-9 (in Russian).

E

eighteenth, and especially in the nineteenth, century barely reached the mass of the people, so great was the cultural gap. Whether these intellectuals were western-type chauvinists, or Christian or atheist humanists of a more indigenous type, the ideologists' or mythologists' public was long confined to the intelligentsia. We must now turn our attention to the tragedy which overtook this intelligentsia.

*   *   *

Intelligentsia is one of the few words that western languages have borrowed from Russian. Its emergence in Russia, in the middle of the nineteenth century, points to the existence of a specific milieu, clearly delimited, and distinguished from the Russian people by its culture, which was of foreign origin. According to the view it took of the Russian people and the plans it made for that people, the intelligentsia was divided into two factions, the "westernizers" and the "slavophiles". Both terms suggest that these men wished to be what in fact they were not; there never have been "easternizing" or "francophile" Frenchmen or even "germanophile" Germans. The same consideration applies to the revolutionary movement of the Populists. These key-words point to the tragedy of the Russian intelligentsia: the profound sense of alienation, of a cultural rootlessness which could even include ignorance of the mother tongue (witness Tatyana in *Eugene Onegin*, or the French conversations with which *War and Peace* begins, or the gibes of Dostoevsky).[38] In the education of the cultivated classes in Russia the peasant nurse, the *nyanya*, was usually replaced at an early stage by a foreign tutor or governess who was responsible for teaching the alphabet and so on.* No doubt this abandonment of the native culture at an early age was one of the primary causes of the sense of guilt, of having betrayed the people, which have left so deep a mark on Russian literature and thought. In the nineteenth century this feeling gave birth to the concept of a Russian or Slav soul which was attributed, quite wrongly, to the Russian people as a whole.

At the beginning of this process, we find the distinctive style of Europeanization imposed by Peter the Great, which called for derision and persecution of everything Russian together with imitation and adulation of everything foreign. The man who turned Russia against her past in this fashion seemed to generations of intellectuals almost like a god who had rescued the country from nullity. Archbishop

* Such was the experience of the author of the present work and of a number of his childhood friends.

Prokopovich, in his panegyric at the Tsar's funeral, declared that Peter had regenerated Russia, or rather that "he had given birth to it and suckled it", and compared him to the Emperor Constantine, to the prophet Moses and to the patriarch Japheth.[39] Michael Lomonosov went even further in 1740, stating that if he were to be compared to anyone it could only be to Almighty God.[40] With only a little less exaggeration, such praises were to be repeated from generation to generation both by the supporters of the autocracy and by its detractors. For the orthodox historian Pogodin, Peter was "the human god"; for the critic Belinsky, "altars should be raised in his honour in all the streets and squares of the Russian Empire".[41] The classic Russian culture of the nineteenth century was believed to have owed its existence to him since, according to a well-known opinion, "Peter threw out a challenge to Russia and she replied with Pushkin". All these images suggest a creation *ex nihilo*, an act of generation by some god or else a primordial rape.

Thus everything had had its origin with Peter. But what had been there before him? Through the window which he opened on to Europe the Tsar was the first to seek the light which western knowledge might cast upon the origins of his people. When Leibniz, who had just peopled the whole of Europe solely with Germans,[42] was asked about this he replied that the Russians were of Asiatic stock and that they were led into Europe by Attila.[43] This unflattering genealogy was merely an anticipation of what was taught throughout the eighteenth century by the German scholars who staffed the first Russian universities. The erudite Schlözer compared the early Russians to the animals and birds of their forests.[44] But it was above all their appeal to the Varangians which produced disagreeable comments on the nature and character of the Slavs. This stimulated the first historians of genuinely Russian stock to protest that, far from being savages, the Slavs were already renowned in the times of Alexander the Great, and even of Herodotus. Indeed, they surpassed even the wildest claims of their German teachers, including their speculations about the "youth" and "age" of peoples. Schlözer had no difficulty in comparing these patriots with the German humanists of the Renaissance.

The first Russian historian Tatishchev (1686-1750), who could be critical enough when dealing with the Biblical genealogies, nevertheless affirmed that the emperors of Byzantium spoke Slavonic, and wondered whether Pharaoh's daughter was not of Slav extraction since she had bestowed the name of Moses (Moi-ssei meaning "This one is mine") upon the infant she found floating in the Nile.[45] Not to be outdone, the grammarian Tredyakovsky (1703-1769) affirmed that the "Slovensque" language was the most ancient in Europe and that both the Germanic and Celtic languages were derived from it (Celts = Yelts = Yellow = blonds).[46] The Celts were therefore a branch of the Slav race, argued the poet Sumarokov (1717-1777), and the Romans must have been another since the monosyllables *dom, noss, oko* and *bratt* must be the roots of *domus, nasus, oculus* and *frater*.[47] The idea that monosyllabic words were the oldest root-words was born like so many others in the Germanic countries* and the more the Russians claimed priority in their origins, that is to say originality, the more in fact they were imitating the Germans. The great Lomonosov (1711-1765) was more restrained when he compared the ancient glory of the Slavs to that of the Romans and, inspired by the latter, affiliated them to the Trojans. Though more cautious than Tatishchev he did not exclude the possibility that their ancestry went back to Meschech and to Noah.[48] These past splendours were the guarantee of future glory, and it seemed to him that the time was approaching when the immemorial and therefore eternally young "land of Russia would produce its own Platos and Newtons endowed with the same agile intelligence".[49] In the field of physics Lomonosov certainly fulfilled his own prediction, but where history was concerned he denounced the academician Gerhard-Friedrich Müller to the authorities because he had dared to question that Russia had been visited by the apostle Saint Andrew, and had attributed a Germanic origin to the Varangians. (Except for the style and for the mention of Saint Andrew, the denunciation could have come from 1950 rather than 1750.)[50]

All these grandiose Russian claims remained cultural rather than racial. It fell to Catherine the Great—who was, it should be remembered, of German origin—to proclaim a hereditary or racial superiority of the Slavs; indeed, it seems she was the first person in Russia to use the word "race". In her review,† she dissented from Sumarokov's opinion that virtues and vices were equally shared by all peoples whether they were French or Tartars, and she attributed the faults of the Russians to their semi-Asiatic or Sarmatian ancestry. But their numerous good qualities seemed to her to be genuinely Slav, and

---

* The Fleming, Goropius Becanus, seems to have been the first to launch this idea; cf. above, p. 90.

† It should be observed that Catherine II fancied herself as a journalist and she edited the monthly review *Vsyakaya Vsyachina* (A Bit of Everything).

towards the end of her life she was one of those who proclaimed that the first language of mankind was Slavonic. "I have collected a great deal of knowledge about the ancient Slavs", she wrote to Grimm in 1784, "and I could show without much trouble that they have provided the names of most of the rivers, mountains, valleys, regions and provinces of France, Spain, Scotland and other places. . . . The Salian Franks and Salic Law, Chilperic I, Clovis and all the Merovingian race were Slav, as well as all the Vandal Kings of Spain." The "Semiramis of the North" came near to publishing those discoveries, which she also pursued with reference to America and to India. Moreover, philology provided her with astonishing corroboration; for were not Osiris, Zoroaster and Odin originally Slav names? And were not the astronomer Bailly, Court de Gébelin and the great Voltaire himself convinced of the existence in Asia of a primitive civilization which had given birth to those of Europe and the Middle East? Only a few months before her death Catherine wrote:

> I personally believe that King Alfred and others of the Anglo-Saxon race were Slavs; that to this day a tribute is paid in England called socage and that the English are aware that this payment was established by the Saxons, who are a Slav tribe. I do not read nor even glance at any book which is not at least three hundred years old. I learn nothing from the others, and as to conjectures I've had my fill of them.[51]

If Russian cultural poverty, especially when measured by the European yardstick, induced these authors to outdo the age-old Germanic pretensions even while imitating them, they had not reached the point as yet of asking themselves about the specific character of the national "soul" or "essence". It was only when a genuinely Russian literary culture was born that the problem of understanding the worth and significance of this culture arose, but it was the West which served as model and provided the scale of values. This was true even when it was a question of Russia distinguishing herself from western culture by rejecting it. A historian who began by being a novelist and who was one of the creators of modern Russian literature, Karamzin, was the first, round about 1810, to put forward a number of perplexing questions. While admitting the outstanding qualities of Peter the Great, he wondered whether the Tsar, in violently uprooting the old Muscovite traditions, had not "debased the Russians in their own hearts". He went on to ask:

Can a man be prepared for great enterprises by self-abasement? . . The leaders have become detached from the common people. The Russian nobility are looked on as Germans by the peasants, the middle classes and the merchants, to the great detriment of the people's fraternal solidarity. . . . We have become citizens of the world but in some cases we have ceased to be citizens of Russia. That is Peter's fault.[52]

As a responsible historian Karamzin did not try, in his classic *History of the Russian State*, to disguise the appeal to the Varangians. He considered it "an astonishing fact almost without parallel in the annals of the human race", and he explained it by the good sense of the Russian people "who were prepared to put aside their national pride in exchange for order and quiet".[53] We shall see how some of his successors exploited this idea.

Pushkin, who was also a historian at times, never bothered about such questions. He was a westernizer through and through, and he viewed the reign of Peter the Great with unstinted admiration. In 1836, when criticizing the Russian society of his time, he wrote in a letter to Chaadaev that "the government [of Nicholas I] is in spite of everything the only European in Russia, and however brutal and cynical it is, it could easily decide to be a hundred times more so; nobody would notice".[54] The ambiguity of Pushkin's relations with Nicholas I is well known. As a Russian patriot he approved the annexation of Poland which he regarded as an internal matter between Slavs,[55] but he was free from racism and he prided himself on the "African blood" which flowed in his veins. In all this he was very Russian. Indeed, his genius enabled him to reconcile all differences, and he represented a unique interlude in the national history, the fulfilment of a long cherished hope. But it was a hope without future; the harmonious integration of all the past and present elements of Russian life remained his incommunicable secret.

The death of Pushkin coincided with the beginning of a debate in which the question of origins ("where do we come from?") was relegated to second place by the quest for a national identity, the absorbing and distinctively Russian question—"what are we?" This question became the principal theme of Russian philosophy, and no doubt that was bound to be the case.[56]

The starting signal was given by Pushkin's friend, Peter Chaadaev, a nobleman converted to Roman Catholicism. In his first "Philosophical Letter", written in the impeccable French of the *Grand Siècle*,* he declared that Russia's only distinctiveness lay in its cultural nullity:

> The general education achieved by the human race has never reached us. . . . We have remained isolated in the world and have contributed nothing to it. Among the mass of human ideas, we have not contributed a single one; we have added nothing to the progress of the human spirit . . . on the arid soil of our country no great truth has been sown among us; we have not taken the trouble to think out anything for ourselves and from the idea of others we have only borrowed appearances which have deceived us and a love of splendour which was useless to us. . . .[57]

After running down his country so thoroughly, Chaadaev, as often happens with reflections of this kind, gave himself up to the most splendid dreams. Because Russia was nothing, she was to become everything.

> I am firmly convinced that it is our destiny to resolve the main social problems, to fulfil the greater part of the ideas which have been born in old societies, to give judgement on the most serious questions which preoccupy the human race . . . like a jury deciding on various disputes argued before the great tribunals of the world.[58]

The letters of Chaadaev, like "a flash of lightning on a dark night", created a sensation in Russia. Nicholas I forbade the publication of the revue in which they appeared and had the author declared a lunatic. Soon afterwards Russia had to face another similar attack which left the government powerless. This was the publication by the Marquis de Custine of an account of his journey through Russia; 200,000 copies were printed, and the book was translated into all the major European languages.[59] The message of this vitriolic book might be summarized in the phrase, "Scratch a Russian and you will find a Tartar". But over the heads of the Russian leadership Custine held out a friendly hand to the Russian people:

> The true, bearded Russians think as I do and they are determined one fine day to make a clean sweep of all those prigs who foreswear the ancient customs, who are indifferent to the true interests of the nation, and who betray their country in order to ape the civilization of foreigners.[60]

* For the purposes of publication the letter was translated from French into Russian in the Moscow revue *Teleskop* (The Telescope).

Against this background the Russian intelligentsia split into camps which, though seemingly opposed, had very similar motivations and objectives. In the words of Herzen, the westernizers and the Slavophiles looked in opposite directions, "like two-faced Janus, but their hearts beat as one". Was Russia's true path to continue her European apprenticeship or to seek in her own past and among her own people the source of her life? But with the second of these alternatives as with the first it was the Germans who figured as precursors or teachers. When the Slavophile Constantin Aksakov grew a beard and donned a Russian smock to walk about in the streets of Moscow, was he not simply imitating German students afflicted by the German obsession? Anyway he was prohibited by Nicholas I's government from carrying on with this mummery.

The dynamic founder of the Slavophile movement, Aleksey Khomyakov, outdid even the most fanciful of the German claims in a field which was specifically concerned with the myth of origins. His philosophy of history implied a contrast between two principles: the Iranian or Aryan, representing moral freedom which was fulfilled in the Orthodox Church (though he also considered the Jews to be "Iranians"), and the Cushite or Hamite, representing magic and scientific necessity, which was embodied in the Romans of Antiquity or in the German philosophy of his period. Khomyakov furthermore (perhaps as a result of investigating the secret archives of Catherine II)* saw the Slavs inhabiting all the regions of the world. He discovered them in Vendée (whence the loyalty of the Vendéens to the monarchic principle) but also in Périgord, Roussillon and Arles. Even more remarkably, he declared that Troy had been a Slav town; that the Angles were a wholly Slavonic tribe and the Saxons partially so. Siegfried and Parsifal, no less than Attila, had been Slav heroes.[61] It must have been claims of this kind which the young Dostoevsky ridiculed when he imagined a meeting of Slavophiles "during the course of which it will be proved irrefutably that Adam was a Slav and lived in Russia."† Most of the other Slavophiles would not go to such lengths as Khomyakov,‡ but he carried them with him on

---

* This would explain the curious title "Semiramis" which Khomyakov gave to his historical writings.

† Draft of the humorous almanac *Suboskal* (The Mocker), of 1845 (a period when Dostoevsky was still a westernizer or progressive").

‡ Khomyakov's followers were only minor historians like Veltmann and Lamansky.

another point. Reverting to the famous question of the Varangians, he interpreted their appeal as a proof of the basic pacifism of the Slavs and of their moral superiority.[62] This superiority seemed to him to be proved also by the "democratic feelings" of the Russians and by their complete lack of racism. Pushkin, for instance, who was descended from an Ethiopian, they regarded "with pride and joy, whereas he would have been denied citizenship in the United States and would not have had the right to marry the daughter of a washer-woman in Germany or of a butcher in England".[63]

It is only a seeming paradox that the Slavophiles should have shown more restraint towards racial theories than the westernizers. For whereas the former envisaged a universal mission for Russia in a predominantly religious role, the latter were governed by the findings of western science which generally postulated an unbridgeable gap between the white and the coloured races. Thus we find in 1868 a radical like Dobrolyubov writing as follows:

> We consider it useless to expatiate on the differences between the skulls of Negroes and other inferior races of mankind and those of the higher races. Everyone knows about the peculiar development, among the former, of the upper part of the cranium leading in some cases, such as the Australians, to almost total absence of the top part of the brain. And no one is ignorant of the fact that, with regard to the development of intellectual faculties, these people are vastly inferior to the Caucasian race.[64]

Some twenty years later, his friend Chernyshevsky wrote that "from the scientific point of view the significance of racial differences is rapidly waning". But he did not doubt that these differences, both moral and intellectual, existed because "for each exterior difference there must be a corresponding difference in the lay-out of the brain".[65] Another radical (or "nihilist") Zaytsev, who translated the works of Marx into Russian, considered that these differences were sufficiently marked to justify slavery for the Negroes, and he wrote ironically about the sentimentality of *Uncle Tom's Cabin*.[66]

Nevertheless, such extreme statements are only to be found in works by second- or third-rate authors, and the lack of racist opinions—apart from anti-semitism—among the great thinkers and writers shows that Russia was lagging behind the West in this respect (though one might equally say that it was well ahead).

Moreover, the times were not really ripe for an outburst of Russian racial pride. We have seen that the national genealogical traditions were of little use for the purpose. Nor was the verdict of anthropologists any more encouraging, since they all agreed that the Russian people were the result of cross-breeding between Slavs and a number of other races. Those races were the indigenous Finnish or "Ural-Altaic" peoples, with whom the Slavs were supposed to have mingled on arrival in the country. Later on, a succession of invasions and conquests had produced other admixtures of blood whether Germanic (the Varangians) or Asiatic (the Mongols).[67] Therefore not only could there be no question of a pure Russian race but a large part of its constituent elements seemed to have come from Asia and were thus "non-Aryan" according to scientific terminology at the end of the nineteenth century. In these circumstances it was no easy matter to be a racist in Russia.

Did Russia indeed belong to Europe alone? This view was opposed around 1870 by the Slavophile Danilevsky who, long before Spengler, was the author of a theory of "historico-cultural types", of which he discerned about a dozen. In his book on *Russia and Europe* he contrasted the "Romano-German" or European type with a "Slav type", and declared that the dominant European culture was neither unique nor enduring. On the contrary, he believed that it would decline rapidly or, to use a stock phrase, that "the West was rotting away". It was therefore incumbent upon other cultures, and on that of Russia in the first place, to take up the torch and to replace "Romano-Germanic aggression" by the genuine Christian humanism which was the specific quality of the Slav people. From the nineteenth century onwards the Russians became the spokesmen of all the subservient cultures which the Europeans had enslaved and dominated, and this criticism of western culture was perhaps the most original feature of the Slavophile movement. The extent to which it anticipated the criticisms which Europe of the post-colonial period was to make against itself in the present century is indeed striking.

Immediately after the Russian Revolution, these Slavophile arguments were taken up by a movement which was formed among Russian refugees with the significant name of the "Eurasian movement". Like their predecessors, the Eurasians kept the "Romano-Germans" of the West at arm's length; but they claimed only to speak for the Russians and not for other Slavs, who were assigned to Europe. A group of brilliant intellectuals, with the talented linguist Nicholas Trubetskoy at their head, thought it possible to round off the traditional geographical divisions by introducing a new continent of Eurasia, distinct both from Europe and Asia. Geographically and historically such a continent might seem to present a coherent whole, unified for the first time under the Mongols and then under the Tsars[68]; linguistically its inhabitants were alleged to have certain exclusively Eurasian phonetic traits in common[69]; racially, it was thought that the Russians ought to admit without false shame that they were just as much Turanians as Slavs or Aryans. In expounding and defending the Turanian heritage which Europe regarded with contempt, Prince Trubetskoy was led, as early as 1920, to exhort all the peoples of the earth to free themselves from "the hypnosis of the benefits of civilization" in order to avoid "the nightmare of Europeanization". "It should always be remembered", he wrote, "that the contrast between Slavs and Germans, or between Turanian and Aryans, does not provide the real answer to the problem. There is only one kind of opposition which is authentic, that between the Romano-Germans and all other peoples, or of Europe and humanity at large."[70]

Later on, when Prince Trubetskoy was comparing the Mongol domination of 1240–1480 to "the Romano-German yoke" of 1700–1917, he pointed out that it was not Asiatic domination which was the most unbearable, judging by the fury of popular revolt in 1917. Another supporter of the Eurasian view, Prince Svyatopolk-Mirsky, declared that the October revolution was no more than a brutal reaction to two centuries of enforced Europeanization: "though, according to its declared intention, the Revolution aimed at achieving the ideal of European atheistic communism, in its unconscious essence it was the revolt of the Russian masses against the domination of a Europeanized and renegade upper class".[71] Indeed the same kind of view had already been expressed during the turbulent years from 1917 to 1920, especially in the work of the famous poet Alexander Blok, for whom the Revolution was a settling of accounts between the Russian or "Scythian" masses and Europe.

The Eurasian movement came to an end on the eve of the Second World War at the very moment when the liquidation of the old *élites* in the great purges seemed to support such views. But, quite apart from their historical interpretations, it is of some interest to note that, from about 1920, these "Eurasian" patriots were criticizing western claims to superiority with the very arguments which half a century later were to become current among western intellectuals themselves.[72] And it is of even greater interest that in our times the process seems to have been partly reversed. Certain trends among

Soviet anthropologists, which to a western intellectual seem old-fashioned or out of place, remind us of the extent to which the myth of origins is still a live problem in contemporary Russia.

An excellent summary of these trends is to be found in a book called *In Search of our Ancestors*, published in Moscow in 1972, by the anthropologist V. P. Alekseyev:

> The ethnic origin of the eastern Slavs is felt as a profoundly personal question by Soviet historians. Behind the objective information unearthed by historical, archaeological and anthropological research, they see the blood which has been shed in defence of the fatherland, the hardworking life of the peaceful peasants, the glories of Russian culture.[73]

At the same time he criticizes western writers who question the existence of any link between peoples, languages and race. While admitting that racial frontiers no longer coincide with ethnical or linguistic boundaries, he insists that they did so in the remote past, *at the origins*. To take the contrary view, he affirms, is a sign of "nihilism" or "bourgeois liberalism".[74]

Is this Soviet anthropology in advance of or does it lag behind that of the West? As to the racial origin of the Russians, V. P. Alekseyev, like his predecessors in the last century, draws attention to the mingling of Slavs and non-Slavs, in the ethnic origin of the Russian people. "The hypothesis which I uphold and which I submit to the reader is the importance of the role of the *inozemtsy*, or non-Slavs, in the ethnic origin of the Russian people." He is referring to Mongoloid, but especially to the Finnish, tribes and he expresses the opinion that the medieval Russians were essentially "slavic Finns".[75] What conclusion does this lead to? In Alekseyev's case, it is to be found in the answer which he gives to the title of his final chapter—"Who are we?" The reply is: "We are Scythians, that is to say Asiatics with avid, slit eyes." His readers will recognize, in this ending, the famous opening lines of Alexander Blok's poem *The Scythians*[76]:

> *You have your millions. We are numberless,*
> *numberless, numberless. Try doing*
> *battle with us! Yes, we are Scythians! Yes,*
> *Asiatics, with greedy eyes slanting!*

Part Two

THE MYTH OF ARYAN ORIGINS

CHAPTER SEVEN

ANTECEDENTS

THE PRE-ADAMITES

Doubts were cast on the Biblical doctrine of a single human race well before the eighteenth century. Indeed, objections to the theory are almost as old as the theory itself. Long before the Christian era, some of the older Jewish exegetes concluded, from certain passages in the Book of Genesis, that the universe might have had an earlier creation and that part of this might have continued to exist—angels, demons or men perhaps better, perhaps worse than the posterity of Adam.[1] These views eventually spread from the Jewish microcosm to the wider environment of classical Antiquity where they fused with the theory of human hierarchies elaborated by Aristotle who held that barbarians were born only to be slaves.[2]

The idea that not all men are descended from a common father was taken up in the tenth century by the historian al-Masudi. In the course of speculating, as the Jews had done, on the twenty-eight letters of the Arab alphabet he postulated the existence of twenty-eight nations before Adam. In support of this view a Persian contemporary, al-Maqdisi, quoted a verse from the Koran (Ch. II, 28), in which the angels seem to accuse Adam of homicide.[3] The idea of separate and successive creations, which modern authors were to promote with the help of an entirely different terminology, penetrated medieval Europe in the wake of Averroism. The main argument, and the basic heresy, lay in the concept of an eternal, uncreated world; and the so-called pre-Adamite theory, which was formulated by the Spanish monk Tomas Scotus, in the fourteenth century, was only invoked accessorily in support of that basic concept. He declared: "There were men before Adam. Adam was made by these men, whence it follows that the world has existed from all time and that it was inhabited by men from all time."[4] We know of only one follower of this heretic during the Middle Ages, the Italian canon lawyer Giannino di Solcia, who was censured by Pius II.[5] But even before the discovery of exotic new continents there were thinkers who, in an abstract and speculative manner, questioned the myth of a world peopled by Adam and Noah.

The critical temper of the humanists on the one hand and Protestant exegesis on the other, but above all the discovery of the New World, multiplied the insoluble problems which in modern times discredited the Biblical genealogies. Alternative genealogies, said to be based on science, were put forward as a result of the general revolution of ideas early in the eighteenth century, when the so-called sciences of Man took root. The doctrine of Aryanism in the nineteenth century could only have been established on the basis of the main racial divisions established by the Enlightenment. Before exploring this anthropology, which was the focal point of all the new learning, let us examine the successive manifestations of the pre-Adamite theory.

In the sixteenth century the theory was supported by two great visionaries. Firstly Paracelsus, who made only a few cautious allusions to it and suggested that the natives of the American islands must be descended from "another Adam".[6] Secondly Giordano Bruno, who was bolder and attributed three great ancestors to mankind—Enoch, Leviathan and Adam, the last being the procreator of the Jews only, who thus became the youngest human grouping or race.[7] Here we can see an antibiblical or anticlerical attitude beginning to take shape. These daring speculations by the martyr of the Inquisition met with some response, especially in Elizabethan England where they were published for the first time. The poet Christopher Marlowe and the mathematician Thomas Harriot adopted Giordano's views,[8] and Marlowe's friend, Thomas Nashe, wrote: "I hear say there be Mathematicians abroad that will proove men before *Adam*; and they are harboured in high places, who will maintaine it to the death, that there are no divels."[9]

In the seventeenth century the intellectual climate was so influenced by the spread of rationalism that the pre-Adamite theory was put forward in France, not for the purpose of undermining established religion but to give it support. The man who became the champion of the theory was Isaac de la Peyrère of Bordeaux, a *Marrano* (a crypto-Jew professing Christianity). He padded out the old rabbinical heresies, which he knew well, with arguments drawn from the New Testament and especially from the Epistle to the Romans, in order to rationalize the chronological contradictions of the Old Testament. He compared himself to Copernicus who had satisfactorily resolved the difficulties to which the calculations of astronomy gave rise. His real ambition, however, seems to have been quite different.[10]

La Peyrère was also the author of a work called *Rappel des Juifs* (1643) in which he urged the king of France to gather together the chosen people into his country so that, once they had been converted to Christianity, he could lead them back to the land of Canaan and re-establish the throne of David in all its splendour. The anxiety to rehabilitate his despised lineage is evident in most of his writings. The special creation of Adam and Eve, just before the seventh day's rest, as ancestors of the Jews only, seemed to him a sign of the supreme distinction of the Jewish race, the race that was subsequently chosen through the call to Abraham.

A sensation was caused in 1655 when La Peyrère's *Systema theologicum ex Preadamitarum hypothesi* was published. Although revolutionary, it attempted to reconcile the Scriptures with the scientific novelties of the century, and it was acclaimed not only by the radicals and free-thinkers of the time. Père Mersenne, the friend of Descartes, considered that "if this hypothesis of several men independent of Adam could be admitted, it would seem that several passages in the Scriptures would be more readily comprehended . . .".[11] But Pascal indignantly de-nounced these ideas as absurd, and the authorities thought it necessary to start proceedings in order to oblige La Peyrère to retract. Never-theless, the polemics which his theory had started continued throughout Europe till the beginning of the eighteenth century, and his name was continually linked with Hobbes and Spinoza as the third member of a diabolical triumvirate. If his name has been forgotten, it was because those who challenged the unity of the human race soon ceased to use theological arguments and could not therefore quote him. The theory of polygenism which, as we shall see, Voltaire in particular advocated during the Age of Enlightenment, claimed the status of a purely scientific doctrine. But the polemical aims were still apparent, for example when the ageing Goethe developed his own polygenist views.

Goethe, in fact, justified his position by personifying Nature, the spirit of which he thought was prodigal rather than miserly. The naturalist von Martius had tried to support the Biblical account by arguing that Nature creates as economically as possible. "I cannot agree", answered Goethe. "Nature is always generous, even prodigal; and it would show more acquaintance with her to believe she has, in-stead of one paltry pair, produced men by dozens or hundreds. When the earth had arrived at a certain point of maturity, when the water had ebbed away and the dry land was verdant enough, came the epoch for the creation of man; and men arose, through the omnipotence of God, wherever the ground permitted—perhaps on the heights first. . . ."

Goethe, half joking, then put forward a second argument, in which some of the main themes of the Aryan theory are already sketched out:

> Holy writ certainly speaks only of one pair of human beings, whom God made on the sixth day. But the gifted men who wrote down the Word of God, as recorded in the Bible, had first in view their own chosen people; and as far as that people is concerned, we will not dispute the honour of a descent from Adam and Eve. But we, as well as the Negroes and Laplanders, and slender men, who are handsomer than any of us, had certainly different ancestors; and this worthy company must confess that we at present differ in a variety of particulars from the genuine descendants of Adam, and that they—especially where money is concerned—are superior to us all.[12]

Here the separate origin claimed by La Peyrère for the greater glory of the Jews was invoked by the illustrious German in order to keep them at arm's length. But whether the value-judgement was one of glorification or of contempt, both expressed the traditional and deeply rooted feeling of the "otherness" of the Jews. The history of the Aryan myth, from its beginnings, rested on emotional judgements of this sort which themselves had obscure, age-old antecedents. It is by no means certain that similar prejudices are absent from modern anthropology.

The Great Discoveries

Ever since the expressive, if imprecise, terms of Renaissance and Middle Ages became universally accepted, historians and philosophers have continually debated the real meaning and scope of the great changes which took place in the West during the sixteenth century. Was the dynamism of modern Europe, and of the world as we know it, caused by the religious, the cosmological or the geographical revolution? The discussion which has raged for fifty years, particularly under the aegis of Max Weber, is far from being settled. Traditional beliefs had been seriously affected by competing religious systems, and they were also shaken by the Copernican revolution. But more germane to our enquiry are the great geographical discoveries.

Early in the sixteenth century two ideologies came into conflict for the first time. Spain was the principal centre of this debate which, in so far as it concerned the American natives, set Christian anthropology at odds with the anthropology inspired by the Classics. For humanists like Juan Sepúlveda, imbued with Aristotle's ideas, the Indians were barbarians and therefore born to be slaves. For the Dominican, Bartolomé de Las Casas, they were a part of Adam's posterity to be evangelized and treated as free men. However, the existence of whole peoples, who had not been envisaged by the Fathers or by tradition and who had lived without baptism or hope of salvation, put a considerable strain on theological imagination. Las Casas himself compared his Indians to beings without the stain of original sin.[13] The discovery of America, therefore, raised extremely important problems of dogma.

The Holy See soon gave its authority to the views of Las Casas and, in the bull *Sublimi Deus* of 1537, proclaimed that the Indians were truly men, *veri homines*, capable of receiving the Catholic Faith and the Sacraments. The Spanish monarchy, under Philip II, supported this interpretation. But the Dominican apostle, so revered in Latin America, might be judged quite differently in Africa today since, in order to spare his well-loved Indians, he proposed importing African slave labour.

In this way, a form of discrimination became apparent which was already perceptible in the first book about the New World (*De Orbe Novo* by Pietro d'Anghiera, 1516) where "white" Indians were contrasted with "black" Ethiopians. It can also be seen in the first attempt at "racial classification" (by François Bernier in 1684) when the Indians were assimilated to the white race.[14] This discrimination still finds an echo in every European language since the contacts between Europe and the other continents gave rise, in the case of the Indians, to the term *métis* or *mestizo*, which is not in itself pejorative, while *mulatto* is derived from mule, and mulattos are therefore half-breeds who until the nineteenth century were commonly thought to be sterile, that is to say, impotent or emasculated.

Black men became the butt of merciless censure by the white man, from Noah's curse on Ham, whom first rabbinic and then Protestant exegesis considered responsible for the crimes of castration and incest,[15] to the classification of Linnaeus and the descriptions of several philosophers of the Enlightenment. Blackness, and with it a great range of evil associations, was contrasted with whiteness, as was innocence with crime, vice with virtue, and bestiality with humanity. The strength of the mutual temptations between black and white can be inferred from the sternness with which they were repressed, and social vetoes suggest the strictness of a taboo which only stimulated the bio-sexual attraction it was supposed to check. Classical Antiquity had also made much of the sensuality and shamelessness of Negroes, to whom recent science obstinately attributed a monstrous penis.[16] World literature, but especially that of Anglo-Saxon countries from Shakespeare to Poe and Melville—all of them in love with whiteness[17]—acquaints us with the leaps of imagination which associated black skin with evil or with lubricity or, more plainly, with the beast. Professor W. D. Jordan, whose magisterial analyses we summarize, has also observed that when the most primitive passions sought expression through pseudo-scientific generalizations, travellers' tales were enough to transform fantasies about the bestiality of the Blacks into anthropological theories. As it happened, the first explorations of the Dark Continent revealed the existence not only of aboriginal tribes but of hordes of large anthropoid apes, and observers were unable or unwilling to distinguish between the two. A more common error than that of Rousseau who asked himself whether these apes were not men[18] was that of Voltaire who assimilated the Negroes to the apes on the strength of these same ingenuous and fanciful travellers' tales.[19]

In contrast there was the theory which, using the American Indians as its chief example, idealized the man who was uncorrupted by civilization, the legendary *Noble Savage*. This Indian, whether he was the Carib of Bernardin de Saint-Pierre or the Huron of Voltaire, became a positive pattern of the enigmatic "natural man", of that non-European who was to serve henceforth as a mirror to Europe, which seemed only to recognize in the Black Man, the hidden and negative side of its character. All these views and judgements, which were debated in cosmopolitan *salons* during the eighteenth century, had their origin in the Iberian peninsula. It was there too that the great key-words—mestizo, mulatto, negro, Indian and caste—originated and from there that they spread abroad, in common probably with the word "race" itself.

Again, it was in the Iberian peninsula that another debate developed, after the Renaissance, which illustrated clearly how societies can in special circumstances establish their hierarchies and formulate their philosophies. The religious unification of Spain from 1492 onwards had given rise to the problem of the *conversos* or converts, either *Moriscos* (Muslim converts) or *Marranos* (Jewish converts), who had been more or less adequately baptized in the fifteenth century. Spaniards of all ranks laid claim to their authentically Christian birth, proclaimed themselves *Old Christians* and imposed on the hapless *New Christians* a discriminatory legislation—the decrees of purity of blood—which relegated the latter to the bottom of the social scale. The doctrine they elaborated was that the heterodoxy or infidelity of certain ancestors, even though they were themselves descended from Adam and Eve, had defiled the blood of their issue, who thus became vitiated by heredity. We shall come across this idea of degeneration again, supported by entirely different arguments, in the anthropology of the Enlightenment. The study of the decrees about purity of blood is of special interest in that it shows how an openly racial legislation could be developed with the help of Christian terminology. We may add that at the end of three centuries of struggle the New Christians, reduced in numbers by expulsion and by the burnings of the Inquisition, merged with the rest of the population. This little known branch of history constitutes a revealing introduction to the study of racialism in Europe.[20]

The New Genealogies

Contrary to what Christopher Columbus supposed, America was not the Indies. However, since the Indians had been adopted by papal decree into the human fold, through what lineage were they to be connected to the common father, Adam, and how did they come to inhabit the New World? That they were not aborigines, and descended from a "second Adam" in America, had already been confirmed to Cortés, the conqueror of Mexico, by the Emperor Montezuma.[21] Cortés' chaplain, López de Gómara, was the first to question whether these people, whose very existence contradicted the views of the Church Fathers, especially those of St Augustine, were not members of the famous Ten Lost Tribes. The great scholar, Arias Montano, concluded that the Aztecs and Incas must be the descendants of Shem.[22] This theory later drew its most able defenders from the ranks of Spanish and Portuguese *Marranos*, because the dispersion of the Jews in all the countries of the earth was thought to foreshadow the end of Exile. The theory was propagated in the Netherlands and in Great Britain by Rabbi Manasseh ben Israel,[23] and it inspired the activities of William Penn at the end of the seventeenth and those of the Mormons, Joseph Smith and Brigham Young, in the mid-nineteenth century. But it found no favour in Spain. There the Jesuits, who controlled education and research as well as the evangelization of countries overseas, preferred to link the Indians with Japheth.

This thesis was first launched by the Jesuit José de Acosta, the

provincial of Peru, one of the great missionaries who had been in-
structed by Ignatius Loyola to adopt the language and customs of the
local inhabitants, the better to convert them. In his *Natural and Moral
History of the Indies* (1590) which was translated into all the main
European languages, Acosta put the question of "how did the first
men reach the Indies?" It seemed obvious to him that these men came
originally from the Old World since "Sacred Scripture teaches us
that all men proceeded from one single man". From this it followed
"that men came hither from Europe, from Asia or from Africa". In
the mind of this enlightened Jesuit that could only have happened by
natural means:

> It is not credible that there should have been another Noah's ark
> . . . and even less so that the Angel should have born aloft the men
> of this new world, held and suspended by their hair, as he did with
> the prophet Habakkuk, for we are not dealing here with God's
> omnipotence but only with what is in conformity with reason
> and order and the disposition of human things. . . .[24]

Armed with these excellent principles, Acosta showed up the inade-
quacy of the semitic genealogy and other fanciful hypotheses of the
times, such as that of a crossing from Atlantis, and concluded after a
hundred pages of closely reasoned argument that the Indians must have
arrived in America by a land route or by passing through some unknown straits. It would be true to say, he discovered the existence of
the Bering Straits by deduction, rather as de Leverrier discovered the
planet Neptune by calculation. The myth of Noah was here revealed
as a pregnant working hypothesis and later, at the beginning of the
twentieth century, it gave birth to certain theories about "cultural
diffusion".[25]

In the present state of our knowledge, the Book of Genesis, excepting
of course its cosmogeny, in many respects affords more satisfaction
to the scholar than the scientific philosophizing of the Enlightenment.
In fact, most of the specialists on pre-Columbian America today
would find little fault with the hypothesis put forward by Acosta:

> I believe that men have inhabited this New World for not more
> than a few thousand years and . . . that the first men who entered
> it were rather savage and probably hunters and neither nourished
> nor brought up in a civilized and ordered republic, and that they
> arrived in the New World through having lost themselves outside
> their own country and needing to find another; which, once dis-
> covered, they began gradually to populate, with no other law

than their natural instinct, still very benighted, and some of the customs they retained from their first country.[26]

If we have dealt at some length with these ideas of Acosta, whom his French translator described as the "Pliny and Herodotus of this newly discovered world", it is because the discovery of America would henceforth dominate the new concepts of anthropology. It is also because this provincial of Peru was the first of the great series of Jesuit missionaries who, by living on the spot in the manner of the twentieth-century anthropologists, tried to identify themselves with the indigenous Americans or Asians, and who, primed with their humanist culture, already began to develop theories of comparative religion.[27] The *Relations* which members of the Society of Jesus like Ricci, Duhalde, Lecomte and Lafitau sent their Superiors proved to be the best source of information in Europe about the inhabitants of other continents.

Meanwhile, in Rome, the guardians of Catholic tradition and dogma soon began to reproach the Jesuits for latitudinarian recruiting of Christians, and the great dispute about the Chinese Rites was the well-known result. It is true that the desire for evangelical success prompted a number of missionaries to impute to their flocks inherent virtues and graces which made it a simple task to qualify them for baptism. A Jesuit of the China Mission, Father Lecomte, justified such a position theologically as follows:

> In the wise distribution of graces made by Divine Providence among the nations of the earth, China has no cause for complaint since there is no other which has been so favoured. . . . China preserved for more than two thousand years the knowledge of the true God and practised the purest maxims of morals, while Europe, and almost every other country in the world, was plunged in error and corruption. . . .[28]

The Jesuits in China were condemned by the Holy See. Nevertheless, they had done no more than adhere, in their own way, to a tendency which became irresistible once the Reformation and the great discoveries had forced European thought to draw conclusions from the plurality of churches and continents. Since it was plain that the message of Jesus Christ could not have reached the newly discovered peoples, Catholic theologians, from the sixteenth century onwards, elaborated a doctrine of "a natural as well as a supernatural Revelation, made to Adam in the terrestrial paradise and transmitted to subsequent generations".[29] The whole human race was thus conceived, according to the teaching of St Paul, to have the same notions of morality and the same natural religion graven in their hearts by God.

> The humanists of the Renaissance for their part came to the aid of the theologians, especially after Marsilius Ficinus and Cosimo de' Medici had popularized neo-platonic disquisitions about the primordial revelations of Hermes Trimesgistus. Both Moses and Pythagoras were supposed to have made use of these.[30]

However, this theory was greeted with much scepticism after the fierce struggles of the Wars of Religion. The English diplomat, Lord Herbert of Cherbury (1583-1648) suggested that the failure of Christianity should be admitted and that universal religion should replace it as the true Faith. According to Herbert, this religion simply required belief in a Supreme God, who would be honoured by a cult based on personal virtue and piety. But of what did this virtue and piety consist, and, above all, where did they come from? The percipient Abbé Gassendi had no difficulty in exposing the weakness of Herbert's idea. "Though you hold these views with sincerity and devotion, I should like you to ask yourself whether, had you not been educated among Christians, such thoughts would ever have entered your mind. . . ."[31]

The idea of a natural religion was used in support of widely varying theories. Among believers, some apologists found traces of the Sinaitic revelation in the common usage of all mankind. This postulate of a common truth for all men was, however, only an indirect corollary of the belief in their common origin. If all had had Adam for their father might they not all have had Moses for their teacher? In terms of modern anthropology the *monogenist* theory was a preparation for a *diffusionist* theory. The typical representative of this view was Pierre Daniel Huet, Bishop of Avranches and a tutor of the Dauphin. He was one of the great scholars of his age and he claimed to have unmasked all the mythologies by showing that they were nothing more than "simple imitations of the Sacred Scriptures".[32] His vast *Démonstration évangélique* drew on all the knowledge then available, and was apparently written as the result of a controversy with Rabbi Manasseh ben Israel. As far as the Noachian genealogies were concerned, Huet adopted the views of his Calvinist fellow-citizen, pastor Samuel Bochart of Caen, according to whose *Geographia Sacra* the French were the descendants of Dodanim, the Italians of Kittim, and the

Spaniards of Tarshish. America had been colonized by the Phoenicians and the Carthaginians. Furthermore, it was also Bochart's opinion that Japheth could be identified with Neptune, Shem with Pluto, Ham with Jupiter Ammon. Following this line of thought to its conclusion, Huet endeavoured to reveal the real Moses in his various disguises: "I shall say it again, nor can it be repeated often enough", he exclaimed. "What could be of greater use to our cause than to show clearly that all the oldest and most well-founded states have revered and regarded as a God the man who gave himself out to be the servant of God whom we adore?" This god, the god Moses, was for Huet the Phoenician Taautos, the Egyptian Thoth, the Persian Zoroaster. He was also Apollo, Aesculapius or Prometheus ("all Greek mythology flows through the books of Israel"). He was Janus and Romulus but also the Gallic Teutates, the Breton Liber, the Mexican Teutlille. Huet identified all the essential dogmas, as well as the story of the Flood, in China and Japan. In fact, everything came from the Jews. Enlightened by divine Revelation, they had given all and dispensed everywhere.

If such a universal identity of cultural origins is no longer entertained today, and if Catholic apologists are the first to ignore the system of the *Démonstration évangélique*, it is no doubt partly due to the fact that the arguments to support it can easily be used against it. For the Encyclopaedists, and particularly for Voltaire, Moses was far from being the original source of religion and science, but had derived everything from the Egyptians. The Jews had given nothing; they had stolen everything. However, Huet's most illustrious contemporaries, whether Protestant or Catholic, were inclined to think otherwise. Bossuet considered that Huet had an invincible case in defence of the true religion. Richard Simon, Bossuet's enemy and victim, intended to publish a summary of Huet's work. In Germany, Samuel Pufendorf proclaimed his admiration. Even more remarkable was the enthusiasm of Leibniz. "You may congratulate yourself", he wrote to Huet, "on having produced an immortal work, and you could not have found a wiser or more splendid outlet for the erudition which has cost you so many sleepless nights. You have succeeded in proving the main point which is that the prophecies have been accomplished in Our Lord. How would it have been possible, indeed, for such a marvellous congruity to be the work of chance?"[33] This was the judgement of the most brilliant intellect in Europe, of the man who was first to formulate as a system the fresh hopes among Christians of progress towards perfection. To complete the picture we should also record the dissonant voice of Antoine Arnauld who with his Jansenist pessimism deplored "horrible things, by which young libertines might be persuaded of the need for religion, but which would show that all religions were equally good and that even paganism can be put on the same footing as Christianity". And such, in fact, were the conclusions reached by many writers of subsequent generations.

The foregoing quotations show that, in spite of the division of Europe into two great religious camps, new genealogies continued to emerge from the general discussion in which Catholics, Protestants and even Jews set forth their conflicting views. The Protestant camp ran into special difficulties quite early on, since it had no tradition to act as a protective screen between Revelation and Reason. It was God's infallible word, textually revealed in the Holy Scripture, which they had to reconcile with the new forms of knowledge and to measure against the yardstick of reason.[34] Generations of exegetes were employed on this task. As a result, great progress was made in many branches of knowledge, notably philology, and especially in the Protestant countries. But this progress was achieved at the risk of withdrawing all credit from the Bible and of concluding—to use the words of Cameron Allen—that "If this book is the basis of faith, there is no basis, there is no faith".[35] The alternative was to throw reason overboard in the name both of faith and of experience, and this, perhaps, was the path taken by English empiricism.

It was above all in the Netherlands, among the Protestant countries, that the question of the origins of mankind and of particular peoples was raised from the end of the sixteenth century onwards. The University of Leyden was then the centre of Protestant science and exegesis. At that time the problem of the origin of the American Indians caused so much concern, we are told, that a young woman, possessed by the devil, repeated incessantly in Latin: "Quomodo insulae animalia acceperint, et eo homines post Adamum pervenerint?"[36] Hugo Grotius proposed an eclectic solution to this problem. North America, he declared, was populated by the Germans who had come from Iceland and Greenland; Central America by the Ethiopians, and South America by the Chinese and Javanese. All Noah's descendants were thus to be found in the New World and, though Grotius did not specify their respective lineages, he too identified Japheth with Iapetus and Ham with Jupiter Ammon.[37] A decisive step forward was taken by his German disciple, Georgius Hornius, a Professor of Leyden and author of *Arca Noae, sive historia imperiorum et regnorum* . . . (1666). According to Horn, the posterity of Noah was divided as follows: the Japhethites became Whites, the Semites became the Yellow Races, and the Hamites became Negroes. History and mythology as principles of classification were now joined by a fresh criterion to which they would progressively succumb—the colour of the skin.[38]

It was from this angle that the French philosopher and sceptic, François Bernier, was soon to tackle the problem. He wrote his *Nouvelle Division de la terre par les différentes espèces ou races d'hommes qui l'habitent* in 1684.[39] In it he declared: "I have observed that there are, in the main, four or five races of men among which the difference is so conspicuous that it can properly be used to mark a division." These races were the European, with whom Bernier linked the Egyptians and the swarthy Hindus ("their colour is only accidental and is due merely to the fact that they are exposed to the sun"); the Africans ("their blackness is essential"); the Chinese and Japanese ("they have broad shoulders, flat faces, hidden noses and small, pig-like eyes") and the Laplanders ("these are vile animals"). As to the Indians, Bernier, as we have seen, aligned them with the Europeans ("I find nothing like enough difference to make them a separate race and distinct from ours"). In this classification, perhaps the first writing in which the term "race" appears in its modern sense, Bernier was not concerned with genealogies and origins, that is to say with the temporal dimension. He was a modern man, already imbued with the mechanistic thought of what was then the *avant-garde* in France, and he divided mankind both according to skin-colour and other physical traits, and according to geographical or spatial considerations.

Leibniz, with his agile mind, immediately seized upon the polygenist implications of this new approach. After summarizing Bernier's thesis he declared: "All this is not a reason for supposing that all the men who inhabit the earth do not belong to the same race, as modified by different climates. . . ."[40]

It seems remarkable that England, which in the second half of the seventeenth century supplanted the Netherlands in every field, did not suggest any universal genealogical theory worthy of consideration during this period. It was content, at times to affiliate itself to Shem as its particular ancestor.[41] As for general history, both Cromwell and John Locke recommended Walter Raleigh's *The Historie of the World* which was still in use at Cambridge University in the eighteenth century.[42] In this work the genealogies of the Book of Genesis were scrupulously recorded but the attempts to bring them forward into a contemporary setting or to relate them to the myths of Antiquity were described as "ridiculous fables".[43] We are, however, familiar with the fertile imagination possessed by the most intelligent of English minds—Newton, Robert Boyle or John Locke—in placing their knowledge at the service of religious apologetics and the greater glory of God. Nevertheless, even if the unity of the human race through Adam continued to be gospel truth for these men, they refrained from advancing any detailed hypotheses. Locke even went so far as to say that no amount of research would reveal the lines of descent of Noah and of Shem.[44] This wise caution may have been an expression of British realism and empiricism—in short, what is usually referred to as "the national genius".

THE UTOPIAS OF REASON

When Galileo proudly called the report on his discoveries *The Messenger of the Stars*,[45] he pointed prophetically to the main theme which was to nourish western prestige in every respect from then on. The Jesuits in China, the better to evangelize the proud Sons of Heaven, were quick to publish in Peking an account of the exploits of "Kia-li-lio". It was by arousing the admiration of the Chinese for their mechanical and astronomical instruments that they found a way of access to Chinese society.[46] The truth of western beliefs was certified by these early examples of technical prowess, and the heavens of the astronomers bore witness in their favour. But arguments intended to impress others become irresistibly convincing to those who use them, and faith in the absolute truths of science grew apace.

Galileo, for his part, while demanding the attention of the philosophers,[47] concentrated his on physics. The philosophers, however, beginning with Descartes, subjected new-born science to Reason, which was henceforth considered infallible. This was a geometrical or mechanistic Reason which claimed both God and man within its sovereign jurisdiction, and which flew from one triumph to another. If the earth no longer occupied the centre of the universe, the pride of Europeans was in no way mortified by this discovery, and Freud for once showed himself to be a poor psychologist in his comments on this subject.[48] This pride, indeed, was to increase unchecked as a result of the contrast between the many European achievements and the inertia which characterized other entire continents. After the end of the seventeenth century those achievements gave rise to the idea of

Progress (which perhaps was merely the reverse of the Christian idea of the Fall),* but the contrast between them and the inertia outside Europe contained the germ of future, highly persuasive racial arguments; because the temptation to attribute a congenital, bio-scientific superiority to white men as the standard-bearers of Progress and the possessors of triumphant Reason became irresistible. In this way, a form of racism which tried to establish itself on a scientific basis— what might be called rational racism—came to be added to an already widespread popular racism, which might be termed "natural" since it was without doubt as old as mankind. Signs of this process may be observed among some major thinkers of the scientific age like John Locke, the author of the idea of the "clean slate" or *tabula rasa* of human understanding, who on this account has been considered the chief precursor of the principle of universal equality (for if all ideas are acquired it is only education which is able to make a man what he is). Moreover, the implications are unconscious—ostensibly Locke was trying to argue something quite different. But let us see how this friend and disciple of François Bernier chooses his examples. Let us hear him explain how, in the eyes of an English child, a Negro, because he was not white, could not be accepted as a man:

> A child having framed the idea of a man . . . such a complication of ideas in his understanding makes up a single complex *idea* which he calls *man* whereof white or flesh-colour in England being one, the child can demonstrate to you that *a negro is not a man*, because white colour was one of the constant simple *ideas* of the complex *idea* he calls *man*: and therefore he can demonstrate, by the principle, *it is impossible for the same thing to be and not to be*, that *a negro is not a man*.[49]

This explanation suggests a prejudice already well rooted in English society, and this prejudice is even more clearly marked in another passage in which Locke affirms that a child, as soon as it starts thinking, is able to distinguish between the wet-nurse by whom it is fed and the Negro by whom it is frightened.[50] Whatever may be the early thoughts of an English child, those of Locke betray an unconscious prejudice which undermines his logical faculty when, dealing with the relationship between ideas, he writes:

* In the sense that the Golden Age, which occurred before the Fall, was transferred to the future. Compare this idea with what we have pointed out above, in the chapter on Germany, about the ambiguity surrounding the notion of time

> ... when I consider [Caius] as a man I have nothing in my
> mind but the complex idea of the species man. So likewise when
> I say "Caius is a white man", I have nothing in mind but the bare
> consideration of a man who hath this white colour. But when I
> give Caius the name "husband", I intimate some other person....[51]

For such an erratic logician, as Locke here reveals himself to be,
the term "white man" became an absolute, just like the term "man"
without qualification.[52] During former centuries, in a scholastic framework of this kind, Caius would have been a Christian and the child
would have been afraid of the devil. The growing secularization of
Europe was exemplified even in such transformations as these.

The philosophers who held all the keys to knowledge in the new
age were mostly, it should be remembered, men of universal learning
and they were by definition anthropologists since all of them dealt
with mankind. The criticisms of Locke by Leibniz in the debate on "acquired ideas" and "innate ideas" shows us how the new classification
of mankind tended irresistibly towards a deep-seated moral absolutism.

Leibniz, in fact, believed in the existence of innate moral truths or
"instincts which prompt, at once and without reasoning, to some
portion of that which reason ordains; just as we walk in obedience to
the laws of mechanics without thinking of these laws. . . . Nevertheless, we agree most frequently with these instincts of conscience", he
added, "and one follows them even when more powerful impressions
swamp them out. The greater and the better part of humanity gives
testimony to these instincts . . . and one would have to be as brutish
as the American savages to approve their customs which are more
cruel than those of wild animals."[53] All the superstitions of the European
age of science seem to be concentrated in these few words. Nevertheless
Leibniz is much more subtle, more "relativist" than Locke since, a
few pages further on, he writes:

> It must be admitted that there are important matters in which
> the barbarians surpass us, especially in bodily vigour, and even
> so far as the soul itself is concerned. In certain respects one might
> say that their practical morality is better than ours since they have
> neither the avarice to hoard nor the ambition to domineer. . . .
> With us there is more of the good and the bad than with them.
> A wicked European is worse than a savage. He puts the finishing
> touches on evil.*

* *New Essays concerning Human Understanding*, I, II, 20. A judgement of this
kind (as to excess both in good and in evil) was sometimes applied to the Jews by
Christian thinkers when contemplating "the mystery of Israel".

But Leibniz falls back at once on his more artificial stand of European Reason by repeating:

> Nothing, however, should prevent mankind from uniting the advantages which nature gives these peoples with those which reason gives us.

It is with reference to morality, which merged with the Reason that was designed to justify it, that the philosophical egocentrism of Europeans was most clearly evidenced, and in this Leibniz spoke for nearly all his fellow-thinkers. Thus, in a passage of capital importance, after referring to Plato and to St Paul to assert with them the existence of natural law and necessary truths (so as to re-establish the credibility of "innate ideas") he wrote: "Metaphysics and ethics, one of which shapes theology and the other jurisprudence, both being natural sciences, are, together with logic, full of such truths, and consequently their proof can come only from internal principles which are called innate."[54] From this it appears clearly that the foundations of Christian theology and European jurisprudence are themselves also innate and *universally* innate. Leibniz specified that only animals were deprived of innate principles: "Animals are purely empirical and conditioned by examples . . . whereas men are able to practice the demonstrative sciences." Similarly, in another part of his work, where he quite wrongly imputed a kind of moral relativity to Locke's philosophy, Leibniz wrote:

> I prefer for myself, to take as the measure of moral good and of virtue the invariable rule of reason which God is charged with maintaining. . . . The good is that which by the general institution of God is conformed to nature or to reason.[55]

Leibniz, at any rate, made the attempt to define the relationship of the three traditional foundation-stones of Christian morality. Others, who repeated what had been said before, no longer bothered to do so. This was the case especially with the deists to whom Gassendi had earlier put the basic question. This question was reiterated henceforth by every great writer and in every text dealing with morality: "Had you not been educated among Christians, would such thoughts ever have entered your mind?" Montaigne's spontaneously relativist maxim — "These laws of conscience which we say are born of nature, derive from custom"[56]—seemed quite forgotten. No doubt, Gassendi's question should be put differently to different authors but we are unable to suggest these variants within the limits of this book. Let us content ourselves with a quotation from Diderot, who was perhaps the clearest French thinker of his time. For him "the moral laws are the same everywhere".[57] This expression is typical of the Enlightenment and might perfectly well be taken to mean "the reason of the strongest is always the best"—for the self-proclaimed universal Reason of the Europeans, was, as the dictionaries clearly demonstrate, at one and the same time judge and party, a sentence from which there was no appeal following a coercive prosecution loaded with threatening implications.[58]

★   ★   ★

The bias of Reason, in the sense described above, was all the heavier in its consequences because pre-racist ideas were in any case likely to be induced by the new methods of experimental science. Experience is observation, but it also implies the instruments of observation, the magnifying-glass, the scalpel, the scales. Until the invention of psychoanalysis, positive science investigated only what was tangible in man, only what could be weighed and measured. Within such limits scientists were quickly induced to postulate, on the basis of physical characteristics to which alone they had access, certain mental and moral qualities and, without realizing it and often in spite of their materialism, to draw moral conclusions from the shape of craniums or the colour of skins. Clearly these aberrations were imposed by some philosophic choice rather than by any scientific necessity or limitation. Voltaire, in his *Traité de Métaphysique*, proclaimed the general principle: "When we are unable to obtain help from the compass of mathematics or from the lights of experience and physics, we shall be unable to take a single step forward."

While pursuing this subject, we should take a look first of all at the progress of anatomy. In spite of being less spectacular, because relatively more circumspect, the discoveries of some of the internal structures and mechanisms of Man exercised quite as much influence on the new philosophy as the external ones in the fields of cosmogeny and geography. Did they suggest the idea of Man as a Machine? Descartes unfolds this idea in a celebrated passage of the *Discours de la Méthode* inspired by Harvey's description of the circulation of the blood.

This [cardiac] movement which I have just explained, follows as necessarily from the mere disposition of the organs which one can see by eye within the heart . . . as does that of a clock from the power, the placement and the shape of its counter-weights and wheels. . . . This cannot seem strange to those who, knowing how many automata or moving machines the industry of man is capable of fashioning compared with the great multitude of bones, muscles, nerves, arteries, veins and all other parts which are to be found in the body of every animal, should consider this body as a machine which, having been made by the hand of God, is incomparably better constructed. . . .

And further:

God has made our body like a machine and has willed that it should function like a universal instrument always working in the same way according to its own laws.[59]

These laws are therefore mechanical laws and are the same laws which control the movement of the stars. They regulate the course of events in a universe from which, once He had created it, God appeared to have withdrawn. This was a technical-mathematical concept of nature reduced to a static geometrical plane, the concept of a totally flattened out, "two-dimensional" world. Such was the price which had to be paid for the triumph of those clear, distinct and effective ideas of Cartesian science supported by an "engineering philosophy" which was both awe-inspiring and oversimplified.

We have analysed some general ideas which may seem very hackneyed. But it would be as well to remind ourselves, if only quite briefly, how, from Spinoza and his ethics *more geometrico*, or Leibniz and his jurisprudence *modo geometrico* or Samuel Pufendorf with his social science *ad analogiam systematis Copernicaei*, down to the judgements of sociology in our universities or of psychology in contemporary laboratories, western thought has been, and still is, fascinated by the successes of the exact sciences, the rules of which it tried to apply to the human sciences on the same grounds as to all the other sciences of life. In spite of this or perhaps because of it, the science of "animated matter" remained in many respects the poor relation of physical science much as the investigation of the latter was for centuries subservient to ancient mythologies and superstitions. This is especially true of the problems of procreation and the mingling of the species. If the nineteenth century still believed in spontaneous generation, the eighteenth was quite prepared to consider the possibility of cross-breeding the most diverse species. Thus Locke, in England, firmly

F

declared that he had seen with his own eyes "a creature which was the issue of a cat and a rat, and had the plain marks of both about it".[60] In France the scientific world was convinced that Réaumur had successfully crossed a chicken with a rabbit,[61] and Maupertuis suggested experimenting on the farms with all kinds of "artificial unions".[62] The veterinarian Bourgelat claimed to have dissected a "jumart", the issue of a bull and a mare.[63] The observations of Fortunio Liceti, according to whom a man could procreate with a cow and even with a hen, were discussed well into the eighteenth century,[64] while at the end of the same century Johann Fabricius, a pupil of Linnaeus, *proved* how Negroes were descended from a cross between men and apes. We shall return to this subject later.

This indeterminate drawing of the frontiers between the species— between cat and rat and man and ape—might be interpreted psychoanalytically as a mechanistic desire to eliminate the borderline between the animate and inanimate.* With its capacity for stimulating fantasies which link Man more closely to Mother Nature, this confusion seems to reign everywhere—except in the Pentateuch. Or perhaps this indetermination of frontiers between species disappeared from the Pentateuch as the result of a process of censorship, since the legendary cross-breeding and impossible ancestries, from god-ancestors to animal ancestors which abound in every mythology, seem to have been replaced by its ferociously anti-sodomite decrees and ritual prohibitions.† We might note, at this point, that though the sin against nature bears no fruit, there is none the less, as Freud has shown, a desire behind the prohibition. Genesis itself tells us how God, who had created all animals *according to their kind*, was careful to fill the ark in the same way so that no animal should be obliterated. This taxonomy, which is scientifically accurate, is of course implicit and has to be

---

* The ideas associated with these words lead one's thoughts to the concept of *animism* which curiously enough used to mean a philosophy of life, both Classical and Christian, until it was taken up by anthropologists and applied to primitive religions and has now remained fixed with this later meaning.

† This is obviously a vast subject. It must suffice to quote Genesis vi, 4-7, where the transgression of the vetoes seems clearest. "There were giants in the earth in those days; and also after that when the sons of God came in unto the daughters of men and they bare children to them, the same became mighty men which were of old, men of renown. And God saw that the wickedness of man was great on earth and . . . the Lord said, 'I will destroy man whom I have created from the face of the earth; both man and beast', etc.". Then came the Flood followed by a kind of new creation.

deduced from various chapters and verses of the Old Testament, the purpose of which is purely didactic or legalistic. Nevertheless, it is a fact that there was never any question in the Bible of cross-fertilizations, bastardies or ancestries that are biologically impossible though western science continued to take them seriously for a long time after Linnaeus's classification.

The basic epistemological problem thus raised would seem to imply a relationship between the Bible's more accurate conception of the sciences of life and the strict monotheistic code which decreed a relentless fight against idolatry and the abominable desire to unite with the great Earth Goddess.[65] But how should this relationship be interpreted? Perhaps the problem can best be approached obliquely, that is to say not by looking at it from the standpoint of what is true but by considering the persistence of mythological errors and relating them to the confusions of animism and paganism and to the great chain of Aristotelian beings?[66] M. Georges Gusdorf has pointed out that polytheism implies a theology of succession not only between the gods themselves but between gods and men as is shown by the demi-gods and heroes who were welcome intermediaries between divinity and humanity.[67] Were not the hybrids and monsters which the thinkers of the Enlightenment believed in—and they were devoted readers of Aristotle and Pliny the Elder—unquestionably the offspring of Zeus and Leda? The intermediate link might be the Christian Middle Ages about which an expert of the period[68] tells us:

> . . . the idea of a common descent of men and animals, the result of guilty passions, is nowise excluded. In this matter one should also recollect the witness of classical writers. Pliny, for instance, recorded that hybrid "semiferos", the product of relations between Indians and wild beasts, were born in India, and Plutarch attributed the birth of minotaurs, dryads, satyrs and even sphinxes and centaurs to such practices. Pope Alexander II was alleged to have shown his visitors a "boy" of about twenty who was dumb and who strangely resembled his father, an ape which had been presented as a gift to a countess and which she had taken as her lover. . . . Of course, the idea of being descended from the union of a man or woman and some infernal creature (a Succubus or an Incubus) was even more frequently entertained. . . . Far from vanishing in the light of Christian revelation, all these anthropomorphic imaginings which thronged the wilder shores of Greek mythology were reinforced by a host of demons and popular

goblins all the more difficult to identify in that their transformations were regarded as being both possible and frequent. . . .

★   ★   ★

If, on the vital question of the creation of life and the barriers between beings, biological experimentation did not finally concur with Biblical ideas until the nineteenth century, what was the position with reference to psychological knowledge? It was towards 1935, on the eve of the general cataclysm, that Edmund Husserl tried to draw up a balance-sheet. His criticism was directed in the first place against Cartesian dualism:

> Formerly psychology had been charged with performing the task of a parallel science which was based on the following concept: that the soul—the object of investigation—was something as real as corporeal nature, the subject of natural science. So long as this age-long pre-conception had not been revealed in all its absurdity there could be no psychology which was a true science of the soul. . . . The modern age, from the beginning, had adopted the dualism of substances and the parallelism of methods of the *mos geometricus* as a model. . . . The world was already viewed in a "naturalist" way. It followed that the soul was envisaged as being a real appendage of the body, to be interpreted by the same methods as were used in the exact sciences in accordance with the categories of physics which served as both a starting-point and a prototype. . . .[69]

Husserl believed that at the root of this error, along with Cartesianism, was Locke's analogical statement about the clean sheet or *tabula rasa*, round which psychic phenomena revolve, controlled somehow by the corporeal processes of nature.[70] Nevertheless, in his disjointed empiricism, Locke seems to have perceived clearly one of the ambiguities which were at the origin of the materialist and mechanistic orientation of modern psychology since it was he who brought into use the term *consciousness* as distinct from conscience[71] (both forms of this inner knowledge being described in French by the one word *conscience*) though it is thanks to Freud that we have been able to grasp all that this distinction implies. One of these forms of knowledge was elaborated by theology and included, in a sense, the complex of the emotions whether conscious or unconscious; the other meaning was later developed by theology's emancipated servant, philosophy, and limited itself rigorously to the field of conscious perception, and this is the *consciousness* of Locke. Perhaps this semantic evolution provides the key to the errors of psychology in the past, for might it not be true to say that the point of departure of modern philosophy, "I think, therefore I am", means in the last analysis "I am nothing else than what I think"? And if this were indeed the case how did this latest Utopia of Reason come about and what does it imply? Why this philosophical desire to reduce Man to his conscious thought only? And what meaning are we to attach to this permanent suppression of the urges of affective being, this determination to ignore the fact (with which the theologian, Bossuet, confronted Cartesian thinking) "that beyond our clear and distinct ideas there are others, confused and general, which contain such essential truths that all would be thrown away if one were to deny them"?[72]

It would undoubtedly have been more methodical, before putting any of these questions, to show how and to what extent theology took account of the depths in the soul which psychoanalysis attempts to explore and, for a start, to try to establish the similarities between "supernatural intervention" on the one hand and "unconscious impulses" on the other. For instance, one might be able to establish a rough semantic correspondence between the doctine of the Fall and the dialectic of culpability. One might go further and, with the aid of anthropologists and mythologists, seek out the same kind of relationship between the demonologies and spiritualisms of different cultures, or examine some modern philosophical insights of the same order.★ Above all it might be useful to question the illustrious shades of past ages, to ask Spinoza, who was the son of a *Marrano*, about that impersonal and icy God who "properly speaking loves nobody and hates nobody"[73] and about the philosopher, who, modelling himself on that God, must "neither laugh, nor cry, not hate but only understand".[74] One might follow up, with Léon Chestov, the mental processes of western philosophy, fascinated by mechanistic Reason, terrorized by the legalism of scientific Necessity[75] and in turn terrorizing its handmaid, the psychology of the pre-Freudian period, to the point of confining it in the dead-end which Husserl described so well.

In our time, when mankind is asking the sciences ever more insistently to give an account of their work, such enquiries might usefully steer this debate to a question of truly historical import: how was it that the resources of the western genius, while transforming the image

★ As in the works of Blaise Pascal and Johann-Georg Hamann.

of the world, have so deformed the image of man? Was it simply through the utopian extension of an intellectual system, which had yielded such dazzling success, that thinkers and philosophers flattened out and mutilated man's image? Or was it the excitement of the fight against what was known as revealed truth, against the dogmas and superstitions of the clergy, that carried them away? Or were their frightening simplifications due to their desire to fabricate a white man to match their idea of morality and of an "ideal self", a man who was naturally pure and good, infinitely perfectible, potentially omniscient? Or were there other more obscure reasons to account for this fundamental aberration in the human sciences?

CHAPTER EIGHT

THE ANTHROPOLOGY OF THE ENLIGHTENMENT

The Moderate Anthropologists
(the monogenists)

It was Max Weber who pointed out the connexion during the eighteenth century between the Protestant ethic of the Anglo-Saxons and an aggressive capitalist outlook. Less attention has been paid to the prodigious upsurge of scientific investigation which followed the Puritan Revolution in England. To contemporaries the pre-eminence of the English in this field was unquestioned. La Fontaine paid tribute to it in his fable of the English Fox:

> . . . *Englishmen*
> *Think deeply; and in this their temp'rament*
> *And intellect betray a common bent.*
> *They dig far down and use Experiment*
> *To throne the Sciences in every sphere.*[1]

This devotion to science drew part of its strength from religious zeal. If science and religion made good stable companions in England at that time, it was because, according to the experts, "the investigation of nature was elevated to the level of a fundamental religious act"[2] and because researchers "had in common a sincere conviction that the works of the Lord were rightly sought out by His people".[3] Let us consider the words of one of them, the parson John Ray (1628–1704), who is often considered the founder of modern botany and zoology, and who expressed admirably the religious enthusiasm of those scientists among whom Newton was the leading light:

> . . . There are those who condemn the study of experimental Philosophy as a mere inquisitiveness and denounce the passion of knowledge as a pursuit unpleasing to God. As if Almighty God were jealous of the knowledge of men. As if when He first formed us, He did not clearly perceive how far the light of human intelligence could penetrate, or were it to His glory to do so, could not have confined it within narrower limits. . . . Those who scorn or deny knowledge should remember that it is knowledge that

makes us superior to the animals, and lower than the angels, that makes us capable of virtue and happiness. . . .[4]

Ray too applied the method of the *tabula rasa* in carrying out his research, in order to free himself from Aristotle's classifications and achieve the complete elimination of "hieroglyphics, emblems, morals, fables, presages or ought else pertaining to Divinity, Ethics, Grammar or any sort of human learning".[5] In other words, he discarded traditional logic and familiar ideas and sought to grasp reality by using his own judgement. Without deference to any preconceived theories or philosophies, Ray was just as concerned to refute atheist Epicurians as the followers of Descartes, those "mechanick theists" as he called them. He used the Bible, which was the only scriptural authority he recognized, merely as a general framework of reference. He would not, like Job, have uttered "That I understood not; things too wonderful for me, which I knew not."[6] As to whether new discoveries, like those of fossils, gainsay the story of Genesis, he confessed ignorance and hoped that others would later reconcile the difficulties.[7] In one of his books he wrote:

> If I am to be quite honest there are many points on these subjects still open to doubt; questions can be raised which I confess I am not competent to solve or to disentangle; this is not because they have not got definite natural explanations but because I am ignorant of them.[8]

Nevertheless, his views on spontaneous generation and the transmutation of the species were uncompromising:

> My observation and affirmation is that there is no such thing as aequivocal or spontaneous generation, but that all animals as well small as great, not excluding the vilest and most contemptible insect, are generated by animal parents of the same species as themselves.[9]

Ray revealed himself as a great precursor when, writing of plants, he stated that a black man was no more different from a white man than a black cow from a white cow:

> Diversity of colour in the flower, or taste in the fruit is no better note of specific difference in plants, than the like varieties of hair or skin, or taste of flesh in animals; so that one may, with as good reason, admit a blackamoor and European to be two species of

men, or a black cow and a white to be two sorts of kine, as two plants, differing only in colour of flower, to be specifically distinct. . . .[10]

The first order of mammals postulated by Ray was that of the *Anthropomorpha* or apes but it did not occur to him to include man in this. His collaborator and competitor, Edward Tyson (1650-1703), indirectly filled the gap by pointing to the structural analogy between a man and a chimpanzee, and for this reason he deserves to be called the founder of Comparative Anatomy. His book bears the title of *Orang-Outang, sive Homo Sylvestris: or the Anatomy of the Pygmie compared with that of a Monkey, an Ape and a Man*. If one disregards the baffling terminology, (Tyson describes the chimpanzee as a Pygmy and the Orang-Outang as a man of the forests) this treatise, according to one authority,[11] is a masterpiece of meticulous and accurate observation, which retains its value to this day. Tyson was among those who, not without humour, kept Cartesian excesses at arm's length:

> . . . the Ancients were fond of making Brutes to be Men: on the contrary now, most unphilosophically, the Humour is to make Men but Brutes and Matter. Whereas in truth Man is part a Brute and part an Angel; and it is that Link in Creation that joins both together.

In general, Tyson refrained from philosophizing or making value-judgements, and it is interesting to note that, in dealing with Negroes, he declared that the colour of their skin "came from vessels in a particular body between the Skin and the Epidermis which were full of black liquor"; and he added that "the Climate might alter the Glands and by this means give a different Hue to the Inhabitants". We shall see that this idea became popular and was adopted, in particular, by Maupertuis and by Buffon.

According to Ashley Montagu, his biographer:

> . . . Tyson's principal contribution to the development of Western thought has been in focussing attention upon the relationship of man to the apes. . . . It would be difficult to overestimate the importance and far-reaching consequences of the revolution in our ideas concerning the descent of man thus initiated. It is clear that Tyson's part in producing that revolution entitles him to a high place among the creators of our present culture.

This encomium appears all the more deserved because, starting from his Pygmy, Tyson rigorously refrained from establishing hierarchies among men. His contemporary, on the other hand, the doctor and poet Richard Blackmore, immediately popularized Tyson's Orang-Outang under the title of *The Lay Monk*[12] and compared monkeys to the basest individuals of our species. He stated that if monkeys were "endow'd with the Faculty of Speech they might perhaps as justly claim the Rank and Dignity of the human Race as the Savage *Hottentot* or stupid native of Nova Zembla".

After the pioneer work of Tyson there were two possible theories and each found illustrious supporters in Great Britain. The first regarded European man as a monkey or a Negro who had been able to better himself. This was the view of Lord Monboddo (1714-1799), a Scottish disciple of Rousseau, for whom the ape was brother to the man; "For it is certain, as you observe", he wrote to a friend, "that the baboon has a desire for our female and . . . that they copulate together." Lord Monboddo, therefore, considered it was man's glory "that, from the savage state in which the Orang-Outang lives, he should, by his own sagacity and industry, have arrived at the state in which we now see him".[13] Such a close relationship between man and ape was not to everybody's taste and Herder, who was given the task of writing an introduction to the German edition of Monboddo's great work, made the following exhortation:

> But thou, O Man, honour thyself: neither the pongo, nor the gibbon is thy brother: the american and the negro are: these therefore thou shouldst not oppress, or murder or rob; for they are men, like thee: with the ape thou canst not enter into fraternity.[14]

The other, more generally held theory, was inclined to consider the ape and the Negro as hopelessly retarded men. In England this theory was defended with special vigour by a surgeon from Manchester, Charles White (1728-1809), who had nothing of the puritan about him:

> Ascending the line of gradation, we come at last to the white European, who, being most removed from the brute creation, may, on that account, be considered as the most beautiful of the human race. No one will doubt his superiority in intellectual powers. . . . Where shall we find, unless in the European, that nobly arched head, containing such a quantity of brain. . . . Where that erect posture of the body and noble gait? In what other quarter of the globe shall we find the blush that overspreads the

soft features of the beautiful women of Europe, that emblem of modesty, or delicate feelings, and of sense? Where that nice expression of the amiable and softer passions in the countenance; and that general elegance of features and complexion? Where, except on the bosom of the European woman, two such plump and snowy white hemispheres, tipt with vermilion?[15]

★   ★   ★

From the time of Conrad von Gessner (1516-1565) down to our own days, post-Reformation Switzerland has produced a remarkably high number of good naturalists. Some, who were authorities during their lives, are now completely forgotten. One such was Johann Scheuchzer, who distinguished himself by discovering the bones of "a man who had witnessed the Flood" (*Homo diluvii testis*)—which reminds us to what an extent, until the eighteenth century, scholars of all descriptions had remained fettered, either from religious conviction or mental habit, by the "short" chronology of the Bible. This explains the line taken by other theorists who have a place among the founders of modern biology, such as Albrecht von Haller (1708-1777) and Charles Bonnet of Geneva (1720-1793).

Both these men were philosophers and scholars of world renown whose names are especially associated with the great debate about the means of procreation of living beings. There were two major theories on this subject, that of dissemination or epigenesis, which was favoured by the partisans of metamorphoses and of "spontaneous generation", and that of preformation or pre-existence which postulated an act of origin by a Creator. "All trees", wrote Mallebranche, "exist in miniature within the germ of their seed" and Vallisneri added, "the whole human race which is and shall be till the end of the world was thus created in Adam".[16] If the question could not be settled by experiment, it could be decided by theology and by philosophy. Both Haller and Bonnet therefore drew support from Leibniz who himself, in his *Système nouveau de la nature*, had referred back to the scientists of the preceding century:

> . . . I was forced to agree that all the forms constituting substances were created together with the world and that they subsist forever . . . and it was at this point that the transformations of Messrs Swammerdam, Malpighi and Leeuwenhoek, who are among the most acute observers of our time, came to my assistance and enabled me the more easily to admit that an animal, or any

other organic substance, does not at all come into existence when we think it does, but that its apparent generation is really a development and a kind of increase.[17]

In short, "The whole world is contained and preformed within the world itself." Bonnet was enthusiastic about the views of "our modern Plato" who "suggested such noble ideas as to the wisdom and beauty of the supreme Being who from all eternity had controlled the destinies of mankind".[18] Haller went on to argue that, at the moment of creation, God placed in the bodies of the first parents the germs of all plants, of all animals and of all human beings who were to follow. This original encasement, a homunculus within a homunculus, implied a truly remarkable degree of human fraternity since "the germs of two hundred million men were originally placed by the Creator in the womb of our first mother Eve in a state so fine and transparent that they could not possibly be recognized".[19] In spite of all this, the good Christians Haller and Bonnet did not deserve the somewhat ironical comments made by certain biologists in the twentieth century,[20] because, during the eighteenth century, the infinite divisibility of matter could be adduced with as much good reason as the converse hypothesis. It must be admitted, however, that the thought of our ancestor Adam's stupendous loins at times led to strange confusions, as in the case of a popular disciple of Leibniz, G. F. Meier, who wrote: "Adam carried all men in his seed including the spermatozoon from which Abraham issued. And in this spermatozoon all the Jews were included as spermatozoa. And when Abraham engendered Isaac, Isaac came forth from the belly of his father carrying within him the whole of his posterity."[21]

Carolus Linnaeus, who dominated the natural sciences in the eighteenth century, shared the orthodox Protestantism of Bonnet, Haller and Meier. Like them he believed that each vegetable or animal species was derived from a single parent, in the case of vegetables, or a couple in the case of animals, all of which were divinely created about five and a half millennia before. The saying "God created and Linnaeus tabulated" perhaps had its origin in the enormous vanity of this famous Swede who wrote about himself—in the third person: "God permitted him to look into His secret Council Chamber. . . . The Lord was with him wherever he went. He has vanquished his enemies and magnified his name as with the great ones of the earth."[22] Perhaps it was this megalomania which enabled Linnaeus to take the decisive step, in his *Systema Naturae*, of including man in the animal kingdom. But *Homo Sapiens* did not go naked into this kingdom. Linnaeus dressed him up in the cast-offs which generations of white travellers and scholars had provided. The order of *Anthropomorpha*, which later became that of the *Primates* and which, as with Ray, included apes, was enriched by four coloured varieties:

> *Europaeus albus:* . . . ingenious, inventive . . . white, sanguineous. . . . He is governed by law.
> *Americanus rubesceus:* . . . happy with his lot, liberty-loving . . . tanned skin, irascible. . . . He is governed by custom.
> *Asiaticus luridus:* . . . proud, avaricious . . . yellowish, melancholy. . . . He is governed by opinion.
> *Afer niger:* . . . crafty, lazy, careless . . . black, apathetic. . . . He is governed by the arbitrary will of his masters.[23]

In a later work, Linnaeus further explored the deep chasm dividing white law-givers from black slaves. Judging by the difference between the European and the Hottentot, "it would be difficult", he wrote, "to persuade oneself that they derived from the same origin".[24]

★   ★   ★

It is obvious that the contrast between the White Man, the Negro and the Ape presented great problems to eighteenth-century scientists. It looks as if European narcissism needed a clear dividing line between "them" and "us". Psychologically a demarcation was required but it could be drawn in different ways. And (as with the hypotheses about procreation) a relationship can be detected between Christian orthodoxy and the choice of the dividing line, as we have seen in the comment of the pastor, Herder, on Lord Monboddo's book. The polemics of the famous Dutch anatomist, Pieter Camper, illustrate this link between religious conviction and scientific options even more clearly.

A first dispute found Camper opposing the German surgeon, Johann Meckel, who was a member of the atheist clique which had formed itself round Frederick II of Prussia. After dissecting some Negroes in 1757, Meckel claimed that their brains were of a darker colour than those of Europeans, and that their blood was black, "so black that instead of making the bandages red, as blood normally does, it made them black"; and he concluded from this that Negroes belonged to "almost another species of man as far as their internal structure is concerned". To this Camper objected that

> The little experience he [Meckel] has had of seeing Negroes no doubt induced in him a repugnance for their colour. . . . I therefore resolved to look into this interesting question so as to throw, if possible, some light upon that truth of the Christian religion which proclaims that, at the beginning of the world, God created only a single man, who was Adam, to whom we owe our origin whatever may be the features or the colour of skin which differentiate us. . . .

In support of his thesis, Camper pointed to the fact that some Jews were dark (the Portuguese) while others were fair (the German) though everybody knew they came from the same stock. Having come to these conclusions, he ended by exhorting Europeans to "hold out a fraternal hand to the Negroes and to recognize them as the descendants of the first man to whom we all look as to a common father".[25]

Since the Negroes were genuine human beings it was vital to distinguish properly between these descendants of Ham and the great apes. For this purpose, Camper adopted the view according to which the human skeleton lacks the upper intermaxillary bone identifiable in the simian species. About 1780, Goethe, who at that time was deeply interested in anatomy, reached a more accurate conclusion which he put to Camper in a memorandum. The latter, so Goethe tells us, "praised the execution [of the work] with much kindness but continued as before to hold to the view that man lacked the intermaxillary bone" and was thus, in this respect, anatomically different from the ape.[26] It looked as though, in this exchange, the Christian in Camper had got the better of the scientist.

Nevertheless, it was the same excellent Christian who was the first to make an observation from which others were to draw the most fearful conclusions. In comparing the skulls of a European, a Kalmuck, a Negro and an ape he thought that he could discern a "facial angle" of variable width which diminished in the same respective order. In other words, it was the European who enjoyed the widest angle. In this way Camper practically inaugurated the former sciences of craniology and cephalometry which flourished up to the first half of the twentieth century and led some scientists to measure intelligence by the cubic capacity of crania and others to boast of the superiority of the "dolichocephalics" over the "brachycephalics". We must add that Camper warned the learned against adopting similar techniques, without ever dreaming of the pitch of absurdity which they would reach in the West.[27]

★   ★   ★

The death of an old and devout king, which is what Louis XIV was when he died, opened up a period of intellectual and literary pre-eminence in France. There are no modern ideas, or few of them, which were not anticipated in the century of the French Enlightenment. Sometimes one has the impression that everything there is to say had been said in the Parisian salons where also everything that has come to pass had been foreseen. If any one person were to be awarded the palm for these intellectual audacities and presentiments no doubt Maupertuis would deserve it most.

In the history of science, the name of Pierre-Louis de Maupertuis (1698-1759) is associated above all with his work in geometry and astronomy, but there is no region of knowledge to which he did not contribute and he certainly merits the title of "one of the creators of genetics" bestowed on him by M. Jean Rostand.[28] He dreamed of "carrying experiments further, as far even as those species which Nature is least acquiescent in seeing united. One would then witness the birth of many a monster, new kinds of animals, perhaps even new species which Nature has not yet produced."[29] Live experiments on human beings were what attracted him even more, however: "perhaps there would be a number of discoveries about that wonderful union of soul and body if one dared to look for the links in the brain of a living man"—preferably a criminal because "a man is nothing compared to the human species; and a criminal is even less than a man".[30] Hence almost all experiments appeared to him to be justifiable. Under the heading of *Recherches à interdire* he only mentioned the philosopher's stone, the squaring of the circle and perpetual motion, while under that of *Expériences métaphysiques* this apostle of the scientific method proposed using children as subjects of experimentation.

> Two or three children, taken at a very early age and educated together without any contact with other men, would most certainly develop a language ... several similar societies should be formed of children of different countries ... above all these small groups should be prevented from learning any other language....[31]

What kind of new language might have emerged? These "experiments to find out" were simply the bold and ingenuous dreams of scientists. In Maupertuis the urge to know and to create was slightly tinged every now and then with bawdy: "Why should this art be limited to animals? Why should not those stale sultans in their seraglios, which enclose every known kind of woman, not procure for themselves the breeding of some novel variety? [If I were in their place] I should soon have recourse to such novelties." Maupertuis believed that, in forming his regiments of giant grenadiers, the "sergeant-king" Frederick William of Prussia was proceeding along the right lines: "A king of the North has succeeded in elevating and beautifying his nation. . . . In these days we are witnesses to a singular example of the power of kings. This nation is distinguished by its superior stature and by the greater uniformity of its human figures. . . ."[32] When he became president of the Academy of Sciences in Berlin, Maupertuis hoped to achieve great things but his august patron and friend, Frederick II, though not restrained by any religious scruple, did not dare to execute the plan "to breed a type of man with a noble nature".[33] It was only after a further two centuries that the research programme which he had dreamt of was put to experimental testing in Germany.

Maupertuis's genius was also exercised in the field of racial theory. In his *Dissertation physique à l'occasion du Nègre blanc* (an albino Black) he reached the following conclusion:

One might perhaps conclude, from these unexpected births of white children among black peoples, that white is the primitive colour of mankind while black is only a variation which has become hereditary in the course of centuries but which has not entirely effaced the white colour, the latter tending always to reappear. For one never sees the contrary phenomenon; one never sees black children born of white ancestors. . . . This would perhaps be sufficient to conclude that white is the colour of primitive man and that it is only due to some accident that black has become the hereditary colour of the great families which populate the torrid zone; amongst which, nevertheless, the primitive colour is not so completely effaced that it does not occasionally reappear.

This difficulty as to the origin of the Negroes, so often reiterated, and which some people would like to use to contradict the story taught by Genesis, that all the peoples of the earth issued from a single father and a single mother; this difficulty is removed if one admits an argument which is at least as worthy of credit as all that which has so far been imagined to explain the problem of generation.[34]

This theory as to the recessive character of black colour, though erroneous, nevertheless provided a forecast of Mendelian genetics and the theory of mutations. It was adopted by Buffon and, under the name of the theory of degeneration, was launched on a most successful career.

Buffon himself was a scientist and philosopher of universal renown and he deserves our attention as the first great explorer of the dimension of time, because he dared to say openly that the Biblical limit of 6,000 years was insufficient (his calculations yielded an age of 74,000 years for the earth). He deserves even more attention as the equal of Charles Darwin if one takes account of the influence exercised for nearly a whole century by his ideas on man and the animals.

With Buffon, indeed, the study of animals can hardly be distinguished from the study of man, because he is really only interested in man. Hence the double tendency in his famous *Natural History* to humanize animals and to concentrate on man whether the context was relevant or not. Let us, for example, take the case of the donkey which is a *despicable* animal because "it appears to be nothing more than a degenerate horse . . . one might attribute the slight differences between these two animals . . . to a chance succession of a number of half-degenerate, wild horses, which in the course of time would have degenerated still more to a point where no further degradation was possible."[35] Buffon then questioned whether it was legitimate to speak of "natural families".

> If it is admitted that there are families of plants and animals, that the donkey belongs to the same family as the horse and only differs from the former because it has degenerated, one might equally say that the ape belongs to the family of man and is a degenerate man, and that man and ape have a common origin. . . .

Is there not, perhaps, a trace here of prudent concern to establish a definite frontier between men and animals? Further on, Buffon returns to the subject of men in order to measure the gap which divides some men from others. "Men vary in colour from white to black; some have double the height, girth, nimbleness, or strength of others . . . and in character they may be endowed with or they may lack all the qualities. . . ." If it were not for the fact that White and Black can "procreate together . . . there would be two quite distinct species. The Negro would be to man what the donkey is to the horse, or rather, if the White was man, the Negro would no longer be man but an animal of another species like the ape. . . ."

It is when dealing with the most *noble* among animals, the lion, that Buffon's anthropomorphous zoology reveals the subconscious feelings and prejudices on which it rests and which were, doubtless, shared by his readers. This key passage deserves some attention. After he had praised the anger of the lion (which is "noble") its courage (which is "magnanimous") its generosity and beauty, Buffon continues:

> In addition to all these noble qualities in the individual lion there is also the nobility of its species. What I mean by the nobility of a species in Nature is that it should be constant, invariable, incapable of degradation. These species are normally isolated and alone of their kind. They are distinguished by such marked characteristics that it is impossible to mistake them or to confuse them with any of the others. Let us take man to begin with, who is the most noble being in creation. Mankind is unique because human beings of all races, of all climates, of all colours, are able to mingle and procreate together, while it cannot be said that any animal belongs to mankind whether proximately or remotely through any natural relationship. In the horse the species is less noble than the individual because it is close to that of the donkey which seems indeed to be a near relative since these two animals are able to reproduce living creatures, though it is true that Nature regards these as bastards, unworthy to procreate and unable to produce offspring of either of the species to which they belong. . . . In the dog the species is perhaps even less noble since it resembles those of the wolf, the fox and the jackal, which may be regarded as degenerate branches of the same family. And moving down by degrees to the inferior species, like those of rabbits, weasels, rats etc., having a large number of collaterals, it is no longer possible to recognize the common stock or main branch of each of these families for they have become too numerous. Finally, in the case of insects which we must consider the lowest of Nature's species, each is accompanied by so many neighbouring species that they cannot any longer be considered individually and it is necessary to lump them together and classify them as a genus if one wishes to name them . . . to class man with the apes and the lion with the cat, or to call the lion a cat with a mane and a long tail,★ is to degrade and to disfigure Nature instead of describing or classifying it.[36]

★ Buffon here recalls, in order to criticize it, the definition of a lion made by Linnaeus.

This zoological classification of merits reminds one of a medieval bestiary. The lion, king of beasts, is compared to man, the lord of creation; the larger mammals, horses or dogs, take the place of the nobility while the small creatures, rabbits or weasels, where "it is no longer possible to recognize the common stock or main branch", resemble the lower orders that have no genealogy or ancestral lineage. Do the "lowest species", the insects, represent the coloured peoples? In fact, Buffon refuses to allow any anthropomorphic quality to insects and describes a hive of bees as follows: "This society is therefore no more than a physical assembly controlled by nature, deprived of sight, of knowledge and of reason. . . ."[37] But his description of the Hottentots is no more flattering since Buffon compares them to monkeys, the difference being that "the Creator at the very instant when he imparted [to the Hottentot] his material shape similar to a monkey's, impregnated the animal body with His divine afflatus".[38]

The real human body, that is to say the body of the white man, is something altogether different for Buffon. His classic description of man, patently borrowed from Aristotle, emphasizes the outward signs of man's aristocracy:

> Everything about man, even his exterior, marks his superiority over all other living beings. He bears himself upright and aloft, his demeanour is that of command, his head is turned to the sky and shows a lordly face which is stamped with the nature of his dignity.[39]

This portrait has nothing whatever in common with that of the crouching Hottentot, whose children drag themselves about on all fours and wallow in their own excreta, or with the description of the Laplander, a real piece of *bravura* with which the *Histoire naturelle de l'homme* opens, where Buffon only concedes one human feature to those primitive people, the ability to recognize their own baseness and to know how abject they are.[40]

No doubt the theory of degeneracy, which he may have borrowed from Maupertuis, enabled Buffon to preserve the dogma of the unity of the human race (for he was not censured by the Church for his anthropology but for his geology). But we shall once more let Buffon speak for himself, simply abbreviating some of his prolixities:

> Ever since man began to settle under different skies and to move out of one climate into another, his nature has undergone changes . . . these changes became so great and so evident that

one might think that the Negro, the Laplander and the White are different species, were it not that on the one hand we are told that originally only one man was created, while on the other we know that the White Man or Laplander or Negro, however dissimilar, are able to unite and propagate. . . . It is certain that each is equally a man . . . if it happened that a man were forced to leave the climate in which he long ago settled, to return to his land of origin, he would with time acquire his original features, his primitive stature and natural colour . . . but it would perhaps require quite a number of centuries to produce this effect.[41]

Buffon himself dreamt of some marvellous experiment *in vivo* which would enable him to verify his hypothesis:

. . . in order to experience a change of colour in the human species, it would be necessary to transport certain individuals of the black race in Senegal to Denmark where, because men normally have white skin, blond hair and blue eyes, the difference in blood and contrast of colour would be the greatest. These Negroes and their families would have to be carefully closeted so as to preserve their race, without allowing them any outside breeding. This is the only way to find out how much time would be needed to restore man's nature in this respect and, by the same reasoning, how much time would be necessary to change him from white to black.

That Buffon was a forerunner of racism is debatable. On the one hand he explained the degeneration of the Negroes by a difference of blood; on the other, he seemed convinced that this degeneration was not irremediable. What are we to conclude from this? Perhaps the question of what age should be attributed to the earth (on which subject Buffon worked very hard) might provide the clue in the sense that a degeneration of recent date would be less serious than one protracted over dozens of millennia especially when as many more would be needed to recuperate from it. Would it take "a number of centuries" or an eternity to *restore man's nature* in the case of the Blacks?

I have had to quote at length from Buffon because, in cultivated European society, his *Natural History* was for nearly a century the main source of information about exotic men and beasts and because the popularity of an author reflects the intellectual climate of the public at large.[42] We can deal more briefly with his French contemporaries. It is fairly easy to find a parallel to or a reflection of Buffon's views in such idyllic, or idealized, authors as Bernardin de Saint-Pierre, who invoked the curse on Ham[43] in referring to the Blacks, or the abolitionist, the Abbé Raynal, who believed that "negro blood is perhaps mingled in all the ferments which transform, corrupt and destroy our people".[44] The article on Negroes in the *Encyclopaedia* of Diderot and d'Alembert is scarcely more favourable.[45] As to Diderot himself, he was to proclaim white superiority through the words of his Tahitian "noble savage",[46] and to follow this by philosophizing on the inferiority of the Laplander: "Who can deny that this misshapen biped, who is only four feet high, who is still called a man in the neighbourhood of the Pole and who would quickly lose that name if he were but a little more deformed, is the figure of a species which will die out?"[47] Other authors, especially Voltaire, whose works we shall consider later, spoke of "exotic men" in even more contemptuous language.

In this way, some of the most notable champions of the Enlightenment laid the foundations of the scientific racism which was to follow in the next century. But other famous French writers of the period supported a resolutely universalist point of view. Among these were Montesquieu (in spite of his tendency towards Germanomania)* and Helvétius, since both held that it was education in the wide sense of the term, namely that of environmental influences or *nurture*, which makes man what he is.[48] Nor should we forget Condillac and, above all, Condorcet whose *Épître aux nègres esclaves* opened with this profession of faith: "Though not of the same colour as yourselves, I have always looked upon you as my brothers. Nature formed you to harbour the same spirit, the same reason, the same virtues as the Whites. . . ."[49] The works of Julien de La Mettrie, the author of *L'Homme Machine*, who was much slandered and little understood, reveal a similar outlook. As to Holbach, his *Système de la nature* might justify his reputation, as the successor of La Mettrie; but his anticlerical fury and his crude ideas of progress led him to attacks upon the Jews.

> This people uniquely favoured by an immutable God, has become very feeble and miserable. The victim, in every age, of its fanaticism, its unsocial religion, its meaningless laws, it is now dispersed among all the nations which regard it as a lasting monument to the dreadful results of superstitious blindness. . . . Dare, therefore, O Europe, to shake off at last the unbearable yoke of the prejudices which afflict thee! Leave these superstitions, as

* See above, p. 25.

debased as they are senseless, to stupid Hebrews, to fanatic imbeciles, to craven and degraded Asians. They are not made for the inhabitants of thy climes . . . close thine eyes forever to such vain chimeras, which for so many centuries have served only to delay progress towards true science and to divert thee from the paths of happiness.[50]

There remains the case of Jean-Jacques Rousseau. It is true that this erratic genius, thirsting for equality and justice, did not make differential judgements on the men and races of the world and that he did criticize the prejudices and presumptuous judgements of such writers as Buffon and Voltaire: "The whole world is inhabited by nations of which we only know the names and we presume to judge the human race!" The well-known passage in the *Discours sur l'origine de l'inégalité* from which this protest is taken ends up with the sketch of a programme of anthropological studies "in the field", which he seems to have been the first to envisage "in a century when men pride themselves on their advanced knowledge".[51] Nevertheless, one cannot help questioning whether Rousseau deserves the status of a patron saint of anthropology, attributed to him by M. Claude Lévi-Strauss,[52] when his "natural man" is constructed on the basis of "hypothetical and conditional reasoning" which is invalidated, in the case of this ex-Calvinist, by his belief in the doctrine of the Fall.

Indeed, on close examination, all Rousseau's arguments and descriptions seem to be no more than a reformulation, in lay terms, of that early belief. His theoretical "natural man" is placed, from an ethical point of view "at equal distances from the stupidity of brutes and the baneful lights of civilized man". Perdition sets in as soon as man becomes an agriculturalist and a smith ("iron and wheat have civilized man and ruined mankind"). Rousseau admits that his "natural man" does not exist, because the exotic peoples known in his day were already far removed from the state of nature. On the other hand, like so many in the Age of Enlightenment, Rousseau was uncertain and gullible about the barriers between species. Thus, when questioning whether the Orang-Outang was a man, he also dreamt of experiments for cross-breeding men and monkeys but rejected them on grounds which were anything but scientific.[53]

*   *   *

Let us now examine the German authors whose authority began to grow from the end of the century. The time was approaching when

German erudition would dominate Europe. We can rapidly pass over a crowd of geographers and naturalists like the two Forsters, J.-P. Pallas, C. de Pauw, and E. A. W. Zimmermann, who mostly shared the views of Buffon as to the influence of climate and environment, with the difference that they spoke of the exotic peoples with far less vehemence, and that, no doubt as a consequence of this, they appeared to be more optimistic about the length of time needed for regeneration.

Immanuel Kant, who thought and wrote a great deal about the subject of the human races, worked out certain principles which were regarded as authoritative until the middle of the twentieth century. As late as 1968, a well-known German anthropologist, W. E. Mühlmann, described him as "the founder of the modern concept of race".[54] If that were the case, one would be inclined to think that this concept, whatever its logical force, was not infallible. This supposition becomes all the more convincing when one considers some of the practical ways in which the philosopher applied his ideas. One finds these in his *Anthropology from the Pragmatic Point of View* (1798) in which Kant summarized the university courses which he had given for thirty years. The platitudes and truisms with which it is filled, especially in the second part ("The characteristics of anthropology"), are astounding.

Almost at the beginning, Kant deals with the character of the sexes:

> It is easy to analyse man; but no woman betrays her secrets even though she is unable to keep those of others (owing to her love of gossip). Man is fond of *domestic peace* and submits easily to its governance so as to be unmolested in his business. Woman has no dislike for *domestic war* for which she is armed with her tongue. . . .[55]

After a similar judgement made by a hardened bachelor about the sex which he avoided, one is less astonished to observe that this metaphysician who never left Königsberg fails to consider, under the headings of "character of the people" and "character of the race", any other than his own white race. Hence we do not know exactly what Kant might have said about the Eskimos or the Negroes. Perhaps one can make a guess as one reads "it is here a question of innate, natural character which has, so to speak, its seat in the composition of the human blood . . ."[56] In the main therefore, it is on the composition of the blood that Kant takes his stand in describing, by means of the most conventional comparisons, the respective characters of the Englishman, the Frenchman, the German and the Italian. His underlying plan becomes a little clearer when he is dealing with the character of the Spaniards. The passage in question opens with the following statement: "The Spaniard [is] born of a mixture of European and Arab (Moorish) blood", and concludes, "as shown by bull-fights, his character is cruel which is proved by the auto-da-fé of former times and this taste shows that his origin lies in part outside Europe."[57] Kant's general approach to anthropology is more clearly defined when, a bit further on, he moralizes as follows: "This is the judgement which one can truthfully make. The mingling of stocks (due to great conquests), little by little erodes the character and it is not good for the human race in spite of any so-called philanthropy."[58] In an unpublished text on the conditions governing human progress, Kant reiterated this view more vigorously, and he congratulated the governor of Mexico for opposing the policy of inter-social breeding which was favoured by the Spanish Crown.[59]

It would seem, therefore, that what is good is purity of stock—but what stock? Here again, a further timid excursion to the confines of Europe shows to what extent Kant, when describing actual types of man, merely rehashed the age-old prejudices of common folk. In dealing, at the very end of his work, with "another Christian people, the Armenians", he praises them for their highly developed commercial sense—"a reasonable and diligent people . . . which knows how to make itself accepted peaceably by all the nations among which it settles . . .".[60] But the peaceful occupations of commerce become criminal when exercised by a non-Christian people, the Jews. Such a people even becomes, in a kind of way, philosophically unimaginable. The following diatribe is taken from *Vermischte Schriften* by Kant:[61]

> The Palestinians who live among us have the well-merited reputation of being sharpers, owing to the spirit of usury which holds sway amongst most of them. It is true that it seems odd to imagine a nation of swindlers but it is equally difficult to imagine a nation of merchants, by far the most important of which, bound together by ancient superstitions and recognized by the State which they inhabit, do not aspire to civic virtue but wish to compensate their shortcoming in this respect by the benefits they derive from deceiving the people who grant them protection, and even by swindling one another. But a nation composed merely of merchants, that is to say of unproductive members of society, cannot be other than this. . . .

Thus "Palestinian" behaviour is Jewish behaviour, and might not Spanish cruelty be the same as the proverbial "Moslem cruelty"?

Admittedly, Kant professed a belief in the unity of the human race for philosophic reasons, but in this also he was, after all, merely conforming to the predominant view of his time.

Altogether more impartial than Kant's anthropology was that of Johann-Friedrich Blumenbach (1752-1840). This professor from Göttingen is usually considered the founder of Physical Anthropology which is a branch of learning as reputable as any other provided that the researchers steer clear of value-judgements and inferences. This temptation which had previously been practically irresistible was resisted by Blumenbach in the most praiseworthy manner. The five great races which he described were, generally speaking, neither good nor bad in themselves. If he sometimes gave way to the temptation it was because of an aesthetic preference as when he praised the face of the white man, "that face which is normally regarded as the most beautiful and agreeable . . .". "I gave to that variety", he continued, "the name of the Caucasian mountains because it is in that region that the finest race of men is to be found, the Georgian race, and if it were possible to assign a birth-place to the human race all physiological reasons would combine to indicate that place. . . . Finally, the skin of the Georgians is white and this colour seems to have belonged originally to the human race, but it can easily degenerate to a blackish hue. . . ."[62] This is reminiscent of the theory of degeneration propounded by Maupertuis and Buffon. In a typically academic vein, after praising the Georgians' faces, Blumenbach commends their skulls, "those beautifully shaped skulls from which all others seem to derive, even those examples that are furthest from them, which are the skulls of Malays and of Negroes".[63] Blumenbach's category of a Caucasian race was used in the first half of the twentieth century as a criterion for selective immigration into the United States and it served to justify the segregation of both the coloured races and the Hebrew race. From an administrative point of view, therefore, the Caucasian race was the Aryan race according to the North Americans before 1939-1945.

In following the German controversies, to which we shall return in the next chapter, great attention must be paid to Johann-Gottfried von Herder (1774-1803) whose outlook is altogether different. In his major work, *Outlines of a Philosophy of the History of Mankind*, Herder led a revolt, ahead of his time, against the "veterinary philosophy" of science and described as ignoble (*unedel*) the very expression of "the human race".[64] He tried by this means to escape from contemporary prejudices. The sympathy with which he wrote of the people of the

Pole, of Eskimos or Laplanders, was only equalled by his sympathy for the people of the Equator. "The Negro", he wrote, "has as much right to term his savage robbers albinoes and white devils . . . as we have to deem him the emblem of evil, and a descendent of Ham, branded by his father's curse."[65] Like Rousseau he emphasized the importance of environment, "What so forcibly discriminates the negro races in Africa itself? The climate, considered in the most extensive signification of the word, so as to include the manner of life and the kind of food."[66] In view of this, it is hard to know why, at the end of this chapter on Africa, he should have allowed himself to repeat the old fable about the lasciviousness of the Blacks, which, step by step, led him to conclude:

> That finer intellect, which the creature, whose breast swells with boiling passions beneath this burning sun, must necessarily be refused, was countervailed by a structure altogether incompatible with it. Since then a nobler boon could not be conferred on the negro in such a climate, let us pity, but not despise him; and honour that parent, who knows how to compensate, while she deprives. He spends his life void of care in a country, which yields him food with unbounded liberality . . . he runs and climbs as if each were his sport. . . .[67]

The thesis of the Blacks' inferiority reappears in Herder at the end of the chapter which he dedicated to the European conqueror: "The negro has invented nothing for the european; he has never once conceived the design of improving or conquering Europe."[68] Thus, even less than Rousseau, does Herder deserve the title of the patron saint of anthropology. If such a tribute were to be paid to any of the great pioneers it should be to the brothers Wilhelm and Alexander von Humboldt each of whom, complementing the work of the other, explored almost every branch of human knowledge without succumbing to the prevailing European egocentrism.

"Whilst we maintain the unity of the human species", wrote Alexander von Humboldt in *Cosmos*, "we at the same time repel the depressing assumption of superior and inferior races of men."[69] He blamed Aristotle for the classification of mankind which had so often been used to justify slavery.* "All men are equally destined for liberty",

---

* "The very cheerless, and in recent times too often discussed, doctrine of the unequal rights of men to freedom, and of slavery as an institution in conformity with nature, is unhappily found most systematically developed in Aristotle's *Politica*, i. 3, 5, 6" (*Cosmos*, op. cit. p. 368).

he added, and, in common with his brother Wilhelm, he declared his aim to be that of "perceiving humanity as a whole, without distinction of religion, or colour; like a great family of brothers, a single body marching towards the same goal, the development of their moral resources in freedom". The Humboldt brothers were never to lose sight of this ideal which isolated them more and more from the general trend of ideas in the nineteenth century. In thanking Gobineau politely for sending him a copy of his celebrated treatise on *The Inequality of Human Races*, A. von Humboldt wrote to him, in 1856 at the age of 88, that the book "was opposed by its very name to my old belief about the unhappy distinction between superior and inferior races".[70]

The Extremist Anthropologists
(polygenism)

The doctrine of the unity of mankind, which had been questioned from pre-Christian times for occult or philosophical purposes, was rejected in the century of the Enlightenment for reasons which were supposed to be scientific. It is not easy, however, to trace the dividing line between the two. One of the first supporters of polygenism, the English doctor John Atkins (1685-1757), himself confessed to being unorthodox though on grounds which may seem in the main religious. "Though it be a little Heterodox," he wrote, "I am persuaded the black and white Race have, *ab origine*, sprung from different-coloured first Parents."[71] Atkins also thought that the black race could breed with monkeys and give birth to sterile hybrids like mules.[72] Soon afterwards, this doctrine gained the adherence of a formidable champion in the person of Voltaire.

For the historian Voltaire presents an enigma. He remains the leading apostle of toleration in spite of a harsh exclusiveness to which both his life and his writings bear witness and which it is hard to describe otherwise than as racist. One of the main reasons for his hatred of coloured people was revealed from the moment he opened his attack on them. Whatever might be said by "a man dressed in a long black cassock", he declared in his *Traité de métaphysique* (1734), "bearded whites, fuzzy negroes, the long-maned yellow races and beardless men are not descended from the same man". So the former pupil of the Jesuits rebelled against their teaching. On the other hand he conformed to accepted views by placing the Blacks at the bottom of the ladder. The Whites were "superior to these Negroes, as the Negroes are to the apes and the apes to oysters", he wrote a little further on in the same work.[73] Twenty years later, Voltaire developed his views on anthropology in his celebrated *Essai sur les moeurs et l'esprit des nations*. After asserting that "only a blind man is permitted to doubt that Whites, Negroes and Albinos . . . are totally different races", he applied the epithet of "animals" specifically to the Negroes. Then, referring to some of the older authorities, he described "the monstrous species [which] could be bred from these abominable passions" by which he meant copulation between apes and negresses.[74] Further on, the existence of the New World furnished him with fresh arguments in favour of polygenism, and polygenism in turn allowed him to put forward a "natural" vindication of slavery.[75] Voltaire's anthropological edifice was crowned by a chapter on India, to which he attributed a degree of antiquity which enabled him to demythologize Judeo-Christian teaching notably by playing with etymologies—was not *Adam* derived from *Adimo* and *Abraham* from *Brahma*?[76] His posthumous editors (probably Condorcet) felt obliged to insert a rather long corrective note in this chapter pointing out that it was impossible for a serious author to decide between the respective claims of monogenism and polygenism.[77] Voltaire himself persisted in this type of polemic till he died, whether in attacks on the Jews in his famous *Dictionnaire philosophique* (1764)[78] or on the Jesuits in the *Défense de mon oncle* (1767) or when, dealing with "Men of different colours", he rounded on Père Lafitau.[79] If no man ever did more to demolish the idols and prejudices of the past, neither has any man done so much to propagate and elaborate the aberrations of the new age of science.

David Hume is also worth considering in this connexion, especially his essay on National Characters published in 1742. In this he declared in passing that "all the nations which live beyond the polar circles or between the tropics are inferior to the rest of the species".[80] In 1754, in the second edition of this work, Hume added a note in which he dealt specifically with the black races:

> I am apt to suspect the negroes, and in general all the other species of men (for there are four or five different kinds) to be naturally inferior to the whites. There never was a civilized nation of any other complexion than white, nor even any individual eminent either in action or in speculation. No ingenious manufactures amongst them, no arts, no sciences. On the other hand, the most rude and barbarous of the whites, such as the ancient Germans, the present Tartars, have still something eminent about

them, in their valour, form of government, or some other particular. Such a uniform and constant difference could not happen,
in so many countries and ages, if nature had not made an original
distinction betwixt those breeds of men. Not to mention our
colonies, there are negroe slaves dispersed all over Europe, of
which none ever discovered symptoms of ingenuity; tho' low
people, without education, will start up amongst us, and distinguish
themselves in every profession. In Jamaica, indeed, they talk of
one negroe as a man of parts and learning, but 'tis likely he is
admired for very slender accomplishments, like a parrot, who
speaks a few words plainly.[81]

Although his tone was harsh, Hume did not explain his concept of
human origins very clearly. Outspoken monogenists like Buffon were
more vehement than he, while the polygenists sometimes displayed
a typically humanist universalism. The contradiction between Biblical
teaching and the progress of learning produced, among some authors,
a strange interplay of light and shade. The most remarkable example
of this was the Scottish philosopher Lord Kames (1696-1782) who, in
his *Sketches of the History of Man*, suggested the following scheme of
history: on the one hand, in the Old World, racial differences arose as a
result of the linguistic confusion resulting from the Tower of Babel;
on the other hand, America was populated thanks to an independent
and "local" creation.[82] But if Lord Kames's anthropography was
complex, the moral to be drawn from it was simple and unambiguous.
Somewhat ingenuously he declared:

> The colour of the Negroes, as above observed, affords a strong
> presumption of their being a different species from the Whites;
> and I once thought that the presumption was supported by in-
> feriority of understanding in the former. But it appears to me
> doubtful upon second thought, whether their inferiority may not
> be occasioned by their condition. A man never ripens in judge-
> ment nor in prudence but by exercising his powers. At home,
> the negroes have little occasion to exercise either: they live upon
> fruits and roots, which grow without culture; they need little
> clothing: and they erect houses without trouble or art. Abroad,
> they are miserable slaves, having no encouragement either to
> think or act. Who can say how far they might improve in a state
> of freedom were they obliged, like Europeans, to procure bread
> with the sweat of their brows?[83]

If the benign Lord Kames's curious theory achieved a certain success
with the English public (his book ran through twelve editions between

1774 and 1825) it was not destined to keep the interest of learned societies as did the simpler system of the medical Edward Long (1734-1813). For nearly a century *Long's History of Jamaica* (1774) was considered authoritative. As late as 1857, Armand de Quatrefages, head of the French school of anthropology, quoted this source with reference to the assumed sterility of mulattos.[84] In his book, Long recorded his observations, which, he claimed, proved mulattos to be as unfertile as mules. He consequently divided *genus homo* into three species; Europeans and related races, Negroes, and Orang-Outangs. However, in their mental capacity the Negroes appeared to be closer to Orang-Outangs than to men because Orang-Outangs "did not seem at all inferior in the intellectual faculties to many of the negroe race; with some of whom it is credible they have the most intimate connexion and consanguinity . . . the negroes themselves bear testimony, that such intercourses actually happen; and it is certain that both races agree perfectly well in lasciviousness of disposition . . .". However, in view of the monstrosity of the creatures thus engendered "the all-wise Creator of the Universe has raised an unsurmountable barrier, which is no other than rendering the offspring of such intercourse STERILE". In short, Long presumed the existence of two kinds of sterile mulattos, of whom one lot were produced by the coupling of Blacks with Whites and the other of Blacks with Orang-Outangs. As to the latter, he added: "I do not think an Orang-Outang would be any dishonour to an Hottentot female. Orangs . . . conceive a passion for the negroe women. . . ." Perhaps the evocation of this tropical love-making contributed to the enduring success of Long's book. On the other hand, it is to his credit that he reported the following anecdote: "[The Negroes] say that God is partial to the Whites and treats them as his own children, but takes pleasure in afflicting the Blacks with a thousand evils".[85]

* * *

The University of Göttingen was founded in 1737 by the Hanoverian dynasty and soon became the chief centre of German erudition. We shall consider later on the orientalists Michaelis and Schlözer who taught there. In the human and natural sciences, in addition to von Haller and Blumenbach, we should also mention the philosopher Christoph Meiners (1745-1810) who devoted much attention to anthropology. After 1933, his name was once again honoured in Germany both as a "founder of the racial theory" who anticipated the "Aryan concept"

(Egon von Eickstedt, 1940)[86] and as a precursor of cultural anthropology whose thinking was marred by racism (Wilhelm Mühlmann,
1968).[87]

Without doubt the views of Meiners cut across many of the generally
accepted ideas of his time. Thus he denied the theory of the *unilinear*
progress of culture[88]; he doubted the feasibility of differentiating
strictly between races, and he criticized the systems proposed by his
colleagues. He was the first modern thinker to put forward the hypothesis that mankind had its origin in Africa and to insist upon the
importance and universality of myths of origin. He also showed a
genuinely independent spirit towards German public opinion in his
time by referring with irony to the respect which was then accorded
to ancient Hebrew traditions.[89] But the idea to which he clung above
all else was that of two great human lineages—a race which was fair
and beautiful and one which was dark and ugly. This division enabled
him to penetrate the secrets of the "superior men"—who were only
to be found among the fair and beautiful peoples.

> Only white peoples, especially the Celtic, possess true courage,
> love of liberty and the other passions and virtues which distinguish
> great souls. . . . The black and ugly peoples differ from these by
> their deplorable lack of virtue, and because of several appalling
> vices. Most of the black and ugly peoples combine an irritability
> due to their lack of character with a crude insensibility to the joys
> and sufferings of others, even when their nearest relatives are con-
> cerned; an unyielding hardness with an almost total absence of
> kindly impulses and feelings. . . .[90]

With Meiners, the transition from beast to man was achieved in
successive stages marked by the presence or absence of "human
merits".[91] His scale started with the *quatos* (monkeys?), followed by
Orang-Outangs, which "are called men of the forest (*Waldmenschen*)
because of their resemblance to man", and by *kimperzeys* (chimpanzees)
which were even more anthropomorphic since, so he affirmed, they
were able to provide a guard of honour to the king of Dahomey.
Next in line were the famous "Negroes of the forest" (*Waldneger*), the
Hottentots, bushmen and natives of the Australian coasts, who, however, "display so many animal features, and so few human, that they
can scarcely be described as men". Step by step, through the copper-
coloured and the yellow races, Meiners reached the Slavs who, in
spite of their fair complexion, also displayed such inferior characteristics that the "German masters were obliged to treat their wendic

serfs much more harshly than other serfs, since experience showed that it was only by the strictest supervision and indispensable punishments that they could be induced to do good and avoid evil . . .".[92]

Other ideas of Meiners caught on by degrees in Germany, like that of the rapid degeneration of noble and European peoples in America, or that of the dangers of racial mingling and cross-breeding.[93] It can scarcely be denied that this philosopher was indeed a precursor on many and varied counts.

At about this time, the "animality of the Blacks" suggested the following argument to one of the pupils of Linnaeus, J.-Chr. Fabricius (1745-1808): Negroes and anthropoid apes are met with in Africa but not in South America where climatic conditions are the same— does it not follow that black men are the issue of cross-breeding between white men and apes? This pious Lutheran was thus able to reassure his readers that the skin of Adam, our common father, was immaculately white.[94] Fabricius also deserves a mention as an entomologist, since he obtained acceptance for the view (which appears to have been Edward Long's) that there existed a "negro louse" (*pediculus nigritarum*) which differed in shape and colour from the "human louse" (*pediculus humanus*).[95]

In revolutionary France, Jean-Joseph Virey (1774-1847) became an apostle of the teaching of Meiners. In the ninth year of the revolutionary era this military pharmacist published his *Histoire naturelle du genre humain* in Paris. In it he announced:

> We shall here describe the general characteristics of each of the human races, which may be divided broadly into those which are fair and white and those which are ugly and dark or black. The Celtic line and those of the Sarmatians and Slavs display a pleasant oval face . . . and a well-rounded head. In other words they present proud and noble features, a generous spirit, a character which is active, frank and beautiful. . . .[96]

In this passage the main lines of Meiners's thought emerge very clearly. But his French disciple drew from it such militant conclusions that they seemed like the echoes of revolutionary drumbeats:

> What would our world be without the Europeans? Powerful nations, a proud and indomitable race, immortal geniuses in the arts and the sciences, a happy civilization. . . . The European, called by his high destiny to rule the world, which he knows how

to illumine with his intelligence and subdue with his courage, is the highest expression of man and at the head of the human race. The others, a wretched horde of barbarians, are, so to say, no more than its embryo. . . .

A little further on in his book Virey wrote: "I have not relied on feelings of national pride when referring to all these foreign races" (by which he meant the coloured races).[97] It is easy to see from this that the Europeans and the French were one and the same for the patriot of the year IX. Without stopping to consider his description of the cruelties of the Mongols or the stupidities of the Blacks we must examine the meaning of his chauvinistic anthropology.

Perhaps a deeper study than the one we are able to undertake would show that, soon after 1815, the French extremists in racial theory were to be found in the ranks of the Bonapartists rather than among the Bourbons. It would be interesting to make a more systematic comparison from this specific viewpoint than I am able to do, of two great encyclopaedias of the natural sciences both published in Paris from 1816 onwards. One was the *Dictionnaire des sciences naturelles*, whose editor was Baron de Cuvier (an important official) assisted by "several naturalists of the king's botanical gardens". The other was the *Nouveau Dictionnaire d'histoire naturelle* by Jean-Joseph Virey (now released from the army) helped by a group of naturalists and agriculturalists. It is certainly true that, in the article on Man, the coloured races were roughly handled in both publications, but while the tone of Comte de Lacépède in the first encyclopaedia was relatively restrained we find the most extreme views expressed in the second, in an article signed by Virey himself; this includes such fables as the copulation between Negroes and apes, the black blood and brains of the Negroes and so on. In order the better to emphasize that the Black was not a man, Virey put forward, among others, the argument of the *pediculus nigritarum*:

> Let me add an inference which is not without importance and which was notified to me by our learned entomologist Latreille. Just as each species of mammal, of bird etc. often has insect parasites which are only to be found in association with it, so it is with the Negro. He has his louse which is quite different from that of the white man. The *pediculus nigritarum* (Fabricius, Syst. antl., Brunsw. 1805, p. 340) has a triangular head, a crimped body and is black like the Negro himself. . . .[98]

G

The above argument was still the subject of serious consideration by Darwin in his *Descent of Man*.[99]

Finally, it should be recalled that the *Histoire naturelle du genre humain* by Virey was translated and published in the United States in 1837 under the title of *The Natural History of the Negro Race*. "The book was read in England as well as America, and the older group of racist pro-slavery arguments took a new lease on life", as we learn from Philip D. Curtin.[100] So ideas made their way, from Göttingen to Charleston, North Carolina.

CHAPTER NINE

THE QUEST FOR THE NEW ADAM

THE MYSTERIES OF INDIA

In the eighteenth century, when the West was seeking to free itself from the confines of Judaeo-Christian thought, many authors recommended the ancient wisdom of China as an example for Europe. None of them, however, thought of locating the origins of mankind or of all human knowledge in the Celestial Empire. India was another matter. The special and mysterious fascination of India has continued to make itself felt right up to our own times. Many an esoteric doctrine claims to derive from India. The Middle Ages and the Renaissance did not look as far afield as this, since their knowledge of antiquity was confined to the Hebraic or Greco-Latin cultures. Nevertheless, it was the Bible itself which suggested that the origin of mankind might be discovered somewhere to the east of Judaea. A pointer in this direction was provided by the description of the Garden of Eden, bounded by four rivers, one of which was the Euphrates. The migration of Abraham from Ur of the Chaldees started in the same area. But even more indicative was the story of the Flood in which Noah's ark was grounded on the heights of Mount Ararat in the Caucasus. These mountains figured with equal prominence in Greek legends in which they were the scene of several famous myths, while some Pythagorean traditions drew attention to countries even further to the East, since Pythagoras himself was reputed to have absorbed the wisdom of both Persia and India.

The origin of *Homo sapiens* was still being sought in those regions at the time when scientific reasoning, without as yet discarding the truths which claimed to be revealed, was trying to come to terms with them. Buffon elaborated a relatively coherent theory according to which "the first people worthy to be called by that name" had emerged, when the earth cooled off sufficiently (thirty thousand years ago in his estimation), somewhere to the east of the Caspian Sea.[1] This people "merited all our respect as the creator of science, of the arts and of all useful institutions". Furthermore, "it was very happy because it was very wise". Later, other men "still ignorant, wild and barbaric" had attacked and destroyed this civilization of Eden and plunged the whole of humanity "into the night of ignorance once again". Only the Brahmins of India were able to preserve a flicker of the old learning. This anthropodicy, which was based on speculations by the astronomers Cassini and Bailly,* seemed to echo the old mythologies of the Golden Age and the Fall.

Buffon tended to interpret Biblical data in an allegorical manner. His great rival, Linnaeus, advanced views which conformed more closely to a literal interpretation of the Bible but which, far from being coherent, seemed to defy all logic. Starting with the story of the Flood, he imagined a very high mountain emerging from the deep somewhere near the Equator. The arctic animals dwelt in couples on the snowy summit of this mountain while the tropical animals, as well as the first human couple, lived round its base. With the emergence of new lands, men and animals took possession of them, increased and multiplied. Linnaeus, however, did not trouble to explain how reindeer and polar bears could, without dying, have crossed tropical zones in order to go and multiply in polar regions.[2]

Without furnishing such exact details as Linnaeus, the scholars of the Enlightenment, who were monogenists for the most part, generally looked to the mountains as the cradle of the human race. This was certainly true of the geographers. In their view, the presence of sea-shells in all latitudes confirmed the hypothesis of a universal inundation and therefore corroborated the story of the Flood. Now it was known that the highest mountains in the world towered over India and China. But the fact remains that tradition, perhaps influenced by the reluctance of the Whites to admit affiliation to the Yellow races, focussed attention on the near side of the Himalayas and of Kashmir, not beyond them.

Apart from these supposedly scientific theories, a totally different kind of argument was developed for polemical purposes with special reference to the origin of culture and religion. The deist school, turning the Bible against itself, tried at first to prove that Moses had filched his revelations from Egypt. "To imagine that a company of poor, contemptible, egyptianized slaves . . . were intended in the divine

---

* On the authority of a certain passage in Josephus, Cassini and Bailly assumed that the Ancients could calculate with precision the movement of the stars. Cf. the notes in Piveteau's edition of Buffon's works referred to above, p. 188 and p. 220.

Counsel and Wisdom as a light to the Gentiles" was for Thomas Morgan the same as "supposing what we speak with scorn, that God was disappointed of his End, and took as wrong means, as Moses himself."[3] Voltaire, who was a disciple of the English deists, turned the theory in favour of India. As a polygenist, he did not place the origin of mankind there but he strove to demonstrate that Adam had taken over everything, even his name, from the Indians.[4] The *Encyclopaedia* of Diderot likewise suggested, in the article on India, that the "sciences may be more ancient in India than in Egypt". To many contemporaries, however, it seemed quite obvious that this was due to polemical bias, "a desire to discover in the ancient Orient a rival society to that of the Hebrew", as Edgar Quinet was to say later.[5] Some importance should also be attributed to the backing which the Indian theory received from the celebrated astronomer Jean Bailly who, on the strength of his mathematical calculations, situated the earliest men in the regions of Greenland or New Zemlya and transferred them at a later date to the valley of the Ganges where they founded the arts and the sciences. The arctic origins were soon forgotten and Voltaire was able to record his agreement with Bailly in the following terms:

> I wholly share your opinion when you say that it is not possible for different peoples to have shared the same methods, the same knowledge, the same legends, the same superstitions, unless all these things had been adopted by a primitive nation which taught, and led astray, the rest of the world. Now I have long since regarded the dynasty of the Brahmins as having been this primitive nation. You must be familiar with the books of Mr Holwell and Mr Dow. . . . Finally, sir, I am convinced that everything has come down to us from the banks of the Ganges, astronomy, astrology, metempsychosis, etc. . . .[6]

John Holwell and Alexander Dow were two English authors who in their writings on India gave prominence to the high level of culture and the ancient wisdom of the Brahmins. More emphatically than Dow, his French translator, M. B.***, declared in 1769 that all ancient cultures and religions were of Indian origin. Moses was an Indian renegade and Mahomet an impostor.[7] The French naturalist, Pierre de Sonnerat, also deserves a mention. For him India was "the legislator of all the peoples". He found analogies between different western mythologies and religions and deduced that they had a common source in India, the birthplace of the human race (*Voyage aux Indes orientales*, 1782).

These ideas, as they appeared in successive translations and travellers' tales, captivated the imagination of Kant, who modified the popular arctic and astronomical theory of Bailly by placing the origin of mankind in Tibet. "This is the highest country", he argued. "No doubt it was inhabited before any other and could even have been the site of all creation and all science. The culture of the Indians, as is known, almost certainly came from Tibet, just as all our arts like agriculture, numbers, the game of chess, etc., seem to have come from India." Here Kant expressed himself hypothetically; but he was less cautious when he allowed himself to be beguiled by etymological fancies. Then he tried to connect Manichaeism with the saying "O mani padme hum" and Abraham with Brahma[8] (an etymology which had already been proposed by some Renaissance writers).* But it was Johann-Gottfried Herder above all who introduced the passion for India into the Germanic lands and who prompted the imagination of the Romantics to seek affiliation with Mother India.

Herder's view about the details of this affiliation changed in the course of time, but basically he associated with the Indian birthplace a kind of "natural revelation" which was also a poetic initiation (poetry was for him the primitive language of humanity) of which the original form had been lost. Nevertheless, this Lutheran pastor did not depart from tradition since he considered the Bible as the most accurate copy of the legendary poem. "Historically, all that we have left in the whole world is the written tradition which we are wont to call Mosaic . . . ."[9]

Herder believed that, ethnically or racially, the Germans could be related to the Persians, which caused him to rejoice[10]; but morally it was to the Indians that he gave the palm, claiming that

> the bramins have formed their people to such a degree of gentleness, courtesy, temperance and chastity, or at least have so confirmed them in these virtues, that Europeans frequently appear, on comparison with them, as beastly, drunken or mad. In their air and language they are unconstrainedly elegant; in their behaviour, friendly; in their persons, clean; in their way of life, simple and harmless . . . they are not destitute of knowledge, still

* I am indebted to Maurice de Gandillac's inexhaustible erudition for this information. He has pointed out that this comparison was met with particularly in the work of Guillaume Postel.

less of quiet industry or nicely imitative art; even the lowest castes learn reading, writing and arithmetic. . . .[11]

In his *magnum opus*, the *Outlines of a Philosophy of the History of Mankind*, Herder strongly opposed the Noachian or Jewish genealogy.

> The pains that have been taken, to make of all the people of the Earth, according to this genealogy, descendants of the hebrews, and half-brothers of the jews, are contradictory not only to chronology and universal history but to the true point of view of the narrative itself . . . nations, languages and kingdoms were formed, after the deluge, without waiting for envoys from a chaldean family. . . . Suffice it, that the firm central point of the largest quarter of the Globe, the primitive mountains of Asia, prepared the first abode of the human race. . . .[12]

He supported this theory of a primeval mountain region with every kind of argument, from the speculations of Linnaeus on the "mountain of creation" to the geographical deductions of Pallas and Zimmermann and the astronomical calculations of Bailly. He revealed the essence of his vision in a poetic flight:

> Let us abandon these regions where our predecessors, like Buet, Buxtorf or Bochart, sought the beginnings of the world! These corners of Arabia and Judaea, these basins of the Nile and the Euphrates, these coasts of Phoenicia and Damascus, where the human race might have come into existence like mice or rats; all these must be left behind! Let us scale the mountain laboriously to the summit of Asia. Where will this lead us? The horizons swing back and forth. History, which has dated all things from that beginning, will have another beginning and another end. Our vision becomes clouded. Whither are we going? . . . Patience.[13]

Adopting Herder's style for a moment, one could say that Germany, striving to extricate herself from Judaeo-Christian fetters, soon responded to this aspiration; with Schopenhauer she longed to be the child of India and Buddhist; with Nietzsche, the child of Persia and a follower of Zarathustra. It is certainly true that Herder, with his longings for the primitive, with his exaggerations and also with his flashes of genius, seems both to have anticipated and sharpened the contradictions of romantic Germany; and not of Germany alone, for it is perhaps with good reason that the orientalist, Raymond Schwab, considered him the main instigator of those "prejudices which, even today, prompt our worship of the infantile and the primitive".[14]

Thus we see that a wide variety of authors and schools located the birthplace of the entire human race between the Indus and the Ganges. It only remained for linguistics to make its contribution, in a decisive though ambiguous manner, by dispelling with one certain truth a fog of adventurous suppositions, and at the same time advancing a new hypothesis as fragile as any of those which preceded it. According to this new theory it was not the whole human race but one particular race—a white race which subsequently became Christian—which had descended from the mountains of Asia to colonize and populate the West. It seemed as if the Europeans of the scientific age, having freed themselves from the conventional Noachian genealogy and rejected Adam as a common father, were looking around for new ancestors but were unable to break with the tradition which placed their origin in the fabulous Orient. It was the science of linguistics which was to give a name to these ancestors by opposing the Aryans to the Hamites, the Mongols—and the Jews.

THE BIRTH CERTIFICATE OF THE ARYAN MYTH

The origin of the human species and the origin of language were related problems, but they were not identical. Though it had been traditionally accepted that Adam was the father of all mankind, the language that he had spoken was disputed, and we have seen how, particularly in the Germanic countries, the legend of a German-speaking Adam had been known from the Middle Ages onwards. But the thesis that Hebrew was the original or mother language was still dominant in the eighteenth century, to such an extent that it was upheld, for example, in the *Encyclopédie*.[15] All the more reason, then, for it to remain dominant in Germany, where the new thinking spread later and more slowly.

We have seen, however, that Leibniz already questioned whether Hebrew was in fact the first language. In this he was followed by Johann-David Michaelis (1717-1791) of the University of Göttingen, who was considered the best Hebrew scholar of his time.[16] Michaelis should be mentioned in a political context for his campaigns against Jewish emancipation. In the field of learning, he was one of the founders of the school of Higher Criticism of the Bible and he refused to take the Noachian genealogies seriously. As to languages, "nothing proves", he wrote, "that they all derive from an original language, let alone that this language was Hebrew. Above all, let not [the book of] Moses be brought forward as proof."

By contrast, his colleague, the historian Gatterer (1727-1799), held firmly to traditional and orthodox views since he considered the Old Testament the best manual on the beginnings of world history. He believed that the Germans were descended from Ashkenaz and that the natives in America were unquestionably descended from Noah. He was less certain whether Hebrew was the original language. In company with most of his compatriots, he followed the Mosaic chronology and dated the years from the creation of the world.

A third name to bring fame to Göttingen was that of Ludwig von Schlözer (1735-1808) who adopted an intermediate position. He regarded the Biblical account of the Flood as a certain truth, but he was less sure about the story of the confusion of Babel. On the one hand, he imposed on German historians the use of modern chronology starting with the birth of Christ,[17] on the other hand, like Leibniz he tried to divide languages into a Semitic and a Japhetic family. Though the first designation was readily accepted by the scientific world, the second enjoyed no such fortune. Europeans were prepared to admit that their languages were related, but were unable to agree on a generic term for them (as though it were harder to define oneself than another). This difficulty has not been wholly overcome in our time, since in Germany the expression *indo-germanisch* is still used to indicate the languages which elsewhere are known as Indo-European.

* * *

Schlözer already included Armenian and Persian among the Japhetic languages. The relationship between different European and Asiatic words had attracted attention ever since India had become accessible to Europeans. The Italian traveller, Filippo Sassetti, had remarked upon it in 1587. A French Jesuit, Père Coeurdoux, devoted a long treatise to this question in 1767.[18] But Asiatic languages remained little known, and the idea of Hebrew as a mother tongue from which other languages were derived turned the attention of scholars in the wrong direction.

The growing interest in India stimulated more thorough linguistic investigation. It was in order to study Zend, the language of the Parsees, that the Frenchman, Anquetil du Peyron, set out for India as a common soldier and finally, in 1771 after many adventures, completed the translation of the Zend-Avesta. The mysteries of Sanskrit were revealed to Europe in a less romantic way. About 1780, the Brahmins of Bengal were given orders to translate into English (at first through the intermediary of Persian) the ancient laws and sacred writings of India. In 1783 the English poet and jurist, William Jones, was appointed a Justice of the High Court of Bengal. He set himself to study Sanskrit and soon realized its affinities with Greek and Latin. The discovery of the family of Indo-European languages is normally dated from his publication of the following passage in 1788:

> The Sanscrit language, whatever may be its antiquity, is of a wonderful structure; more perfect than the Greek; more copious than the Latin, and more exquisitely refined than either yet bearing to both of them a stronger affinity, both in the roots of verbs and in the forms of grammar, than could possibly have been produced by accident; so strong, indeed, that no philosopher could examine them all three without believing them to have sprung from some common source which, perhaps, no longer exists: there is a similar reason, though not quite so forcible, for supposing that both the Gothick and the Celtick, though blended with a very different idiom, had the same origin with the Sanscrit. . . .[19]

Furthermore, Jones believed that he was able to trace close analogies between Greco-Latin and Indian mythology. "There exists a striking similitude between the chief objects of worship in ancient Greece or Italy and in the country which we now inhabit. . . ."

The linguistic historian, Benfey, remarked that William Jones was lucky in discovering the affinity of Sanskrit with the European languages, or perhaps that he divined correctly thanks to his "intuition", since the state of knowledge in his time might have led him to suggest other analogies as, for example, between Sanskrit and Hebrew; also because real scientific proof, namely that of structural affinity, was only established by the German, Franz Bopp, thirty years later.[20] In fact the discovery was contested, particularly by the celebrated German grammarian, Adelung, who held to the theory of an original common language which began, at the same time as the human race, in Kashmir where he placed the Biblical Garden of Eden.[21]

Most orientalists, however, approved Jones's discovery. At the beginning of the nineteenth century it penetrated into cultivated society, thanks in the first place to Friedrich Schlegel, who immediately gave it an anthropological twist by deducing from the relationship of language a relationship of race. It was this brilliant author of the first generation of Romantics—the generation which believed that art and science must serve the development and progress of humanity

—who, by suggestions put forward at exactly the right moment rather than by direct statement, was able to galvanize German youth with the myth of an Aryan race. Among his other activities Schlegel was a novelist, a historian and a diplomat but he was not in any sense an extreme German nationalist. He campaigned in favour of Jewish emancipation, and historians of Nazi Germany, not knowing how much they owed him, thought they were doubly entitled to reproach him with a lack of "racial instinct"[22] because he married the daughter of the Jewish philosopher Moses Mendelssohn.

Schlegel had an opportunity of learning Sanskrit during a visit to Paris in 1802-1803, and, to begin with, he used this newly acquired knowledge in a series of lectures on universal history, which he gave from 1805 onwards at the University of Cologne.[23] "Everything, absolutely everything, is of Indian origin,"[24] he declared, and he carried this conviction to the point of believing that Egyptian civilization itself was the work of a group of Indian missionaries. Enlightened by the latter, so he taught, the Egyptians in their turn founded a civilizing colony in Judaea; but the "Tartar" nation of Moses was only partially indoctrinated with the Indian truths, since it was ignorant of metempsychosis and especially of the immortality of the soul. (In this way Schlegel paid his tribute to Voltaire,[25] but it was a tribute which clearly showed that he remained mid-way between the tradition of the Enlightenment and whole-hearted German Romanticism.)

Schlegel continued his Indian apostolate by publishing his well-known *Essay on the Language and Wisdom of the Indians* (1808). The first two sections of this book developed the theme of the beauty and antiquity of Sanskrit and of its aptitude for expressing philosophical ideas. In the third section, entitled "Historical Ideas", Schlegel became an anthropologist and boldly portrayed columns of masterful men marching down from the roof of the world, founding empires and civilizing the West.

Schlegel supposed that, as a result of obscure mingling, a new people had formed itself in northern India and that this people, goaded "by some impulse higher than the spur of necessity",[26] had swarmed towards the West. The greatness of this people was attested by "the gigantic grandeur and durability of Egyptian and Indian architecture in contradistinction to the fragile littleness of modern buildings. This consideration will enable us," he continued, "by analogy to grasp the idea . . . that all these famous nations sprang from one stock, and that their colonies were all one people directly or indirectly, of Indian origin. . . ." This is the key idea which was to be promoted before long to the rank of scientific truth. Schlegel went on to question whether these colonies were established by warriors or, as he suspected, by priests. But whichever it was, he wondered what force could have set them in motion, "what inconceivable desolation of the human conscience?" By way of reply, he developed an even more astounding hypothesis (perhaps suggested by the *Metamorphoses* of Ovid),[27] that of some primeval crime which had transformed the kindly Indian vegetarians into carnivores and driven them to distant lands by some mysterious instinct. "Must not this unknown anxiety of which I speak have pursued fugitive man, as is told of the first murderer whom the Lord marked with a bloody sign, and have flung him to the ends of the earth?" This vegetarian anthropodicy, purged of all reference to Biblical myths, was to be taken up again later and developed by Richard Wagner.[28]

Schlegel was careful to add that he was referring to "facts which preceded history", and further on he wrote: "Nothing can arouse so much doubt as the way in which the population of the most contented and fertile region of Asia reached the northern extremities of Scandinavia. . . ." He nevertheless discovered in Indian legends "the tradition of a miraculous mountain . . . a deep reverence for the holy mountain of the North. . . ." It was for this reason that "some supernatural idea of the high dignity and splendour of the North" had drawn the Germanic peoples like a magnet along their historic path.

Schlegel's vision of the world concluded with these words: "It is not suitable here to pursue this enquiry any further, important though it is for the history of our country." This final touch reminds us that the *Essay on the Language and Wisdom of the Indians* was published at a time of uncertainty and troubles, in the same year as Fichte's *Address to the German Nation*. On close inspection it will be seen that there are no clear affirmations in it; statements are carefully hedged; every idea is suggested poetically. Finally, in this work Schlegel did not yet use the terms *Aryans* or *Indo-Germans*. Nevertheless, his vague generalities were enough to stimulate his readers to the boldest of speculations.

THE MYTH DEVELOPS

The first follower and propagator of the ideas of Friedrich Schlegel was his brother, August-Wilhelm, who drew the same patriotic conclusions from them. "If the regeneration of the human species started in the East", he wrote in 1804, "Germany must be considered the Orient of Europe."[29] Wild, not to say frantic, speculations spread rapidly in those years of nationalist excitement. Görres expounded his theories in 1810, and his terminology is surprising since he described the future Aryans as "Semites of the Far East", while he thought Abraham came from Kashmir which he regarded as the birthplace of humanity and religion.[30] In 1810-12 the works of Creuzer, who advanced the best known of these theories, were published attributing Judaism to a primitive Brahmanism which was the true natural religion. In his view Abraham-Brahma and Sara-Sarasvadi were Brahmins.[31] Kanne developed these identifications in 1808 and 1815, equating Esau with Ahriman, Jacob with Ormuzd and Joseph with Ganesha.[32] At about this time, Schopenhauer began to formulate his system which was undoubtedly to become the most important philosophical corpus of pro-Indian or pro-Aryan—and at the same time anti-Jewish or anti-semitic—arguments. Soon afterwards the terminological weapons began to be forged. The term *Aryan*, borrowed a little earlier from Herodotus by Anquetil du Peyron to designate the Persians and Medes, and used by several German authors in this sense, gained widespread authority thanks, once again, to Friedrich Schlegel in 1819. Schlegel justified his choice by connecting the root *Ari* with the German word *Ehre*, or honour (philologically he was no doubt correct for one finds the same root, with a similar meaning, both in the Slav and the Celtic languages).[33] The term *Indo-Germans* was coined by the orientalist Julius von Klaproth in 1823 and was immediately adopted by most German authors,[34] while other countries preferred the term *Indo-Europeans* suggested in 1816 by the Englishman, Thomas Young.[35] But *Indo-Germans* was also disputed in Germany, even in its linguistic sense. Thus the scholar, Franz Bopp, in 1833 found good reasons for preferring *Indo-Europeans*,[36] and as late as 1851 the orientalist Boetticher-Lagarde, who was anti-semitic but a convinced Christian, used the expression "Japhetic languages".[37] This linguistic research had its significance and it produced fateful results in a field where everything depends on words. What matters is who uses the words, and it is common knowledge that, once in circulation, they quickly escape the control of the linguists who coined them.

Henceforth, the authentic and useful science of linguistics became absorbed in the crazy doctrine of "racial anthropology". Worse still, political passions influenced the course taken by these anthropological distortions. Moreover, it was at the time when these new words and new theories began to abound that the Jewish question was being discussed with special fury. At this point a rapid digression is required.

Jewish emancipation took place in most Eastern countries between 1789 and 1815. Thereafter the Jews aspired to become citizens like everyone else. But Christian society, especially in Germany, trusted them even less, as usually happens when slaves are freed. Now, in a scientific age, the theological argument based on a curse could no longer justify the re-establishment of ghettos; therefore the "deicide caste" of the Jews was transformed in the aftermath of emancipation into an "inferior race". The new anthropology of the Enlightenment provided the general framework for a semantic and sociological phenomenon which I have examined thoroughly in previous works and which may be summarized in a few words: *the ineradicable feelings and resentments of the Christian West were to be expressed thereafter in a new vocabulary*. In Germany the emancipation of the Jews, having been achieved under French occupation, was doubly unpopular and German patriotism was bound to take an anti-semitic turn, even if this was only a secondary stimulus. Anti-semitism existed before the Aryan myth and helped to give it a hold but, if the Germanomaniacs were nearly always anti-Semites, they were not necessarily followers of the new Indian genealogy. The fact that the latter were opposed to the old patriotic tradition, according to which the Germans were descended from their own race, made them all the less inclined to accept it.* Later on, in the first half of the twentieth century, the same tradition held the field; the term *Aryans* was preserved but deprived of its Indian connotation. At the beginning of the nineteenth century also, typical Germanomaniacs like E. M. Arndt or F. L. Jahn, not to mention Fichte with his theory of an original German people, altogether ignore the Indian affiliation. The latter may be considered, in the final analysis, as a traditional mythology between the Biblical genealogy of creation and Darwin's evolutionary genealogy.

As nineteenth-century positivist science gradually became prevalent, scholars set the hall-mark of scientific truth on those philosophical or politico-religious yearnings, the birth of which we have noted above with special reference to Herder. Three great names illustrate the extraordinary range of theories, options or attitudes which were possible while these yearnings and dreams were maturing.

From 1803 onwards, the philosopher Schelling publicly paid tribute

---

* Cf. above, the chapter on Germany.

to the Indian obsession without, however, subscribing to Indian parentage of language or race. If Indian religion attracted him it was because he considered it the source of "the oldest idealism". He thought that the "books which are called Biblical" were an obstacle to the perfection of Christianity and that they could not even remotely be compared "in truly religious content" with the sacred books of India."[38] "What is Europe really but a sterile trunk which owes everything to oriental grafts?" he wrote in 1805.[39] Later on, as he drew closer to Lutheran orthodoxy, Schelling ended up as a declared adversary of the Indian obsession.[40]

Goethe had always been opposed to it. He felt a deep-seated antipathy for the Indian Pantheon and could find no language strong enough to show his disgust for the "Indian monsters" and their idolators (Götzendiener). It seemed to him that Indian religion was fatal to art and poetry. The devout interest which he had shown in his youth for Biblical traditions was directed in his late years to other oriental mythologies. But he refused to cross the Indus. By way of a personal compromise, he became an adept of the "noble and pure" wisdom of the Parsees as a means of escaping from the "narrow circle of Hebraic-Rabbinic thought and of reaching the depth and amplitude of Sanskrit". Thus the ancient Indian language escaped his strictures. Goethe had made a careful study of the leading orientalists of his time. It is all the more interesting to note that in the long and erudite appendix with which, in 1819, he followed his West-Östlicher Divan, he nowhere mentions the discovery of the family of Indo-European languages, though he might well have done so in the short chapter which he dedicated to William Jones. Since he felt no racial affinity with the Indians and since he was anyway disdainful of the rowdy agitation of German patriots, he was badly out of step with his contemporaries.[41]

Hegel showed a far more modern approach when, during the same period, he compared the discovery of Sanskrit to that of a new continent because, in his view, it established "historic ties between the German and Indian peoples with all the certainty that can be required in dealing with such a subject".[42] It was for this reason that he promoted the grand conception of the Indians as colonizers of Europe to the rank of irrefutable fact, in contrast to the fabulations (Erdichtungen) with which history is familiar:

> In the cohesion between the languages of peoples so widely separated from each other . . . we are faced with an outcome

which shows us that the dispersion of these peoples, starting from Asia, and their distinct evolution beginning with the same common ancestry, is an irrefutable fact (*unwidersprechliches Faktum*). This has nothing to do with hypothetical combinations of circumstances, great or small, which have enriched history with so many fabulations presented as facts, and which will continue to do so, since fresh combinations of the same circumstances, or of these with others, will always be possible.[43]

The augur had spoken; only linguistic proof was a scientifically valid test of the origins of nations. In the case of Hegel, this confusion between race and language is the more remarkable in that, according to his *Philosophy of History*, India was a prehistoric country. Moreover, Hegel had nothing but contempt for the philosophy, character and customs of the Indians.[44] He wrote ironically of the "view current in our times" (citing Bailly, Schelling and Schlegel) according to which a primitive Indian people could have been the creators of all wisdom and the arts. "This picture", he observed, "revives that of the earliest state of Man in Paradise, which theologians earlier on elaborated in their own fashion by saying, for example, that God had spoken to Adam in Hebrew, but adapts it to other needs."[45]

We must finally refer to some of the scholars who perfected the pseudo-scientific form of the Aryan myth at the time when, if we are to believe Heine, the German devil himself undertook the study of Sanskrit and of Hegel.[46]

The first, chronologically, is the geographer, Karl Ritter, who from 1820 described in great detail how Indian armies led by Buddhist priests and missionaries had burst into the West through the Caucasus, "the country of the Asas".[47] If India was thus singled out by Ritter, it was not as yet set against Judaea. That dualistic view, which was hinted at in the same year by Johann Gottfried Rhode, who asserted the superiority and priority of Zoroaster's teaching over that of Moses,[48] was not expressed in its final and modern form until a quarter of a century later by the Indologist, Christian Lassen.

This pupil and *protégé* of the Schlegel brothers wrote about 1845:

> Among the Caucasian peoples, we must certainly award the palm to the Indo-Germans. We do not believe that this is due to chance but that it flows from their superior, more widespread talents. History teaches us that the Semites did not possess the harmonious balance of all those forces of the spirit which characterized the Indo-Germans.

Neither is philosophy a strong point with the Semites. All they have done is to borrow from the Indo-Germans, and it was only the Arabs who did this. Their views and notions so absorb their intelligence that they are unable to rise with serenity to the contemplation of pure ideas. . . . In his religion the Semite is egotistical and exclusive. . . .[49]

Further on, Lassen contrasted the *Aryans* of India with the people of Deccan, and the latter with the natives of Australia and America who had been conquered by the Europeans. In this connexion he asserted that the highest castes in India were also the whitest. "The Aryans", he concluded, "are the most highly organized, the most enterprising and the most creative among the peoples; they are also the youngest, because the earth only produced the most perfect species of plants and animals at a late date. This relationship will ultimately reveal itself in a similar way in the political field. . . ."[50]

Here are all the basic elements of the myth: the emphasis on biology, the deserved triumph of the strongest, the pre-eminence of youth, the superiority of the Whites. Only the terminology was faulty since Lassen included the Semites among the Caucasian people.

His colleague, August-Friedrich Pott, *proved* the Asiatic origin of the Europeans on linguistic grounds, but to support his views he used poetic images such as the course of the sun or the maternal breast of Asia.

Ex oriente lux: the march of culture, in its general lines, has always followed the sun's course. The people of Europe at first nestled in the bosom of Asia; like small children they played around this mother. There is no longer any need for us to invoke obscure memories in this matter. We can rely on the factual proof which European and Asiatic languages provide. There, and nowhere else, were situated the playground and school of the earliest material and spiritual energies of the human race. . . .[51]

Other German professors were to strike the same note with even more resounding effect—such as the grammarian K. F. O. Westphal, in dealing with modes of speech which, he affirmed,

our Indo-German ancestors learned, with the same artlessness as when they seized their first food for sustenance, or when, for the first time, the Indo-German man took the Indo-German woman into his arms so that she would, without his knowing it, give birth to another human being like himself. . . .[52]

By far the most influential promoter of the Indo-German or Aryan myth, however, was Jacob Grimm, the originator of the famous dictionary, who was considered an oracle by all the authors of literary and historical textbooks. It was from this source, above all, that the myth was to be taught to a large public in the second half of the nineteenth century. Let us, for instance, look at the classic *History of the German Language* (1848) which Grimm himself described in his preface as a book published at a critical time in history, adding that it was a "political work to the marrow of its bones".[53] It contains a chapter entitled "Immigration" (*Einwanderung*) in which Grimm gave, with the dates, an account of the successive waves of settlers in Europe —first the Greeks (1800 B.C.) followed by the Romans and the Celts. "As to the history of the Germans," he went on, "who are the fourth people to advance into Europe, it is customary to begin this with the account given by Pytheas in the time of Alexander the Great."[54] There followed, still in order of succession, the Lithuanians, the Slavs, the Thracians and the Scythians. Grimm also tended to attribute an Asiatic origin to Finns and Iberians. All these colonizers were propelled by some irresistible instinct:

> All the peoples of Europe and, to begin with, those which were originally related and which gained supremacy at the cost of many wanderings and dangers, emigrated from Asia in the remote past. They were propelled from East to West by an ir-resistable instinct (*unhemmbarer Trieb*), the real cause of which is unknown to us. . . . The vocation and courage of those peoples, which were originally related and destined to rise to such heights, is shown by the fact that European history was almost entirely made by them.

It is worth noting that Grimm did not use the term *Aryans* nor that of *Indo-Germans*. He preferred *Deutsche* to *Germanen* to designate the Germans, among whom he included the Franks, the Burgundians and the Lombards.[55] Neither of these terms occurs in the writings of the amateur mythologist, Richard Wagner, who nevertheless was the first to set the foundations, between 1848 and 1850, of the anti-semitic apocalypse. He evoked the image of the Jew as an agent of corruption, a "ferment of decomposition" and also that of the tragic destiny of the nobler elements of humanity, as exemplified in the royal Passion of the "marvellous Frankish race".[56]

Once they were united about the main lines of their new myth of origins, German thinkers, though drawing the rest of Europe in their wake, were still uncertain about the terms with which to give it the most perfect expression. This can be seen in the works of the leading Sanskrit scholar of the nineteenth century, Max Müller who, towards 1860, wrote:

> As the person mainly responsible for the use of the term *Aryan* in the sense of *Indo-European*, and since the term has not encountered the same acceptability in Germany as in England or in France, I am going to develop below some considerations which might justify its use. . . .[57]

Before beginning this demonstration, Max Müller enumerated the rival terms—Indo-German, Indo-European, Japhetic, Sanskritic and even Mediterranean (*mittelländisch*). It remains to be seen why "Aryan" was adopted with more favour in England and France than in Germany. We shall start with France.

THE ARYAN MYTH IN EUROPE

The cosmogony which was worked out in Germany spread through France with astonishing rapidity. As early as 1817, Cuvier used the linguistic argument to support his classification of mankind, and made a favourable comparison between the branch of it to which he thought he belonged and the Aramaean branch in the Near East.[58] Some ten years later Michelet already knew the key words, since, in his *History of Rome* he wrote of the "long struggle between the Semitic world and the Indo-Germanic world". He was certain that India was the birthplace of humanity.

> Follow the migrations of mankind from East to West along the sun's course and along the track of the world's magnetic currents; observe its long voyage from Asia to Europe, from India to France. . . . At its starting point, in India, the birthplace of races and of religions, *the womb of the world* . . ..[59]

The philologist, Eichhoff, was even more incisive when he wrote in 1836 as follows: "All Europeans came from the Orient. This truth, which is confirmed by the evidence of physiology and of linguistics, no longer needs special proof. . . ."[60] India seemed to have a powerful attraction for Michelet. In the "Journal" he kept, the following note is to be found:

> The little ruins of the Mediterranean world can no longer assuage the craving for ruins which is felt by my ravaged heart. I need the desolations, the cataclysms of the Orient, the annihilation of

whole races, the deserts. . . . The Hall of the Nibelungen is not
enough. I need the great plain of the Indian world where the
Gurus perish by the hundred thousand. . . .[61]

The genius of Michelet, which was infallibly revealing where Michelet
himself was concerned, drew this avowal from him in a moment of
great melancholy. Another Romantic, Gérard de Nerval, wanted to
undertake an enquiry into the European myths of origin just after his
first crisis of madness:

> The Cantal of Auvergne* corresponds to the Cantal of the
> Himalayas. The Merovingians are Indians or Persians or Trojans.
> . . . Is it not highly important to clarify these relationships, migra-
> tions and filiations, at least with somewhat more care and research
> than has been devoted to them so far?[62]

Balzac's *Louis Lambert* was also a prey to madness. This character
addresses the author in the following terms:

> It is impossible any longer to question the priority of the Asiatic
> writings over our Holy Scriptures. For those who are able to admit
> this historical fact in good faith, the world grows astonishingly
> greater. Was it not on a plateau in Asia that the few men who
> survived the cataclysm found refuge? . . . The history of the
> origin of man in the Bible is only the genealogy of a swarm
> which came out of the human hive hanging on the mountain-
> sides of Tibet between the summits of Himalaya and the Caucasus.
> . . . A great history rests beneath these names of men and places,
> behind these fictions which attract us irresistibly without our
> knowing why. Perhaps we breathe in them the air of our new
> humanity.[63]

Louis Lambert was a hero in whom Balzac had put much of himself.
The genealogical myth which his nascent madness, or that of de
Nerval, fastened upon, was a collective myth. Pierre Leroux, a follower
of Saint-Simon, tells us about its political and religious implications
in an article written in 1832, in which he emphasized the importance
of Oriental studies.[64]

For Leroux, as for the majority of his contemporaries, the new
Indian genealogy—or, to use his own words, "the long pilgrimage
of our ancestors which led them from the plateaux of Asia to the ice-
fields of the North, and scattered them later in fertile dissemination
through Germany, England, France and Spain"—was self-evident and

* A mountainous department in the Auvergne (Tr. note).

did not need to be proved. "We had forgotten all this," he continued, "we had abandoned our heritage and repudiated the legacy with which nature provided us." Since Oriental studies had enabled white humanity (Leroux seemed to be ignorant of any other) to rediscover its genealogy and became conscious of its family ties, Saint-Simon's disciple proposed a new Reformation of an all-embracing character:

> Why should we now restrict ourselves to the Jewish Pantheon when we have been illuminated by this light which has begun to spread right across the horizon? . . . Should we only recognize in humanity that isolated branch which is called Christianity, the revelation of Moses and that of Jesus? No. We desire a more ample Pantheon, one which answers to the name, so recently coined, of HUMANITY. . . . We are not sons of Jesus or of Moses; we are sons of humanity. . . . On what principle of distributive justice can you place all the great religious lawgivers of humanity at the feet of one of them who lived in a comparatively recent age? . . .

Proudhon was later to contrast *Jewish polytheism* [sic] with *Indo-Germanic monotheism*, in a similar context, and he too seemed oblivious of the existence of different human colour groups.[65] We shall see that the rediscovery of "more ancient ancestors" whom Pierre Leroux, as a free thinker, cited in evidence against the established religion, could be equally well invoked in its support. But, first, we are faced by the question why, immediately after Waterloo, the *élites* of the new generation, from the Saint-Simonians to the *ultras*,* were prepared to go to school with Herder and Schlegel.

This question is best answered by examining the spread of ideas. The spoken word is more persuasive than the written one and sometimes the spread of its influence can be detected. For instance, we learn by chance, from a correspondence published with a commentary,[66] that a certain Jacques-Roux Bordier had set himself up in Lyons during the eighteenth century as the apostle of German supremacy. He combined the anti-Biblical views of Voltaire with the ideas of Klopstock and Herder. The group which formed round him contained at least two young men destined for a great future, the physicist, Ampère, and the poet, Ballanche. Under the Restoration, Ballanche was to be found in the circle of friends of another propagandist, Baron d'Eckstein, though it is hard to recall any writers of note who were not associated

* The ultra-royalists under the Restoration of the Bourbons in France after Waterloo. (Tr. note.)

with this half-German, half-Jewish contact-man between the Paris salons.[67] Victor Hugo was one of them; Lamartine, Sainte-Beuve and Lamennais (to whom he revealed the mysteries of the Orient) were others, not to mention the Romantic historians, Augustin Thierry, Henri Martin and Michelet. Eckstein, known as the Sanskrit Baron, was a restless personality whose erudition, however, could not be denied. In 1824 he founded a paper, *Le Catholique*, which reflected the views of the *ultras*. In this he argued that a "natural revelation" had been made to the Indians, and he completed this, as occasion required, with the picture of a Europe which owed the best of its blood, culture and institutions to the Germans.[68] In this circle we find the young Frédéric Ozanam, founder of the Society of Saint Vincent de Paul, who wanted to prove "the Catholic religion by the antiquity and universality of the beliefs of mankind".[69] But rather than subordinate these beliefs to Moses, as Bishop Huet had done earlier, this movement "for the restoration of Christianity by Science"* tended to derive the special revelation of Moses from the universal revelation of India. Thus Eckstein, the "Baron Buddha" as Heine dubbed him, with his unceasing flow of words and his clumsy, pedantic pen, strengthened the obsession with India. The impression which he made on his contemporaries is revealed in a curious note by Hegel, who saw in him the dispenser of funds for governmental neo-Catholic propaganda.[70]

Meanwhile, a restricted circle of French specialists had taken up Indian studies without waiting for German initiative in this field. The *Asiatic Researches* of Jones were translated in 1803 and it was in Paris that the first university chair of Sanskrit was inaugurated in 1816. It was not until 1825, however, that the great German philosophic treatises began to be translated—in 1825 the *Mythology* of Creuzer; in 1828 Herder's *Ideas*; in 1837 the *Wisdom of the Indians* by Schlegel. Edgar Quinet translated Herder; Michelet translated Grimm; Heinrich Heine became the salesman of the religions and philosophies of Germany. Nevertheless, these translations and conversations were not decisive. What counted was that French minds were ready to absorb the new ideas, that they were looking for keys to open up new ways of understanding the world. Gradually, the mixture of idealistic nationalism and scientific materialism began to take shape, from which racial determinism was to emerge.

France was in search of novelty. The leaders of the new generation

---

* This description is by Sainte-Beuve. Cf. Schwab, *op. cit.*, p. 344.

asked for nothing better than to dismiss both the God of Sinai and the Goddess of Reason with an equal lack of ceremony. As Edmond Vermeil wrote: "Romanticism had declared war upon those fraternal enemies, Roman Catholicism and the Philosophy of the Enlightenment."[71] On the Catholic side, Joseph de Maistre concluded with the following reflection: "Every Christian philosopher has to choose between two hypotheses; either a new religion will appear on earth or Christianity will be renewed in some extraordinary manner."[72] Now the Indian genealogy permitted a curious reconciliation between a religion which wished to renew and enlarge itself and the universalist revolutionary idea. The extension of the Indian genealogy in Germany enabled many Frenchmen who professed the principles of 1789 to affiliate themselves secretly to the noble Frankish line. Patriotic feelings were not averse to this. After Waterloo, vanquished France was able to align herself the more easily with a partitioned and inoffensive Germany because England, the perfidious Albion, appeared as the official victor.

Given this general climate, what led particular individuals to become Indomaniacs or Germanomaniacs in the time of Louis Philippe,* and who were the chief exemplars of this tendency? Can we agree with the historian R. Schwab, himself a poet, and contrast the "feminine" Indian enthusiasm of Lamartine and Michelet with the more virile scepticism of, for instance, Victor Hugo? On this question Schwab wrote as follows:

> Hugo defends the Greco-Latin tradition as if it were his life's blood. . . . He has a rock-like quality and this is lacking in the femininity of Lamartine and Michelet; some rudimentary instinct warns him against such female influences. . . . He expresses perfectly what he means when he calls Germany an India because he senses the same dangers for the spirit in both.

In the "great tidal wave from the East" coming in through Germany, Schwab saw "a call for another Flood, which Michelet and Lamartine repeat without knowing it, in their clamour against western narrowness".[73]

On further examination, it would appear that the controversies of the period were summed up in certain personal disagreements like that between Tocqueville and his friend Gobineau (as we see from their correspondence) or that between the two Franco-German inter-

---

* Louis Philippe I who reigned from 1830–1848. (Tr. note.)

mediaries, Heinrich Heine and Eckstein. To talk of feminine influences or virile forces does not seem, at first sight, to mean much. In the last analysis, however, we believe that all these debates and contradictions lead us back to a permanent conflict which dwells in the heart of every human being.

By this we mean the struggle between regressive maternal images (projected through Mother Nature) and another relationship with the universe, which in the child is experienced later on and is a less destructive or anarchic development in the adult. This consists in an identification with the paternal image (projected through religious and cultural institutions). In a psychoanalytical perspective, and in the historical context under discussion, the obsession with India would seem to be the literary and political expression of a subconscious desire to abolish the social yoke of law and culture by making an appeal to the rights, duties and laws of "Nature" with all its wide semantic connotations. Thus a primary and archaic outlook could be embodied in systems of ideas which were variable and often contradictory as, for example, the libertarian impulses of Leroux or Proudhon and the scientific fatalism of Gobineau. There is surely something suggestive in the lines by Leroux and Michelet which I have quoted above, where the Christian-spiritual and "masculine" genealogy is rejected ("we are not sons of Jesus or of Moses" was Leroux's phrase) and maternal or material India (*mater* = *materia,* and India according to Michelet is the *womb of the nations*) is adopted as the racial parent, all in the name of science which can handle matter but is unable to cope with the spirit.

It is well known that maternal images are a basis for dreams about the return to a golden age or about integration with the universe (i.e. a return to the womb), whereas the father is a model to be imitated (identification) and surpassed. The latter image is the more constructive in the sense that it finds an outlet in realities and makes plans for the future. But having said this, we still need to clarify the relationship between individuals and the collective world with its sequence of generations. For, on the one hand, both series of images are latent in each individual: the tension between them is resolved by the compromises which mould each individual's temperament or outward "character"; on the other hand they attain a final and plenary expression in "world visions" which are likewise subject to variation in the course of history. The way in which some authors of the eighteenth century (and principally Rousseau) appealed to Nature was a portent. The Romantics in the nineteenth century gave even freer rein to these regressive tendencies. Contemporary writers referred to them as the "sickness of the century" or the "malady of the times". Tocqueville expressed this point of view when criticizing Gobineau:

> ... After thinking that we could transform ourselves, we now think that we are incapable of reform; having displayed excessive pride, we have now plunged into a humility which is no less exaggerated. We believed that we could accomplish everything and now we believe that we can achieve nothing, that every struggle and effort henceforth is useless and that our blood, our muscles and our nerves will always be stronger than our virtues and our will. This is the great malady of our times, the opposite of that of our fathers. Your book, whichever way you marshal your arguments, will intensify rather than cure the ill. . . .[74]

This reproach appears to have been directed, through Gobineau, at the materialist physiologists, Cabanis, Broussais or Bichat. In Germany, meanwhile, the popular anthropologists, whose outlook was decidedly romantic, divided mankind into "active" and "passive" races or "virile" and "feminine" races, as we shall see later on. Naturally they conferred the palm of virility on the Germans or Aryans which shows how every attempt to clarify this confusion ran into a labyrinth of false trails and surprise traps. Here, it is worth recalling an interesting distinction, which was pointed out by Thomas Mann, between pure Romanticism and "Romanticism" in inverted commas:

> Novalis and Schlegel are "Romantics" in inverted commas. At bottom they belong to the eighteenth century; were contaminated by Reason and, therefore, were poor Romantics. Arndt, Görres, Grimm, Bachofen, were the real Romantics, for they alone were completely dominated and motivated by the idea of a great retrogression, by the maternal and nocturnal idea of the past, whereas with the others the masculine idea of the future—and how masculine it was—was still pre-eminent. . . .[75]

In the light of the above, the configuration of "space-time inversions" from 1789-1815, which we have already referred to,* might well be divided into an inversion or projection of past→future, yielding the "masculine idea", and an inversion of right→left, opening the door to archaic or "nocturnal" drives. In a word, what we are dealing

* Cf. p. 29, above.

with is a massive penetration into politico-social life, under the banner of Romanticism, of regressive tendencies which until that time had been more securely held in check, or censured with greater severity.

I would add that this insight needs further definition, verification or adjustment by means of a thorough-going historical and analytical investigation which, it must be hoped, will one day be undertaken by courageous and properly equipped research workers. As for ourselves, we must now carry forward our own enquiry. We shall not expatiate in this chapter on the ill-starred Gobineau, who was resolutely ignored by his contemporaries, nor on the main source of his inspiration, the Saint-Simonian Courtet de l'Isle, a worshipper of the "blond race" who deserves as much—or as little—posthumous fame as his emulator. The chief scientific sponsor of the Aryan myth in France was Ernest Renan, a man who, by becoming the channel for all the main intellectual currents of his time and by seeking to please everyone, ended up as the almost official ideologist of the Third Republic.

As a propagandist for the Aryan Myth Renan deserves to be placed side by side with his friend Max Müller. If the influence of one was exercised in Latin countries and that of the other in the Anglo-Saxon and Germanic world, Renan was nevertheless regarded as an authority by the whole of international learned society. The warnings which both of them issued after 1870-71 against seeking political advantage from the confusion between languages and races must be placed to their credit.[76] This implied self-criticism had little effect, however, while their writings before the Franco-Prussian war continued to make headway in one encyclopaedia after another and to spread their influence through a series of textbooks.

The part played by German philosophy and philology in the intellectual formation of Renan is common knowledge; less well known is his admiring friendship for Baron d'Eckstein, whom he suggested to Müller as arbiter of their scientific dispute in 1855,[77] and whom he described as the "crystal-gazer of science".[78] Love of Germany went deep in the young Renan. "Germany, which had been my mistress for several years, moulded me too closely in her likeness", he admitted in 1890, while in a letter of 1856 to Gobineau he justified this passion philosophically as follows:

> You have written a most remarkable book full of vigour and originality of mind, only it is not at all written to be understood in France, or rather it is written to be misunderstood. The French intelligence does not adapt itself easily to ethnographic considera-

tions. France does not believe overmuch in race, precisely because the fact of race has been practically erased from her consciousness. I find the same difficulty in linguistics. The fact that the French language is no more than a detritus of the fourth or fifth zone, is certainly one of the causes why the French mind has not been directed to, and accepts with difficulty, the true principles of comparative philology. These could only have come to life among a people like the Germans, who still cling to their primordial roots and speak a language which has its origin in itself. . . .[79]

Renan's approval of Gobineau is as self-evident as is Tocqueville's disapproval. There is a remarkable affinity between the idea of a language which has "its origin in itself", and the idea of *Abstammung aus sich selbst* or "creation of the self by itself" which the German humanists had put around in their attempt to glorify Germany.* On the other hand, it was not a reading of Schottel, Herder or Grimm which inspired Renan with his contempt for the coloured or "savage" peoples[80] since such judgements were common in France at the time. But it was certainly from German thinkers that he drew the substance of his Aryan doctrine, though he may have coloured this with theological ideas from which he never really freed himself.

One might well think that it was this "remnant of Catholicism"† which led him to assign a common birthplace to the two "great and noble races, the Aryan and the Semitic",[81] while differentiating sharply between the two as to their periods of influence. "The Semites have nothing further to do that is essential . . . let us remain Germans and Celts; let us keep our 'eternal gospel', Christianity . . . only Christianity has a future."[82] Or again: "Once this mission [monotheism] was accomplished, the Semitic race rapidly declined and left it to the Aryan race alone to lead the march of human destiny." The ex-seminarist, Renan, reveals better than anyone else, in this comparison of the Semites as a decadent people with the Aryans as the newly chosen race, the confusions which had arisen between race, language and religion, between a "new Israel" for Christians and the fantasm of "Arya". But it was both as a disciple of Schlegel and Grimm and as a poet that Renan proposed the following anthropodicy as he contemplated "mount Imaüs" (the Himalaya?), the imagined birthplace of white humanity:

* See above in the chapter on "Germany".
† The expression in Renan's when reviewing his past, in 1890. *Œuvres*, III, 721.

We salute those sacred summits, where the great races, which carried the future of humanity in their hearts, contemplated infinity for the first time and introduced two categories which changed the face of the world, morality and reason. When the Aryan race, after thousands of years of striving, shall have become the masters of the planet which they inhabit, their first duty will be to explore that mysterious region. . . . No place in the world has had a comparable role to that of the nameless mountain or valley where mankind first attained self-consciousness. Let us be proud . . . of the old patriarchs who, at the foot of Imaüs, laid the foundations of what we are and of what we shall become.[83]

Here we have a patriarchal genealogy which supplants that of the Chaldeans. The Aryan race became "Masters of the planet", thanks to reason and science, or, in other words, thanks to "a search which was thoughtful, independent, strict, courageous and philosophical, in a word a search for the truth, which seems to have been the characteristic of this race".[84] Renan contrasted these qualities of the Aryans with the "fearful shallowness of the Semitic spirit, narrowing the human mind and closing it to all subtle ideas . . .".[85]

Renan was already a recognized scientific authority when, in 1863, he became an internationally famous author with the publication of his *Life of Jesus*, which was rapidly translated into ten languages. In this book the choice of subject caused him to make use of the terminology of his younger days, and the *Semitic race* soon became once more the *Jewish people*, which he described in the traditional manner so that Jewish unbelievers joined orthodox Catholics in their protests: "[Renan] asks the Catholics to excuse him for diminishing Jesus, whom he makes out to be a man, by insulting the Jews, who made Him a martyr" (Adolphe Crémieux).[86] In other works, too, Renan showed some uncertainty in his choice of terms, using *Semitic race* or *Jewish race* on the one hand, and *Indo-Germanic race*, *Indo-European* or *Aryan race* on the other, though his preference was for the latter term.

The amazing success of the *Life of Jesus* (the 100,000 copies sold in a few months were followed by 321 critical pamphlets or refutations)[87] produced a number of imitations. The following year, the aged Michelet joined the ranks with his *Bible de l'humanité*.

> . . . My book is born in the full light of the sun among our forefathers, the sons of light—Aryans, Indians, Persians and Greeks. . . . This trinity of light quite naturally met with opposition from the sombre genius of the South by way of Memphis, Carthage,

Tyre and Judaea. Egypt in her monuments, Judaea with her scriptures, established their Bibles, tenebrous but of lasting influence. . . . Now that our parent Bibles have come to light it is more apparent to what extent the Jewish Bible belongs to another race. It is a great book, without doubt, and always will be—but how gloomy and full of gross equivocation—beautiful but full of doubt like death. . . .[88]

It was not long before other Aryan Bibles appeared. We may note the *Bible dans l'Inde* (1868) by Louis Jacolliot, a prolific writer on many subjects. Though he does not figure in the encyclopaedias, his popularity in his own day is attested by the amount of space he occupies in bibliographies and catalogues. Jacolliot, after saluting "India, the birthplace of the human race and ageless mother with bountiful breasts" put forward another version of the universal Indo-Aryan religion. Moses became Manu (Manu→Manes→Minos→Moses). Jesus was derived from Zeus (Zeus→Iezeus→Isis→Jesus). By such daring etymologies, supported by apocryphal "laws of Manu" which he claimed to have discovered, Jacolliot was able "to ascribe the origins of the Bible to the highlands of Asia and to prove that, the influence and memories of the birthplace having been prolonged throughout the ages, Jesus Christ had come to regenerate the new world as Iezeus Christna had regenerated the old". The Old Testament was regarded by Jacolliot as no more than a collection of superstitions, the Jews as a degraded and stupid people, and Moses as a "fanatical slave charitably educated at the court of Pharaohs".[89]

All these books made their contribution to the Aryan myth. The *Bible dans l'Inde* went through eight editions in a few years and captivated at least one eminent adept in the person of William Ewart Gladstone. He thought he had found in this Bible fresh arguments against Darwinism, to the dismay of Max Müller who, as we shall see, had some difficulty in enlightening the British prime minister.

★   ★   ★

The conception of India as the great ancestress did not, however, recommend itself greatly to the British. Admittedly the Aryan myth, in as much as it was considered a scientific truth, ended up by gaining acceptance in the British Isles. But when its distinguished god-father, Max Müller, declared from the vantage point of his Oxford University chair that the same blood ran in the veins of English soldiers "as in the veins of the dark Bengalese"[90] he seemed to be criticizing the national pride which refused to admit any such relationship. The classic contempt for the "native", that of the colonizer for an indigenous people, was certainly responsible for the unpopularity of the Indian affiliation, and R. Schwab even refers to an Indophobia of the British, quoting Macaulay and Kipling[91] in support. But this attitude can also be attributed to older and more significant insular traditions.

When reviewing the "new genealogies", we considered that, in the case of the English, a link could be found between the national attachment to the Bible and the scientific caution of such writers as Ray, Locke or Newton with his *"hypotheses non fingo"*. This devotion to the Bible, which was just as lively in Victorian times and came to be known as "bibliolatry", led to a censorship of such ideas or research as were thought to be overbold. William Lawrence, a brilliant precursor of Darwin, had his career broken; Lyell, the founder of geology, was socially ostracised. In the field of philosophy, Dugald Stewart refused to admit that "the classical languages were intimately connected with the jargon of savages" and even denied the existence of Sanskrit. It was his view that William Jones had been deceived by Brahmin forgers.[92] As to the origins of the human race, the account in Genesis was still considered authoritative by the masses and by educated people alike. It seemed to have the force of good sense, and this in itself suggested a further reason, if one were needed, for believing in the supernatural character of the Bible.[93] But rather than talk of the "hypothesis of Genesis" it might be more appropriate to refer, as Thomas Huxley did, to the "Miltonic hypothesis" as it was developed in *Paradise Lost*:[94]

> . . . *The Omnipotent,*
> *Eternal Father (For where is not hee*
> *Present) thus to his Son audibly spoke.*
> *Let us make now Man in our image, Man*
> *In our similitude, and let them rule*
> *Over the Fish and Fowls of Sea and Aire*
> *Beast of the Field and over all the Earth*
> *And every creeping being that creeps the ground,*
> *This said he formed thee, Adam, thee O Man.*
>
> (*Paradise Lost*, Book VII, lines 516-24)

The British Adam was all too ready to extend the superiority which had been granted to him over the rest of creation to all coloured races —among these he included the races of the European continent—

while the imagination of novelists, especially Walter Scott, contributed greatly to the increase of racial doctrines in the nineteenth century. These authors, however, did not tackle the prohibited question of the origin of mankind. Bulwer Lytton's *Zanoni* (1842) sang the praises of the Normans, "the Greeks of the Christian world . . . born to be the masters of the world . . ."[95] while in 1844 Disraeli's Sidonia took up the challenge and applauded the superiority of the Semitic spirit,[96] but neither of them makes any reference to India and its primeval mountains. The scientists for their part were advancing even more remarkable hypotheses. James Cowles Prichard, by far the most popular anthropologist of the first half of the nineteenth century (who was a monogenist on the authority of the Scriptures, as he himself expressly admitted)[97] had elaborated, round about 1810, a kind of evolutionary theory according to which Adam and Eve were Blacks. It was only in the course of time that their descendants, as they became civilized and changed their way of life, had acquired a white colour.

In later editions of his work, in 1826 and 1837, Prichard rounded off his theory in the light of German philosophical research by espousing the classical tripartite division between the Hamite or "Egyptian" race, the Semitic or "Syro-Arabian" race, and the Japhetic or "Aryan" race, though he did not allow any moral superiority to the latter. If anything, he preferred the Semitic race "which", he wrote, "all its branches, the Hebrew and Phoenician being included, must be considered as the first and greatest of the whole human family".[98] Even more paradoxical, in view of the European science of that period, was the position of Prichard's successor, the ethnologist Robert Gordon Latham, who was the first to throw doubt on the Asiatic origin of the Europeans (*Man and his Migrations*, 1851).

The English, indeed, were decidedly averse to being affiliated to Mother India. There are grounds for thinking that it was due to this very fact, namely the lack of any mythology of transition between the Bible and Darwin, that the *Origin of the Species* and the *Descent of Man* provoked such a scandal in conventional England. "Only let our scientific friends show the people that there is no Adam", we read in a scientific journal dated 1861, "that nothing certain is known, and . . . we shall have no laws, no worship and no property, since our human laws are based on the Divine".[99] Not all those who argued against Darwin expressed themselves like this. Disraeli, for instance, merely announced that he was on the side of the angels and against that of the apes.[100] Put this way, the problem obviously excludes the division between the Aryan and the Semitic species with all its attendant value-judgements. After exciting notorious antagonism, evolution was finally accepted in England. It was in the wake of this moral and intellectual revolution that the idea of Aryanism was propagated there, but it was not accompanied by any ideological ferment or political agitation and therefore did not give rise to any anti-semitic campaign.

In England, old Adam was relegated to the museum of antiquities much later than on the Continent and in quite a different way. Schlegel's original theory was never taken seriously there. English scientists and philosophers never (to use a happy phrase coined by Huxley) "laid down the routes of the successive bands of emigrants with as much confidence as if they had access to the records of the office of a primitive Aryan Quartermaster-General".[101] In the same vein, this brilliant advocate of Darwinism waxed ironic over the quarrels among physical anthropologists, and claimed the right to arbitrate between them since "the combination of swarthiness with stature above the average and a long skull confers upon me the serene impartiality of a mongrel".[102] Not that Huxley doubted the existence of an Aryan and a Semitic race since, by the end of the nineteenth century, international scientific opinion had promoted this division to the status of an axiom; but, with an effort at impartiality, he attributed to the Aryans "our art (except, perhaps, music) and our science" and to the Semites "the essence of our religion". Thereupon, this champion of agnostic science quoted the prophets with fervour and, in the name of primitive Judaism, criticized the religious beliefs of his contemporaries.[103] Elsewhere he said: "It appears to me that if there is anybody more objectionable than the orthodox Bibliolater it is the heterodox Philistine, who can discover in a literature which, in some respects, has no superior nothing but a subject for scoffing. . . ." There followed an impassioned defence of the Bible "the national Epic of Britain" and Huxley concluded:

> Assuredly, the Bible talks no trash about the rights of man; but it insists on the equality of duties, on the liberty to bring about that righteousness which is somewhat different from struggling for "rights"; on the fraternity of taking thought for one's neighbour as for oneself.[104]

At the other end of the British intellectual spectrum, Huxley's greatest opponent, William Gladstone, mustered novel arguments in favour of Revelation from *La Bible dans l'Inde* of Louis Jacolliot.

"Would you believe that Gladstone was reading it in the midst of the Irish debate", wrote Max Müller to the Dean of Westminster, and he also stated: "That book of Jacolliot's is as silly, shallow and impudent a composition as ever I saw".[105] To Gladstone himself Müller wrote in more diplomatic language.[106] The learned philologist's indignation against the statesman was the more understandable since the latter had stopped him in the street shortly beforehand to reproach him for not having "told us of those wonderful discoveries in India".[107] This happened in 1869. For years Max Müller had been advocating in England his version of the birth of the Aryans "under the same roof". ("The first ancestors of the Indians, the Persians, the Greeks, the Romans, the Slavs, the Celts and the Germans were living together within the same enclosures, nay under the same roof.")[108]

Later on, the Aryans were to become the rulers of the world at the cost of unceasing battles: "In continual struggle with each other and with Semitic and Turanian races, the Aryan nations have become the rulers of history".[109] It is possible that Gladstone's reproaches stimulated in Müller his earliest reflexions on the political responsibilities of men of learning. He certainly felt such a responsibility after the Franco-Prussian war. He wrote to his friend, Ernest Renan, in 1871:

> I know you are as strongly French as I am German, but that does not prevent both of us, I think, from feeling deeply the shame and degradation which this war has brought on the race to which we belong as men. . . . We must all hide our faces in shame and grief. . . .[110]

A year later, this man of goodwill publicly proclaimed his revision of the anthropological ideas he had held until then.

His self-criticism may, it is true, have been so timid as to be practically inaudible. But the following episode, which shows the moral impotence of scientists, is worth recording in detail. Soon after the annexation of Alsace, the University of Strasbourg was germanized with great ceremonial, and Max Müller was invited to give a course of lectures there. His international fame was considerable and the Kaiser invited him to dinner.[111] On 23 May 1872, Müller pronounced his inaugural lecture. He began by calling attention to the solemnity of the hour, declared that he had never, while abroad, forgotten that he was a German at heart, and affirmed his patriotic convictions. He then asked himself whether Germany was not losing the simple and admirable virtues of past times and warned his hearers against the lure

H

of money and the excessive growth of nationalism. "You know that abroad they do not prophesy a great future for us . . .." The moral lesson was followed by an appeal to scientific caution. It was necessary to remember that linguistics was one thing and ethnology another. It was important to keep the two disciplines strictly separate and to avoid confusions of race and language; to talk of an Aryan skull was as ludicrous as to talk of a dolichocephalic language.

> How many misunderstandings and how many controversies are due to what is deduced by arguing from language to blood-relationship or from blood-relationship to language. Aryan and Semitic languages exist but it is antiscientific, unless one realizes the degree of licence which one is employing, to speak of an Aryan race, Aryan blood or Aryan skulls.[112]

What Müller failed to make clear was that, for the last quarter of a century, he himself had been taking this degree of licence in a systematic manner and had sown confusion among his Anglo-Saxon and continental readers who had followed him with enthusiasm. Needless to say, his timid retractation passed almost unheeded. The textbooks and encyclopaedias continued to quote the Max Müller of the earlier period. This was the case, for example, with the *Imperial Dictionary of the English Language* in 1883 or another encyclopaedia, *The Americana*, in 1903-1906. Another American example is that of Müller's follower at Harvard, John Fiske, who in his Aryan Manichaeism compared the Australian aborigines to lions and wolves because of their mathematical faculties, and to dogs and baboons because of their moral development.[113]

It was to be expected that the chief discordant voices came from those scientists whom popular opinion identified as sponsors of a Semitic Adam or from those who would not wholeheartedly support the German Adam. Thus the countries generally considered backward at that time, like Russia, Italy or Spain, were the ones which kept furthest away from the Aryan concert. But of this we shall have more to say later on.

CHAPTER TEN

GOBINEAU AND HIS CONTEMPORARIES

REVOLUTION, IDEOLOGY AND PHYSIOLOGY

Bertrand Russell has pointed out that Darwin's theory was, in substance, the extension of the doctrine of *laissez-faire* to the animal and
vegetable worlds. In an altogether different political context, nearly
half a century earlier in 1809, the other great herald of evolution,
Lamarck, put forward the following hypothesis in his *Philosophie
zoologique*:

> If we should now suppose that a race . . . thus perfected had
> acquired, by the force of constant habit among all its individual
> members, such a configuration as I have described above . . . then
> it may be granted:
>   1. That such a race, so perfected in its faculties that it was able
> at last to dominate all others, would have gained possession of
> all the places in the world which it desired;
>   2. That this race would have driven out all the others . . . and
> forced them to take refuge in those regions which it did not
> occupy;
>   3. That . . . by keeping other races confined to forests or deserts
> it would have impeded them in the process of perfecting their
> faculties while itself . . . developing new needs which would
> stimulate its industry and gradually improve its resources and its
> faculties;
>   4. Finally, that this pre-eminent race would have achieved ab-
> solute supremacy over all the others. . . .[1]

The superior race here described was not, however, specifically the
European or white race. Lamarck, under the heading of "Quelques
observations relatives à l'homme", contrasted the role of the *Bimanal*
with that of the *Quadrumanal* beings, of men with monkeys.
Nevertheless, from the way in which his theory was formulated,
the vision of a conquering race is easily identifiable with French
expansion in Europe at that time. Furthermore, Lamarck was influenced by the philosophy of Cabanis and, like him, he appeared to

attribute to "physical facts" all manifestations of life and intelligence.[2]

Let us now turn our attention to another prophet of the new age, Saint-Simon, the founder of the "religion of science" or *physicisme*. His *Mémoire sur la science de l'homme* which was published in the same year as Lamarck's *Philosophie zoologique*, contains the following suggestion about putting an end to wars:

> The great mass of the European population is involved in the most terrible war there has ever been. Those physiologists who study the science of Man are the only scientists in a position to analyse the causes of this war and to discover the means to put an end to it by making clear how the interests of all may be reconciled.[3]

Several authors from the Abbé de Saint-Pierre to Kant had worked out plans for permanent peace during the course of the eighteenth century but none of them thought of using physiology, an exact and experimental science, in support of these projects. Were scientists properly equipped to undertake such a task? "Physiology", Saint-Simon admitted, "is not yet worthy to be classified among the positive sciences though it is only a step removed from this." Thanks, however, to the work of Cabanis, de Richat and Vicq d'Azyr, "physiology which had for long floundered in a flood of charlatanism is today founded on facts which are observed and discussed. Psychology is beginning to be based on physiology rather than, as hitherto, on religious prejudices", in this respect following the example of astronomy and chemistry.[4] The pro-scientific, anti-clerical bias of this passage is noticeable and it may have been a significant factor in the tremendous events which had taken place in Europe during the preceding twenty years. These events required a radically new explanation which, to quote Saint-Simon once more, might be sought in "the most powerful efficient cause". In attempting to refute theological systems Saint-Simon adhered to the main tradition of the Enlightenment but he pressed the attack more vigorously. At the same time, his work began to reveal an uncritical scientific spirit overlapping with militant racism. Thus Saint-Simon's fantasy induced him to declare that the animal most closely resembling man was not the ape but the more industrious beaver. Whence, he asked, did the traditional error of scholars derive? Quite simply from religious obscurantism, since the error

> is founded on the belief that the world was made for man and that man was created in the image of God. Hence that which

most resembles man is that which, after him, is most perfect. Physiologists, like others, learn this as their first lesson. . . . Scientists, studying comparative anatomy, responded to the beliefs they imbibed when they first began learning, rather than to any impulse of reasoning, when they placed the ape after mankind in the hierarchy of social organization.[5]

This kind of argument, from a man who is considered as one of the founders of modern sociology, is most astonishing. It remains to be seen to what extent and in what way the refusal to recognize man as being created in the image of God strengthened determinist and racist thought in the nineteenth century.

We have already drawn attention to this refusal in the writings of some of the better known authors of the Enlightenment, especially in relation to the upholders of polygenist theories. The experience of revolution added something new: a tendency to draw concrete, political conclusions from that refusal. So we find Saint-Simon once more criticizing the principle of equality in 1803 because, when applied to Negroes, it had caused disaster in the colonies. The revolutionaries made a great mistake in emancipating an inferior race:

> The revolutionaries applied the principle of equality to Negroes. Had they consulted the physiologists they would have learned that the Negro is organically incapable, in a situation where he can obtain the same teaching, of being educated to the same level of intelligence as the European.[6]

This sounds like an echo of anti-abolitionist propaganda put out by planters who from 1790 onwards made use of frankly racist arguments.[7] Further on, in one of the "visions" about the new scientific religion which Saint-Simon included in his writings, he compared the Europeans to the children of Abel and the coloured peoples to the offspring of Cain. "See how bloodthirsty those Africans are; observe the indolence of the Asiatics." The founder of the new religion (that is to say Saint-Simon himself in his fantasies) would assemble an army and "make the children of Cain submit to religion". We have already seen how another son of revolutionary France, Virey, sketched out somewhat differently a similar mission for Europeans because they were "at the head of the human race". We have also glimpsed a reflection of the atmosphere of this period in the biological views of Lamarck.

It remains to examine the anthropological doctrines of the "physiologists" on whom Lamarck and Saint-Simon relied. Among the authors they referred to Pierre Cabanis was the most representative of the new revolutionary generation. He was without doubt the most influential of the "ideologists" whom the new élites of the Directory and the Consulate regarded as their intellectual masters and who were to influence so profoundly certain currents of French thought, particularly that of militant secularism (the word *ideology* itself was coined during this period by his friend Destutt de Tracy, the editor of his works after his death). In the Institute,★ which had just been founded, Cabanis declared: "I ask that the name of God should never be mentioned in these precincts." Even more famous was his theory that the brain secretes thoughts in the same way that the spleen secretes bile, or, as he wrote, in a passage that was often referred to by the nineteenth-century materialists, "the brain digests impressions in such a way that it achieves the organic secretion of thought".[8']

Cabanis developed this idea in a work produced between 1795 and 1798 with the title *Rapports du physique et du moral chez l'homme* from which it is clear that in his mind the physical predominated over the moral. In the field of biology he anticipated Lamarck's ideas on the transmission of acquired characteristics by inheritance. "If", he wrote, "the determining causes of an early habit continue to act for several generations, a newly acquired nature will be formed."[9] He combined this idea with the old teaching of Hippocrates on climates and temperaments. He recognized six of the latter. He called the most contented of these *sanguin-bilieux*, which he thought was most common among the French and explained why they had pioneered the advancement of Reason. For him the Revolution was a shining example,[10] and in his desire to extend its benefits to the entire world, he recommended that man should "dare to revise and correct the work of nature" by mixing together different races. This would produce "an equality of talent which does not exist in primitive societies and which, like the equality of rights, would be the creation of enlightenment and of perfected reason".[11]

Cabanis did not analyse the respective qualities of the different races. He merely referred to the project of a certain Draparnaud,

★ The *Institut de France* was founded in 1795 after the suppression of the old academies of learning which had existed under the monarchy. It now comprises several academies, among them the famous *Académie Française* and the *Académie des Sciences*.

whose purpose was to "determine the respective degree of intelligence and sensibility of different races and thereby to establish their level, so to speak, in the ideological scale".[12] Here, at any rate, we have an optimistic and revolutionary conception: for even if the races are of unequal worth, reason will find a remedy and bring about true equality. However, in the edition of 1824, the editor decided to introduce a note of critical disillusionment:

> Beyond the fact that this equality is likely always to remain a chimera, one may question whether it would even be desirable. Is it not precisely because of the inequality and diversity between men that society exists, that is to say, that there is an exchange of services among them?[13]

This criticism was directed not at the anthropological doctrine but at the political conclusion drawn from it. Under the Restoration the inequality of nature seemed to Cabanis's editor to be in conformity with the social order. This point of view was developed with greater originality in 1832 by Victor Courtet, the future secretary of the Ethnological Society of Paris who was then barely twenty. He noted that for Europeans liberty was associated with an abstract concept of equality, and he proposed as a remedy the accentuation of racial differences in order to prevent any further claims to equality.

This idea he expressed as follows:

> . . . I say that the crisis in Europe will not cease until its different societies are recomposed so as to display natural inequalities, or racial differences more or less marked. I am not putting forward an opinion which will offend feelings of human dignity; I am proclaiming a fact which has been verified in the annals of all the peoples of the world.[14]

We shall be returning to the views of this young enthusiast for racism. His ideas were basically not unlike those of Cabanis. The difference lay in their practical conclusions. However, the transformation of revolutionary optimism into the pessimism of the Restoration also found expression in the evolution of genuine anthropological concepts. This was clearly the case with Cuvier, the originator of comparative anatomy. In 1790, when he was young, he criticized the writers who maintained that the Blacks were a congenitally inferior race and who compared them to monkeys. A quarter of a century later, in his book called *Le règne animal*, he himself made the following classical comparison:

The negro race is confined to an area south of the Atlas. Their colour is black, their hair crimped, their heads squashed and their noses flat. Their protruding mouths and thick lips are strikingly similar to those of apes. The peoples which compose this race have always been savages . . ..[15]

Cuvier had a better opinion of the yellow race since it had created great empires, but "its civilization was always stationary". The development of civilization had therefore been the attribute of "the Caucasian race to which we belong, a people distinguished by the beautiful oval shape of their heads". So the idea that progress was the prerogative of the West, and that the white race had a superior value, persisted from the previous century, while the pessimism of the post-revolutionary era created an ever-deeper distinction between the Whites and those races which remained stationary, or were imprisoned in barbarism.

Cuvier, who was a convinced Christian, derived the different human races from a common stock. It was perhaps out of deference to the tripartite division in the Bible that he split mankind into three great races, the white, the yellow and the black. Nevertheless, religious belief no longer stopped a growing number of writers from choosing the theory of polygenism. Bory de Saint-Vincent, who was one of the most popular anthropologists during that period, declared that "Revelation . . . nowhere prescribes that we are to believe exclusively in Adam and Eve; the 'inspired' author evidently intended to deal only with the Hebrews and by referring to the other races with such brevity seems to have intended to leave their history to the naturalist." In developing this history, Bory de Saint-Vincent distinguished fifteen different human species, each separately created, and classified them in a descending scale of value. First place was given to the white or "Japhetic" race in which "there shone the greatest geniuses humanity can boast of". The "Arabic race", including the descendants of Adam who were the subject-matter of Biblical Revelation, came second. Like Christoph Meiners, Bory placed "the Australian race, the last to be formed by nature, without religion or laws or the arts" at the end of the line. Moreover, the Australians were utterly shameless: "They are completely unaware of their nudity and it never enters their heads to hide the organs by which they reproduce themselves".[16]

Another polygenist, Desmoulins, also used the Australians as an example of how difficult it was to educate and improve the races described as savage. He called attention to a conclusive experiment which he alleged took place in Sydney. Some sucklings were taken away from their native parents and brought up with English children of their own age in circumstances which would seem to guarantee the success of their education. The results were disastrous. "No sooner were they strong enough for their natural instincts to assert themselves than they rejected all instruction with the utmost violence. Before even growing out of childhood, they escaped and were never seen again." Desmoulins, convinced in spite of this that man could be improved thanks to the natural sciences, concluded: "This showed an instinctive urge, comparable to that which causes the migrations of birds".[17]

Even among militant abolitionists the same kind of prejudice could be observed. Though Victor Schoelcher thought the potential capacity of Whites and Blacks[18] to be exactly equal, his companion-in-arms, the Saint-Simonian Gustave d'Eichthal, seemed to think otherwise. On the authority of the physiologist, Flourens, he maintained that there was a constitutional and radical difference between the two races; they were to be seen, in his view, as a couple in which the white race represented the male and the black race the female—a dichotomy which the German Romantics were to take up with enthusiasm.[19]

The head of the French school of physical anthropology, Armand de Quatrefages, who was also an abolitionist, was careful to distinguish between the argument of principle and its anthropological application. "To fight slavery by appealing to an equality which does not exist", he wrote, "is to play, by this very exaggeration, into the hands of those whose opinions one is attacking." He was in favour of the abolition of slavery because of "the immorality which it necessarily brings in its train among the Whites"; not from any "sympathy for the black race". His dislike for that race went so far that, soon after a visit to the United States in 1842, he described it as scientifically monstrous, "an eccentric quirk of nature":

> The Negro is an intellectual monstrosity, to use the term in its scientific sense. In order to produce him, nature has employed the same means as she uses to give birth to those physical monstrosities which we see on show in glass cases . . . to achieve this result all that was needed was for certain parts of the creature to be arrested at a certain stage of development. The result is to be seen in those foetuses without heads or limbs, those infants who bring to life the fable of the Cyclops. Now the Negro is a White,

whose body acquires the well-defined form of the species, but whose whole intelligence is halted along the way. . . .[20]

Such was the view of Quatrefages as an anthropologist who specialized in the study of physical characteristics. The philosopher in him, who was idealistic and for that reason monogenist, declared that with the Blacks "animal functions take the place of all the noble conceptions of the spirit". These impressions he derived from a journey to Florida and very probably from the descriptions of planters' talk. Scientists are not spared instinctive reactions of this kind. The correspondence of another well-known naturalist, the Swiss Agassiz (1807-1873), shows how his contacts with black slaves at Boston made him a follower of the new American school of anthropologists.[21] It was in the United States, for obvious reasons, that anti-Negro racial theories were developed during the last century in their more extreme forms. These theories are connected with the names of Morton, Gliddon and Nott, all of them followers of the new science of craniometry or of the cephalic index. Their school became known in Europe and had some influence there. The German Carus, for example, supported his views on the inequality of races by reference to the craniography of Morton, while Renan voiced his agreement with the classification suggested by Nott and Gliddon in their *Indigenous Races of the Earth*.[22]

In Britain, on the other hand, ideas of this kind met with the most powerful resistance in the first half of the nineteenth century. Hostility towards the materialism which was spreading from the Continent, particularly from France, was reinforced by the Biblical fundamentalism which we described in the preceding chapter. No doubt white supremacy was generally recognized, but at the same time primitives were thought capable of improvement and regeneration through the Christian faith. The anthropologist William Lawrence (1783-1867) was actually persecuted because in 1819 he had developed views, in his *Lectures in Physiology, Zoology and The Natural History of Man*, which foreshadowed those of Darwin. His critics did not reprove him for denying that Negroes had "what we regard as noble feelings, manly virtues and a moral sense" but for equating man with the beasts, for arguing that the rules which determine moral and intellectual qualities in both species are the same and, more generally, for stressing the all-importance of heredity.[23] His superiors, in the hospital where he worked, declared his book immoral and a danger to the social order, and he had to withdraw it from circulation.[24] In this climate of opinion, so moderate a French author as Cuvier was criticized by implication, in 1827, by his translators who were at pains to show that man was moulded above all by education.[25] Prichard's anthropology, which he harmonized with the Scriptures, was typical of the English outlook at the time. But these pious critics of racial determinism occasionally showed remarkable insight, as was the case with the parson, Richard Watson. He denounced the tacit alliance between planters and "philosophers" in the following terms:

> The first class is composed of those who have had to contend with the passions and vices of the Negro in his purely pagan state, and have applied no other instrument to elicit the virtues they have demanded than the stimulus of the whip, and the stern voice of authority. . . . The second class are our minute philosophers, who take the gauge of intellectual capacity from the dispositions of the bones of the head, and link morality and the contour of the countenance; men who measure mind by the rule and compasses; and estimate capacity for knowledge and salvation by a scale of inches and the acuteness of angles.

Philip D. Curtin, from whose book, *The Image of Africa*, we have taken the above quotation,[26] writes that it was not until nearly halfway through the century that racial determinism began to be the dominant theory in Britain. Such well-known, influential writers as the utilitarians John Stuart Mill and Thomas Buckle, both of them apostles of reason and progress, as late as 1850-1860 still professed a complete "environmentalism", and attributed all differences of a cultural or ethnical nature to diversities in the climate or in ways of living.[27] Moreover, Dr James Hunt, the founder of the Anthropological Society, stated in 1863 "that facts relating to the physical, mental and moral characters of the Negro have never been brought before a scientific audience in London, while in France, America and Germany these subjects had been freely and fully discussed".[28] This "scientific backwardness" provides a further indication of the special climate of opinion that prevailed in England.

But let us return to the continental origins of racism. In France, Auguste Comte's writings provide a good example of general opinion in the second quarter of the nineteenth century.[29]

The founder of positivism also took it for granted that the leadership of humanity belonged to the white race and especially the peoples of western Europe. He therefore believed that the only historical enquiry of any interest was that which concerned itself with "the ancestors of this privileged population". The Oriental studies, which were so popular in his day, seemed to him a waste of time if not positively harmful.[30] Apart from this, he recognized only three great races—the white, the yellow and the black, "the only ones between which a distinction can positively be made". To the first of these he attributed the quality of intelligence; to the second, industry, and to the third, emotion. However, he prophesied an age of universal harmony in which these differences would disappear, since "the complete harmony of the Great Being requires the closest support of these three races, the speculative, the active and the affective". All the nations and all the races would, therefore, be represented in the Supreme Council envisaged by Comte's "religion of humanity: even the black race, although our pride assumes that the latter is condemned to irreversible stagnation".

Comte also expressed views on the old dispute about the relative influence of heredity and environment. The former, that is to say race, was in his opinion a more important "factor of social variation" than the climate. Nevertheless, he would not accept that it had a predominant role and strongly criticized the views of those who did. Though he may have been exaggerating when he wrote, about 1850, that "our so-called thinkers all attribute a major role to this strange explanation",[31] this is worth noting as evidence. For it shows that there were already many authors, especially in France, who discovered in the existence of different races a partial, or even total, explanation of historical development, which was one way of substituting a scientific for a theological interpretation of human life, or, in other words, of replacing Providence by "physiology". The question, then, was no longer whether different races had a different value (as most people believed at that time) but was one of drawing historico-philosophical conclusions from these differences, as was done by Gobineau and a few others. Let us now deal with the first writers who put forward such views.

RACE AS A MOTIVE POWER IN HISTORY

We have seen in previous chapters how European peoples in all periods considered their origins or their "race" to be of prime importance. We have also seen how, during the Restoration in France, some French historians and political controversialists, when uniting old traditions with new anthropological or "physiological" ideas, interpreted revolutionary changes in terms of race conflicts without indicating very clearly what meaning the concept of race had for them. One of these was Charles Comte (1782-1837), whose name deserves to be rescued from oblivion. He went so far as to attribute the main political quarrels in Europe to "racial pride". In Germany it was the Napoleonic wars which gave a new and militant twist to the old idea of Germanic racial supremacy, though this was still subordinated to Christian values and remained associated, in one way or another, with religious tradition. The German people, like the English across the Channel, still regarded themselves as being entrusted with a divinely ordained mission. Thus racial determinism was effectively born in France where, as a result of the ideological influences we have described, the laws of science, which were supposed to regulate the future of mankind, were released from divine control at the beginning of the nineteenth century. When Augustin Thierry wrote that the preponderating influence of race was demonstrated both by physiology and by history, he was already attributing to it the function of a prime force. What remained to be done, however, was to build a bridge between the old (and imaginary) races of European mythologies and traditions, and the races which anthropologists throughout the world were cataloguing.

This impossible task could only increase the number of intellectual dead-ends. The "historic" races, usually derived from a mythical ancestor, were nothing else than the ancient populations of Europe, which the great classifiers of the eighteenth century were content to include within the white race. Now, prompted by rising nationalism and popularized by newspaper polemics, a new historical outlook stimulated the search for "physiological" subdivisions in the white race, and these subdivisions usually led to the confusion of races with the old "peoples" or the old cultures and languages in Europe. French and English authors came to the conclusion that two or more races existed on their national soil. German anthropology, not having to grapple with this false problem, was free to elaborate more consistent theories.[32]

The Anglo-French anthropologist, F. W. Edwards, who was to become the founder of the Société Ethnologique of Paris, raised the problem of the relationship between "historic" and "physiological" races in a letter of 1829 to Amédée Thierry.[33] "You have established", he wrote, "historic races which may be quite independent of those which are familiar to natural science. You have a right to do so since each science is governed by its own principles. However, it may happen that in following these principles you will arrive at the same result as that to which one might be led by the application of another science." And, indeed, confusion arose at once; for, in an effort to "meet" the historian, the anthropologist suggested trying to discover "how far the distinctions which history establishes among *peoples* may be made to agree with those in nature".

Edwards noted, on the other hand, that "peoples which have settled in different climates are able to preserve their distinctive types for centuries". While critical of the old "theory of climates" (which he believed was undermined by linguistics) he raised a double problem: first the hereditary permanence of racial characteristics and, secondly, a rigorous correlation of physical and moral factors much as had been postulated by such authorities as Cabanis or Broussais. What he himself endeavoured to do was to establish distinctions as required in each case. The example of the Jews seemed to him to indicate an absolute "racial stability",[34] but he was not certain that it was always so in other cases. "Not every people", he declared, "would have the same power of resistance."

It is worth noting that, for Edwards, the Jews were a race. That too was a sign of the times. During the preceding century writers usually related the Jewish nation to the white race, and attributed its singular destiny either to the decrees of Providence or to its own debased condition. Now we find this caste or "historic race" promoted to the rank of a "physiological race" which was soon to be renamed "Semitic". Other writers also singled out the case of the Jews (we have seen how the conviction that they were a pure race led Michelet to attribute their misfortunes throughout history to this purity).

Today we should describe Edwards' approach to the problem of racial determinism as interdisciplinary. Other authors of the period, going beyond his doubts and scruples, tried to make racial determinism into a universal or monist explanatory principle.

Such at first sight appeared to be the system suggested in 1827 by the militant republican, Charles Comte, to explain the exploitation of man by man, of the slave by his master, and of the serf by his lord. Nevertheless, on closer inspection, the "races" which he defined seem rather to be social classes held together by their condition as much as by their common origin. "Once different races are thrown together by conquest on the same soil", he wrote, "each of them preserves and transmits to its descendants the customs and prejudices born of domination and servitude." In his view, the physiological derivation of these people or castes was of no special significance:

> If both castes belong to the same species and if, as a result, they cannot be distinguished by physical characteristics, they may be differentiated by artificial signs . . . what the European values is not such and such a name or sign in itself, it is the fact of being able to claim among his ancestors a member of the conquering race.

In the French context this seems a clear attempt to evoke the "controversy about the two races". Comte thought, however, that history was moulded by such confrontations on a global scale. "Not only in the Ocean archipelagos . . . but in all the countries of Europe", indeed everywhere, he discovered two antagonistic groups: "He who was the first owner, who cleared the land and who still cultivates it and he who, coming later, gained possession of the land and of its cultivators." His sympathies clearly lay with the cultivators, the Gauls of every country who were used as "instruments": "under such domination conquered people are put into the category of things". The tone of this observation is much closer to Marx than to Gobineau. Comte was very sceptical about differences in value between different races, though he hesitated to make any pronouncement on the subject on the grounds that information was still inadequate. He was an independent thinker and was always able to distinguish between the reality of race and imaginary representations of it (between nature and culture one might also say). In characteristic language, he described the persistence of racial myths beneath their successive disguises:

> The last kind of pride to be extinguished in the spirit of man is the pride of race: a man may renounce individual pride, family pride, even pride in his country, but pride of race is not so easy to give up. Our ideas about the formation and division of peoples are attributable to this feeling. . . .[35]

His friend, the economist Barthélemy Dunoyer, on the other hand, emphasized racial inequality and, as befitted a child of his century, attributed a primary role in this matter to physiology. Political realities, he thought, supported his views. "Why is it not the black race which rules? Why are not the Whites servants?" Dunoyer, a man of liberal convictions like Charles Comte, deplored this universal inequality.

> There is no denying that men are unequal. The same is true of race and it is no use closing one's eyes to the fact. . . . From the unequal perfectibility of races a number of painful results may follow, as for instance the impossibility for all to become equally industrious, rich, enlightened, moral or happy.

These reflections induced him, though without enthusiasm, to regard the Germanic peoples as a superior race. Did not history show that they must be "considered as the first and only founders of modern societies"? He was convinced that the rules of aesthetics, whether applied to ancient or to modern art, established yet another kind of superiority of the "Teutonic type". A controversy developed between Dunoyer and Charles Comte. The former significantly reproached the latter with denying the inequality of human races in spite of the verdict of science. Charles Comte replied that he had not yet pronounced a definite judgement on a matter which was still uncertain.[36]

The Saint-Simonian, Victor Courtet de l'Isle, also recognized the Germanic peoples as constituting the master race, when he was enquiring into the primary impulses which regulate the history of human society—"the organic causes", as he put it, "inherent in man's existence".[37] This race was formerly spread out over Europe "like the oil of the nations"; it was "big, strong, beautiful" and represented "the finest ideal of man's physical nature". It was because of this that it had been empowered by Nature to subjugate the races which formed the Roman Empire. All this, however, in Courtet's view, could be dismissed as past history. Since that time a fusion of races had taken place in the West, arousing an "egalitarian spirit" which he believed was attested by Christianity as well as by the French Revolution. We have seen how Courtet proposed to break down this complex of races in order to bring peace to Europe. He referred to this plan again in his principal work, *La Science politique fondée sur la science de l'homme* (1837). This book was intended to be realistic. The main indicator of the quality of a race was stated to be its power to dominate; masters were by definition superior to slaves, and Europeans, however mixed they might be, had amply proved their supremacy throughout the world. The same reasoning led Courtet to assert the superiority not only of the Asians but also of the American Indians over the Blacks; like writers of his century, he placed the Blacks at the bottom of the human scale, their absolute inferiority being demonstrated by the fact that "they have enslaved no foreign race; they have only enslaved one another".

One of Courtet's original ideas was that human history was determined not merely by interracial struggles, that is to say "physically", but also in a more intimate way through a welter of combinations or injections of different bloodstreams, or "chemically". He seems to have been the first to clothe this idea, which was to become, thanks to Gobineau, a dogma of modern racism, in scientific language. Typically, he regarded this as a "progressive" idea when contrasted with older theories. This emerges from his criticism of Thierry:

> Thierry's method, unfortunately, has a reactionary and ex-clusive character. He deals only with the primitive conflicts of races and tries to discover in the remembrance of their violence, that is to say in the perpetuation of hatreds caused by this violence, the cause of all our present-day contests . . . but the mingling of blood, the gradual identification of interests, have gradually destroyed these elements of antagonism, and later revolutions, those in our own time, are no longer caused by the same hatreds and the same memories. . . .[38]

The mingling of blood was, in the opinion of the Saint-Simonian Courtet, beneficial so far as industry and progress were concerned, since "nothing is more favourable to the division of labour, which is the first cause of general prosperity. Social functions are and will always of necessity be graduated: differences in rank are and always will be the consequence of the diversity of functions. If, then, nature has provided, in the most comprehensive way, for the fulfilment of this double need through the inequality of races, we should, on that account, magnify the author of all things."[39] In stating his conclusion, Courtet adopted the position of the impartial scientist who is con-cerned only to enlighten his contemporaries about the laws governing racial matters, while inviting them to choose between the order and stability obtained by the dictatorship of one race over another and the disorders and rebellions of societies which are just and egalitarian, and in which racial individuality has been totally effaced. To judge by his final summing-up—"You will find freedom at the heart of slavery and slavery at the heart of freedom"—the advantages and disadvantages would be evenly balanced from a moral standpoint, whichever view humanity adopts.

In working out such pseudo-scientific systems, more or less monist, these obscure precursors were in various ways giving extreme ex-pression to the views which were vaguely impregnating the atmosphere of the time. Some echo of these views is also found in the works of several well-known writers. Even such an intransigent Catholic as

Joseph de Maistre paid them an unexpected tribute. When seeking to explain the "lowest stage of brutishness of savages", whom he regarded as born criminals, beyond hope of improvement,[40] he suggested that their ancestors must have committed some outrageous crime, "an original sin of the second degree". This had resulted in their exclusion from the human race whose unity was thereby shattered. The conviction that races are fundamentally unequal found a place in de Maistre's idea of the divine plan and induced him to propose an entirely new theology. Men were no longer equals before God since the savages, bowed beneath the weight of two original sins, were doubly perverted; and this "lay theologian of Providence" reproached established theology with "throwing a cloak over the appalling state of the savages; the immense charity of the Catholic clergy has often, when speaking to us of these creatures, substituted its hopes for the reality".

Joseph de Maistre, however, stands alone in his approach to this question. In general, it was not considered necessary to follow such theological detours in order to sustain belief in the importance of the racial factor. On the other hand, in the liberal camp, the belief was sometimes felt to represent an embarrassing truth. Writing in praise of Dunoyer's book, Benjamin Constant observed:

> This system contains its portion of truth: it is stimulating to explore it and science may be enriched thereby, but we believe that it should be kept rigorously apart from politics. . . . Let us leave it to the physiologists to investigate these primordial differences which sooner or later will be overcome through the perfectibility with which the whole human race is endowed, but let us beware of arming politics with this new pretext of inequality and oppression.[41]

Among contemporary comments on race, the following passage of Lamartine may also be cited: "The more I have travelled, the more convinced I have become that the races are the great secret of history and of morals."[42] The dominant tendency was for a kind of pluralist interpretation such as was later methodically expounded by Taine. In his theory of three factors—race, environment and time, the most important was race, "the first and richest of the factors from which historical events derive".[43]

★   ★   ★

From about 1840, racial interpretations of history began to appear in Great Britain too, That of Thomas Arnold, the famous headmaster of Rugby, had moral and spiritual accents. In substance, he put forward a panoramic view of universal history which conferred on the Teutonic race the role of a specially designated instrument of Providence. According to Arnold, the torch of civilization passed successively from one race to another, each of them, as soon as it had accomplished its task, disappearing from the scene of history. The Greeks had enjoyed their moment of supremacy; then came Rome. But the real impulse to Christian and western culture had been provided entirely by the Germans. It was they who had preserved the heritage of classical times and developed medieval civilization. It was thanks to them that European expansion had covered the whole world (this, of course, emphasized the special contribution of the Anglo-Saxon nation). Arnold did not reveal who would take up the torch after the Germans. In a somewhat Hegelian manner, it seemed as if history would reach its fulfilment in them. As far as he was concerned Germany was

> the land of our Saxon and Teutonic forefathers; the land uncorrupted by any Roman or other mixture; the birthplace of the most moral races of men that the world has yet seen—of the soundset laws—the least violent passions and the fairest domestic and other virtues.[44]

Arnold's Christian belief did not prevent him from leaning towards the polygenist theory. It did not seem to him improbable, he wrote, that the Greek and the Australian were not descended from the same ancestor. Casting his thoughts as far back as de Maistre, though in a different way, he accepted that the Almighty might at some time have chosen the Greek people, like that of Israel, as His instrument, "communicating all religious knowledge to mankind through the Jewish people, and all intellectual civilization, through the Greeks".[45] As far as the latter were concerned it was they who exemplified "the power of reflection and of questioning things". It is clear that even among believing Christians the old dogmas were changing and weakening, overwhelmed by the prestige of science. Nevertheless, the main influence for men like Thomas Arnold was still Divine Providence which had chosen the Germanic people as the instrument of its plans. Not long afterwards, the young Disraeli took up the racial theme once more. He relegated Providence to the background and with quiet audacity replaced the keys of human destiny in Jewish hands.

No sooner had he entered political life than Disraeli revealed his ideas and his vision of the world in his great trilogy of novels (*Coningsby*,

1844; *Sybil*, 1845; *Tancred*, 1847). His philosophy of history might be summarized in the formula: *"All is race; there is no other truth."* He included the Jews in the "Caucasian race" in conformity with the anthropological views of his age, and he described their occult power in the following terms:

> The fact is, you cannot destroy a pure race of the Caucasian organization. It is a physiological fact. . . . And at this moment, in spite of centuries, of tens of centuries, of degradation, the Jewish mind exercises a vast influence on the affairs of Europe. I speak not of their laws, which you still obey; of their literature, with which your minds are saturated; but of the living Hebrew intellect. You never observe a great intellectual movement in Europe in which the Jews do not greatly participate. The first Jesuits were Jews; that mysterious Russian Diplomacy which so alarms Western Europe is organized and principally carried on by Jews; that mighty revolution which is at this moment preparing in Germany, and which will be, in fact, a second and greater Reformation, and of which so little is as yet known in England, is entirely developing under the auspices of Jews, who almost monopolise the professorial chairs of Germany. . . .[46]

If the future Lord Beaconsfield was the first to transfer the debate in England to the political field (in a later work he attributed the revolutions of 1848 to the underground plots of the Jews), his fantasies were to produce a louder echo on the Continent where they provided a variety of arguments for the vulgar propagandists of anti-semitism. The British public regarded his bragging as a harmless whim. In any case, he reserved the second place in his hierarchy for the Saxons, the race best able to receive the "light of Jewish spirituality."[47]

With the surgeon Robert Knox, whom Philip D. Curtin described as the "real founder of British racism",[48] it was no longer a question of spirituality, whether Jewish or other. In his "philosophical enquiry" on human races published in 1850, the Jews were described as sterile parasites, while Disraeli's views were reproduced and developed as follows:

> . . . that the race in human affairs is everything, is simply a fact, the most remarkable, the most comprehensive, which philosophy has ever announced. Race is everything: literature, science, art — in a word, civilization depends on it.[49]

Knox called his system "transcendental anatomy" though it had no trace of transcendentalism. He thought that the most gifted races, especially from a philosophical point of view, were the Goths and the Slavs, followed by the Saxons and the Celts (he was not afraid to criticize the "inordinate self-esteem of the Saxon"). At the other end of the scale were the Blacks to whom, however, he conceded warlike qualities which might imperil white supremacy in Africa. All this was a new language. Great Britain was beginning to adjust itself to continental thinking, and Knox's book made its mark. Darwin quoted it with approval, and historians of anthropology see Dr Knox as a precursor of the theory of evolution who anticipated Darwin's and Spencer's theories of natural selection and the survival of the fittest.[50] Equally novel, in his country and in his age, were Knox's anti-Jewish arguments, which were directed in part against Disraeli. He attributed the parasitism and cultural sterility of the "Hebrews" (which he traced back to remotest antiquity) entirely to their race not to their religious beliefs, and in this he provides a foretaste of modern anti-semitism. But in the case of half-Jews, he was inclined to admit that their Saxon or Celtic blood dominated their Jewish blood. This was a particularly English point of view.[51]

★   ★   ★

Historical and literary studies about Gobineau since the end of the last century have often speculated about his sources. One curious hypothesis put forward by a German author in 1926 suggested that Gobineau was initiated into the mysteries of race by Disraeli during meetings which might have taken place between them in Paris.[52] A more solidly based attribution was proposed by Jean Boissel, who showed that some of the key ideas of the *Essai sur l'inégalité des races humaines* were derived from Courtet de l'Isle. But however they were transmitted, Gobineau merely systematized in a very personal way ideas which were already deeply rooted in his time. His own contribution consisted mainly in his pessimistic conclusions, which sounded like the death knell of civilization. With a pretence of science, he gave vent to bitterness and disappointment of every kind. He himself admitted that science was for him "only a means to assuage a hatred of democracy and of the Revolution".[53] He expressed his message even more clearly in the following phrase in a letter which he sent in 1856 (just after his book was published) to Tocqueville: "I do not say to people: *you are to be forgiven or condemned*, I say to them: *you are dying.*"[54]

Gobineau's ideas have little in common with the legend that has grown up around him. By all the rules of logic, his racial hierarchy should have got his book burned in the Third Reich.

The range of Gobineau's reading was vast and he enlisted all the anthropological literature of his time as well as the writings of the leading "physiologists" in support of his thesis. But, as far as the historical sources of his inspiration are concerned, the Bible must take first place. He followed the Biblical chronology (the human species, if not the universe itself, was five or six thousand years old); he borrowed his essential ideas about mankind from the Book of Genesis. According to him, this dealt only with the white race, which held "the monopoly of beauty, intelligence and strength".[55] This race, which had been guided by Providence from the start, had emerged from northern Asia and had divided into three branches, those of Ham, Shem and Japheth (the future Aryans). All three were equally endowed with talents and virtues but, according to Gobineau, the white race was blessed from infancy with "the two main elements of all civilization: a religion and a history".

As to the origin of the inferior or "secondary" coloured races, Gobineau, not wishing either to contradict the old tradition of the Church or to affiliate them to the chosen white race, sought refuge in inconsistency. He admitted, without attaching much importance to it, the existence of "a man of a first creation called Adam", but he preferred to leave this mysterious personage "out of the controversy".[56] In his eyes, an abyss divided this "Adam" from the black and yellow races which he thought were indigenous to Africa and America respectively. In a word, he was a monogenist in theory and a polygenist in practice.

On the other hand, Gobineau assumed the existence, in all branches of the human species, of a "racial instinct" which was opposed to cross-breeding ("the law of repulsion"). But the very qualities of the white race, its civilizing urge towards social intercourse and its expansion through conquests, ended up by creating an opposite tendency ("the law of attraction"). It followed that the white race, and therefore civilization itself, were fragile and ephemeral, since these "alloys" or infusions of inferior blood soon produced devastating effects. The laws of "historical chemistry" decreed that the mixed "ternary" or "quaternary" sub-races must be degenerate.[57] Thus the Hamites were the first to "saturate themselves in black blood",[58] as a result of expansion and conquest, and became thoroughly degraded. Such was also the destiny of the Semites, though to a lesser degree. Only the sons of

Japheth, the Aryans, remained more or less completely pure, at least until the beginnings of the Christian era. Thereafter they too embarked, in the course of their expansion, on the same downhill course.

However, it would be a mistake to think that Gobineau regarded coloured people as objects of contempt or as mere brutes. On the contrary, his judgement of them is surprisingly moderate. He insisted on the gulf which separated them from the great apes,[59] and he reproached the anthropologists of his period for their exaggerations. "Most scientific observers up to now have displayed a marked tendency to debase the lowest types of humanity more than the facts warrant. Almost all the early information about a tribe of savages portrays it in falsely repellent colours."[60] He attributed to the Blacks in particular "a universal force of imagination" which the civilizing Whites did not have and which he saw as the source of all the arts.

> The black element is certainly indispensable for developing artistic genius in a race, for we have seen what outbursts of fire, flames, sparks, vivacity and spontaneity are intrinsic to its soul and how much the imagination, that mirror of sensuality, and all cravings for material things prepare it to receive those impressions which are produced by the arts.[61]

As for the Jews, to whom Gobineau attributed relatively unadulterated Semitic blood, his description of them might easily have been inspired by Disraeli. It ends with what is almost a panegyric of the Chosen Race:

> The Jews were encircled by groups which, speaking dialects of a language related to their own, also had for the most part quite a close blood-relationship with them. Yet they outstripped all these groups. They appeared as warriors, agriculturalists and merchants. Under a singularly complicated form of government, which reconciled not only monarchy and theocracy but also the patriarchal power of the heads of families and the democratic power of the people as represented in the assemblies and by the prophets, they could be observed moving across the centuries in prosperity and glory and overcoming, by one of the most intelligent systems of emigration, the obstacles to their expansion imposed by the narrow limits of their domain. And of what did this domain consist? Modern travellers are able to assess at what a cost of enlightened effort the cultivators of Israel maintained its artificial productivity. For since this chosen race ceased to inhabit these mountains and plains, the well where Jacob watered

his flocks has filled with sand, Naboth's vineyard has been overrun by the desert, and the site of Ahab's palace covered by brambles. What figure did the Jews cut in this miserable corner of the earth? I repeat, they were a clever people in all their undertakings; a strong, a free, an intelligent people who before losing, in courageous combat, the title of an independent nation, had provided the world with almost as many scholars as merchants.[62]

The fact was, as Gobineau informs us later on in his work, that the "Hebrew, in the alloyage to which his race was subjected, had a greater share in the essence of the Whites" than his neighbours.[63] Indeed throughout his book Gobineau indulged in endless operations of racial blood-counts which were supposed to explain the course of man's history at all times and in all places. Thus the miracle of Greece, with its flowering of art and philosophy, but also its final decline, were due to a mixture of:

1. Hellenes—Aryans modified by yellow elements but with a great preponderance of the white essence and some Semitic affinities;
2. Aborigines—Slavo-Celtic peoples saturated with yellow elements;
3. Thracians—Aryans mixed with Celts and Slavs;
4. Phoenicians—Black Hamites;
5. Arabs and Hebrews—very mixed Semites;
6. Philistines—Semites perhaps of purer stock;
7. Libyans—almost black Hamites;
8. Cretans and other islanders—Semites more or less resembling the Philistines.[64]

Clearly, cross-breeding of the kind described above, when carried on for centuries, could only cause a deterioration of stock; and, if at the beginning of our era the Germanic invasions produced a temporary respite, the Aryan blood which they introduced was soon to be diluted with the old Roman, Hellenistic or Semitic compounds.[65] It comes as a surprise to find in Gobineau's work no analysis of the blood compound which led to the French Revolution. For him all the bloodstreams of the European nations were equally and inextricably mixed. The final chapters of his book are dedicated to a description of the bastardization of the Aryans; nor is any exception made (as is generally thought) in favour of the Germans, who were also contaminated by residual European blood-types as well as by

"Finnish blood". Still more tragic were the prospects in the New World, whose inhabitants "are the products of the detritus of all the ages, of Irishmen and Germans thoroughly cross-bred, of some French who are no less so and of Italians who are more so than all the others". Furthermore, to this mixture would be added before long the blood of Blacks and Indians from which there could only result the "juxtaposition of the most degraded beings".[66]

The same fate was in store for the whole world, and the *Essai* concludes with the following peroration:

> The white species will disappear henceforth from the face of the earth. After passing through the age of the gods when it was absolutely pure; the age of heroes, in which the mixtures were moderate in strength and number; the age of the nobility, where human faculties remained considerable though they could not be renewed from dried-up sources, it has descended, more or less swiftly according to the environment, to a final confusion of all the elements. . . . The portion of Aryan blood, already subdivided so frequently, which still exists in our countries and which alone sustains the edifice of our society, advances daily towards the last frontier before total absorption. When this result is achieved the age of unity will have been reached . . . this state of fusion, far from being a consequence of the direct marriage of the three great archetypes in their pure state, will be no more than the *caput mortuum* of an infinite series of mixtures and, consequently, of attenuations. It will be the last stage of mediocrity in all its aspects; mediocrity in physical strength, mediocrity in beauty, mediocrity in intellectual aptitudes, one might almost say annihilation[67].

Gobineau believed that he could assess the duration of this final stage. Since the flowering of civilization had lasted five or six thousand years, its decline, which had begun several centuries ago, would probably continue for a similar period. Three or four millennia should therefore "precede the final spasm of our species, when the lifeless earth will continue, without us, to describe its apathetic orbits in space".[68]

One finds the same lugubrious poetry in Gobineau's letters, as for instance in the passage quoted above: "I do not say to people: *you are to be forgiven or condemned* (and he added: 'I am no more a murderer than the doctor who says that the end is near'); I say to them: *you are dying* (and he added: 'Winter is coming and you have no sons')."[69]

Such visionaries as Saint-Simon and Auguste Comte—and Ernest Renan with reservations— hoped that a worldwide racial fusion would open up an era of harmonious happiness, an undefined form of eternal life for the human race, thus secularizing the ancient Christian hope of the *parousia*. With Gobineau, who thought himself a good Catholic, any hope of a second coming of the Christ-Messiah had definitely disappeared and the human race had no other prospect than complete annihilation. In this sense his disciples have not misinterpreted him. He was indeed the great herald of biological racism, a man in whom regressiveness seemed to be inspired by the desire to lead humanity back to its point of departure.

METAPHYSICIANS AND MEGALOMANIACS

When trying to console Gobineau for the setback which his book received in France, Tocqueville and Renan promised him more success in the Germanic countries. The former stressed the German characteristic of "enthusiasm for what they regard as abstract truth", and assured him that his book "would return to France, above all by way of Germany"[70]; the latter referred to the Germans' understanding of race problems and their attachment to "their primordial roots".[71] Time proved both of them right. More and more from now on the main strands of our enquiry will lead to Germany, the most favourable breeding-ground of European racial fantasies and the stronghold of an idea of purity which under the impact of the Napoleonic wars, had taken on a militantly nationalist character. There is no better example of this new trend than Fichte's paranoid doctrine, which, as we have seen, relegated all the non-Germanic white peoples to the outer darkness—which was, after all, in keeping with the constant confusion between "historic races" and "physiological races". It is none the less true that, unlike his fellow countrymen, Fichte stuck to the criterion of language, so that his attack remained indirect; and indeed the bio-materialist philosophy of French writers never did command much of a public in Germany. The foggy language of German idealism, however, made it possible to glorify the Germanic race in other ways as the quintessence of the white race, and to condemn other human groups without appeal—as Fichte condemned the Jews.[72] In a country of poets and thinkers, metaphysical judgements were considered by ordinary mortals as authoritative in every field.

So German philosophy continued to approach the "relations between the physical and the moral" from the angle of the "moral".

The "invisible" was called upon to explain the visible; matter was in some sense secreted in thought. This contrast with French ideology found its most radical expression in a *Naturphilosophie* in which all natural phenomena were but a symbol, or material manifestation, of the "Idea". The detailed manifestations of a universal relationship had to be worked out, the secret significance of natural phenomena had to be discovered, and this allowed the Romantic imagination to launch out into the most extravagant fantasies, punctuated here and there by a flash of genius.

Friedrich Wilhelm Schelling (1775-1854), often described as the father of *Naturphilosophie*, seemed at first to consider the different races of humanity in the classic spirit of the Enlightenment. Without doubt, the white race was the noblest of all races, but how had it become so? Was it because, unlike the coloured races, it had preserved in full its primitive dignity (as Buffon thought) or had there been a worldwide degeneration which only the Whites had been able to withstand, thus attaining a "higher spirituality"? Whatever the truth, he took it for granted that "European humanity could in no sense be described as a race". At first Schelling also suggested that "the differences which separate the peoples are not racial differences . . . among some peoples there are class differences at least as great as racial differences". The philosopher, therefore, asked himself "if differences of physical development, far from being a cause, were not rather an accompanying phenomenon of great spiritual movements which must have been closely related to the earliest formation of peoples".[73]

However, with the passage of time this semblance of "cultural anthropology" gave way to quite different ideas. In the second part of the *Philosophy of Mythology*, Schelling divided the human race "in two great masses, in such a way that the human element seems only to exist in one half of it". In the other half he placed not only the tribes of Africa and America, which were "bordering on the animal", but also the "intermediate types" in Asia. In an attempt to reconcile Blumenbach with Holy Writ, he concluded that "only the ancestor of that race which was ready to endure all, the Japhetic, Promethean, Caucasian race . . . could be the Unique Man capable by his own act of breaking through into the world of Ideas". As for the other races, Schelling thought they were destined either for slavery or for extinction. He was prepared to justify this view, of which he saw a practical demonstration in the colonial systems of his time, on metaphysical grounds.

> For the first man, for man properly so called, the different races
> are no more than matter . . . with the consequence that the action
> of a superior race may be twofold: the elevation of a part of them
> towards the divine, or the degradation of others below the human
> level.

Schelling apparently saw the slave-trade as one of the means for
achieving an "elevation towards the divine". "A benevolent spirit",
he wrote, "might have discerned therein the only means of salvation
for this race of humans abandoned to the most terrible barbarism and
for these souls destined, almost without reprieve, to an eternal death."
Such might be the ways of Providence—or the resources of idealist
philosophy—and if the lot of the slaves had become appalling in fact,
that was because "everything which is touched by human hands is
destined to corruption. . . . It is not a question of knowing what is
real but what is possible. . . ."[74]

We shall not delve into the theosophical speculations about the Soul
of the World, or the identity between the Unique Man and the Whole,
by means of which Schelling justified his position. His anthropology
is notable for being distinctive in another respect. According to him,
all white men have access to the world of Ideas by the same right,
and the Jews, whom he classified as a "non-people" or as "representatives of pure humanity", had even readier access to this world than
others.[75] Moreover, this fellow-pupil and youthful friend of Hegel
refrained from assigning to the Germans any special responsibility for
bringing the human species towards its true country, namely, towards
Heaven.

Another follower of *Naturphilosophie*, Lorenz Oken (1779-1851),
was the pioneer of a form of German naturalist symbolism which
combines all the extravagances and fantastic absurdities that the mystico-
philosophical imagination could invent. Oken taught that nature was
a single body whose members were living beings. Man *symbolized*
nature because he was the supreme being in creation and he "reunited
in a single body all the bodies of the animals". Consequently the
human body could be subdivided in the same way as the animal
kingdom, the main classes of which "corresponded" to the organs of
the five senses—the mammals, as the highest animal class, corresponded
to man's sight, the birds to his hearing, and so forth, until one reached
the insects which corresponded to the sense of touch. The human races
were categorized by a symbolism connected with the elements. The

black race was terrestrial or simian; the white race, luminous or human; the Mongols and the Amerindians were symbolized by air and water respectively. In support of his thesis, Oken pointed especially to the *opacity* of the Blacks who, being unable to blush, could not express an interior life. "He who can blush is a man; he who cannot is a Negro."[76] In addition to this, Oken, whom his compatriots willingly credited with genius,[77] glorified "the divine art of war". He thought it should be conducted according to the laws of nature, and he reproached the Germans of his day for continuing to rely on philosophy.

We shall consider later on similar fantastic comparisons and ideas in the writings of the most popular anthropologists in Germany during the next generation. But first we must glance at the anthropology of the author whose thought, after illuminating the nineteenth century, continues to be a philosophic beacon in the twentieth.

The idealism of Hegel, as a philosophical system, is inherently poles apart from the teaching of bio-materialism. While he supported the theory of Indo-Aryan origin, as we have seen, he rejected with contempt the claims of the "physiognomists" or "cranioscopists" who, in studying physiology, sought to extract its secrets from the human soul.[78] Hegel's standpoint was exemplified by his views on the Jewish question which was then being passionately debated. Unlike Fichte, he was in favour of the emancipation of the Jews, precisely because he could see no other way of getting them to renounce their detestable beliefs—which implies that these beliefs were not rooted in their bodies.[79]

Nevertheless, Hegel described the coloured races, especially the Blacks, in a way which inevitably suggested the idea of congenital inferiority. "The Negro", he wrote, "exhibits the natural man in his completely wild and untamed state. We must lay aside all thought of reverence and morality—all that we call feeling—if we would rightly comprehend him; there is nothing harmonious with humanity to be found in this type of character." It was unnecessary to look far afield to find proofs of the baseness of the Negro. "They have no Knowledge of the immortality of the soul . . . the devouring of human flesh is altogether consonant with the general principles of the African race." Such a creature was worth no more than Oken's simian man, the man "unable to blush". His was a hopeless case. "This condition is capable of no development or culture, and as we see them at this day, such they have always been."[80] Africa was for Hegel beyond the bounds of world history, which for him started in Asia and ended in

Europe. The formula in which he summed up the "march of God on earth" is well known. "The Orient only recognized the freedom of *one* man; the Greek and Roman world, that of *a few* men; the Germanic world that of *all* men." In this progression towards freedom for all, he successively aligned despotism, the combination of democracy-aristocracy, and monarchy.

Another classification of periods in world history suggested by Hegel was that of the three great stages in Germanic-Western history —from its beginnings to Charlemagne, from Charlemagne to the Reformation, and from the Reformation to the period which found its consummation in his own philosophy. These three periods also corresponded to the three reigns of the Father, the Son and the Holy Spirit. So far as the first two dispensations were concerned this Joachimite eschatology was susceptible of various interpretations. As to the third, however, Hegel departed from his cardinal principle, and subscribed to the racial alchemy of his age. The stumbling-block was the Reformation. Why had the Spirit been able to establish his reign only among the Germans and not among the Slavs and the Latins? The Slavs, he pointed out, had remained peasants and serfs because they "could not share the benefits of dawning freedom". But there was no lack of culture among the Latin nations: "on the contrary they were in advance of Germany in this respect". Some other explanation must be found, and it was at this point that Hegel made a scarcely disguised appeal to the purity of German blood.

"The pure inwardness of the German nation", he wrote, "was the proper soil for the emancipation of the Spirit; the Romanic nations, on the contrary, have maintained in the very depth of their soul—in their spiritual consciousness—the principle of *Disharmony*; they are the product of the fusion of Roman and German blood, and still retain the heterogeneity thence resulting." He was to take up this idea again later in language more explicitly Hegelian:

> On the other hand, among the Romanic peoples we immediately encounter that internal schism, that holding fast by an abstract principle, and, as the counterpart of this, an absence of the Totality of Spirit and sentiment which we call "Heart"; there is not the meditative introversion of the soul upon itself;—in their inmost being they may be said to be alienated from themselves.[81]

This judgement on the *Welsche* can be compared with some writings of the youthful Hegel, where one is led into a peculiar mystical world.[82] The condemnations, sometimes of unparalleled virulence,[83] with which he denounced the Jews in his *Theologische Jugendschriften*, contain a passage where he deplores the way the Germans ignore their own traditions and legends:

> Christianity has emptied Valhalla, felled the sacred groves, extirpated the national image as a shameful superstition, as a devilish poison, and given us instead the imagery of a nation whose climate, laws, culture and interests are strange to us and whose history has no connection whatever with our own. A David or a Solomon lives in our popular imagination, but our country's own heroes slumber in learned history books. . . .

Hegel felt, however, that the battle for the Germanic gods was lost:

> The project of restoring to a nation an imagery once lost was already doomed to failure; and on the whole it was bound to be even less fortunate than Julian's* attempt to inculcate the mythology of his forefathers. . . . Is Judaea, then, the Teutons' fatherland? . . .[84]

If a thinker of Hegel's stature succumbed like this to the prevailing Germanomania, less solid personalities were easily carried a good deal further. The Catholic publicist Görres (1776-1848) held that Germanic sap had biologically revivified moribund Latinity:

> Constantly renewed waves of Germanic blood spread through the arteries of the Italian people and as a result of this transfusion all that was exhausted, worn out, corrupt and lifeless was swept away and replaced by young and vital lymph; the old decrepit body was thus re-animated for centuries, regenerated and filled with life. . . .[85]

In the Hegelian school, and particularly among the young revolutionaries who were eager to outstrip their teacher, ideas of this kind enjoyed differing fortunes. The atheist humanist, Ludwig Feuerbach (1804-1872), whom Marx reproached for dealing only with "abstract man", certainly refrained from categorizing different kinds of blood or race and from differentiating between civilized men and savages. (Even the human stomach was for him a "universal essence" different from the stomach of beasts. He thought this was established by the

---

* The Apostate.

fact that, unlike the animals, man is omnivorous.)[86] In Feuerbach, the Germanomania of his student days was only aroused, if at all, in a spirit of conciliation, as when he contrasted a philosophic principle which was masculine and essentially German, with a feminine principle which was essentially French[87]—a theme which, as we shall see, had an irresistible attraction for the Germans.

By contrast, the anarchist Max Stirner (1806-1856) urged his contemporaries to conquer a heaven reserved for "Caucasians" alone. His strategical analysis remained more or less Hegelian:

> The history of the world, whose shaping properly belongs altogether to the Caucasian race, seems till now to have run through two Caucasian ages, in the first of which we had to work out and work off our innate *Negroidity*; this was followed in the second by *Mongoloidity* (Chineseness), which must likewise be terribly made an end of.

This violence, as Stirner made clear in his book *Der Einzige und sein Eigentum* (*The Ego and His Own*), must be deployed in the first instance against established beliefs. "Nevertheless the point aimed at, often as it may vanish at every new attempt, is the real, complete downfall of heaven." But such a plan could not be carried out unless "heaven-storming men of the Caucasian blood throw off their Mongolian skin" since "the consciousness of sin was our Mongolian torment that lasted thousands of years."[88]

We now reached the instructive case of Karl Marx and Friedrich Engels, who wanted to put Hegelianism "on its feet". Here one immediately breathes a different air. Yet the founders of "scientific socialism" were bound to place civilized men, morally and intellectually, on a higher level than savages, precisely because they accepted the practical verdict of science in their time. They did not always draw the same conclusions from that science, and this led them on occasion into controversy with one another. As a result, their case is doubly instructive.

It was clear to both Engels and Marx that the white race, as the bearer of progress, was more gifted than all the other races. In his *Dialectics of Nature*, for instance, Engles wrote that "the lowest savages" could revert to "an animal-like condition". A more detailed consideration, supported by references to Hegel and Lamarck, led him to conclude that the Blacks were congenitally incapable of understanding mathematics[89]. At least he refrained from establishing hierarchies from the

European peoples, and he placed the Semites and Aryans, whom he recognized as the two most advanced races, on the same level.[90]

Marx's thought, on the other hand, was influenced by the hierarchies of the Germanomaniacs, and this was in no sense exceptional among German Jews at that time. In 1865, he became interested in the views of a certain Duchinski, according to whom the Russians were of Mongol origin, and he concluded: "They are not Slavs, and therefore they do not belong to the Indogermanic race. They are intruders and must be thrown back beyond the Dnieper."[91] The next year, he thought he had discovered the scientific explanation for the superiority of Europeans over Russians in the book of a French traveller, Pierre Trémaux, which he recommended to Engels in the following terms: "In practical and historical application, Trémaux is far richer and more important than Darwin. Thus certain questions, such as nationality, etc., he explains simply on a natural basis."[92]

This natural basis or "environment" was the geological structure of the soil. Trémaux affirmed categorically that in Africa the white man became black and vice versa.[93] "Go on and mingle together, transform yourselves, O nations; unless the environment changes there will always be Englishmen on the Thames, Frenchmen in France, Romans on the Tiber, Egyptians in Egypt and Negroes in Africa, Red Indians in America, etc. The extent of the change demands more or less time, that is all".[94]

After this Marx thought he understood that it was "because of the geological formation which predominates in Russia [that] the Slav is becoming tartarized and mongolized".[95] Engels, however, preferred to stick to Darwin and denied that Trémaux's theory had any value whatever. He openly ridiculed it. "How does this person explain that we Rhinelanders on our secondary Devonian mountains (which long before the formation of coal were no longer covered by the sea) have not long ago been turned into idiots or niggers"?[96] But Marx returned to the charge: what did errors of fact amount to if the philosophical principle was the right one?

> The fundamental idea of Trémaux about the *influence of the soil* (though he naturally does not take account of the historical modifications of this influence; and among these historical modifications I would place even the chemical transformation of the earth's crust by agriculture, etc.) this idea, I believe, has only to be enunciated in order to acquire once and for all its rightful place in science, and this quite apart from Trémaux's exposition.[97]

I

This geo-racial determinism, which convinced Marx of the inferiority of the Blacks or of the Russians, was not easily applicable to the wandering race of the Jews. Nevertheless unlike Engels, who in this respect was the better Marxist, Marx shared the increasing prejudice of his century against the Semitic race. In his work on *The Jewish Question* this intolerance was still muted by Hegelian dialectic but in his description of his friend and rival, Ferdinand Lassalle, all his prejudices and all the fury of vulgar racism seem to have combined:

> I now see clearly that he is descended, as the shape of his head and his hair clearly indicate, from the Negroes who were joined to the Jews at the time of the exodus from Egypt (unless it was his mother or paternal grandmother who mated with a Negro). But this mixture of Judaism and Germanism with a Negro substance as a base was bound to yield a most curious product. The importunity of the man also is negroid. . . . One of the great discoveries of this Negro, which he confided to me, is that the Pelasgians are descended from the Semites. His main proof is that, according to the Book of Maccabees, the Jews sent messengers to Greece to ask for help and appealed to their tribal relationship. . . .[98]

Lassalle at least endeavoured to dignify his Semitic ancestors by affiliating them to the Pelasgians. As to Marx, his anti-Jewish obsession can no doubt be adequately explained by psychoanalysis,[99] though it is worth adding that the history of ideas in his case also leads back to the original confusion between social classes and historic races. Marx elaborated his ideas about class war and the mission of the proletariat, at least as far as his historical vision was concerned, under the influence of French historians and notably Augustin Thierry.[100] When, in his *The Jewish Question*, he confused Judaism with the *bourgeoisie* of his time, he was giving vent to resentment of a quite different order from that of the Romantic champions of the "Gallo-Roman race"; but he was guilty of the same kind of methodological error.

Marx did, however, in principle consider the mode of existence (culture) more important than biological essence (nature). One can also see two contrasting sides to him: the more racist Marx of the letters, where he opened his heart as a man and a son of his age (in one of his letters he referred to the "sexual swinishness of the savages")[101] and the universalist Marx of the philosophical and sociological writings, for whom all the natural differences of the species were to disappear in the socialist city of the future.[102]

Theoretically speaking, it would appear equally wrong to call Schopenhauer racist, yet no author did more to popularize the Manichean distinction between "Aryanism" and "Semitism" in Germany. It is true that this contemporary of Hegel and of Oken did not as yet use these terms. In the main, he emphasized the opposition, as he understood it, between the two types of religious thought. And in placing the origin of the white race in India and in attributing true wisdom to the Indians alone, he went no further than the Romantic mythologists whose works we have already considered. Far more radical was the way he dissociated the Old from the New Testament. He endowed the New Testament with Indian origins: and the imagery he employed was seductive:

> Just as ivy in search of support entwines itself around a thick prop, adjusts itself to its contours and exactly follows its shape, though it retains its own life and its particular charms, and looks most attractive, so Christian doctrine issuing from the wisdom of India has covered over the old trunk of gross Judaism, which is completely dissimilar to itself. What has been preserved of the fundamental form of the latter is something entirely different, something true and living which has been transformed by this doctrine. The trunk looks the same but is quite different.
>
> The Creator outside the world, which he has made out of nothing, is identified with the Saviour and through him with mankind; he is mankind's representative, it was redeemed by him as it had been lost in Adam, since when it has been enchained by the bonds of sin, corruption, suffering and death. For this is the attitude of Christianity as it is of Buddhism. The world can no longer be seen in the light of Jewish optimism which found that "all is well". No, rather is it the devil who now calls himself "prince of this world". . . .[103]

Schopenhauer had adopted the Spanish proverb: "*Detrás de la cruz está el Diablo*". This theology was remarkably successful in Germany. So it was the devil who had won the day. Schopenhauer initiated his public into the mystique of anti-semitism and cursed the hold which Jewish ideas had in the West, asphyxiated by a *foetor Judaicus*, the Jewish putrescence—by which he meant, in philosophical terms, belief in the goodness and rationality of Creation as well as in free will.[104] He proposed to leave these ideas "to the synagogues and philosophical assemblies which are not fundamentally so different",[105] though the Jews were much worse than the Hegelians.[106] His eschatology resembled that of Gobineau in that the Indians of long ago represented in his eyes "the most noble and the most ancient of peoples",[107] whose great virtues he set as an example before his decadent contemporaries. For Schopenhauer as for Gobineau man was "the wickedest of animals".[108] Nevertheless, in spite of his metaphysical pessimism, he did not exclude the possibility of the regeneration of the West. "We may hope", he wrote, "that Europe will free itself some day of all Jewish mythology. Perhaps the century is approaching when the peoples of Japhetic stock, originating in Asia, will find the sacred relics of their native land, because, after going astray for so long, they have reached sufficient maturity for this."[109]

Before long these aspirations and views began to attract followers, and from 1850 onwards Richard Wagner echoed them. The idea of a German-Christian mission gained ground even more rapidly and gave rise to an increasing number of esoteric sects and Aryan cults of every description. As shown in the first part of this book, this typically German phenomenon was derived from an age-old tradition. But henceforth it developed in a socio-political context which made the myth of domination of the community by the Jews or by Jewish ideas seem more credible. The patriotic exaltation of the Napoleonic wars, the glorification of the Germanic language, religion and blood found a fertile breeding ground in the universities and in revolutionary circles which dreamed of a united Germany from which aliens were to be excluded, i.e. the *Welsche* and the Jews who were already boycotted by most of the student corporations. As a result, along with the suspicions of the authorities and their repression of the students' agitation, criticisms and sarcasm soon began to be heard from the Jews, as they found themselves threatened immediately after their emancipation, by further discriminatory measures. In 1817, students and professors who had assembled to celebrate the third centenary of the Reformation burned two symbols of an imagined coalition of the enemy—a corporal's baton and a pamphlet entitled "Germanomania" by a certain Saul Ascher.[110] Soon afterwards far more redoubtable controversialists such as Ludwig Börne and Heinrich Heine joined the fray with their gibes about the Germans emerging from Tacitus's forests, about the virtues of the holy water of baptism and other sacred objects. For this reason, they figured among the principal instigators of a politico-literary opposition group which adopted the name of "Young Germany" but which was described by its adversaries as "Young Palestine".[111] The exclusiveness of the Germano-Christians constituted a powerful stimulus to the critical and contentious tendencies of a marginal minority which was forced to side with the pacifist, internationalist and above all anti-racist camp. In the eyes of their enemies they naturally seemed to incarnate the opposition which indeed was partly under their leadership. In the end the "Semitic race" came to be seen as an "anti-race" (*Gegenrasse*).

The result was a strong outcry, during the whole of the nineteenth century, for the withdrawal of civic rights from the Jews. The dispute which reached a climax between 1815 and 1830 was the counterpart of the French dispute about the two races. Like the latter it was supported by arguments (or pretexts) of an economic kind. If, according to Saint-Simon, financial power in France was in the hands of the Gauls,* a chorus of voices was raised in Germany to deplore the mortmain by which the Jews kept their hands on this same source of power. What Karl Marx wrote in his *The Jewish Question* merely echoed a widespread opinion. This turn of events influenced the historical and anthropological doctrines of the age. Consequently the Jews—who may once more be compared to the "Gauls" in that they were the ones to fight wholeheartedly for equality of rights—were allotted an especially important place in "Germanic" thinking. As Ludwig Börne wrote about 1830, "some reproach me for being a Jew, others praise me for it, still others forgive me for it but all are thinking about it . . . they are all fascinated by the magic Jewish circle, no one can escape from it . . .".[112]

*   *   *

It only remains for us to examine some of the anthropological systems, both simple and complex, which were elaborated in Germany in the middle of the nineteenth century.

Oken's theory of symbols was adopted and developed by a prodigiously erudite philosopher-physician, Carl Gustav Carus (1789-1869), who wrote on subjects ranging from gynaecology (a term which he introduced into Germany) to painting (which was a hobby of his). In his *Psyche* (1846) Carus developed a theory of unconscious life which anticipated psychoanalysis (and more particularly the "analytic psychology" of C. G. Jung). Some remarkable insights are to be found there along with a theosophy of the Unconscious; for this late Romantic the Unconscious was the point where the *Idea* takes root in human beings, and he attributed a divine nature to it. Incidentally, Carus distinguished between an "objective" or "divine"

---

* Cf. above p. 32.

point of view according to which an infusorium was a being as perfect as man, and a "subjective" or "human" attitude which placed man above the infusorium and above all other living beings.[113]

Soon after this, Carus published an essay on "the inequality of the intellectual capacities of human races" which was followed by other writings on this theme,[114] in all of which he adopted a resolutely human standpoint. It was in this connexion that he defined his theory of symbolism. The universe was for him a unique organism endowed with a soul, while man was "the symbol of the divine idea of this soul". In the beginning, therefore, there existed this soul or Idea which gradually took on material form and gave birth first to interstellar ether and then to the solar system and the planet Earth. The latter in turn, proceeding from one metamorphosis to another, fulfilled its end and asserted its value by forming man, "the final and supreme goal of all the metamorphoses of the formation of this earth".[115] Now it was well known that there existed varieties of men, some fairer and others darker; Carus took this to be a reflection of the degree of "their interior illumination". The illumination of the earth was also variable and, as every phenomenon had its symbolic meaning, he deduced that the four great races must be the races of dawn (yellow), day (white), sunset (red) and night (black). These races were related to bodily organs, as they were for Oken though in a different manner. The yellow race represented for Carus the stomach, the Whites the brain, the Red Indians the lungs, and the Blacks the genitals. He tried to support these resemblances by highlighting the greater fecundity of the Blacks (whom he compared to the proletarians in this respect) and the more highly developed brain of the aristocratic race of Whites.

On this question of brainpower, Carus was able to use comparative tables and to propose a further set of symbols introducing a hierarchy among Europeans. The Germans, for instance, had the broadest skulls. The Italians were the most artistic, the French the most eloquent, the English were men of action, while his compatriots were endowed with the highest intellectual capacity.[116] He was able to support the superiority of his nation's genius by citing both the number of illustrious men which Germany had produced, from Luther to Goethe and Hegel, and by the case of Georges Cuvier "whose German origins rather than his name (which was changed from *Küfer* into Cuvier) are proved by the great size of his head, and whose German mould of thought is clear from the evidence of his works".

Carus wrote for specialists and he refrained from drawing political conclusions from his system. The case of Wolfgang Menzel (1799-1873), a more popular writer, was quite different. He was one of those chauvinistic students who, in Heine's phrase, "even when they have taken off their old-German vest cling to their old-German pants".[117] In his *Geist der Geschichte* (1835), Menzel began with the dialectic of slavery and liberty with which he established cosmic similarities.[118] Was not the earth a "slave" in relation to the sun, though "free" in relation to the stars? Man, in Menzel's view, was both slave and free and he took part in the cosmic relationship in that he was more free in the North, where he stood under the polar star, than in the South, where he found himself in the sun's axis. The conclusions, as far as inhabitants of the tropics are concerned, seemed obvious. With regard to the yellow races, they were intermediate, and Menzel, who considered them old and "etiolated", subordinated them to the moon, a dead star. Having established this premise he was not too particular about how he worked out the results. According to the demands of controversy and of the political situation, he submitted the Latin peoples, and particularly the French, to the slavery of the sun. His opinion varied with regard to the Jews whom he likened at first to the Germans,[119] but whom he eventually considered the most dangerous "ferments of decomposition". Moreover, Menzel delighted in visions of an apocalyptic kind:

> Man breaks the horizontal line of natural history in turning himself vertically towards the ideal world. Hence the clash between the eternal and the temporal, a struggle without end. It will last forever and will ever become more magnificent but we shall perish in the fight. Not on earth but in the world above shall we celebrate our victory.

Little by little he abandoned his cosmic speculations to throw himself whole-heartedly into militant Germanomania. In 1853 he reproached Carus for having written that the Germans were a people of thinkers. It was not so; they were better than that.

> Today, Herr Carus affirms that the English are the men of action and that we remain a people of thinkers. Both these affirmations are false. Whatever is operative in the English, as in the French, does not derive from their Celtic but from their Germanic elements. In the course of the Christian Middle Ages, as in Pagan Antiquity, there was no more active people than the German people. . . .[120]

This activity was evidenced by the expansion of the Germans. Intensi-
fying his eulogy of German military virtues, Menzel ended up by
confronting them with the rest of the world. If the French, English
or Italians were ever able to stand up to the Germans it was thanks to
their French, Saxon or Lombard blood:

> We Germans were in the past the leading people of Europe,
> we were the most warlike people ever to have existed on earth.
> We dismembered the world empire of the Romans, we conquered
> all Europe and founded new empires, we pushed back the Muslim
> hordes, we established the Holy Germanic Empire and our
> emperor held first place throughout the entire world. . . .

It was on this note that Menzel set out to demolish "the pedantic
lie to the effect that the Germans were no more than a people of
thinkers".[121]

The bipolar principle was developed in an altogether different way
by Gustav Klemm (1802-1867), an author who was reputed for his
scientific learning and avoided political controversy. A century ago,
Klemm's *General History of Civilization* was considered authoritative
by all cultivated Germans.

Without going into detailed speculation, Klemm assumed that
"humanity in its entirety is, like man, one being which is divided into
two parts each necessary to the other, the active and the passive part,
the male and the female".[122] In his view these two parts were of
equal value and in the last resort they tended to fuse:

> I see in this fusion of active and of passive races which were
> originally separate, the realization of the purpose which is pursued
> by nature in all the domains of its organic creation. Just as the male
> or female individual, once isolated, does not conform to nature's
> purpose, so a people which is made up only of members of the
> active or members of the passive race remains imperfect and in-
> complete. . . . It is only by mingling the two races, the active
> and the passive, by the marriage of peoples if I may put it thus,
> that humanity is completed, it is only thus that it awakens to life
> and brings forth the flowers of culture. . . .[123]

The world, however, is so constituted that men conceive a better
opinion of themselves than they do of women, and the nineteenth
century pushed this tendency to extremes. In reading the observations
of Gustav Klemm, we learn that "the character of passive humanity is
gentle and patient, pliant through weakness and tolerant through

idleness".[124] This passive humanity, which was native to the plains, had been conquered by "active humanity", which had swooped down from the mountains and raped it. "Just as the hard crust of the earth is strained and broken by volcanic forces, so the peaceful and primitive populations spread over the earth were taken unawares, while engaged in their pacific dreams, by the heroes of the active race who fell upon them."[125] The active peoples were distinguishable from the passive peoples by "their love of freedom, their great courage, their awareness of their human dignity and of their human rights, by their sense of poetry and their love of power".[126] To these masculine attributes were added forms of bodily beauty of which the Apollo Belvedere was the ideal. There was no mention of Venus in relation to the feminine and passive race. The latter, according to Klemm, included not only the coloured peoples but also the Slavs and especially the Russians, with the exception of their "ruling class". As to the "mass of common and servile people their state resembles that of the Blacks. . . . The serfs display the signs of their passive origin in their ample cheek-bones, their eyes which are small and slanting, their thick flat noses and their dark or livid complexion."[127] Klemm included the Latins among the active races, although the German tribes, numerically inferior, "had always vanquished them, thus demonstrating their moral and intellectual superiority". It was to the Germanic tribes that Providence "seemed to have entrusted the task of watching over the progress of the human race, since it is they who occupy all the Christian thrones of Europe".[128] This argument was very popular then and was parodied by Heine as follows: "We Germans are the most powerful and intelligent of peoples. Our princely dynasties sit on all the thrones of Europe, our Rothschilds control all stock markets of the world, our scientists dominate all the sciences; we have invented gunpowder and printing. . . ."[129]

In the end, it was this doctrine which was adopted by German public opinion, perhaps for no other reason than that the symbolism of masculine and feminine races had always been the one most widely used throughout the world, and that in the nineteenth century it became the corner-stone of anthropology. Thus Lippert stated in 1886, in his *History of Civilization*, that the distinction between active and passive races was generally adopted because it "was in line with the facts".[130] This division between a masculine and a feminine principle can be found in the works of Carlyle, who used it to point out the contrast between Germans and Latins; and in those of Bismarck, who used it to distinguish the Germans from the Slavs and the Celts. But it was carried to the furthest extremes by the young Viennese philosopher, Otto Weininger (1880-1904): he differentiated Aryans from Semites on the basis of this doctrine, and later committed suicide. "He was the only Jew fit to live" was how Hitler described him.[131]

CHAPTER ELEVEN

THE ARYAN EPOCH

THE TYRANNY OF LINGUISTICS

Although the Biblical account of creation had already been called in doubt by the great discoveries in the sixteenth century, it was not until the nineteenth century that the universe was recognized as being apparently infinite both in time and space. Charles Lyell was still criticized in about 1835, as Buffon had been in 1760, for proclaiming that the world had existed for more than 6,000 years. Progress in a number of different branches of knowledge, from geology to archaeology, rapidly undermined nearly all the old beliefs. As a result, the origin of the human race was pushed back indefinitely and the study of man was pursued along quite different lines. Anthropology achieved the status of an independent science from about 1860. France led the way when, in 1859, Geoffroy Saint-Hilaire, Quatrefages and Paul Broca founded the *Société d'anthropologie de Paris*. Scientists in other capitals followed suit, beginning with London, Moscow and Madrid in 1863, though there were occasional difficulties—for example the controversies in England or the early demise of the Spanish society. In the course of these polemics, Dr John Hunt, the president of the Anthropological Society, declared that anthropology was feared and persecuted because it had declared the theological and political utopias of equality and fraternity to be false.[1] No doubt the methods of the new science, especially in France, tended to be experimental and quantitative and therefore seemed materialist or even anti-Christian. But on closer examination it became clear that, however dependent it was on the use of balances, compasses and other instruments of measurement, its main tenets were based on existing branches of knowledge, especially linguistics. Thus the division between Aryans and Semites was accepted as dogma by the majority of researchers. By about 1860 this conviction was already a part of the intellectual baggage of all cultivated Europeans.

Marcelin Berthelot is an example. In 1863, when discussing scientific methods, he referred to "the symbolic language of our ancestors, the Aryes and the Hellenes".[2] During the same year, Hippolyte Taine glorified "the ancient Aryan people . . . [which] in its languages, religions, literatures and philosophies, shows that a common blood and spirit linked all its offshoots".[3] The debates in the *Anthropological Society* of London show that, from the very year of its foundation, the term Aryan was in general use. In 1871 Darwin in his *Descent of Man* accepted the classification, though he expressed some doubts about the "racial unity" of Aryans and Semites. Nietzsche in Germany, in his earliest work the *Birth of Tragedy*, which also dates from 1871, distinguished between an Aryan and a Semitic essence which were symbolized respectively by the Promethean Myth and by Adam's Fall, or by the ideas of sacrilege and of sin. In Germany, the term Aryan was less common since the words Germanic or Indo-Germanic were often used instead. This was the case in Gustav Freytag's series of novels called *Die Ahnen* or Felix Dahn's *Die Könige der Germanen*. Anti-semitic propaganda, when using scientific arguments, liked to contrast the "Indo-Germanic" race with the Semitic to the advantage of the former. Articles under the heading *Arier* were included in the big popular encyclopaedias of Brockhaus and Meyer from 1864 and 1867 respectively, and the *Arier* is defined from the start as Indo-Germanic. The 14th edition of *Brockhaus* states specifically that it is better to apply the term *Arier* only to "Asian Aryans" and to use the term Indo-Germanic or Indo-European to describe the "European Aryans".

It will be seen that, in its original form, the belief in Aryan origins presupposed a twofold article of faith: Europeans are members of the Aryan race, and this race is derived from the high plateau of Asia. In the event, the first of these ideas, that of an origin distinct from the Jews, proved to be far more tenacious (more "resistant" in the psycho-analytical sense) than the second, that of an Asiatic origin. This latter belief was questioned by the majority of scientists from the end of the century. One of these, the English philologist Isaac Taylor, at the end of his book on *The Origin of the Aryans*, rejoiced in the overthrow of the "ancient tyranny of the Sanskritists".[4] This brings us to the un-doubtedly tyrannical influence of linguistics on anthropology. It was not merely in the mid-twentieth century, in the era of structural anthropology, but throughout the nineteenth century, in the wake of romantic orientalism, that linguistics imposed its methods and authority on the other sciences of man. Anthropologists were aware of this ascendancy. Some found it deplorable while others thought it legiti-mate; and their comments are not without interest if only because they show that difficulties and misunderstandings in the relations between the sciences are nothing new.

In 1862, Paul Broca, the leading anthropologist of the "physical" school in France which developed the work of Cabanis and Bichat, noted that

> the linguistic specialists have one great advantage over us: they can do without us whereas we cannot do without them. . . . We are, therefore, the vassals of linguistics and grateful vassals; but we must not be, we cannot be, its slaves.

Broca regarded the Aryan theory as probably, but not certainly, true,

> Hitherto the philologists in seeking to establish the origins of our races and languages, have discovered probabilities but nothing definite, and in the present state of our knowledge I am afraid that the names which have been advanced as a substitute for that of Indo-Europeans are statements of theory rather than of fact.

In view of this, Broca regarded the use of the term *Aryan races* as "perfectly scientific" though he described its counterpart—the expression *Semitic races*—as a "gross error" and found good reasons for proposing the neologism *Hebroids* to indicate "the peoples who by their physical conformation, their language, their intellectual and moral character, their traditions and their histories, are naturally grouped around the Hebrew people".[5] However, his authority was not great enough to ensure that the Arab peoples were included in the Hebroid group.

A similar suspicion with regard to the decisions of the philologists may be observed in the works of a great pioneer of cultural anthropology, Edward B. Tylor (1832-1917). "A man's language is no full and certain proof of his parentage", he wrote. "Much bad anthropology has been made by thus carelessly taking language and race as though they went always and exactly together." But, in spite of his caution, Tylor succumbed to the common mistake—when describing the Gypsies—of referring to "our Aryan forefathers".[6] He gives the impression of writing as a scientist in the first case and using the language of his time in the second. The same impression is derived from a manual by Broca's pupil Paul Topinard (1830-1911), called *l'Anthropologie*. He was the first influential writer to suggest that the French were not "Aryans by blood, but a mixture of races superimposed on one another". Nevertheless, this did not prevent him, when describing the congenital or "physiological" lack of aptitude of coloured peoples for "counting beyond 2, 3, or 5", from contrasting them with "the so-called Aryan races which have a great aptitude for mathematics".[7] When making this comparison he clearly regarded the French as being collectively Aryans.

The most interesting comments about the influence of linguistics on anthropology are to be found in the work of the German Theodor Waitz (1821-1864), whose book *Anthropologie der Naturvölker* had a double claim to originality in its day: it did not use the expression "Aryan race" and it questioned whether Europeans were in any way superior to primitive peoples. Waitz justified the influence of linguistics on two grounds. On the one hand, he pointed out that the characteristics of language are more stable than racial or ethno-racial qualities and thus provided a more reliable guide to historical continuity. On the other hand, he considered that the methods of comparative philology had reached a higher degree of exactitude than those of physical anthropology, especially craniology. Proof of this superiority was furnished, in his view, by the relative agreement among the students of linguistics as to the main results of their science, while the physical anthropologists, when dealing with the human races, seemed engaged in a general affray. In a word, the strength of the philologers was in their unity.[8]

Another German anthropologist, Adolf Bastian (1826-1905), looked with favour on the "tyranny of the Sanskritists". Anticipating Teilhard de Chardin, he wrote:

> Taking into consideration the fact that civilized peoples are in the course of developing spiritually towards an unquantifiable end, all classifications depending on the corporeal are bound to be sterile and contradictory. Philology, with its auxiliary branches, replaces craniology (applicable to primitive peoples).[9]

Bastian himself dealt at length with the nomadic Aryans, as ancestors of the "civilized peoples", though the quest for their "cradle of origin" seemed to him to be derived from a mythology "in no way superior to that of the Zulus, who believe that the nomads of South Africa emerged one after another out of a cave".

Bastian's famous compatriot, Rudolf Virchow, stressed the usefulness of craniology and the study of other physical characteristics. Without such data, he wrote, soon after the war of 1870-1871, "decisions on the ethnical situation of peoples will be placed unquestionably in the hands of the linguists". The latter in their purism had originally postulated "pure" races, which was indefensible in anthropology, and now they were introducing politics into the debate by relating both Aryans (like the Celts) and non-Aryans (like the Sardinians and Iberians) to the same Latin race, thus confusing races, nations and languages. "Language may nationalize and de-nationalize", he concluded, "but it cannot be an indication of blood-relationship."[10]

We must now examine more closely the raw material which the philologists provided for their vassals, the anthropologists, the prehistorians and the archaeologists. We have already seen what happened to Ernest Renan and Max Müller, the two great popularizers of the Aryan theory. A host of minor writers who followed displayed their linguistic imperialism even more crudely. Let us take the examples of F.-G. Bergmann (1812-1895), for whom the origins of "the primitive peoples of Japheth's race" should be investigated by "sciences which are part physical and part philosophical"—by which he obviously meant the sciences of language[11]; or of his Belgian colleague, Honoré Chavée (1815-1877), who thought he had scientifically demonstrated "by the facts of the natural history of language, the essential differences in mental constitution and therefore in cerebral organization" between Aryans and Semites.[12] The philologist A.-F. Pott, whom we have mentioned before, was prompted by his reading of Gobineau to write an essay on the *Inequality of human races, especially from the point of view of philological science, based on a consideration of the work of Count Gobineau which bears the same title.* He thus contributed to the posthumous fame of the latter.[13] Other scientists who seemed to show no interest in the question of human origins revealed their uncritical acceptance of the Aryan myth. The great linguist August Schleicher (1821-1868), for example, after summarizing in a few lines J. Grimm's thesis about "successive waves of immigrants", drew the following conclusion: "We must, therefore, look to the highlands of central Asia to find the homeland of the original Indo-Germanic people."[14] This laconic phrase was itself part and parcel of those "assertions of the linguistic experts [who], on this as on other subjects, have influenced the judgements of anthropologists which were no sooner formulated than they were in turn appealed to by these experts"— to paraphrase a pertinent analysis by the archaeologist, Joseph Reinach, of the way in which this "oriental mirage" was formed.[15]

An altogether different case was that of the Genevan philologer, Adolphe Pictet, who was clearly influenced by Renan and who, in turn, influenced Max Müller.[16] In his voluminous *Essai de paléontologie linguistique* published in 1859, Pictet showed himself to be particularly well informed about the *primitive Aryas* whose origin he situated in Iran:

> In a period before all historical knowledge, which is lost in the darkness of time, a whole race, destined by Providence to reign one day supreme over the entire earth, grew up slowly in the primitive cradle, preparing for a brilliant future. Favoured above all others by nobility of blood and the gift of intelligence, in a natural setting which was beautiful but harsh and which yielded up its riches without lavishing them, this race was destined from the outset to create by its labours the basis of a lasting industrial organization, which would raise it above the elementary necessities of life. From this there emerged an early development of thought. . . .

This was followed by a hundred pages of philological speculation at the end of which Pictet summarized his ideas as follows:

> . . . this was the race of the Aryas, who were endowed from the beginning with the very qualities which the Hebrews lacked, to become the civilizers of the world; and nowhere does the evidence for a providential plan emerge more clearly than in the parallel courses of these two contrasting streams, one of which was destined to absorb the other. The difference between the two races could not be more marked. . . . The religion of Christ, destined to be the torch of humanity, was adopted by the genius of Greece and propagated by the power of Rome, while Germanic energy gave it new strength, and the whole race of European Aryas, under its beneficent influence, and by means of endless conflict, raised itself little by little to the level of modern civilization. . . . It is thus that the race of the Aryas, more favoured than any other, was to become the main instrument of God's plan for the destiny of mankind.[17]

Pictet tended to confuse the Aryan race, in its capacity as an instrument of God's plan, with the Christian people. This confusion was not unusual at the time. Renan, in 1882, gave it the support of his authority when he wrote that "the view that Christianity is the most genuine form of the Aryan religion is to a great extent true". And he added: "St Bernard, Francis of Assisi, St Teresa, Francis of Sales, Vincent de Paul, Fénélon, Channing . . . are people of our race; they feel with our hearts and think with our brains."[18] This idea was developed more directly and more ingenuously in 1867 by the treasurer of the Anthropological Society of London, the Rev. Dunbar Heath. In a book entitled *On the Great Race-Elements in Christianity*, this parson endeavoured to show that "all Aryan mythologies delight in depicting the descent of gods upon earth to combat evil. . . . The Aryan spirit considers law to be evil and supports the rights of conscience." The Semitic race had proclaimed in its day that Jesus was the Devil while the Aryan race continued to revere him as God. This race had elaborated the doctrine of the Trinity—a concept far removed from "all the instincts of the Semites". In conclusion, Heath declared that "Christianity is a religion derived principally from Aryan sources . . . being professed by Aryans now and not being professed by Semites now" and being "in a fair and full sense of the word a truly Aryan religion".[19]

Already in 1867, this obscure ecclesiastic, like the child in the Andersen fairy-tale, revealed the core of the problem. It would take professional scholars several generations to become aware of the king's nakedness, and it is by no means certain that they are all agreed about it even now.

ARYANISM AND THE FRANCO-PRUSSIAN WAR

The head of the French school of anthropology, Armand de Quatrefages, shared the general agreement about the Aryan origins of the Europeans.[20] During the siege of Paris he witnessed the Prussian army's bombardment of the civil population and scientific institutions. He at once tried to explain this conduct, unworthy of a civilized people, in terms of anthropology. Such barbarity, he wrote in about February 1871,[21] could only be attributed to the existence, postulated a short time before by Swedish scholars, of the primitive inhabitants in northeastern Europe who had preceded the Aryans. Far from being real Germans, the Prussians, from the anthropological point of view, were *Finns* or *Slavo-Finns*, that is to say "men who preceded all history" and contemporaries of the period when "there lived in Europe the rhinoceros and the elephant, the reindeer and musk-ox". They had retained "a truly national imprint" of their past:

> The Finn will never forgive an insult whether real or imagined. He will avenge himself at the first opportunity without showing any scruple as to his choice of means. This explains the numerous murders which take place among the peasants who belong to this race.

This made everything clear. "Not content with subjecting the Germans to the Slavo-Finns, Germany has adopted the hatreds and furthered the instincts of those whom she has appointed her leaders." This was the real explanation of the bombardment of the Museum of Paris and the burning of the Strasbourg Library in particular, for "nowhere was the black hatred of the Finns, the jealous hatred of the semi-barbarian for a superior civilization, more clearly displayed". After this Europe must expect some dark days in the future. "Will the Slavo-Finns now want to dominate the Latins as well as the Germans? And will the world submit in silence to being divided in this way?"

For some time after the war, Quatrefages's theory met with a certain success in France. In 1872 an illustrated textbook by Louis Figuier called *Les Races Humaines* echoed his views. This writer, who continued to place the "Teutonic family" at the head of the human race, was of the opinion that Quatrefages had "proved scientifically" that the Prussians were not members of this family. "These Finns, the primitive inhabitants along the shores of the Baltic, were characterized by trickery and violence combined with a remarkable tenacity. Modern Prussians revive all these vices of their ancestors."[22] In Germany this "Finnish theory" naturally aroused indignation. The main newspapers took a hand in the affair and the *Kölnische Zeitung* accused Quatrefages of being an "ignorant naturalist" and a "learned liar". International scientific opinion was divided into two camps. But France was isolated. Italian and English scientists disagreed with Quatrefages who was supported only by his colleagues Hamy and Broca. The latter paid the Germans back in their own coin, stating that it was they who were the first "to excite racial patriotism, which was certainly more vigorous than ordinary patriotism, among the German nations".[23] Quatrefages was obliged to make a partial retreat. In his lectures in 1872, he declared that his objective had been a purely scientific one.

> No doubt I was not loath to remind the Germans that the Prussians are not their brothers. . . . But if Prussia had been as devoted a friend of France as she has shown herself to be an implacable enemy, I should have acted in the same way.[24]

Later, in his classic *Histoire générale des races humaines* Quatrefages was anxious to rehabilitate the *Finnish Race* which he classified as a special and ancient branch of the white race:

... the Finnish races have a special importance from several points of view. Since they derive from a past which is far more remote than that of the Aryans and the Semites, properly so called, and are probably contemporaries of the pre-Semites, their blood must have mingled with that of many other races which came after them. In any case, if only because they are the first-born, one cannot refuse them a place alongside their fellow races, even though the latter may have had a greater history.[25]

The scientific counter-attack was organized by the two outstanding figures in German anthropology, Adolf Bastian and Rudolf Virchow. The former, ironically, came to the defence of the Finns, those "poor orphans of anthropology" who had already been roughly handled by Gobineau in his *Essai*. There were no longer, declared Bastian, any Finns or Slavs in Prussia. They had been absorbed or destroyed by the advance of Germanism. "In the same way as the Indians, they have disappeared, like snow, beneath the rising sun of history . . .", and Bastian already relied on the great Darwinian argument: "The flood of Germans advancing towards the East had implacably rolled back the weaker race following the law of victory to the strongest, the law of the *struggle for existence*." It was no use being befogged by "Celto-Latin verbiage", especially in the nineteenth century when the Germanic people had become the standard-bearers of scientific culture in Europe. The Germans, he concluded, had built themselves a new dwelling in the eastern marches, and what their fathers had conquered the sons would be able to keep. "Prussia is a country of warriors; so it was and so it will remain as long as it is necessary to protect the marches of the East, but above all those of the West, against the trouble-makers."[26]

This martial tone mirrored the nationalist excitement which seized hold of Germany immediately after its reunification. Henceforth the old tendency to Germanomania was to combine with new patriotic responsibilities, and this combination gave birth to certain obligations which were considered imperative. We may recall the timid warning which Max Müller sounded in Strasbourg in 1872.[27] Even more significant was the disavowal by the Jewish historian, Heinrich Grätz. In 1868 Grätz had described the German people as "the German Michael" (a simple and harmless figure of German folklore), but in 1879 he retracted this opinion in the following terms:

Glorious victories, the unification and the success of Germany under brilliant leaders took place later. Earlier on, the German

people in general had the reputation of being like the German
Michael. . . . Though true before 1870, this judgement is now
false.[28]

A yet deeper symptom of the change of mental climate may be seen
in the cult of "blond virility". A careful study informs us that this is
a recent phenomenon which invaded German letters only after 1870-
1871.[29]

The second critic of Quatrefages was Rudolf Virchow (1821-1902).
He was a scholar of the widest learning and a deputy in the Reichstag.
As an anatomist and craniologist, Virchow's approach to the dispute
was a good deal more serious than Bastian's.

This science of "craniology" in the nineteenth century is worth considering briefly. On closer inspection it looks like an offshoot of the
"phrenology" of Lavater and Gall. It was when criticizing their views
around 1845 that the Swedish scientist, Andreas Retzius, introduced
the idea of a *cephalic index*. At that time he thought he had established
that it was the dolichocephalic peoples such as the Scandinavians, the
Germans, the English and the French who were "endowed with the
highest faculties of the mind". "Brachycephaly" was an indication of
a different origin which he described as Turanian, as distinguished
from Iranian or Aryan, and which was typical of retarded peoples
such as the Lapps, the Finns or Finno-Slavs and the Bretons.[30] The
theory of craniology, carried to a high pitch of sophistication by the
Paris school, was built around the concept of the cephalic index and
other indices which were gradually added to it. Extraordinary measur-
ing instruments, which mostly sprang from Broca's ingenious mind,
came into use in ever increasing numbers. All manner of special
characteristics, like the "complexity of cranial dentures" were put
forward as proof of the superiority of European skulls over those of
inferior races, and it was the common opinion that the wizards in Paris
could distinguish at a glance between a Roman, a Frankish and a
Saracenic skull.[31] Within the space of ten years, European science was
everywhere convinced that skulls would yield more accurately than
languages the information necessary to define human races, with their
respective qualities.

Virchow must have felt himself especially concerned since he was a
native of Pomerania, a region which had been germanized only in the
twelfth and thirteenth centuries. Thus, while he reproached Quatrefages for exclusivism and Prussophobia, he criticized him more in form
than in substance and seemed not to find his "Finnish hypothesis" in

the least extravagant.[32] But he wanted to make quite sure. The ink was barely dry on the Treaty of Frankfurt before this conscientious scholar called his colleagues together to form a commission "to establish a statistical record of the shapes of skulls throughout Germany, following a method to be formulated by the commission".[33] Their first idea was to measure the skulls of all soldiers, but the army chiefs refused to collaborate with Virchow and his friends. They were obliged to fall back on what were considered "associated" characteristics such as colour of hair, eyes and complexion. With this new approach, the enquiry was assisted not only by the German educational authorities but by those of Austria, Switzerland and Belgium.[34]

Questionnaires were sent to all the teachers in these countries, with the explanation that the theory that European peoples came from a common Asiatic country of origin was now open to doubt. According to a new hypothesis, the Indo-Germanic or Aryan immigration had encountered and mingled with an aboriginal population in Europe. The main weight of opinion favoured the view that the Aryans were blond and dolichocephalic, the natives dark and brachycephalic. Information about the distribution of the colour of eyes and hair in Europe would, it was hoped, show whether there was any truth in this assumption. Scientific accuracy required a careful examination of all children with the exception of Jews and foreigners. The questionnaire ended with an exhortation: "Teachers will not hesitate to make their contribution to a scientific enterprise whose purpose, like that of schools, is the gaining of self-knowledge; for the knowledge of our origins is an essential part of the study of our own human nature."[35]

The investigation assumed gigantic proportions, lasted more than ten years and involved something like fifteen million school-children. Meanwhile, the indefatigable Virchow had gone to Finland where he was able to establish that, contrary to the prevalent belief, the overwhelming majority of the Finns was blond.[36] In 1885, he communicated the general result of the enquiry to the Prussian Academy of Sciences. These results were "as decisive as they were surprising". The so-called French theory was demolished. The predominance of blond hair and blue eyes in northern Germany including the territory East of the Elbe showed that the people there were of essentially Germanic stock. In contrast with the Germanic migrations to the West and South — of Goths, Franks and Burgundians who were finally submerged by the native populations — those in the East had resulted in a definitive Germanization, "the formation of a new, purely German, Volkstum.

The fact that the dynasties of both the Hapsburgs and the Hohen-
zollerns should have had their real origins in that region is certainly
not without significance."[37] The Germano-Aryan honour of Prussia
was saved; and the patriots, who had been concerned by the threat
of the "Slav invasion", were satisfied.

Virchow, however, was far from being a chauvinist. As a political
man he fought against the rising tide of pan-Germanism and anti-
semitism; as a scientist he deplored the misuse of science for political
agitation and warned his colleagues: "The questions which we are
dealing with, when taken over by the people, soon become national
questions."[38] He restrained the racist enthusiasm of his friends at
various times. What is more, Virchow seems to have been the first
great scientist to suspect that "dolichocephaly", the new totem of the
Germanomaniacs, was a malleable and mutable standard and therefore
lacked all historic-anthropological value.[39] As time went by his faith
in craniology was shaken, though he did not completely abandon it:
in 1891, for example, he expressed an opinion on some skulls which
were dug up in Hungary—"similar to Aryan skulls. There is nothing
to prove that they do not belong to an Aryan people but, in any case,
they are not Mongolian and not Australian. I can be sure of that."[40]

On the Finnish-Slav front, French science had suffered a setback, but
the battle continued to rage in other sectors. The English philologist,
Isaac Taylor, described its vagaries in 1890:

> The question has been debated with needless acrimony. German
> scholars, notably Pösche, Penka, Hehn, and Lindenschmidt, have
> contended that the physical type of the primitive Aryans was that
> of the North Germans—a tall, fair, blue-eyed dolichocephalic race.
> French writers, on the other hand, such as Chavée, De Mortillet,
> and Ujvalfy, have maintained that the Aryans were brachy-
> cephalic, and that the true Aryan type is represented by the Gauls.
> The Germans claim the primitive Aryans as typical Germans
> who Aryanized the French, while the French claim them as
> typical Frenchmen who Aryanized the Germans. Both parties
> maintain that their own ancestors were the pure noble race of
> Aryan conquerors, and that their hereditary foes belonged to a
> conquered and enslaved race of aboriginal savages, who received
> the germs of civilization from their hereditary superiors. Each
> party accuses the other of subordinating the results of science to
> Chauvinistic sentiment.
> Thus Pösche, in somewhat inflated language, writes: "The true

scientific theory, which uplifts itself, calm and clear, like the summit of Olympus, over the passing storm-clouds of the moment, is that a noble race of fair-haired, blue-eyed people vanquished and subjugated an earlier race of short stature and dark hair. In opposition to this is the new French theory, without scientific foundation, originating in political hatred, which asserts that the primitive Aryans were a short and dark people, who Aryanized the tall fair race."

M. Chavée, on the other hand, contends that the intellectual superiority lies with the other race. Look, he says, at the beautifully formed head of the Iranians and Hindus, so intelligent and so well developed. Look at the perfection of those admirable languages, the Sanskrit and the Zend. The Germans have merely defaced and spoilt the beautiful structure of the primitive Aryan speech.

Ujvalfy says "if superiority consists merely in physical energy, enterprise, invasion, conquest, then the fair dolichocephalic race may claim to be the leading race in the world; but if we consider mental qualities, the artistic and the intellectual faculties, then the superiority lies with the brachycephalic race".

De Mortillet also is strong to the same effect. The civilisation of Europe is due, he contends, to the brachycephalic race.[41]

Taylor himself conferred the title of *primitive Aryans* on the "Ural-Altai Brachycephalics" to whom, by a series of hypotheses, he related the Finns and the Celts—which was at least proof of his originality. One idea that never occurred to him was that the Aryans might have been a figment of the imagination. This notion was expressed in 1892 by the archaeologist Salomon Reinach. "To speak of an Aryan race existing three thousand years ago", he wrote, "is to put forward a gratuitous hypothesis; to speak about it as though it still existed today is quite simply to talk nonsense."[42] But this statement was as little understood as the criticisms of Italian scientists, who referred to a "scientific myth", or the reflexions of another Jewish scholar, Siegmund Feist, who in 1915 developed the Italian idea as follows:

> The alleged Aryan origins may be safely compared to the fables about the origins of Troy which grew up in Rome in the second century before our era. That myth survived for a remarkably long time, since it was adopted by the Franks who by this means affiliated themselves to the Trojans. Let us hope that the Aryan myth, as it is still accepted today, will soon be replaced by a more reasonable and scientific conception of the past of European peoples.[43]

Feist's comparison could quite reasonably be carried even further since the Aryan myth, just like the Trojan, became an apple of discord between France and Germany. For the latter, the main development between 1871 and 1914 consisted in domiciling the Aryans in Germany or in Scandinavia. This operation was carried out under the cover of science, and was favoured by the natural prudence of real scientists like Virchow, Kollmann, Von Luschan and others who, by the end of the century, agreed that they knew less about the matter than they thought they did twenty years earlier; that the hopes of finding the ancestors of European peoples in India had vanished; even that, in fact, the Aryan race no longer existed.[44] Their doubts and scruples were drowned by the strident voices of such authors as Pösche, Penka and Kossina who, as Virchow observed sarcastically, "derived all civilized peoples, the Greeks, the Italians, etc. and, how could it be otherwise, the ancient Trojans too—from the prehistoric Germans".[45] This was the school of thought which was to become dominant in Germany in the twentieth century and which, in Hitlerism, abandoned any pretence at scientific impartiality. Let us listen to the observations of its most famous spokesman, the anthropologist Georg Heberer, about a prehistoric site in Thuringia:

> These stones are linked with one of the most significant phenomena of history, the birth of Indo-Germanism! That this German territory, this Germany should have been the homeland of the race which has been called to the highest cultural achievements cannot leave us, who are its heirs, indifferent. We cultivate a heritage which is indeed our own, which did not reach us from elsewhere, and did not come to us from the Orient. It was here that it was founded and here that it developed throughout the millennia. This truth faces us with obligations. . . . Once more, a new humanity is being established today, in the course of a titanic struggle in the heart of Europe. . . .[46]

By such means was the old Germanic tradition of "the creation of the self out of itself" perpetuated or renewed. It is worth noting that under the Third Reich it was the idea of Nordic man which commanded agreement rather than that of *Aryan man* or *Germanic man*. Indeed, the over-estimation of dolichocephalic blonds reached such a point that the Party authorities issued a circular ordering that the susceptibilities of swarthy Germans, or of those with round heads, should be spared.[47]

The far more complex anthropological debate which took place in

France at the end of the nineteenth century seemed to be a continuation of the Controversy about the Two Races. The Third Republic had undoubtedly chosen to be altogether Gallic, but it looked as though the rejected Germans were returning to the charge disguised as "dolicho-blonds". This at any rate seemed to be the implied attitude of Paul Topinard, Broca's successor, who was a firm supporter of the peaceful bourgeois Republic:

> The truth is as follows: the Gauls of which history speaks, from Brennus to Vercingetorix, were a people formed of two elements —the leaders or conquerors who were blond, tall, dolichocephalic, leptoprosopes, etc., and the mass of the people who were small, relatively brachycephalic, chamaeoprosopes. The brachycephalic were always oppressed; they were the victims of the dolicho-cephalics, who carried them off from their fields and forced them to follow their invasions, as at Delphi. The least unfortunate sought refuge, as poor and obscure people in the mountains. In time their fate changed. The blond people changed from warriors into merchants or industrial workers. The brachycephalics breathed again. Being naturally prolific, their numbers increased while the dolichocephalics naturally diminished. Today, in France among other countries, in Southern Germany, etc., they constitute the laborious, sober, farsighted, peace-loving and patriotic population. Must we not conclude that the future belongs to them?[48]

Let us now examine the views of Georges Vacher de Lapouge(1854-1936), the main champion of the dolicho-blond Franks. He was most despondent about the future of his country:

> The confusion of ideas runs deep. The failure of the Revolution is obvious. . . . [The Revolution] was above all a replacement of the dolicho-blonds by the brachycephalics as the holders of power. . . . The brachycephalics gained power by the Revolution and, as a result of democratic development, this power tends to be concentrated in the lower classes, those which are most brachy-cephalic. The Aryan, as I have defined him, is something quite different. He is the *Homo Europaeus*, a race which made France great, the members of which are rare among us today, indeed almost extinct.[49]

All the misfortunes of France were attributed by Lapouge to the extinction of the Aryans. With the passing of time his craniology, which he called *anthroposciology*, became more spiteful.

It is a serious matter that in our times the curse of the cephalic index should make the brachycephalics, all the races of brachycephalics, born slaves, seeking out new masters when they have lost their own—an instinct which is common only to brachycephalics and to dogs. It is a very serious matter that, wherever they are, they live under the domination of the dolicho-blonds and, in the absence of Aryans, under that of the Chinese and the Jews. . . .[50]

Lapouge went on to point out that: "The ancestors of the Aryans cultivated wheat when those of the brachycephalics were probably still living like monkeys."[51] But if he sounds delirious his delirium fostered in him a presentiment of other kinds of madness on a world-wide-scale:

The conflict of races is now about to start openly within nations and between nations, and one can only ask oneself if the ideas of the fraternity and equality of man were not against nature. . . . *I am convinced that in the next century people will slaughter each other by the million because of a difference of a degree or two in the cephalic index. It is by this sign, which has replaced the Biblical shibboleth and linguistic affinities, that men will be identified . . . and the last sentimentalists will be able to witness the most massive exterminations of peoples.*[52]

Looking through the scientific reviews and publications of the period convinces one that "anthroposociology", which was an offshoot of the theories known as Social Darwinism, was taken very seriously. Lapouge was certainly revered in Germany where William II considered him to be "the only great Frenchman"[53]; but he also had followers in other European countries. His scientific method consisted largely in the preparation of tables comparing the cephalic index, religious beliefs, the extent of urbanization and tax receipts from one region to another.[54] On close inspection, some of these correlations are the same as those which were preoccupying Max Weber at about that time; but it was from skulls alone that Lapouge sought to wrest the secrets of ethics and conduct. In France, Célestin Bouglé was impressed by Lapouge's work and attacked him only on the level of principles and not of scientific truth.[55] Another contemporary, the influential French philosopher Alfred Fouillée, wondered about the future of France and of Europe because of the "retreat of the dolicho-blonds":

We are becoming more and more Celto-Slav and "Turanian" once again, as we were before the arrival of the Gauls, whereas the so-called Aryan element in our midst is diminishing in importance and influence. This is the phenomenon which causes anxiety to some anthropologists. It is happening, moreover, to all other European peoples, though less quickly. . . . There is, so to speak, a slow and general russification of Europe, including Germany itself, a spontaneous pan-Celtism or pan-Slavism. It is as yet impossible to foresee the fortunate or unfortunate results of this change, but it is certain that the balance of our three constituent races has been compromised. . . .[56]

It was in a harmonious proportion of German, Celtic and Latin blood that Fouillée discerned the special genius of France. This idea had been elaborated at the time of the Restoration by the romantic historians and had taken a strong hold during the period of the Dreyfus affair, to the extent of provoking a split between nationalists and racists among the opponents of Dreyfus.

It is worth taking a look at the contradictions of the *Action française* in this connexion. This party, which emerged as the result of the Dreyfus affair, was often compared to German national-socialism with which it shared an idealization of an archaic past, an appeal to "instincts" and a cult of hatred and violence.[57] Its ancestor-cult was so all-embracing that it only stopped short at the Jewish race. The *Action française* welcomed Celts, Ligurians, Galatians, Greeks, Germans and Romans to its pantheon. Its failure to formulate a monolithic, elementary myth of origin (mere allegiance to the French kings as "fathers of the nation" was no satisfactory substitute) may well have been responsible for the relative political powerlessness of the party. Moreover, one notes again in this instance the contrast, which was emphasized in the first part of this work, between an authentically western tradition in France, and the Germanic or Slav claims to "autochthony". Charles Maurras went so far as to speak of the "Latinity" of the English. On another occasion this frustrated racialist glorified the lineage of the *Roi Soleil* in the following terms:

> In that "great Frenchman" Louis XIV . . . the Spanish and Italian ancestries must neither be exaggerated nor belittled. They exist. Perhaps they were less a hindrance than a help to some of the more marked and constant features of a very pure Celto-Galatian. Louis Bertrand says "of a Latin". But one could go further back, to that Gallic pre-Latinism which in part explains our most ancient ties with Greece and Rome.[58]

It will be observed that Maurras glossed over the traditionally and officially *Frankish* lineage of the king. The same contradictions or paradoxes as those of the *Action française* may be found in the lines (which might have been written by Michelet) with which Jacques Bainville opens his *History of France*:

> . . . the Ligurians and the Iberians, dark and of medium height, still provide the basis for the French population. The tradition of the Druids teaches us that the Gauls were in part indigenous, in part immigrants from the North and from beyond the Rhine. Thus a fusion of races began in prehistoric times. The French people is an amalgam. It is better than a race. It is a nation. . . . Clovis still had to be converted. . . . It may be said that France began at that time. Her civilization was strong enough to survive the fresh influx of the Franks, while leaving material power in the hands of these barbarians. And she needed Frankish power. She was able to assimilate men, to refine them. As with her civilization, her religion is Roman. . . .[59]

It is scarcely surprising that in 1940-1944 the pro-Hitler anthropologists of Paris dubbed the *Action française* "Action Marrane" (i.e. Marrano, or crypto-Jewish), and that Maurras himself was described by a Nazi sympathizer, the anthropologist Montandon, as the prototype of the Latino-Semite.[60]

RACIAL MANICHAEISM

By the second half of the nineteenth century all the sciences had become so complex that most scientists were forced to specialize. Popularizers and writers of textbooks acted as intermediaries between the universities and the public, and it was these popularizers in particular who informed the public not only about the "Aryan race" but about its antitheses, the most obvious being the "Semitic race". But there were others. On close inspection the true Aryan appeared to be a Westerner of the male sex, belonging to the upper or middle classes, who could be defined equally by reference to coloured men, proletarians or women. Even as liberal a scientist as Thomas Huxley, though he favoured the emancipation of women and Negroes, remained convinced of the congenital inferiority of both.[61] Other scholars went further. The French orientalist, Émile Burnouf, to take only one example, maintained that the skull formation of the Chinese and

Semites made them incapable of understanding the beauties of meta-physics—and of Christianity.[62]

Renan, in 1890, discussing the progress of science, concluded that: "The general laws governing the process of civilization are under-stood. The inequality of races is established. . . ."[63]

All these views of the late nineteenth century were mirrored in a historical encyclopaedia which was considered authoritative in the Germanic countries, the great *Kulturgeschichte* of von Hellwald. This was compiled by some twenty well-known authorities. The most eminent was Ludwig Büchner (1824-1899), the author of the materialist manifesto *Kraft und Stoff* (*Strength and Matter*), who was responsible for the introductory chapter on "Races and History". When trying to show the congenital incapacity of primitives to raise their minds to the level of abstract ideas, Büchner killed two birds with one stone by taking as his example, not the Australian man, but his mate, "the savage and degraded Australian's wife, who is exhausted by work, uses few abstract words and is unable to count beyond four, has no self-awareness and cannot reflect upon the nature of her existence".[64] Moreover, Büchner, who was imbued with ideas of human progress, declared that the intellectual gap between Whites and Blacks was bound to increase since the former would always advance more rapidly than the latter.[65] Karl Vogt, a follower of Darwin, applied the following law to women: "The difference between the sexes, so far as the cranial cavity is concerned, increases with the development of the race, so that the European male surpasses the female to a far greater extent than the Negro does the Negress".[66] It was Büchner's view that the uncivilized and brutal "lower classes" could be compared in many ways to the primitive peoples.[67] But for him the essential thing was "blood relationship". This *Blutsverwandschaft* was the "real and unbreakable bond which ensures the cohesion of the individual cells of which the social organism is composed", and it was in the blood relationship between the generations that "the inheritance of physical and moral faculties, aspirations and needs was rooted".[68] This accounted for the chasm between the races. Not merely was it impossible for two different races like the Aryan and the Semite to fuse, but "unity can only be achieved between like and like in the human as in the animal and vegetable world. Nature is and remains essentially aristocratic and punishes implacably all attempts upon the purity of blood."[69]

Von Hellwald's *Kulturgeschichte* did, it is true, find room for other opinions also. One of its collaborators, Professor Otto Henne am

Rhyn, who wrote the general introduction, hoped for the harmonious fusion of all human races.[70] In his eclecticism, von Hellwald surprisingly entrusted Professor Salomon Lefmann with the chapter on the "Aryans in ancient times" while he himself and Friedrich Schwally informed readers about the history and customs of the Semites. For von Hellwald, the opposition between Jew and Christian reduced itself to that between Semite and Aryan. Everywhere and always, the Jew remained a stranger and an intruder and his conversion could in no way change the animosity which he aroused. "Anti-Jewish prejudice is a kind of instinctive and natural feeling which is revealed wherever men of different races come in contact with one another."[71] Schwally remarked that nearly two thousand years after the destruction of the Jewish nation "the Jewish race has flooded the world", and he dwelt at length on the pride and arrogance of this "inexhaustible race".[72] Even if he had wanted, it would have been difficult for Salomon Lefmann to repay his uncharitable colleagues in their own coin—especially as, since 1879, anti-semitic agitation had been penetrating into the universities under the aegis of the famous historian Heinrich von Treitschke, the author of the slogan "the Jews are our misfortune".

Another less voluminous German *Kulturgeschichte* produced by Julius Lippert contrasted Aryan agriculturalists with Semite shepherds. The absence in Judaism of any myth of a mother-goddess seemed to him to prove the inability of the Jews to invent agriculture, and he described them as a "completely desiccated branch" of the white race.[73] There were very varied ways of proving Semitic inferiority and they were not practised in Germany alone. In translating the books of the popular German naturalist, Alfred Brehm, his French publisher had the idea of completing his *Life of the Animals* with a supplementary volume of *The Races of Mankind*. The task was entrusted to the anthropologist René Verneau. The Hebrew tribes, that sprig of the "Semitic branch" of the "white trunk", did not emerge from this book with great credit:

> "In France especially, the life of a Jew is outwardly the same as anyone else's. He is only distinguishable by his lack of cleanliness, his cupidity, his obsequious character, his observance of the sabbath, his habit of only eating certain meats. . . . What has been said above may be applied, in large measure, to Jews all over the world. Everywhere their morality is summed up in the idea that the world belongs to the people of God. Whatever

infidels possess has been taken from the Jews. The latter are within their rights to recover it by deceit since they cannot do so by force. If they are successful they are merely recovering goods of which they have been deprived."[74]

In the development of French scientific thought Gustave Le Bon has a place as a thinker of some originality. But his anti-Jewish diatribes were totally unoriginal in the sense that everything he said had been said with a good deal more verve by Voltaire—save only the term "Aryan".[75]

It has often been said that French anti-semitism served to distract attention from the national humiliation of 1871. A commonplace article in *Figaro*, written in 1883, was a remarkable illustration of this. The author, René Lagrange, was attempting to evoke the triumphal entry of Prussian troops into Paris. Far from denying their Aryanism he appeared, when describing them, to be paying tribute to the shades of Clovis and his companions:

> They were dressed for the most part in the brilliant uniform of the *cuirassiers*. Crowned by helmets of which the crests were decorated with imaginary animals; armed with breast-plates on which coats-of-arms were depicted in relief or armorial bearings were chased in metal, these riders sparkled in the first rays of a March sun. The faces of these aristocratic warriors were in harmony with their manly armour. The spectacle was grand. Their hair was blond and reddish, their moustaches were strong and bold in outline, their complexion was fair and at the same time ruddy, their eyes clear and sky-blue with a fierce gleam, recalling most convincingly the portrait of these men which was painted in ancient times by the pen of Tacitus. . . .

The resentment of the vanquished was shown further on in Lagrange's description of the event:

> The military group was followed immediately by another composed of civilians. This second group was certainly even more curious than the first. Behind the Centaurs, covered with armour and gleaming metal, there advanced like pairs of tongs astride their horses, a strange group of persons dressed in long, padded brown great-coats. They had drawn faces and golden spectacles, long hair, dirty auburn beards twirled into cork-screws, wide-brimmed hats. These were the Jewish bankers, so many Isaac Laquedems,* following the German army like vultures. It was

* A name for the Wandering Jew. (Tr. note.)

easy to guess their profession in this garb. Here, clearly, were the Jewish accountants and financiers charged with encashing our millions. . . .[76]

In *La France juive* Édouard Drumont also testified to having seen this procession of eagles and vultures. We might add that in 1940 the entry of the German army into Paris was described in much the same way, though without the inclusion of the fantasy about the Jews.[77]

A Swiss scholar, Alphonse de Candolle, had another even more extraordinary vision in 1873. It was that of Europe entirely inhabited by Jews and, moreover, happy and peaceful because of this.

> If Europe were entirely inhabited by Jews we should indeed witness a singular spectacle. There would be no more wars and our moral sensibilities would be less often outraged; millions of men would not be snatched from their useful work of all kind; taxes and the public debt would be seen to diminish. Because of the well-known bent of the Jews for literature, sciences, art and above all music, these would be highly developed. Industry and commerce would flourish. There would be few attacks against people, while those against property would rarely be accompanied by violence. Riches would increase enormously due to intelligent and regular work combined with economy. These riches would be distributed through plentiful charity. There would be no conflict between the clergy and the State, or at worst this would be about secondary matters. There would, unfortunately, be some misappropriation of funds and a certain pliancy on the part of civil servants. Marriages would be contracted early, there would be many of them, and in general the marriage vow would be observed. The evils resulting from loose morals would, therefore, be few. Add to this sound rules of hygiene, and the consequence would be a healthy and handsome population. . . .

Nevertheless, continued Candolle, this ideal Jewish city could not last long because the Aryans would soon launch a deadly attack upon it. "However small in number, if there remained in Europe or in the neighbouring countries some children of Greeks or Latins, of Cantabrians or Celts, Germans, Slavs or Huns, the immense population which we have envisaged would soon be subdued, raped and pillaged. . . . If there were no barbarians in Europe, others would come in from overseas. . . . Such are the laws of natural history."[78]

It may well be asked why this pro-Semitic utopia figured in a book called *The History of Science and of Scientists*. In fact, Candolle was attempting to prove the overwhelming power of "atavisms", namely, of heredity. He therefore emphasized, in a sequel to his parable, the paradoxical contrast between Jewish gentleness and the savagery of the Christians or Aryans:

> The Old Testament . . . accepts the hard law of the Talion: eye for eye, tooth for tooth. The New Testament, on the other hand, is imbued with gentleness, charity and humility. . . . If only religious teaching had educated the peoples, the Israelites might be violent and the Christians submissive whereas what we observe is precisely the opposite. . . . The Jewish race is one of the oldest and most civilized and has not mingled with any other. . . . The gentleness of the Israelites is, therefore, due neither to their religion nor to the treatment they received. Natural history affords a much better explanation.

Thus, despite his good will and even though he stood the usual scale of values on its head, Candolle still looked to nature or race to provide the main key to history. In the scientific world this kind of racial determinism dominated the field until the end of the nineteenth century. And it was just when it began to give ground to other views that it was adopted as an article of faith by the public at large. This was illustrated in 1904 by a critical thinker, the Frenchman Jean Finot:

> What is more, these products of the scientific imagination, blindly adopted without the least criticism, were introduced into manuals of history and school textbooks. Today, out of 1,000 educated Europeans, 999 are convinced of the authenticity of their Aryan origins. . . . This has become almost an axiom. Following this doctrine, so profoundly rooted in the European consciousness, modern sociology, history, politics and literature have continually contrasted the Aryans and other peoples, whether Semitic or Mongol. The Aryan origin has become a kind of beneficent source from which the high morality of Europe and the virtues of its principal inhabitants are supposed to flow. . . . : When making a comparison, in contemporary sociological jargon, between two mentalities or two kinds of morality it is usual to distinguish them by saying "Aryan" or "non-Aryan". With that one is supposed to have explained everything.[79]

FROM THE PRE-ADAMITES TO PSYCHOANALYSIS

We have seen how, at the beginning of the nineteenth century, a polygenist like Bory de Saint-Vincent was at pains to show that his

K

scientific beliefs in no way contradicted Christian tradition. Half a century later things were very different. Some Christian traditionalists now saw in polygenism a last resort against the all-conquering theory of evolution; for, extended to animals, polygenism could be invoked to support the Biblical account of the Creation (in the sense of the species being created "pair by pair"). The first authors to revive the old pre-Adamite theory for this purpose were the two American pro-slavery writers, Nott and Gliddon. Using science as their only authority, they resolutely adopted a separate classification for the Jews in their book *Types of Mankind*, describing them as the people who "in obedience to an organic law of animal life have preserved, unchanged, the same features which the Almighty stamped on the first Hebrew pair created". The other races, particularly the Blacks, had also clearly had a separate creation: "The Almighty, no doubt, individualized all human races from the beginning."[80] In Nott and Gliddon's case the political conclusion to be drawn from this was perfectly plain.

The celebrated naturalist, Louis Agassiz, who spared no effort to attack evolution by means of his theory of "separate creations", wrote the preface to Nott and Gliddon's book and was its principal scientific guarantor. Agassiz explained that it was essential to maintain the distinction between man and monkey as had been done in the past.[81] In fact, on closer inspection, the cause which he defended was only half lost because, in an attempt to close the gap and find the missing link, the evolutionists were using various scientific pretexts to erect new barriers between different human races. A speech by the anatomist Schaafhausen (whom Darwin regarded as one of his precursors)[82] makes us realize what psychological satisfaction white Europeans were to derive from this process.

In 1866, Schaafhausen declared that "the wall of separation between the early world and the present world, between man and the animal, has crumbled", and he explained that

> the abyss which separated them seems to us less profound since we have acquired knowledge of apes of a higher order. . . . This abyss is filling in more quickly since the physical structure of inferior races and, what is highly significant, that of fossilized man, has made us understand that we should undoubtedly consider certain of their characteristics as being very proximate to animal nature.

The fact that some natives were not accessible to the "lofty ideas of religion" was one of these characteristics. Schaafhausen, therefore, accepted the "thesis of the multiple origins of man. . . . This opinion is further supported by certain resemblances between the monkeys of Asia and Africa and the various races of humans which inhabit these regions."

This anatomist, who was also a believing Christian, insisted that "Our science does not contradict our morality. It does not deny the soul in man nor God in nature; it is in no wise minded to deny man the consolation he derives from his faith in the immortality of the soul."[83]

It began to look as if the *balance which had been upset by the approximation of man to animals was being re-established by a distinction between men who were accessible to the highest ideas of religion or morals, and others who "were very close to animal nature"*. Before long, a materialist follower of Darwin, Karl Vogt, who was as concerned about moral principles as the idealists Agassiz and Schaafhausen, and for whom "the range of human types" began with the Negro and reached its culmination in the German,[84] laid the foundations of the "polyphyletic theory" of human origins.[85] This modified polygenism, which was developed by various disciples, affiliated each human race to one of the main races of big anthropoid apes, and can be summarized in the following table:[86]

Theory put forward by	GORILLA	CHIMPANZEE	GIBBON	ORANG-OUTANG
Klaatsch	Negroes		Mongols(?) {	Malays Europeans
Sergi	Negroes		Yellow Races in general	
Sera	Andamans		Negroes	Mongols Yellow
Arldt	Negroes	Whites		Races

These authors tended to relate the white man to some ape of a reputedly higher intelligence than the others. Thus the anatomist Klaatsch related the Indo-German to the Orang-Outang through the Aurignacians, and the Negro to the Gorilla through Neanderthal man.[87] At the same time other speculations which one hesitates to describe as more fanciful (the last being those of the biologist Lecomte du Noüy)[88] supported the new polygenist theories by reference to Biblical exegesis. Thus at the height of the Darwinian controversy several English authors attempted to revive the old pre-Adamite theory. Some, like

Dr Vivian at the anthropological congress of Dundee (1867), appealed to the theory of Agassiz and concluded that there had been a plurality of separate Adams, of whom the Jewish Adam was merely the last.[89] Others, like the Rev. Dunbar Heath or George Harris, F.S.A., ignored Agassiz and natural history and were content to rely upon the time-honoured resources of Biblical exegesis—for was it not written that Cain, after killing Abel, had become a fugitive from men, which proved the existence of people before Cain and his parents, and so on?[90] But this kind of pre-Adamitism was too contrary to the scientific spirit of the age to rally more than a few Anglo-Saxon supporters, whereas another theory, which assumed a radical difference between the nature of Jews and other men, was to enjoy far greater success.

Since Jewish-Christian conflict had henceforth, in the light of scientific knowledge, to be explained "naturally", i.e. in terms of a Semitic-Aryan conflict, it was easier to appeal to physiology than to genealogies. Dr Jean-Christian Boudin (1803-1867), the President of the Anthropoligical Society of Paris and one of the pioneers of medical statistics, was the first to state the laconic principle: "Nowhere is the Jew born, nowhere does he live or die as the other men among whom he dwells. This is a question of comparative anthropology which is now beyond discussion."

In his great *Traité de géographie et de statistique médicales*, Boudin, relying principally on Prussian statistics, elaborated on this statement. He subscribed to the commonly held opinion that the Jews increased more rapidly than other peoples, though he thought this was due to a lower mortality rather than to a higher birth rate. As far as the latter was concerned, the Jews very rarely had children born out of wedlock. Even more than by their astonishing longevity, Jews were singled out by their physical resilience. They were able to adapt themselves to all environments and climates; they were the

> only truly cosmopolitan people. This quality which they alone, among all the peoples of the earth, possess, confounds human reasoning and one might well ask oneself whether it is not rather an indication of a providential mission than the effect of chance?[91]

Most decidedly the "people who were to bear witness" seemed to Boudin to have been biologically adapted in advance to carry out their theological role. His views were taken up by scientists who had no knowledge whatever of theology. Karl Vogt took them up when he wrote in his *Lessons on Man* that of all the human peoples there is one only, the Jewish race, which is able to acclimatize itself with equal facility in two hemispheres, in the hot and in the temperate regions, and to live there without the help of the indigenous population.[92]

During the period of colonial expansion this was a much discussed problem and Virchow, for example, thought that he had definitely established that the Germanic race was congenitally incapable of acclimatizing in the tropics.[93] The idea that Jews were constituted differently from other men, and specifically from Christians, after inspiring so many medieval legends,[94] now became part of modern science. A Jewish sociologist from Vienna, Ludwig Gumplowicz, reproached the Jewish people with their "inability to disappear"[95]; a French anti-semitic doctor, Georges Vitoux, tried to prove statistically that their days were numbered.[96] To writers like Vacher de Lapouge in France and Karl Pearson in Great Britain, who were concerned about the "twilight of the Aryans", it seemed that the Jews by contrast, thanks to their special physique, were in the strongest possible position to be the Aryans' successors.

The chief popularizer of the Aryan idea in France, Édouard Drumont, also commented on this strange situation: "Alone among all the races of the world, it [the Jewish race] enjoys the advantage of being able to live in all climates yet, at the same time, it is unable to survive without damaging others. . . ."[97] Drumont, who was a careful reader of the scientific publications of his time which he quoted accurately, was relying on a study published in 1881 in the *Revue Scientifique*, in which all the available information about Jewish populations throughout the world had been collated. The anonymous author of this work believed that the physiological advantages and immunities of the Jews showed that they had "either a particular congenital vitality or a marvellous aptitude for adjusting their hygiene to the climatic exigencies of each region. . . . These immunities will stand up to the usually miserable condition which many observers attribute to them." By way of explanation Drumont suggested either the racial purity of the Jews, or the healthiness of their hygiene and family life, or even their material wealth carefully disguised "under the appearance of misery. . . . All these hypotheses are admissible", he concluded.[98]

In 1881 also, a German geographer, Richard Andree, declared that there was only one arguable hypothesis. This was the strength of Jewish blood which, always and everywhere, had been able to *overcome* any transfusions of foreign blood so as to preserve intact and unchanged "the old and monumental Jewish body, and the Jewish spirit which was hereditarily transmitted by this body".[99] "From the anthropological point of view", wrote Andree, "the Jews represent one of the most interesting subjects of study because no other racial type can be so easily identified through the centuries, no other displays such organic stability, no other has withstood so well the effects of time and of environment." This expresses in scientific jargon one of the main themes of anti-semitic writing from La France juive to Mein Kampf.

It also translates long-standing human fears into scientific language. In 1900 textbooks and encyclopaedias of natural history devoted considerable space to the phenomenon of remote impregnation or telegony. Examples of this imaginary phenomenon were mostly alleged to have taken place in connexion with dogs and horses, man's faithful companions and the mainstays for the projection of his anxieties. According to this belief, a female thoroughbred crossed with a male mongrel was tainted forever and destined to bear an impure progeny in the likeness of the first male—a superstition which was the reverse side of the jus primae noctis. Under the title of "Certain Anomalous Modes of Reproduction" Darwin compiled a list of cases of this kind. These were explained by Claude Bernard as cases of "incomplete fecundation" while Herbert Spencer suggested that the foetus changed the mother in its own image.[100] Thus fortified by the prestige of science and philosophy, telegony entered the realm of human relations and it was alleged that an Aryan woman, if only once soiled by a Jew, was destined to breed only Jewish (or "Hebroid") children. The same virulence was attributed in the United States to the blood or sperm of the Blacks though the idea was never developed, as it was in Germany, in a best-selling novel.[101]

This extreme form of the theory of penetration or of the special nature of Jewish blood, and more generally of non-Aryan blood, was reflected in the legislation of the Third Reich. It was also to be seen in other forms, such as the belief in the infecundity or lesser fertility of "mixed unions", or in the inevitable victory of "inferior blood", and these variants were applied to all the peoples of the earth. Vacher de Lapouge, in France, referred to Gresham's law of political economy in this context: "Bad blood drives out good, just as bad money displaces good money." Broca had already experimented with "phenomena of hybridity in the human race" (which, as a good polygenist, is what he called these mixed unions) and his conclusion was that in nearly all cases the results were biologically disastrous.[102] This was the prevailing view and even Darwin, after weighing the pros and cons, was prepared to back it.[103]

It is quite true that at the end of the nineteenth century (partly through the influence of the doctrine of Evolution which favoured the monogenists) all these superstitions began to disappear in the world of genuine science. And as far as the Jews were concerned, some progress was certainly made in the field of physical anthropology. Before the failure of its principal ambitions, this science had been able to establish by means of detailed research that the Jews did not enjoy any special physiological advantages.[104] As to their better resistance against infant mortality and certain diseases, the tradition of Moses seemed so clearly responsible for this that in 1893 Anatole Leroy-Beaulieu was to be heard regretting "that the controversies of the Early Church about ritual observances had not resulted in the triumph of the Law and of the Judaeo-Christians" and asking whether "the writer of the Pentateuch had not anticipated M. Pasteur".[105]

⋆   ⋆   ⋆

By the end of the nineteenth century, however, the demography of Jews and Christians began to converge. The progress of medicine and the general improvement in habits were putting an end to the statistical anomalies which had struck Boudin and his contemporaries so forcibly. But the theory of "Jewish otherness" was not abandoned; it was merely supported by fresh arguments and by researchers in other disciplines. It is noticeable that, at the end of the nineteenth century, the development of ideas and the evolution of scientific methods was marked by a double and contradictory trend. On the one hand more and more specialized branches of knowledge developed, and the gaps between the various disciplines grew ever greater while the new sciences of man, which were bent on establishing their independence, tended consequently to emphasize what was special to them. On the other hand, the Darwinian revolution vividly re-established man's relation to nature through his own flesh and blood. One could almost say that having been driven out by various windows, nature was re-entering by the wide open door of a belief in the all-importance of heredity.

This ancient belief, now supported by the concepts of atavism and instinct, was even promoted by some thinkers to the rank of a general law of cosmic significance. The philosopher Théodule Ribot (1839–1911), who was the author of a classic treatise on the subject called *L'hérédité psychologique*, described this law as follows:

> From a philosophical standpoint, heredity seems to us to be a fragment of a much wider law, of a universal law, and its cause must be sought in the mechanism of the universe. . . . It is an aspect of that final law which in physics is called the law of the conservation of energy, while in metaphysics it is known as the universal law of causality.[106]

In accordance with this general principle, "in the same animal or human species, actual races preserve their psychic as well as their physiological characteristics". As far as the character and customs of the Jewish race were concerned, Ribot followed the favourable judgement of Candolle, while directing against the "Gypsy race" the criticisms usually hurled at the Jews. He wrote: "This race, filled with hatred against civilized peoples, is the slave of certain hereditary vices which it cherishes and defends like a religion. Thus their highest ambition is to steal from Christians. . . ."[107]

Combined with the axiom "nothing creates itself, nothing destroys itself", the evolutionist concept of heredity brought forth some astonishing fruits. Thus according to Ernst Haeckel, the great ancestor of the theoreticians of Nazi biology, who became the apostle of a new monist religion, the human soul was no more than a gradual development of the "soul of unicellular protista".[108] But let us leave this evolutionary reincarnation of *Naturphilosophie*, and deal with the ideas and the men who gave a completely new impulse to the study of the human soul.

To begin with, there was the obsession of French psychiatrists with certain therapeutic methods based on the obscure phenomena of hypnotism and suggestion. The leading schools at the end of the nineteenth century, those of Nancy and Paris, also placed great emphasis on the genealogies, whether of family or race, of neuropathic patients though they differed as to how pathological heredity was transmitted. The Nancy school postulated a purely psychic mode of transmission and Liébault, its founder, went so far as to adopt a psychic interpretation of *telegony*. According to this view, a mother's thoughts affected the anatomy of the embryo.[109] The Parisian school remained more conventionally attached to physiology, and its celebrated leader, J-M. Charcot (1825-1893), actually held that Jews were racially predisposed to the "neuropathy" of travelling and nomadism. The legendary Wandering Jew merely typified this "irresistible need to move around, to travel without being able to settle anywhere".[110] In view of this, Charcot commissioned Henry Meige, one of his assistants, to carry out a systematic study, under his own supervision, of the Wandering Jew.

In his doctoral thesis, Meige described the latter as "the prototype of the neuropathic Jews wandering around the world". And he continued: "Let us not forget that they are Jews and that it is in the character of their race to move about. . . ." Later, in describing the cases which he and his colleagues had had under clinical observation, he attempted to distinguish between the influences of character and causation:

> What were the contingent reasons for this malady of travelling? Were they traumata as in the case of K... or violent emotions as in the case of S...? This is the very essence of their attacks. Was it not as the result of a violent emotion, the sight of Jesus Christ suffering the tortures of Calvary, that Cartaphilus* fled from his home and started on his wanderings?

Torn between Christian superstitions and medical positivism, Meige concluded:

> The Wandering Jew exists to this day. He still exists in the same manner as in past centuries. . . . Cartaphilus, Ahasuerus, Isaac Laquedem are derived from the same nervous pathology as the patients whose case histories we have examined.[111]

The popular works of Gustave le Bon on collective psychology and the racial soul show how rapidly these "recent discoveries of physiology"[112] were beginning to spread and how easily they could be utilized by extreme forms of racism.† An even better example is that of Drumont's *La France juive*, in which the terrible revelations of Charcot about the Jewish neurosis, as well as its dangerous possibilities of contagion, are discussed. "This neurosis, strangely enough, has been transmitted by the Jews to the whole of our generation. . . ."[113]

Admittedly, the wanderings of the Jews might also be explained by

---

* The earliest name for the Wandering Jew which was used in the Chronicles of the Abbey of St Albans, copied by Mathew Paris. (Tr. note.)

† On Le Bon's anti-semitism, see above, p. 275; on his concept of racial souls see especially *Les Lois psychologiques de l'évolution des peuples*, Paris 1894, pp. 11-28.

recourse to other sciences. Thus the German orientalist, Adolf Wahr-mund, attributed the dangers of "the dominating Jewish nomadism" to the racial maturity of the Jews, playing with the youthful Aryan peoples "like a cat with a mouse", and he was even more emphatic about the contrast between the people of the desert who despoil nature and those of the forest for whom it is sacred.[114] These contrasts were amplified in the influential "anthropogeographical" theories of Friedrich Ratzel for whom the soul of the various peoples was the reflection of the scenery which surrounds them.[115] This was popu-larized later on by Werner Sombart. *The Jews and Modern Capitalism* (1911) by this friend and rival of Max Weber was peculiar in that it opened with a eulogy of the children of Israel, who were defined as the creators of capitalism and as such compared to the sun,[116] only to continue with the usual descriptions of the Jews as talmudic, nomadic, calculating, a product of the oriental desert, and totally contrasted with the true Germans, born of bountiful Germanic nature and its moist forests. It is hard to say which of these themes was the richest in anti-semitic significance but it is known that *The Jews and Modern Capitalism* was used by Hitler as a documentary source when he was writing *Mein Kampf.*[117]

If this kind of psychological speculation has now been definitely discarded, another kind persists. It first appeared early in the twentieth century, when the debate shifted to the new ground of psychoanalysis—a field in which, without always disclosing their intentions but with all the passion which characterizes disputes about wills or claims to primo-geniture, some adepts continue to press the same arguments in our own times.

From the beginning, discussion was bedevilled by personal complica-tions. All Freud's struggles were conducted under the shadow of the Aryan myth. On a personal level one need only recall his dramatic relations with his brilliant "eldest son" and heir presumptive, C. G. Jung. In fact, this disciple, soon after his first visit to Freud, dreamed that he had emerged from an uninhabitable ghetto.[118] Equally sig-nificant by comparison were the fainting fits of the master during his discussions with his secessionist disciple.[119] But we can leave interpretations to the analysts and ourselves deal with the doctrines and ideas involved.

Freud tried to interpret the tension between the Jews and their neighbours (or, as he once put the question, "how the Jews have come to be what they are and why they have attracted this undying hatred"[120]), in the historical light of Jewish monotheism and its struggle against archaic fantasies which were repressed but had partly re-emerged again in Christianity.[121] He explained the question as a sequence of "religious illusions" which made it a purely cultural problem. We should remember that in *Totem and Taboo*, his major anthropological myth, he attributed morals, religion, the arts—all that humanity is made up of—to the same source (the "original parricide", followed by the formation of the Oedipus Complex).[122] The breach with "nature" which this suggests became, or perhaps became once again, fundamental. This is all the more remarkable because Freud hoped that the latest discoveries of psychoanalysis would reduce "the gulf which earlier periods of human arrogance had torn too wide apart between mankind and the animals".[123] Some passages in Freud's correspondence suggest, however, that he accepted the reality of a constitutional or hereditary difference between Semites and Aryans. "After all, our Talmudic way of thinking cannot disappear just like that", he wrote to Karl Abraham in 1908, warning him against their common tendency towards "racial preference".[124] Thirty years later, in his *Moses and Monotheism*, he attributed "a peculiar psychical aptitude" to the Jews of Antiquity which enabled them to endure the "burdens of the religion of Moses".[125] Such ideas were in agreement with the neo-Lamarckian belief in the inheritance of acquired mental characteristics (the hypothesis of "mnemonic traces") which Freud was still defending at the end of his life, in total defiance of biological science.[126]

However, he did not extend this hypothesis to the animal kingdom any more than he did his other concepts; and the Id was for him the bearer of a secret which was lost in the abyss of ancestral or phylogenetic heredity.[127] He showed the same scientific prudence in pausing on the threshold of problems which in one way or another engaged him as a person. He explained this casually in 1931 when dealing with the cultural potentialities of women which, like most other people of his time, he thought inferior to those of men. He concluded that the verdict of psychoanalysis on a question which was so rich in polemical implications risked being like Dostoevsky's famous stick with two ends.[128] Freud's greatness lies in the skill with which, immediately after a break-through, he stops or pulls back, and in the humility which enables him to say: "I can go no further."[129] And this is why, when he attempted to define himself in his capacity as a Jew, he was content to speak of "a clear consciousness of an interior identity, a deep realization of sharing the same psychic structure" and of "obscure emotional forces, which were the more powerful the less they could be expressed in words".[130]

Jung, on the other hand, even before his break with Freud, began to search for a vocabulary which might reveal "that deeper layer which is common to all men", to which Freud never penetrated.[131] In the work which preceded his secession, he posited that "The unconscious, on the other hand, is universal: it not only binds individuals together into a nation or race, but unites them with the men of the past and with their psychology."[132] This was the beginning of his great concept of the *Collective Unconscious*. He defined this in 1917 as "the deposit of all the world's experience in all times, and hence an image of the world which has been built up through the aeons".[133] Jung thought he perceived a manifestation of this image in the universality of religious beliefs—which reminds one of the theologies of "natural revelation"*—but he was dealing with something quite different really, because the Collective Unconscious is by definition incapable of conscious formulation, and above all because, far from restricting himself to the human species, Jung went at least as far back as the age of the dinosaurs. In this way the tree of biological evolution was endowed with a spiritual superstructure.

> We carry with us in the structure of our bodies and of our nervous system all our genealogical history. The same is true of our soul which likewise reveals the traces of its ancestral past and of its future . . . all that which once existed is still present and operative within us.

From this proposition Jung went on to his theory of *archetypes*. The archetype of the dragon, for instance, was due to "nature having passed through two great experiences", through the successive creation of invertebrates and vertebrates. Because of this, "we are both crustacea (through the sympathetic nervous system) and sauria (through the spinal chord) . . .".[134]

Here, under the guise of spirituality, we see that a complete return has been made to *Naturphilosophie*, in the wake of Haeckel's "soul of the protista", or of "the soul of the world". A Collective Unconscious which was derived phylogenetically from the origin of all life had, however, to submit to the laws of evolution, and diversify itself along the successive stages of development. As for the last stage, that is Man as understood by Jung, a warning of what was to follow can be

* See above, pp. 140-141.

detected in his criticism of Freud's "psychology of neurotic states of mind" which, together with the concept of the super-ego, attempted to "smuggle the time-honoured image of Jehovah in the dress of psychological theory".[135] This criticism dates from 1929. Four years later, soon after Hitler's rise to power, Jung went on to make a systematic comparison between "Germanic psychology" and "Jewish psychology",[136] and contrasted "the Aryan Unconscious" with the "Jewish Unconscious" at all levels. His writings suddenly revealed the categories and antitheses which had been developed by European thought since Fichte, Schlegel and Renan—virility and femininity, nomadism and stability, creativity and sterility, youth and age. Only the conclusion was new:

> He [Freud] did not know the Germanic soul any better than did all his Germanic imitators [Nachbeter]. Has the mighty apparition of National Socialism, which the whole world watches with astonished eyes, taught them something better?[137]

It should be made clear, however, that Jung's Aryan mythology was full of nuances and that by conceding so much to the Nazis in 1934 he hoped to protect his own school and to help his German colleagues including Jews. To this must be added his ingenuous ambition, as a therapist, to exercise a moderating influence and exorcise the rising demons.[138] Nevertheless, the concept of a collective or racial soul, independent of time, has a logic of its own, and when, in 1948, Jung's French disciple, Dr Cahen, wrote in praise of his master that "Jung . . . in his biological and even more in his psychological nature has remained a German"[139] he was correctly applying a doctrine whose followers still proclaim its scientific virtues.[140]

It is interesting to note that the first critical voice raised against Jung, the commanding voice of Freud himself, revealed the aggressive intention, both scientific and Jewish, which motivated the formation of his own anthropological myth. Soon after Jung's defection in 1913, Freud wrote to Abraham: "The totem job is finished, apart from revisions and appendices from the literature. It is to appear before the Congress in the August number of Imago and will serve to cut us off completely from all Aryan religiousness. Because that will certainly be the consequence."[141] Once again Freud was right. When, during that Munich Congress, Jung was astonished to see the English psychoanalyst, Ernest Jones, supporting Freud, he said to him: "I thought you were a Christian."[142]

As to their respective methods, Dr Frey-Rohn, a Jungian, seems to be right in commenting that "at the decisive moment Freud always tended to see things in individual and concrete terms whereas Jung concentrated on the impersonal and the general".[143] In the context of values, the mistakes of Jung illustrate the dialectic which leads from universalism, whether pantheistic or other, to racism, and the old adage *summum jus, summa injuria* comes to mind. But these are slippery paths; and we too would do well to remember, following Freud's example, with what ease philosophical dialectics even more than psychoanalytical dialectics can become a "stick with two ends".

The Survival of the Fittest

Contrary to general belief, the two famous principles of the *survival of the fittest* and the *struggle for existence* were formulated not by Darwin but by Herbert Spencer. In fact, the author of the *Origin of the Species* was in many respects but a spokesman for his age. Whether or not the concept of evolution was the work of many hands, it integrated both the old idea of the superiority of so-called advanced races and that of human progress into a grandiose scheme, which included the ascending line of all living beings, from the infusoria to man. As far as the idea of unlimited progress was concerned, Spencer had been a leading advocate of this since the middle of the century. In keeping with the positivist spirit of the times, he associated the law of conservation of energy with that of evolution. He believed that he could prove that man's advance towards a better future was the result of a universal law, and that evolution "could only end in the establishment of the greatest perfection and the most complete happiness".[144] At the same time it was perfectly clear to Spencer that this advance was to be made under the leadership of the white race, and that other races would for a while be left behind in a primitive or backward state. Pending the final but still remote apotheosis of *Homo sapiens*, he was resolutely opposed to any mingling of the widely divergent strains.[145] Thus the link between the idea of progress and that of racial hierarchy, which we have noted in so many earlier authors, emerges particularly clearly in this typical thinker of the Victorian age.

By and large, the same optimism was shared by Darwin to whom the division of the human species into superior and inferior races was also clearly apparent. These opinions are to be found in a number of passages in *The Descent of Man*, perhaps not stated obtrusively, but forming a kind of undercurrent. For instance, he considered that the variation in mental development between different races was greater than between men of the same race.[146] In a curious passage about the vigour of the English colonizers, Darwin adopted the view of an obscure clergyman, the Rev. Zincke, who held that the history of the West seemed directed towards a clearly defined end, the worldwide expansion of the Anglo-Saxon race.[147] Later on in his book, when dealing with the extinction of human races through natural selection, Darwin displayed some caution and confined himself to a description of the Tasmanians and some other populations in the Pacific, which at the time were well-known cases of the kind, without risking speculation on a world scale.[148]

A decisive step was taken in 1862 by the co-author of the theory of natural selection, Alfred R. Wallace. While exploring in the Malayan jungle, he pondered on the way in which the laws governing the human species had developed "the admirable intelligence of the Germanic races" (by which he no doubt meant the white races). Experience had shown that these races had already eliminated a certain number of "populations that were mentally undeveloped", and from this Wallace concluded that the process was sure to continue till all the coloured races disappeared or gradually faded away. The laws of the struggle for existence required that the Germanic races should finally absorb or replace all the others.[149]

It remained to be seen whether the refining influences of civilized behaviour and ethical principles would upset the pattern of natural selection. Darwin was the first to admit that they might alter its development by preserving the lives and the children of human beings who would otherwise have been destined to disappear in the hard struggle for existence. But although this might harm the quality of civilized races, Darwin remained cautiously optimistic because of the higher rate of breeding among the strongest and healthiest elements.[150] On the other hand, even before the publication of *The Descent of Man*, there had been writers who claimed that civilized customs threatened to favour degenerate races or inferior stock. For instance, in 1868, a certain W. R. Greg, comparing the demography of the Irish and the Scots, declared that the "dissolute Celts" were breeding more rapidly than the virtuous Saxons, and concluded that the inferior race was getting the upper hand not because of any virtue but because of its defects.[151] This seems to have been the first childish cry of alarm of what was to become the science of eugenics.

A year later the founder of this science, Francis Galton (1822–1911), who was Darwin's cousin, entered the lists with his book *Hereditary Genius*. His aim was to show that mental characteristics, and primarily intelligence, were hereditary in the same way as physical qualities. Observing the unequal distribution of gifts and talents in the history of different families, he worked out a system of numerical coefficients for their measurement which he believed could be applied to the great races of humanity. According to him the Negro race, for instance, was "two grades" lower than the White race, while the aborigines of Australia were "three grades" lower.[152] A knowledge of these facts, followed by appropriate measures could lead to the breeding of "a race of highly gifted men". He went on: "I shall show that social agencies of an ordinary character, whose influences are little suspected, are at this moment working towards the degradation of human nature, and that others are working towards its amelioration." A study of these social factors was incumbent on the present generation as a duty to their descendants.[153]

Galton accused the Roman Catholic Church of being the principal agent of "the degradation of human nature" in Europe. By imposing celibacy on the priesthood it had cut short the lineages which might have been morally and intellectually the best. With similar results the Inquisition had eliminated heretics who represented the boldest spiritual groups. "The Church brutalized the breed of our forefathers. She acted precisely as if she had aimed at selecting the rudest portion of the community to be, alone, the parents of future generations." This nefarious policy had been continued in France by Louis XIV in persecuting the Protestants, though some other countries, and especially England, had benefited by their seeking refuge there.[154] In old age, Galton expressed an equally favourable view of Jewish immigrants fleeing the persecution of the Tsar.[155] At this time, however, he began to display some pessimism about the future of his own country:

> We are ceasing as a nation to breed intelligence as we did fifty to a hundred years ago. The mentally better stock in the nation is not reproducing itself at the same rate as it did of old; the less able and the less energetic are more fertile than the better stocks. ... The only remedy, if one be possible at all, is to alter the relative fertility of the good and the bad stocks in the community.

But how was this to be done? Not only was public opinion indifferent to these problems but scientists themselves, he confessed, had not yet obtained sufficient mastery of the laws of heredity. "When the desired fullness of information shall have been acquired, then, and not till then, will be the fit moment to proclaim a 'Jehad' or Holy War, against customs and prejudices that impair the physical and moral faculties of our race."[156]

In the Anglo-Saxon countries, however, the climate of opinion was not particularly favourable to a crusade which was not only incompatible with religious traditions but also with the cult of individual freedom. The law of natural selection, indeed, could be invoked in different ways. Spencer, in his optimistic vein, held that the best way to improve the human race was to give free rein to the spirit of competition.[157] With equal optimism, Alfred Wallace believed that humanity would evolve spontaneously to the practice of customs which might assure the survival of better breeds and the increase of super-Shakespeares and super-Goethes.[158] The most influential of the American social-Darwinians, William Graham Sumner, was also a believer in the free play of natural selection—though it was in millionaires, whom apparently he preferred to poets, that he discerned its most advantageous products.[159] Because of their ultra-liberal mentality the Anglo-Saxon followers of Galton, however, had good reason to feel pessimistic about the future of the supposedly superior races. The mathematician Karl Pearson, who was the most energetic of them, sounded the death-knell of Aryan-Christian civilization in 1893:

> We were struggling among ourselves for supremacy in a world which we thought as destined to belong to the Aryan races and to the Christian faith; to the letters and arts and charm of social manners which we have inherited from the best times of the past. We shall awake to find ourselves elbowed and hustled, and perhaps even thrust aside by peoples whom we looked down upon as servile, and thought of as bound always to minister to our needs. The solitary consolation will be that the changes have been inevitable. It has been our work to organize and to create, to carry peace and law and order over the world, that others may enter in and enjoy. Yet in some of us the feeling of caste is so strong that we are not sorry to think we shall have passed away before that day arrives.[160]

In Germany, where national tradition tended to respect the wisdom of government and where scientists were held in high esteem, the prospects of the eugenic movement looked brighter. The German public greeted the theory of natural selection with such enthusiasm that several political parties tried to make use of it for their own ends.

Social democracy appealed to it; Engels wanted to interpret it dialectically.[161] To this, Darwin's famous disciple, Haeckel, replied that natural selection was neither socialist nor democratic but aristocratic.[162] *The Descent of Man* had hardly been published before Darwinism was being used for anti-semitic propaganda. The writer O. Beta, in his book *Darwin, Deutschland und die Juden* (1876), asked the authorities to take account of the "revelations of the Darwinian doctrine"; to recognize that a "struggle for existence" was going on between a productive Germano-Aryan race and a parasitic Semite race, and therefore to take such anti-Jewish legislative action as would be scientifically justified.[163] A more famous propagandist, Professor Eugen Dühring, considered that the Jewish problem was insoluble in a bourgeois society and placed his hopes in socialism which, as he wrote, paraphrasing Marx, was alone able "to emancipate society from the Jew".[164] In the political field the doctrine of natural selection, with its insistence on victory for the fittest, provided theorists with the widest possible choice as to who was fittest and what the results might be in civilized society of the struggle between the "most prolific" and the "best". There was much speculation about which stock or what class, or what Aryan sub-race, was the best; about the value of "inter-racial mingling" and so forth. Thus the founder of the eugenic movement in Germany, Dr Alfred Ploetz (1860-1940), reproached Christianity and democracy with having blunted the racial feelings of the people; he placed the "Western Aryans"—and the Jews to whom he also attributed Aryan descent—at the top of his racial scale (1895).[165] But his views changed later: in a journal which he published, he restricted his interest to the Germans alone, even going so far as to found a secret Nordic Society. In 1936 Hitler fulfilled the ambition of a lifetime when he appointed him a university professor.[166]

The spread of eugenics, to which in Germany Ploetz gave the name of "race hygiene", was greatly furthered by the Krupp family who "in the interest of the nation and for the advancement of science" sponsored a competition in 1900 for the best essay on the theme: "What lessons can be drawn from the principles of the theory of heredity in its relation to the evolution of internal politics and state legislation?" The prize for the winner was to be 50,000 marks. A jury was formed of six famous scientists, including Ernst Haeckel. The essays flowed in, some sixty in number, and the best among them were published at Krupp's expense. The jury's report emphasized the importance of the laws of heredity which refuted the "old theories of equality", and asked whether civilization was not in danger of bringing about a "deterioration or degeneration of the natural qualities in man". The report also pointed out that all but one or two of the competitors placed their hopes in State intervention, which the jury interpreted as indicating that "our times demand a policy of social progress, only possible if there exists a strong central power which is bold enough to limit individual liberty in the name of the common good and which is able to intervene in the mechanisms of economic life".[167]

The first prize went to Dr Wilhelm Schallmayer, who envisaged state direction of the medical services so that these could exercise permanent eugenic control over the German people. In his politico-racial ideas Dr Schallmayer showed great moderation: although he classified races in the usual way, that is to say, allowing a certain superiority to the Nordic race, he was severely critical of the extravagances of pan-Germanism; these, he feared might lead to wars with harmful eugenic results. He went so far as to advocate the unification of Europe, but he thought that German political leaders ought meanwhile to follow a prudent policy with long-term aims. He concluded that, "The statesman who does not merely pursue immediate successes and whose horizon is enlarged and illuminated by the principles of heredity will realize that the future of his people depends on the good administration of procreative power."[168]

Another prize-winning contribution, by Dr Ludwig Woltmann (1871-1907), one of Haeckel's principal pupils, was conceived in an altogether different spirit. This follower of Vacher de Lapouge was utterly convinced of the supremacy of the "Nordics" or dolicho-cephalic blonds, amongst whom he included all great men past and present, from Dante to Napoleon and from Renan to Wagner. He devoted two further books to proving the point.[169] Cross-breeding with races of less value, such as the Alpine, the Mediterranean and the Semitic—not to speak of unfortunate unions with Mongols and even with Blacks—had changed the quality of the superior race. And there was another reason why the future looked black to Woltmann—the Germans were impelled by their aggressive nature to fight constantly against one another: "the German is his own worst enemy", and this would end in their mutual destruction. There was no way of escaping this slaughter which was required by the law of progress. "To put an end to this hostility would be to suppress a basic condition of cultural development, and any attempt to substitute empty dreams for the laws of nature would be childish." This opposition between "the laws of selection" and "the laws of progress" was a cause of anxiety to many thinkers. What, for instance, was to be the attitude towards war? Another German eugenist, Dr Steinmetz, supplied one answer: "Without war, men would all become crafty, selfish and cowardly like the Jews today."[170]

In Woltmann's opinion, however, the situation would be restored by a vast programme of social reforms. In particular, he envisaged the breaking up of the estates of the squirearchy and a distribution of land among peasants of good stock so as to preserve "the organic source of urban culture and spiritual nobility". Even more important for him was the protection of the workers against "the anti-selectionist tendencies of capitalism". He also believed in promoting the working class politically. To give the workers a share of power would cure them of the illusion "that the world could be conquered by means of peaceful competition".[171]

Eugenists and geneticists of the next generation, which flourished during the Third Reich and included Eugen Fischer, Fritz Lenz and Otmar von Verschuer among others, derived their ideas mainly from Woltmann and Ploetz. Fischer, the most famous of them, who was the first to apply Mendel's laws to "racial hygiene", declared in 1934 that he had also been the first to propagate Woltmann's ideas in a university faculty and to have "inflamed young hearts with enthusiasm for racial science".[172] By 1913 he was prophesying "with absolute certainty" the extinction of all European peoples in default of a coherent racial policy.[173] His colleague Fritz Lenz propagated the ideas of Ploetz, his "spiritual guide".[174] He was one of the main collaborators of the *Archiv für Rassen-und Gesellschaftsbiologie* founded by the latter in 1904. This review published contributions representing a variety of views, but Ploetz did not disguise his preference for those of the Germanomaniacs and he often lavished praise on the works of writers such as Theodor Fritsch in Germany or Lanz von Liebenfels in Austria, who are considered today as the intellectual mentors of Hitler.[175]

On the eve of the First World War, Ploetz's review, overshadowing Woltmann's *Politisch-anthropologische Revue*, became the main vehicle of an aggressive "biological philosophy" then fashionable in Germany.[176] Max Weber thought it worth while to engage in argument with Ploetz; he accused him of not realizing that biological characteristics could only influence historical and social events as symbols or, in other words, of confusing race with the idea of race.[177] Such cases illustrate the ease with which men of learning give way to the temptation to exaggerate the range of their respective disciplines. In a century of specialization, the old quarrel about the relative importance of heredity and education, of biological and of psychological factors, was exacerbated by the specialists themselves. Nevertheless, it is significant that the overriding importance of heredity or of the "racial factor", which was generally accepted at that time, should have had even more enthusiastic and active support in Germany than elsewhere.

There was a proliferation of projects and studies for the improvement of the human race. Thus the psychiatrist, August Forel, one of C. G. Jung's teachers in Zürich, examined the comparative value of the Aryan and Mongolian races in *Archiv* and wondered what would be the result of cross-breeding them. In order to make sure he proposed placing a few dozen Japanese orphans in German institutions for children and *vice versa* and keeping them under observation. He was confident that some millionaire would finance such an experiment, which he thought would prove conclusive.[178] Another contributor to the *Archiv*, Professor Christian von Ehrenfels (the author of the *Gestalttheorie*), carried on a campaign in favour of polygamy which he thought would produce good eugenic results.[179] An even bolder project by a certain Dr Müller-Lyer would have limited the right of procreation to 20 per cent of the men and 75 per cent of the women; while some socialists, with whom the first of the wilder Freudians associated themselves, were already preaching free love in the biological interests of race.[180]

In 1905 the indefatigable Ploetz founded an International Society for Racial Hygiene with the aim of improving the quality of the white race. Its Committee of Honour was soon to include such names as E. Haeckel, A. Weismann and F. Galton while its membership reached several hundreds. The Eugenics Education Society in Great Britain (1908), and the Eugenics Record Office in U.S.A. (1910), the only two organizations of the kind outside Germany, cut a poor figure by comparison. In 1908 Ploetz announced the foundation of an associated society inspired by the anti-semitic agitator Theodor Fritsch; this Community for German Renewal (*Deutsche Erneuerungsgemeinde*) envisaged a return to the land as the principal means for regeneration —for Aryans only, of course. In 1913 a third society was formed, the German Union (*Deutschbund*) which was to dedicate itself especially to the "extirpation of the inferior elements of the population" and the fight against "Jewish and Slav blood".[181]

So, though born in Great Britain, eugenics found in Germany its ideal habitat, as an ideology first of all. In 1922 G. K. Chesterton, in a violent pamphlet entitled *Eugenics and Other Evils*, condemned it as a diabolical German science, and particularly as a Prussian science, because Prussia "had long been the model State of all those more rational moralists who saw in science the ordered salvation of society". And he recalled how in 1914, when Great Britain "gave battle to the birth-place of nine-tenths of the professors who were the prophets of the new humanity", the entire world had been privileged to see these Prussian theories being put into practice.[182] Though these arguments may have seemed polemical and exaggerated at the time, it was not long before it began to look as though Chesterton had only mistaken one war for the next. At the beginning of the Second World War in 1939, Professor Otmar von Verschuer was able to announce the opening of the new eugenic era which "gives us the possibility of influencing the biological destiny of our children". The eugenists had indeed finally converted those who held power in Germany. "The history of our science", wrote von Verschuer, "is intimately connected with recent German history. The head of the German ethno-empire is the first statesman who has made the tenets of hereditary biology and eugenics a directing principle of state policy."[183]

★   ★   ★

While scientists were trying to unravel the future of the human race, in the light of natural selection, and discussing how best to arrange this future, a number of politicians were looking to Darwinism to support their political philosophy. It is true that the "survival of the fittest" looked much the same as the rule that "might is right", which had been recognized in international affairs for thousands of years; but nevertheless the theory of natural selection, as popularly understood, did seem to endow aggressive instincts and imperialistic ambitions with all the dignity of scientific truth. As early as 1889 Max Nordau observed that Darwin was well on the way to becoming the supreme authority for militarists in all European countries. "Since the theory of evolution has been promulgated, they can cover their natural barbarism with the name of Darwin and proclaim the sanguinary instincts of their inmost hearts as the last word of science."[184]

If we take as examples the speeches of Theodore Roosevelt and of the Emperor William II of Germany—both of whom glorified national power with more than usual vehemence—we note that the former continually invoked the laws about the struggle for existence and similar "laws of nature"[185] while the latter spoke of the divine election of his people and quoted the old Lutheran Bible in support.[186] But if the Kaiser preferred to describe his subjects as the salt of the earth rather than to bring in Darwin, many of his people were prepared to remedy the omission. One way or another, the similarity between the trend of scientific thought and the style of political pronouncements is evident. The gospel of power was preached above all in imperial Germany and in the Anglo-Saxon countries. In the latter, too, theories of social Darwinism were readily associated with the Germano-Aryan idea, also called the "theory of Teutonic origins".

In which country did these ideas strike deepest? J. A. Cramb (1862-1913) was an English historian who, like so many other European intellectuals of his generation, idealized both his country and warfare. He foresaw a tragic final conflict between the two branches of Germanism, with the old god of the Teutons serenely contemplating a war to the death between his "favourite children, the English and the Germans".[187] In 1881 Cramb's well-known predecessor, Edward A. Freeman, also obsessed by the Teutonic mania, had had to face a different dilemma. During a lecture tour in the United States he had publicly expressed the hope that every Irishman would murder a Negro and be hanged for it for the greater good of the Germanic race. The scandal aroused by this remark obliged him to declare later that "while all Teutons are very near to us, no European Aryan is very far from us".[188] The popular English psychologist William MacDougall, also deserves a mention as a propagandist for "the great Nordic race".[189] But perhaps most typical of the British mentality were the speeches of Joseph Chamberlain. Though he refused to concede any superiority to the Teutons, he envisaged an alliance of the "Anglo-Saxon races" and the "Teutonic race" as one between equals.[190]

These few examples remind one of the diversity of ancestral allegiance in the countries with an English culture. The sons of old "mother Germany" were better placed to claim their racial rights and they enjoyed the services of a spokesman of quite a different calibre. Indeed the most cogent prophets of the Third Reich were not the outstanding exponents of the new philosophy but a few obscure and forgotten authors.

One cannot, however, overlook the contribution of Nietzsche. The way his thought was exploited in Fascist and racist propaganda is well known. On a careful reading, it does indeed become clear that at one time Nietzsche demanded an enquiry about the regions "where the human stock has grown with the greatest vigour",[191] and at another that he recommended "what is ripe for death should be allowed to die and should not be sustained, rather those who are falling should be struck down so that they fall the more quickly—for is anything worse (said Zarathustra) than degeneration?" It was perhaps not without reason that Rickert in his day described Nietzsche as "the most interesting biologist and the one who remains the most influential".[192] It must be added, however, that as a visionary this biologist also forecast the practical results of doctrines which he described as "true but deadly":

> But if we have the doctrines of the finality of "becoming", of the flux of all ideas, types, and species, of the lack of all radical difference between man and beast (a true but fatal idea as I think), —if we have these thrust on the people in the usual mad way for another generation, no one need be surprised if that people drown on its little miserable shoal of egoism, and petrify in its self-seeking. At first it will fall asunder and cease to be a people. In its place perhaps individualist systems, secret societies for the extermination of non-members, and similar utilitarian creations, will appear on the theatre of the future.[193]

Yet Nietzsche's classifications of mankind were disconcerting, because he seemed to assign the first place to the Jews. He therefore wished his German contemporaries the strongest possible injection of Jewish blood. This is the real meaning of the well-known saying: "The future of civilization depends on the sons of Prussian officers."[194] The "blond beast" and the "master race" are not the only Nietzschean slogans which, taken out of context, can be fitted into racist catechisms. Indeed, some of the veteran anti-Semites were not in the least deceived. Eugen Dühring insinuated that Nietzsche was a Jew, and Theodor Fritsch warned youthful students against this "insolent Pole".[195] We might add that while there was one Nietzsche who, with Francis Galton's *Hereditary Genius* in his hand, asked himself whether the regeneration of Jewish Poles through Zionism was not a possibility, there was another who, mostly out of hatred against the Christian religion, boasted of his Aryan origins; and there was yet another who, already a prey to madness, we are told, scribbled with a trembling hand: "I want to have all anti-Semites shot."[196] But one could go on forever about Nietzsche.

By contrast, little ambiguity is to be found in the thought of Heinrich von Treitschke (1834-1896), the German patriot who was most influential among the student youth of the period. He considered the white race the aristocracy of the human species whose mission was to divide and rule the planet. The share which each white nation took for itself would be the measure of its worth.[197] These Aryan rivalries were necessary because "nations . . . cannot prosper and flourish except by intense competition like that of Darwin's struggle for existence".[198] This led Treitschke to declaim an almost religious paeon in praise of war:

> That war should be forever banished from this world is not merely an absurd hope but something profoundly immoral. If it were to happen, it would lead to the atrophy of many of the essential and sublime forces of the human soul and would transform the world into a vast temple of egoism. . . .

War was a "salutary drought". It reminded every man of "how petty is the value of his life compared to the majesty of the State. . . . This is the reason for the depth of religious feeling during any war in which the nation is seriously committed."[199]

It was Treitschke who invented or popularized certain catch phrases like "perfidious Albion" or "the Jews are our calamity" or the one (which is not easy to translate) about the invasion by the *strebsame hosenverkaufende Jünglinge**. Nevertheless he was inspired more by religious than by racial motives in dealing with all these questions, and he hoped that the union of the German *Volk* would be achieved with the assimilation of his "Israelite fellow-citizens"; he did not advocate more drastic measures.

General Friedrich von Bernhardi (1849-1930), who was the best-known of Treitschke's disciples abroad, also believed that only a vast colonial empire could assure "to the German nation and the German intelligence the world-wide respect which was their due". He too thought that war was "an indispensable factor of civilization" as well as "a biological necessity of the greatest importance". He added, quoting Heraclitus, that the philosophers of Antiquity had been aware of this long before Darwin.[200]

---

* A literal translation would be: "ambitious youngsters buying and selling trousers". This was one of the ways in which Treitschke conjured up the bogey of the control of Germany by Polish Jews.

Such writings, however militant, did try to conciliate imperialist or bio-imperialist claims with Christian tradition—von Bernhardi, for instance, recalled Christ's saying: "I am come not to send peace but a sword." But others emphasized the new racial values above all other considerations. Often enough the dividing line was hard to distinguish, as we can see from examples in the works of lesser writers. A certain Klaus Wagner in his book *Krieg* (1906) also referred to the religion of Jesus though his was a "Germanoid Jesus" or "Siegfried-Jesus" whose teaching on the separation of the holy from the wicked in the Last Judgement symbolized the selective merits of war. Wagner envisaged a "policy of racial power" in order to extend the German *Lebensraum*—the eviction of *Fremdlinge* (foreigners), and the fusion of all related Germanic tribes into a single politico-racial entity. "Have Gobineau, Darwin and Chamberlain lived in vain?" he asked.[201]

Alongside this completely forgotten work, another book, now equally unknown, set out in a greater detail what was to become in due course the racial policy of the Third Reich. It was called *Ein Pangermanistisches Deutschland* and was written by Josef Reimer. After paying tribute to his preceptors—to Gobineau, Klemm and Carus in the first place, and then to Darwin, Lapouge and Woltmann—Reimer went on to show how Germany should be organized when it had conquered the European continent and Siberia. The population of this region was to be divided among Germans and peoples who could be assimilated to the Germans on the one hand, and to elements which could not be thus assimilated (*Agermanen*) on the other. The weeding out of the sub-men from the men was to be the work of commissions (as actually happened in 1939-1945)[202] composed of anthropologists, doctors, and specialized "breeders". It was taken for granted that Jews and Slavs, with some exceptions, were to be considered as non-assimilable, while the French stood a far better chance. A statute for the *Agermans* assured them a few limited rights but it was based on the fundamental principle of their "exclusion from the [Germanic] community of procreation (*extra connubio*) coupled, in certain cases, with a total prohibition of all intercourse (*extirpatio*)".

This was considered by Reimer the only way of achieving a truly socialist and internationalist programme, since "the Germanic race is the only driving force and element of decision among those European nations which, in the existing climate of capitalism, are fighting to improve their condition. Therefore international socialism must be extended to the nations which contain elements of the Germanic race. . . . Forward then, Germanic workers of all the peoples of Europe!"[203] In this connexion, it is worth noting certain hopes voiced by the Social Democrat Party about increasing German *Lebensraum* for the greater good of the workers. These are to be found in some of the speeches and articles of Bebel and Kautsky, both of whom were convinced of the "superiority of the white race as a civilizing force".[204]

The spiritual ancestors of National Socialism were innumerable, and it will suffice to mention only two others whose influence was exercised more by their organizing abilities and political action than by their writings.

In the summer of 1890, William II ceded Zanzibar and its hinterland to Britain in exchange for the island of Heligoland. This strategic withdrawal intensified the outburst of indignation which had been provoked by the recent dismissal of Bismarck, and inspired a young collaborator of Krupp, Alfred Hugenberg, to create the famous Pan-German League (*Alldeutscher Verband*). The expansionist programme of this organization soon received the support of tens of thousands of Germans of all shades of opinion, some of whom, like Ernst Haeckel, Max Weber and Gustav Stresemann, achieved real distinction, while others, like Houston Stewart Chamberlain, Ludwig Schemann and Ludwig Wilser, are only remembered as ideologues of racism. The views of the latter triumphed in 1908 when Hugenberg's friend, the lawyer Heinrich Class, became the leader of the movement. In 1912 under the ambitious title of *If I were the Emperor* he published his political programme.[205]

In home affairs Class advocated a merciless struggle against Social Democracy including, if necessary, a *coup d'état*. The Jews, those ferments of Marxist decay, would in any case have to be deprived of their civic rights and isolated from the Aryans. Safeguarding the purity of the race called generally for heroic measures:

> That a bastard people (*Mischmaschvolk*) should become the beneficiary of Bismarck's work is an intolerable thought—it would be better to come to a horrible, though honourable, end than to prolong an existence which dishonours the German name. . . . So-called "humanity" can be re-established once we have been reformed politically, morally and hygienically. Until then we should show our love by being strict, and later we shall always have to set limits to our "humanity" in deference to the law by which no sacrifice is too great to safeguard the health of our people.[206]

As far as international politics were concerned, projects involving great transfers of population (the repatriation of Germans from abroad or the expulsion of Jews to Palestine, etc.), the annexation of all territories to the west of the Dnieper or the holding of Toulon as a surety were also a foretaste of Hitler's early achievements. In order to realize his schemes, Class hoped to establish a military dictatorship between 1914 and 1918, but his appeals to von Bernhardi and later to Ludendorff went unheeded.

During the Weimar Republic, the Pan-German League, strengthened by Class's and Hugenberg's ties with heavy industry, provided most of the financial support for the propaganda machinery of anti-semitism and for the distribution of the Protocols of the Elders of Zion. An excellent description of these activities is to be found in Norman Cohn's book on the history of this myth.[207] It is also worth remembering, in this connexion, the meeting in 1920 between Class and Hitler when the young agitator deferentially kissed the hands of his mentor and made embarrassed comments on the unsuitability of a too open and aggressive propaganda against the Jews.[208]

THE ARYAN MYSTIQUE

The notion of religion is so hard to define that it is sometimes difficult, in retrospect, to draw a clear dividing line between religion and nationalism as between religion and scientism. The German doctrines we have been considering illustrate the difficulty. In this connexion, Max Weber spoke of the "hair's breadth division which separates faith from science". This difficulty, of course, was not confined to German thought alone: in the Anglo-Saxon countries too, where Protestantism encouraged the proliferation of every kind of sect, unclassifiable doctrines and movements abounded. There, too, the atomization of religion favoured religious or pseudo-religious apologies for the white race, of which so many examples are to be found in the writings of Protestant authors. Theological exegesis ingenuously adapted the Bible to make the most of the curse on Ham. It is true that when Europeanism was at its most self-centred, in the second half of the nineteenth century, even the Vatican Council refused to remove this anathema, and Cardinal Lavigerie, the apostle of Abolitionism, maintained that only by their conversion would the black races escape the curse.[209] None the less, Protestant sectarianism was prepared to carry this kind of theology a great deal further than the Catholic

Church. Yet there was an important difference between the Anglo-Saxon and Germanic sects in this respect.

To examine this in more detail we must refer back to those national characteristics which we considered in the first part of this book. The English and American sects, from the Puritans to Jehovah's Witnesses, relied for the most part on Old Testament sources which in Germany were relatively neglected, at any rate after the Enlightenment. Of course, in the infinitely rich fabric of history everything is connected with everything else. Some link must have existed between the rise of Jewish economic power in Germany and certain theological outbursts, just as there was a connexion between the exegesis of the curse on Ham and colonial preoccupations. Nevertheless, it is impossible to explain the German-Aryan mystique by reference to the Rothschilds.

We believe that a particular idea of Christ can help to explain the German attitude. No Anglo-Saxon movement ever dreamt of asking what race the God-Man belonged to. Fichte, however, raised the problem, as we have seen.* Semantics provide another clue. The expressions "English religion" or "Anglo-Saxon religion" are mere juxtapositions of words as arbitrary as "French religion" or "Swiss religion", and having no generally accepted meaning. On the other hand, there was a German religion or faith which was formed over a period of several generations. We shall begin our enquiry with two authors to whom that prodigious propagandist of the Aryan myth, Richard Wagner, appealed in 1878 when he tried to define the concepts of *Germany* and *German*.[210] Frantz and de Lagarde mark the limits of that vague territory, in which "German religion" developed, a territory bounded on one side by the religion of Jesus and on the other by German racism.

The older of these writers, Constantin Frantz (1817-1891), was forgotten soon after he died. His writings were reissued in 1945 by certain well-intentioned people who hoped, in the period after Hitler, to give Germany an intellectual leader of peaceful inclinations.[211] Frantz indeed had carried on a campaign, especially after the Franco-Prussian War, against Prussian hegemony and militarism. "We have acquired glory", he wrote in 1874, "because all the nations study our military institutions and because Krupp has become a company of world-wide renown. If that is the universal mission of Germany we have now achieved our objective. . . ."[212] But his own ambition for

* See above, p. 101.

his country was entirely different—that it should become a centre for a European and Christian federation which was to ensure perpetual peace in the world.

Frantz thought that this was Germany's predestined vocation because the Holy Roman Empire ruled by Germans had taken over the inheritance of Rome and had served as "a bond of temporal union for all Western Christendom" in its capacity of an "international institution" of which "the German nation was the bearer".[213] The vocation of modern Germany was to renew this tradition and to establish a true Reich to take the place of Bismarck's "pseudo-Reich". Germany was an exception to the general rule.

> Germany has never been a "state" and it will never become one unless it ceases to be Germany. We have to look beyond the boundary of statehood and imagine a community of a quite different kind destined to accomplish far greater tasks. This is a condition precedent for resolving the German problem because Germany is in itself and for itself an international entity. It is necessary to rise from the political to the metapolitical point of view.[214]

Frantz illustrated this idea by a scientific comparison. Side by side with ordinary mathematics was there not also higher mathematics? A glance at the map made everything clear. The homeland of the Germans could not be geographically defined, as for instance France could. It spread out in every direction across neighbouring boundaries (*Nachbarschaft*). And was not Prussia the home also of a mixed population with a strong Slav influence? (Here Frantz's diagnosis was similar to that of Quatrefages.)* In short, the universal character of Germany had destined her to become, or to become once more, the base for the "international organization" of Christian peoples. This was because "for modern Christian peoples, nationality is only of secondary importance, so that they are primarily not German or French but *Christian*, which is how the Christian religion teaches them to consider themselves in the first place".[215] European Christianity, however, in order to rise above national and religious differences, would have to be purified and modernized, and Frantz quoted some of the leading intellectuals in this connexion, especially Schelling: "Neither a state religion nor a high church, but a religion of humanity which, in this

---

* Cf. above p. 261.

kind of Christianity, would also have the support of supreme science."
He also quoted Saint-Simon and the Humboldt brothers.[216]

Germany would not be able to exercise her Christian vocation,
continued Frantz, without freeing herself from Jewish domination.
After further quotations from such authorities as Kant, Fichte and
Schopenhauer, he developed his own philosophy of history, which
can be summarized as follows[217]:

After receiving a special Revelation, Judaism was unique in basing
itself first on a religion and then on a race, thereby perpetuating itself
in a way which was contrary to the normal course of events. He
called attention to the fact that even Islam had made converts among
peoples of all races whether Semitic, Aryan or Negroid. After the
Messiah had been put to death, the Jews, as a result of the divine curse,
had become a people of wanderers as well as being the instrument
chosen by Providence for the chastisement of other peoples. Moreover, the wars between Christian peoples had consolidated the power
of the Jews. A Christian federation would put an end to these fratricidal
wars, but only on condition that real progress took the place of "Jewish
progress". Germans had to have their eyes opened so that they might
at last "see themselves as a Christian nation and act accordingly".
Another war, too, would have to be waged. It was necessary

> to win another battle like that of Arminius to free us from the hold
> of Roman law, before we can look for a rebirth of our people.
> If this victory is won its consequences will be felt far beyond the
> boundaries of Germany. It will be a step towards the liberation of
> all Western Europe. . . .[218]

Roman law, in Frantz's view, was an emanation of the domineering
statecraft of Rome; he contrasted it with German law which was
supported by the peaceful will of free men.[219]

In this way Frantz summarized one of the encyclopaedic currents of
German thought which, as we have seen, stretched back to humanism
and the Reformation. His younger contemporary Paul de Lagarde
(1827-1891) covered much the same ground, though from a slightly
different point of view, and became the prophet (who was duly
canonized by the Third Reich) of a new "Germanic religion".

This enormously erudite orientalist was the son of a pastor, one
Boetticher. Family circumstances induced him to take the name of
one of his uncles of remote Lorraine ancestry. He justified this by
maintaining that the people of Lorraine were Germans,[220] and he

showed a marked hostility towards other races. In 1871 he expressed the hope that Paris would be totally destroyed,[221] while a political programme which he drew up for the Prussian Conservative Party envisaged the liquidation of several of the Slav peoples which he described as "the burden of history" and "material for use in constructing new German formations". He added: "The sooner they perish the better it will be for us and for them." The same considerations inspired his attitude to the Hungarians whose disappearance he thought all the more justified because they were an ancient people of Turanian race and no better, therefore, than Turks or Lapps—"the Hungarians will perish as the Celts are now perishing before our eyes".[222]

De Lagarde, nevertheless, has the reputation of having been an idealist in philosophy, and his saying *Das Deutschtum liegt nicht im Geblüte, sondern im Gemüte*,[223] by which he meant that Germanism was a thing of the spirit rather than of the flesh, is often quoted; and he recalled that Leibniz and Lessing were Slavs by descent. In many ways he may be thought of as a Fichte brought up to date by the anthropological knowledge of the late nineteenth century. In theology he was, like Fichte, radically anti-Pauline; like his friend Ernest Renan,[224] he revered Jesus only as a man, born among the stiff-necked race of Semites through some mysterious decree of the Deity, and whose genius was expressed in his "not-wanting-to-be-a-Jew".[225] Though he expressed no clear view about the genealogy of Jesus, de Lagarde asserted that Christian dogma itself refuted the idea that "the existence and essence of Jesus were rooted in the Jewish people".[226] His thought became more precise when criticizing the religious beliefs and institutions of his day. All that the Lutheran Church did was to carry forward "the rotten remains of Christianity".[227] The Catholic Church was "the born enemy of all States and nations",[228] and there could be no question as to the urgent need for abolishing the Synagogue and its members.

De Lagarde wanted above all to be the herald of a new Germanic religion and of the man with "a pure and strong" will who would be its founder.[229] Since all nations had been created by the will of God, all religions, in his opinion, ought to be national religions.[230] In his book, *The Religion of the Future*, he wrote that their national faith (*deutscher Glaube*) should enable the Germans to find the path of true liberty:

> ... We want liberty, not liberalism; Germany, not Judaeo-Celtic theories about Germany; piety, not dogmatics...; we

want our own nature to be acknowledged, educated and trans-figured; we do not want to be driven by a Russian coachman holding French reins, or flogged by a Jewish whip.[231]

De Lagarde sometimes made curious admissions when proclaiming that the Germany of his time was not genuine and exhorting a return to its real character. After repeatedly demanding "the destruction of Judaism" in Europe, without which the continent would become a vast cemetery, he went on: "The Jews will cease to be Jews to the same extent that we become ourselves."[232] Here an incitement to massacre goes hand-in-hand with the realization of a spiritual or moral deficiency, and the same association may be found in the following passage: "Every Jew is a proof of the weakness of our national life and of the small worth of what we call the Christian religion."[233]

These considerations prompted de Lagarde to hope that the Jews might be exiled to Madagascar,[234] for one does not argue with bacilli and threadworms; one exterminates them.[235] In 1942 a similar idea was formulated by Hitler: "The battle in which we are engaged today is of the same sort as the battle waged, during the last century by Pasteur and Koch."[236] It gives one a shock to read in de Lagarde's *Deutsche Schriften* the passage where, after expressing the hope that non-German peoples would soon disappear from central Europe, he adds: "There can be no doubt that a Kingdom of Lodomeria or a Duchy of Oswieczyn (Auschwitz) or a Grand-Duchy of Ruthenia are impossible."[237]

It should be added that de Lagarde, long before Hitler and Rosenberg, had other admirers such as Thomas Carlyle, Thomas Mann (who described him as *praeceptor Germaniae*), Paul Natorp and Thomas Masaryk (who, however, did not agree with Lagarde's opinions about the Czechs).[238] This focuses attention on a certain intellectual atmos-phere at the end of the nineteenth century which deserves to be better known. In Germany the search for a new religion became an endemic phenomenon and it is no exaggeration to describe it as a philosophical psychosis. The titles of a few books published during the period will give an idea of the atmosphere—*The Auto-destruction of Christianity and the Religion of the Future*, by the philosopher Eduard von Hartmann; or *Religion as the Self-Awareness of God*, by Hartmann's pupil, Arthur Drews; or better still, Eugen Dühring's *The Substitution of Religion by Something More Perfect and the Elimination of Jewishness by the Modern National Spirit*.[239] The First World War introduced a note of pessi-mism into this quest. Summing up in 1927, the philosopher Helmut

L

Groos deplored the contradiction between the German-Aryan and the Christian spirit and wondered whether the German people would survive the realization of such a tragic reality. If they succumbed, he concluded with pathos, nothing could be more worthy of them than to make such an end.[240]

The German theologians of the nineteenth century aided the philosophers by widening the breach which their predecessors of the Enlightenment had made between the Old Testament and the New,[241] and the fathers (sometimes in the literal sense of the word) prepared the ground for the heresies of the children. Thus Franz Delitsch (1813-1890), the Lutheran apostle of a conversion of the Jews, associated himself after some hesitation with the Higher Criticism of Wellhausen. His son, the Assyriologist Friedrich Delitsch (1850-1922), described Judaism as a "pagan religion" and an "immense fraud" from the Christian viewpoint.[242] The learned diplomat, Christian von Bunsen, a patron of Max Müller and de Lagarde, tried by means of a theology of "natural revelation" to reconcile religion and science[243]; his son, Ernst von Bunsen (1817-1893), employed considerable ingenuity in inventing an Aryan form of sun-worship based on Biblical traditions (Adam was Aryan and the Serpent semitic).[244] The titles of some of these works are also significant. Thus we have *Wotan or Jesus, Baldur or the Bible* by a certain Friedrich Döllinger, a namesake (or perhaps a relation?) of the great Catholic theologian Ignaz Döllinger (1799-1890).[245] Such works, from *Die Armanenschaft der Ario-Germanen* of Guido von List (perhaps the secret inspirer of Hitler)[246] to the *Germanenbibel* by Wilm Schwaner (a friend of Walther Rathenau),* together with a mass of "revelations" of every kind (such as the "unveiling of the secrets" of Holy Writ or of Runic lore or of Paradise itself)[247] must have constituted a considerable proportion of the printed works produced in Germany at this period. Of course, a great deal of this religious questing was associated with speculations and experiments in occult phenomena or in theosophy and spiritualism, which were taken much more seriously in all western countries than they are at present, now that psychoanalysis has satisfied some of the needs and clarified some of the motivations to which they were a response. But it was only in Germany that they took such an aggressively pagan as well as patriotic and nationalistic turn. The inevitable spongers who climbed on to the band-wagon earned a living by pretending to reincarnate

---

* Cf. below, p. 323.

the Germans of Tacitus[248] or by forging documents to prove the Aryanism of Jesus.[249]

It is noteworthy that Richard Wagner first emerged in this field as an obscure young author who, about 1850, identified Christ with Wotan, the supreme God.[250] It was only later, when he had outlined the plan of his "New Art" that he began writing music and introducing large audiences throughout Europe to the Germanic legends. His work, which was a mixture of musical, ideological, theatrical and religious themes could not have been better suited to the needs of the time and, in a society searching for new myths and avid for undiscovered thrills, it aroused a frenzy of enthusiasm. Thomas Mann, himself a passionate Wagnerian, explained the mystery of this music, which was something more than its purely musical expression, when he wrote in 1932: "When one hears Wagner being played one is persuaded that music will never be able to have another purpose than that of interpreting a myth, and that it was created for this purpose only." And this was the myth about which Mann was to say a few years later that it had unleashed the savagery of the Nazis.[251] As early as 1860 Baudelaire had praised the magic of Wagnerian sound. "This is the final cry of the soul borne aloft in its paroxysm. . . . It seemed to me that this music was my own. . . . Every moment of it carries you away, seems to reach ever higher, is marked by the excessive and the super-lative. . . ."[252]

The Wagnerian movement in France maintained its influence for two or three generations. In literature, the symbolist, as well as the naturalist, school was profoundly affected; there was Mallarmé's famous sonnet on "le Dieu Wagner",[253] and the infatuation of Maurice Barrès for the prophet of a new "universal ethic" is well known.[254] Catulle Mendès in the *Revue wagnérienne*, meditating on the message of Parsifal, saw the "shades of Antiquity", the ancient Aryan past with its "splendid and gigantic divinities", rise up before him.[255] In the same review Baron Hans von Wolzogen undertook to explain the essence of Aryan Art and held out a fraternal hand to Frenchmen. "This race which binds us together is the Aryan race . . . the most noble species in nature . . . all of whom can be called sons of the gods. . . ."[256] The enthusiasm of Edouard Dujardin, the director of the review, knew no bounds. Wagner had "conceived a new religion and preached it like a Gospel in a new, universally read, Bible"; his scores were a kind of celestial Jerusalem and he had instituted Bayreuth to be "the terrestrial Jerusalem, a precursor of the other" for the uninitiated masses.[257] In the words of a Catholic Wagnerian from Barcelona, Parsifal became "the third man of history, the third Adam . . . the form in which Jesus Christ will appear at the end of the world".[258]

The extravagances of the *Revue wagnérienne* were, of course, the product of a group of musical fanatics. Nevertheless they revealed an aspect of the common belief in Aryan or Christian-Aryan superiority, substantial evidence of which is to be found in the work of Marcel Proust, another Wagnerian.* An even better example, however, was provided by Alfred Naquet in a speech in the Chamber of Deputies: "As a Jew and in no way anti-semitic, I believe . . . that with the Jews there was inferiority in relation to the Aryans. . . . In contrast to the Jews, the Aryans have been intellectually fecund . . ." (1895).[259]

In Germany, Wagner himself undertook to proclaim his message or his religion, the corner-stones of which were the anthropodicy of Schlegel and the anti-Jewish metaphysics of Schopenhauer, later reinforced by other authors including Gobineau. Wagner's world vision can be summarized briefly:[260]

Long ago, in the golden age, men lived in a state of primitive innocence as vegetarians on the high plateaus of Asia. But they were tainted by original sin when they killed the first animal. Ever since then a thirst for blood had taken possession of the human race, so that murders and wars increased and were followed by conquests, exiles and migrations. Christ, who was either Indian or Aryan, had tried to save mankind by showing the way back to the innocence of primitive vegetarianism—whose significance he revealed to men at the Last Supper by changing bread into wine and flesh into bread. Finally, "he gave up his life to expiate the blood shed by carnivorous men since the beginning of the world". A Church, influenced by Jewry, had perverted the sense of this message, with the result that mankind had continued to degenerate, polluted by animal flesh and by the poison of Jewish blood. The Jew being "the devil incarnate of human decadence" and western civilization a "Judaeo-barbaric jumble", an apocalyptic end could not be long delayed. Only one hope remained—a new purification, a new receiving of the holy blood according to the rites of the mystery of Parsifal, the Germanic redeemer.

Wagner developed this theology in a number of writings which are still of great human and historical importance,[261] but which show him

---

* The conduct and mishaps of the "disgraceful Jew", Albert Bloch, in *La Recherche du temps perdu*, are especially instructive in this connexion.

to have been a muddled thinker and a poor writer. Moreover, although his incitement to anti-semitism had a vast and immediate response, the same could not be said for his vegetarianism. Most of his admirers drew their sustenance from other philosophical or ideological sources: but the Bayreuth cult gave rise to innumerable exegeses as the complete Wagnerian bibliography apparently contains more than 45,000 items.

Among these books the work of Leopold von Schröder, a Professor of Vienna University and an erudite scholar on India, was singular in that it honoured Judaism equally with Aryanism. In his *Aryan Religion and Fulfilment of the Aryan Mystery at Bayreuth*,[262] von Schröder described the nature cults of the "primitive Aryans", to whom he attributed the gift of contemplative and philosophic thought. These ancient cults became spiritualized when the Jews enlightened the Aryans with their monotheistic ethics, rejected all the nature cults and even persecuted them. According to von Schröder, the genius of Wagner lay in his ability to synthesize these disparate elements. In the *Ring of the Nibelungen*, for instance, he had portrayed the tragedies of envy and the thirst for power, with which Aryan destiny was cursed. *Parsifal* was on a higher level, since it united the Indian ethic of compassion with the Christian idea of redemption against a background of the old-Aryan nature cult, revived by the magician of Bayreuth. "Redemption through love! Redemption through pity!" cried von Schröder with feeling.

> After a separation of more than five thousand years, the Aryan tribes can meet together for the first time in a designated place to contemplate the ancient mysteries fulfilled in a new form. Thanks to Wagner, Bayreuth has become the centre of all the Aryan peoples, and this very fact guarantees an astonishing supremacy to Germany and the Germans. . . .[263]

In spite of this patriotic conclusion, Schröder's analysis met with no success. This learned man seems to have had no understanding of the Aryan myth in modern form. His celebrated friend Houston Stewart Chamberlain (1855-1927), who helped him to find an editor, reproached him for having publicly praised certain talented Jews. Such judgements should only be expressed in private, wrote Chamberlain, for otherwise it would be a betrayal of the Aryan cause (as though the Aryans had unmentionable defects to conceal).[264] It was this step-son of Richard Wagner who, in his own words, was prompted by interior demons to become the chief prophet of Aryanism.

Chamberlain was the son of an English admiral; was educated in France and fell in love with Germany as an adolescent. He was the most cosmopolitan of the Wagnerians. He was also a very sick man who was prevented by a mysterious illness from completing his studies in biology. Only the excitement of polemics in defence of Germanism brought him relief.[265] This stimulated him to produce studies on Wagner, Kant, Goethe and, above all, his *The Foundations of the Nineteenth Century*, a work of some fifteen hundred pages, in which he pronounced on all the learning of his time.

This work certainly possessed the qualities required to command the attention of a cultivated audience. Writing in a brilliant style, Chamberlain attacked scientific pedantry and specialization by showing that every specialist, whether he wanted to or not, had to borrow from other branches of science than his own. This justified him in doing likewise, as a self-confessed dilettante who nevertheless seemed to have read everything. In dealing with the exact sciences, for example, he included non-Euclidean geometry and relied for support on the scientific philosophy of Henri Poincaré. The vision of the world which he thus conjured up seemed to him to support his Aryan mystique, for was not modern science exclusively the work of the "Celto-Slavo-Teutons", more conveniently called "Germans"?

> . . . The faultlessly mechanical interpretation of nature is unavoidable and the only true one. When I say "the only true one", I mean that it can be the only true one for Teutons; other men may—in the future as in the past—think differently . . . so long as the Teuton predominates, he will force this view of his even upon non-Teutons. . . . By this—and this alone—we have acquired a mass of perceptions and a command over nature never equalled by any other human race.[266]

According to Chamberlain, this sovereign knowledge of science was acquired thanks to an understanding of the laws of scientific necessity, enlightened by the religious instinct of the Aryans. This was dealt with in a chapter on "Religion".

> Take, for example, the conception of the Godhead: here Jehovah, there the old Aryan Trinity. . . . Thanks to the influence of Hellenic sentiment, the Christian Church . . . had, in the moulding of its dogma, steered successfully past that most dangerous cliff, Semitic monotheism, and has preserved in her otherwise perilously Judaised conception of the Godhead the

sacred "Three in Number" of the Aryans . . . all human knowledge rests on three fundamental forms—time, space, causality. . . .
In short, the threefoldness as unity surrounds us on all sides as an
original phenomenon of experience and is reflected in all individual
cases. . . .[267]

This was a matter of "spontaneous intuitive development into a
myth of a general, but not analytically divided, physical and at
the same time metaphysical cosmic experience . . ." or of "nature-
symbolism".

It followed that

> he who mechanically interprets empirical nature as perceived by
> the senses has an ideal religion or none at all; all else is conscious
> or unconscious self-deception. The Jew knew no mechanism of
> any kind; from creation out of nothing to his dreams of a
> Messianic future everything is in his case freely ruling, all-powerful
> arbitrariness; that is also the reason why he never discovered
> anything.[268]

This racial philosophy of science had vast ramifications. Chamberlain started a controversy about the theory of relativity which became
acrimonious, with the result that the attacks made on "Jewish psychology" under the Third Reich were soon matched by those on
"Jewish physics". The scientists backed by the régime, among them
two Nobel prize-winners, reproached Einstein and his German imitators (to repeat C. G. Jung's expression) for having developed the
model of an arbitrary and artificial universe, against which they set the
natural and tri-dimensional universe of "German physics".[269]

If the exact sciences provided Chamberlain with arguments to support Aryan superiority, the use which he made of the human sciences
in his day may well be imagined. He was all the more plausible
because he repeatedly insisted on the uncertainties of these sciences
and criticized the fanatical propagandists of both scientific positivism
and anti-semitism. Like many other personalities of the time he
asserted that he was not really anti-semitic because he counted a
number of Jews among his friends.[270] As a student of biology he had

> been taught in the school of facts by an incomparable master,
> Charles Darwin. . . . I accompany the great naturalist to the
> stable, the farmyard or the garden and there I see all that which
> gives real meaning to the word race—an unquestionable reality
> which must be plain to all men.

He also appealed to Descartes.

> All the world's wisest men, said Descartes, would not be able to
> define whiteness, but I have only to open my eyes to see some-
> thing white. The same is true of "race".[271]

Chamberlain cited Robertson Smith on the religious sterility of the
Semites,[272] while August Forel was his authority for proclaiming the
inferiority of the Blacks.[273] Chamberlain was also the first influential
author to quote Freud with approval, though he did not understand
him.[274] Beneath this cloak of universal erudition Chamberlain indulged
his two major obsessions, the hatred of "Rome" and of "Judah".

In attacking the Roman Catholic Church Chamberlain employed
the familiar bogey of the Jesuit menace. But from his racial theories
he developed a totally new argument on the subject, namely that
Ignatius Loyola, being a Basque, must have been a *non-Aryan*. Was
not his case that of a primitive race seeking to obtain revenge against
its conquerors "through the sturdiest of its sons", of "animal nature"
attempting to vanquish "intellectual nature"? This hypothesis seemed
all the more convincing since it was the Jesuits who had launched the
best organized and therefore the most dangerous attack ever directed
against the Germanic spirit, or rather on the Aryan spirit in general.
Moreover, Loyola was not a unique phenomenon in this respect.

> There are hundreds of thousands of people in Europe who speak
> our Indo-European tongues, wear the same clothes, take part in
> our life, and are excellent people in their way, but are just as far
> removed from us Teutons as if they lived on another planet; here
> it is not a question of a cleft such as separates us in many respects
> from the Jew, and which may be bridged at this point and that,
> but of a wall which is insurmountable and separates one land
> from the other.[275]

In spite of this, it was the "cleft" which really frightened him and
the Jews seemed far more dangerous to him than the Finns or Basques.
It was clearly the Jews who provoked the main symptoms of his
neurosis, the dread of pollution and insidious contaminations. The
most revealing passage is that in which, under the heading *Consciousness of Sin against Race*, he dealt with the "physical genesis" of the Jews.
According to Chamberlain the Jewish race was the result of unnatural
cross-breeding between the Bedouins of the Semite deserts, and
Hittites, Syrians and Aryan Amorites. In the course of time the Jews
became aware of their original blemish and realized that

. . . their existence is sin, their existence is a crime against the holy laws of life; this, at any rate, is felt by the Jew himself in the moments when destiny knocks heavily at his door. Not the individual but the whole people had to be washed clean, and not of a conscious but of an unconscious crime.[276]

Because of this the Jews long ago conceived the heroic plan of breeding a pure but artificial race; and this resolution, which was upheld for thousands of years, was the cause of Jewish strength and greatness. In a chapter on "The entrance of the Jews into Western History", the longest in the book, Chamberlain showed how Jewish strength of character had enabled them to dominate the "Celto-Slavo-Teutons" in spite of their evident inferiority in number and intelligence. Their great design apparently began to take effect at the time of the rebuilding of the Temple under Cyrus:

> . . . But not long after Ezekiel's death the noble Persian King Cyrus conquered the Babylonian Empire. With the simplicity of the inexperienced Indo-European he permitted the return of the Jews and gave them a subsidy for the rebuilding of the temple. Under the protection of Aryan tolerance the hearth was erected from which, for tens of centuries a curse to all that is noblest and an everlasting disgrace to Christianity, Semitic intolerance, was to spread like a poison over the whole earth.[277]

In spite of all the persecution and all the burnings, the Jews were able to impose their terrible will upon Europe.

> . . . Olympus and Walhalla became depopulated because the Jews so wished it. Jehovah . . . now became the God of the Indo-Europeans.[278]

In the nineteenth century the influence of the Jews was exercised in every field:

> . . . The possession of money in itself is, however, of least account; our governments, our laws, our science, our commerce, our literature, our art . . ., practically all branches of our life have become more or less willing slaves of the Jews. . . . The Indo-European, moved by ideal motives, opened the gates of friendship: the Jews rushed in like an enemy, stormed all positions and planted the flag of his, to us, alien nature—I will not say on the ruins but on the breaches of our genuine individuality.[279]

How was this situation to be remedied and the true nature of the Aryans to be restored? Chamberlain too considered Jesus as being at the heart of the question and he devoted about a hundred pages to showing that the God-man was not a Jew.[280] Somehow, to ease the anxiety of Aryan minds, it was vital to uproot Judaism from Christianity. Robert Godet, the writer of the preface to the French version of Chamberlain's book, summarized this attempt as follows:

> If Chamberlain is right, it is we who have created the Jewish peril by accepting in our organism a body which it could not assimilate, seeing that the Indo-European conscience had already anticipated the nature of the revelation which was fully realized in the doctrine and example of Jesus. We must therefore free ourselves from the Jewish yoke by spiritual means of our own. Whether we free ourselves or not depends on us; and we shall do so if we detach the Gospel from the links which bind it to the Old Testament, if we untie the knot, by which ... two antagonistic ideals, two worlds which cannot be reconciled, are bound together. This, in short, is what Chamberlain asks us to do.[281]

In 1903-1904, Chamberlain wanted to compose the new Aryan gospel himself and he wrote to his editor as follows:

> In applying oneself to such a task I think that it is necessary in the first place to have a deep and far-reaching realization of the needs of mankind. ... It is not enough to delude oneself that a profession of faith might give birth to a new religion. The true historical process has always been the exact opposite. The new religion appears first; then comes the profession of faith, or various professions of faith adapted to the different needs of different minds.[282]

The Foundations of the Nineteenth Century did indeed seem to be a very personal profession of faith, and one remarkably well adapted to the needs of innumerable minds during the first half of the twentieth century. It was with good reason that the philosopher of the Nazi Party, Alfred Rosenberg, called his major work *The Myth of the XXth Century*, and the many ties between Chamberlain, the Bayreuth circle and the rise of Hitler are well known. The immediate success of *The Foundations of the Nineteenth Century* has been forgotten; it became the new Bible of hundreds of thousands of Germans. What did they see in it? The Emperor William II was perhaps speaking for a majority when, in an enthusiastic letter, he thanked Chamberlain for having freed him from the false beliefs of his youth and for showing him the way of salvation. The Kaiser wrote:

> I knew by instinct that we youngsters had need of another education in order to serve the new Reich. Our stifled youth needed a liberator like yourself, one who revealed to us the Indo-German origins which no one knew about. And so it was only at the cost of a hard struggle that the original Germanic Aryanism (*das Urarische-Germanische*) which slumbered in the depths of my soul was able to assert itself. It showed itself in my open hostility to "tradition" and it often tried to emerge in strange inarticulate ways since it was, to begin with, an obscure and unselfconscious presentiment. And now you come and with a wave of your magic wand create order where there was chaos and light where there was darkness. You explain what was obscure, you show the way of salvation to the Germans and to all the rest of mankind. . . .[283]

The correspondence which began with this letter lasted more than twenty years, and it soon became evident that William II was influenced by Chamberlain in a number of his speeches and plans. Some of the peaceful projects and declarations of this muddled monarch might perhaps be attributed to his new-found Aryan faith, but whatever its effect in the realm of politics, in 1924 he was still asserting that Christianity had grown out of paganism and not Judaism, that it came from the Persians and not from the Hebrews.[284]

In Anglo-Saxon countries *The Foundations of the Nineteenth Century* was very well received when it appeared in translation in 1911. Most British newspapers mentioned it. The *Spectator* praised it as a "monument of erudition"; the *Birmingham Post* found it "glowing with life, packed with fresh and vigorous thought"; the *Glasgow Herald* declared that it would be difficult to "over-estimate the stimulating qualities of the book". The commentator in the *Times Literary Supplement* hailed it as "one of the books that really mattered".[285] Bernard Shaw in *Fabian News* was even more enthusiastic. He called the book a historical masterpiece which had cleared away much confusion. Whoever failed to read it, he declared, would be unable to talk intelligently about political or sociological problems for some considerable time.[286] In America Theodore Roosevelt, more cautiously, pointed out the extreme bias of the author, but all in all he saw no great harm in this since it was a case of denouncing egalitarian doctrines which were as false as they were pernicious, and which were transmitted from generation to generation by men of goodwill but feeble intelligence.[287]

It was otherwise in France. The French translation of *The Foundations of the Nineteenth Century* was published in the autumn of 1913 and was only reviewed during the First World War, in articles denouncing pan-Germanism. Some of the reviews suggest, nevertheless, that had it been published at a different time the book would not have lacked French admirers also. In the *Revue bleue*, for instance, the musicologist Maurice Kufferath deplored "this abysmal aberration of a once intelligent man . . . this spiritual downfall of a thinker who often showed a penetrating and independent mind".[288] A more intriguing article was to be found some fifty pages on in the same issue of *Revue bleue* where the Rosicrucian Joséphin Péladan wrote of the failure of Christianity in Germany.

He began by recalling how he had been beguiled by "Wagnerian magic" and evoked his former affection for the Germany of Oberammergau and Bayreuth. He asked how the barbarity recently shown by the "Teutonic race" could be explained. "How did the Cross come to be shattered?" The high-priest Péladan had the answer: "In the dark soul of the German, the Asiatic Jehovah has taken the place of the Divine Preacher of the Sermon on the Mount. . . . The religious structure of the country remains strongly hierarchic but the sermons speak only of the Jewish Torah."

But there was worse to come. Unfortunately the Germans were not content to follow the Mosaic Law. Having gone to school with the Rabbis they applied the Talmudic teaching which was far more ferocious: "The Gemara, a veritable code of hate, taught that the killing of Gentiles was legitimate and described it as a good work." It was not therefore to the "bad faith of Wotan's followers" that the de-Christianization of Germany must be attributed since *Deutschland über alles* had been borrowed from the Talmud. Was it then surprising that German soldiers, fired by inspiration of this kind, should finish off the wounded in battle with their daggers and cut the throats of the maimed or disembowel the dying? Péladan ended up by putting Allah and Islamic militarism into the dock as well. "It is clear that this war has been declared against Christ and his Word. . . . They call this *Kultur*, this cult of race where the conscience of the whole of mankind is sacrificed on the altar of the State along with the true principles of civilization." Obviously mankind and the members of the Christian Church were synonymous for this author.[289]

So, in the midst of war, Péladan projected his own nationalistic frenzy on to the old Jewish scapegoat. Here we could perhaps leave the history of the Aryan myth, except that it would not be complete without a short account of how certain members of the Jewish community, which provided its future victims, first adopted the theory and then proclaimed their own special versions of it. As might be expected it was only in the Germanic countries that Jewish dreams of total assimilation and protestations of patriotism assumed these distinctive characteristics.

In the case of Hermann Cohen (1842-1918), the founder of the neo-Kantian school of philosophy, the dense language of German idealism encouraged this kind of intellectual legerdemain. From a religious and philosophical point of view Cohen was a believer in Jewish mono-theism, but he thought that there was nothing to prevent "the total German naturalization of the Jewish religion". On the one hand he adjured the Jews to remain faithful to the religion of their ancestors and on the other he promised the Germans that the Jews would be completely assimilated. "Considerations of principle and, even more, our most sacred desires must urge us to identify ourselves completely with the *natural feelings* of the people with whom we wish to unite." As if this was not sufficiently clear, he added:

> We Jews have to admit that the racial instinct is not a mere form of barbarism but a natural and legitimate aspiration of national feeling. . . . I sincerely maintain that all of us want to be like Germans. . . . In this matter, all we have to say is: Be patient . . . (1880).[290]

Thus the religion of Moses dwelt side by side with a Germanic faith in Cohen's soul. During the First World War he tried to justify the amalgamation of these two beliefs philosophically by asserting the existence of a "profound brotherhood between Judaism and Germanism", a brotherhood which was a "basic characteristic of the German spirit". In pursuing this idea he even applied Fichte's anthro-pology to the Jews, for was not Yiddish a Germanic language? It was, after all, spoken by millions of Jews in Russia and America and by the ancestors of most of the Jews in France and England. Hence the obligation for all Jews "to regard Germany with pious respect as their spiritual home; for it is from his language, however mutilated it may be, that a man draws the original powers of reason and of intelligence".

It was up to Jews in the Germanic countries to remind international Jewry of this bond, and of German rights of spiritual primacy over the Jews who had their origin in Germany. Cohen himself carried out this duty by criticizing Henri Bergson who "claims to be an original philosopher. He is the son of a Polish Jew who spoke Yiddish. What goes on in Bergson's mind when he thinks of his father . . .?"[291]

If a religious Jew was able to push his patriotic loyalty to such lengths, what was to be expected of those who, in increasing numbers, cursed the fate which made them Jews? Some were even led openly to profess a wholesale belief in Aryanism.

This is what happened to the Viennese philosopher Otto Weininger (1880-1904) whom we have already mentioned. His short life was a model of its kind. When he ended it by committing suicide he was only drawing the final conclusion from the accusations he made against the Jews, that is to say against himself, in his writings. Not that he openly professed anti-semitism. On the contrary, he declared that true Aryans could on no account be anti-Semites.[292] His masochistic obsessions were mainly centred round a Manichean contrast between women and Jews, on the one hand, and men and Aryans on the other. His book, *Sex and Character*, was devoted principally to the denigration of women, and his theory can be summarized in his axiom. "The best woman is inferior to the worst man."[293] Thus there could be some human beings inferior even to the Jews whom Weininger supposed to be related to the pig-tailed Chinese and to the Negroes who were unable to produce a genius. But in one sense the Jew was inferior even to woman, since the latter at least believed in man while the Jew believed in nothing and was, therefore, a nullity. This negative man, unable to conceive of the eternal life of the spirit, seemed to Weininger to incarnate the materialist decadence of his century. In his anguish he foretold an imminent struggle between flesh and spirit:

> The human race awaits the founder of a new religion and the struggle approaches its crucial phase, as in the first year of our era. Once again humanity has the choice between Judaism and Christianity, between commerce and culture, between woman and man, between the species and the individual, between non-value and value, between nothingness and divinity; there is no third kingdom. . . .[294]

It should be added that Weininger, as an idealist philosopher, considered "race" as a half-biological and half-spiritual fact. Judaism, in his eyes, was "a tendency of the intellect, a psychic condition which could appear in any man but whose greatest historical manifestation was in historical Judaism".[295] Equally, it was in the German race that Aryanism found its highest expression. He followed this declaration by stating: "The author has to point out that he himself is of Jewish origin." Soon after the publication of his book his philosophy reached fulfilment in suicide.

He was not the only Jewish enthusiast of the Aryan myth to excuse himself for being a member of his race. In 1909, Walther Rathenau (1867-1922) introduced himself to the Chancellor, von Bülow, with the words: "Your Excellency, before you receive me I must make a statement to you which is also a confession. Your Excellency, I am a Jew!" In 1897 when he made his appearance as a writer, the future statesman described his fellow Jews as an "oriental horde" camping on German soil:

> . . . What a strange sight! A foreign tribe set apart within the confines of Germanic life, warm-blooded and gesticulating. An Asiatic horde camping on the soil of the March. The forced good-humour of these men cannot hide the ancient unsatisfied hatred which weighs upon them. They do not realize that only a century which has mastered all the elemental forces is able to protect them from such trials as their fathers had to endure. . . . They live in an invisible ghetto partly of their own choosing. They do not form part of the German people, they are a foreign organism in its body. . . .
>
> Look at yourselves in a mirror. This is the first step to self-criticism. Nothing can change the fact that you resemble one another very closely and that the bad behaviour of one is visited upon all. And nothing can prevent your oriental aspect from making you unattractive to the Nordic tribes. . . .[296]

Rathenau accordingly urged the Jews to discipline themselves like the Prussians and so to re-educate themselves that they would no longer be derided by the Germans. And although he later decided that his strictures had been too harsh, his views on anthropology, as they were to develop in his writings, continued to contrast two races, opposed in the same way as the Germans and the Jews. In his essay, *On Weakness and on Fear* (1904), he distinguished between a courageous and aggressive, and a frightened and defensive race, and it was the latter which bore the mark of Cain.[297] From his *Critique of the Times* (1912)[298] it emerged that the courageous and virtuous race was the Germanic. This work dealt with the problems of industrial civilization, for which

Rathenau predicted a joyless, prosaic future; and he called the period of mechanization and levelling out the era of *de-Germanization*. In the same context he declared that the countries of southern Europe, in which Germanic blood had been diluted through the centuries, were no longer capable of cultural progress while the western nations and particularly Germany, where this blood had been better preserved, were for this reason "the world centre and school of cultural values".[299]

Finally, in his aphorisms, which are yet to be published in full, Rathenau described the "tragedy of the Aryan race" in terms more eulogistic even than those of Chamberlain:

> A magnificent blond nation is born in the North. Its over-whelming fertility spreads in waves to the South. Each migration is a conquest, each conquest enriches the customs and civilization of the conquered. One day the South gets the upper hand; an oriental religion is introduced into the countries of the North. The latter defend themselves with their old spirit of courage. But in the end the worst threat supervenes; industrial civilization conquers the world and with it the forces of fear, intelligence and cunning, embodied in democracy and capital, take over. . . .[300]

In his public or private life, as in his writings, Walther Rathenau was fascinated by the Aryan myth. When he was attacked by anti-Semites this forceful man defended himself clumsily as though unable to disagree with his adversaries, and indeed it would have been impossible for him to do so when he found their theories so convincing. He took one of these adversaries, Wilm Schwaner, the author of the *Germanic Bible*, as his friend and confidant. In their correspondence he continued to affirm his "Germanity":

> For me the Jews are a Germanic tribe like the Saxons and Bavarians. You may smile, knowing all about racial doctrines. But I don't care what science says. To my mind it is the heart and the soul which decide what nation one belongs to . . . (1916).[301]

Rathenau believed that with the passage of time he had acquired this Germanic soul, which his friend denied him on grounds of racial science, because of his loyalty and patriotism. In his *Mystical Breviary* he wrote that "The majority of men are born with a soul but all can gain one by noble endeavour. The soul is the reward of all men of goodwill"[302] (1906). In his efforts to serve his country as best he could, he fearlessly assumed the role of a Cassandra in the autumn of 1914, and predicted a long and exhausting war. Later he enabled Germany to stand up economically against the Allies, thanks to the organization for stockpiling raw materials (*Kriegsrohstoffabteilung*), which he founded and of which he was the first head. He was a patriot to the end and, late in 1918, he called for a heroic final uprising of the whole German people. Under the Weimar Republic, after the capitulation, he accepted the risky post of Foreign Minister and suddenly emerged as a symbol of reconciliation. That was enough to make this Jew an Elder of Zion, a man to eliminate. During the spring of 1922 he was assassinated in a terrorist attack, the first and a highly symbolical victim of the Aryan myth.[303]

CONCLUSION

Now that we have reached the end of our enquiry, what lesson can be drawn from it? We said at the beginning that the search for origins, the attempt to find one's identity through one's ancestors, has always been the concern of human groups in every age and culture. This may be inferred *a priori* by analogy with the individual, and it is confirmed in the writings of the anthropologists quoted in the introduction to this book. We have not attempted to investigate this subject in every human culture but have confined ourselves to examining the myths of origin of the principal European nations. One might describe these myths as compromises between pagan memories, dynastic ambitions and the teachings of the Church. These compromises were influenced by the strength of ancestral memories and by historical vicissitudes and they took the most varied forms; but usually they showed distinct preference for Germanic stock or blood. We have also seen how the tendency embodied in the ruling dynasty to claim a distinct and superior descent always clashed with the myth of Adam as a universal father—a myth which according to a rabbinical apologist, was intended to teach all men that they are in reality equal.*

The Judaeo-Christian tradition was both anti-racist and anti-nationalist, and the social structure and barriers of the Middle Ages, with its feudal, horizontal hierarchies, no doubt helped the Church to translate this ideal into reality. If all men were equal before God, vertical and geographical distinctions should make no difference to the value of human beings. Nevertheless, one exceptional case (which we should perhaps have examined more closely)† showed how re-

---

* This was certainly the teaching of Hebraic anthropology. Contrary to a widely held belief, the exclusiveness of the Mosaic law was religious not racial. The barrier between the "chosen people" and "the nations" was intended to preserve the former's function as a priestly people.

† We have done so in Vol. II (*De Mahomet aux Marranes*) of *Histoire de l'anti-sémitisme*.

stricted were the limits of this universal equality. During the Renaissance, the Spanish statutes relating to "purity of blood" brought about
a type of segregation similar to that of the racial laws promulgated
in the twentieth century by the Nazis and Fascists. This case is highly
instructive since it shows how, given appropriate circumstances,
religious bigotry, under cover of a perverted theology, was able to
bring about discrimination against Christians said to belong to a
biologically inferior stock. Even so, though the "inferior race" of the
conversos (i.e. Christians of Jewish or Moorish descent) was persecuted
by the Inquisition and, in the case of the Moors, expelled from Spain,
it was not exterminated. No doubt the anthropology of the Church
acted as a brake in the last resort, thus saving Christian honour.

The doctrine of the unity of the human race, about which people
always had secret misgivings, was directly attacked by a number of
leading philosophers of the Enlightenment. We have discussed the
new anthropological ideas put forward in the eighteenth century at
some length because such writers as Buffon, Voltaire, Hume or Kant,
each in his own way prepared the ground for the racial hierarchies of
the following century. We believe that we may thereby have put
straight certain widespread misconceptions about historical development. When, among the ruins of the *ancien régime*, Adam died as a
universal ancestor, first scientists and then philosophers affiliated
Christian peoples to other patriarchs, and these were no longer Biblical
but Indian. It should be emphasized that, at least to begin with, this
genealogy did not imply any political exclusions. In fact the real
founder of the Aryan myth, Friedrich Schlegel, was a supporter of
total emancipation for the Jews. Once launched by the orientalists and
the German myth-makers, the new theory gained ground rapidly to
become internationally accepted and acquire, during the second half
of the century, much the same status as the theory of spatial ether.
Thereafter the theory of Aryan origins was propagated among the
masses, mainly in support of anti-semitic campaigns, though other
political passions such as Franco-German rivalry also helped it to
spread. From about 1890 the theory began to be questioned, in part
because of the widespread discussion which it aroused. It then passed
from the scientists to the demagogues to become at last the official
doctrine of the Third Reich when men designated as non-Aryans were
sacrificed to the gods of racialism.

Before its final degradation, in the course of less than a century, to
such depths of infamy, the Aryan theory was in the main current of

scientific progress and appeared to be corroborated by linguistic discoveries. Hegel is an outstanding example of how it carried conviction with the most acute minds of the past. We have argued that the attraction which it exercised was due in part to the desire to abandon the anthropodicy of the Bible with its "Jewish fables", and we noted the lordly disdain with which Goethe attributed descent from Adam to the Jewish people alone. The Indian fables, which had acquired popularity before the discovery of linguistic ties between India and Europe, could be used to diminish the influence of the Bible, as the writings of Voltaire or Herder show. So the Aryan theory does indeed belong to the tradition of anti-clericalism and anti-obscurantism; it is a product of the first gropings of the sciences of man as they tried to model themselves on the exact sciences and so strayed into a mechanistic and determinist blind-alley where they remained for a century.

In dealing with these questions we have drawn attention to the remarkable fact that the Bible took some account of the principles and distinctions which have been adopted by biological sciences only in the nineteenth century and by the sciences of man only in our own times. But scientists whose subject was biology often thought in terms of anthropology. When, for instance, Linnaeus heard that Réaumur had fertilized a chicken with a rabbit he at once exclaimed that this cast a disquieting light on the origin of the Negroes—though he added that, as a good Christian, he refused to attribute an animal origin to mankind.[1] Less fervent Christians did not share such scruples. Many gave their support, especially on grounds of polygenism, to those legendary beliefs on which the classical authors had already embroidered innumerable variations and which the Church, as the heir to Jewish tradition, had never been able to eradicate completely.

In what way did the Biblical account anticipate the theories of modern science? It did so by establishing, alongside the gulf between God and His creation, a similar gulf between man and the animals or between man and nature, as well as the gaps between the species. The only Biblical passage which assumes a different order of things seems like an echo of a pagan myth. It is in Chapter VI of Genesis where, in the story of the Flood, we are told that the "sons of God" (bᵉnê 'elōhîm) "came in unto the daughters of men" and bore children to them and that these "became mighty men which were of old, men of renown". This reminds one of the descendants of Wotan or Zeus; but this race of demi-gods, once mentioned, is immediately suppressed, one might say censored, together with all other life on earth. That

Creation survived is due to Noah's Ark alone. After this the censorship is absolute throughout the whole Bible text and in the commentaries. The species, according to the Talmud, promised as they left the Ark, not to fornicate with each other, and they never mingled again. The real meaning of the religious exclusiveness of the Mosaic law is its constant reminder to man, in all the circumstances of his life, of his unique position in the world.

It would probably be useless to ask why the Biblical account rejects the fantastic unions with which all mythologies are filled and why, by thus isolating man from other creatures, it appears to designate him as a creature apart—a "cultural" as opposed to a "natural" being—who has cast off certain biological bonds to set out on a journey from which there could be no return. At most one might compare Biblical anthropology to the insights of some Greek authors, as has been suggested by the Hellenist Pierre Vidal-Naquet. But it is more to the point to stress the persistence of the mythological error and to relate it to the animistic confusions of paganism and to the Aristotelian "great chain of being".*

The problem then becomes one of explaining the constant and universal tendency to identify man with his environment or with "nature". What is the basis of this tendency (which every society has expressed in its own language whether poetical or pseudo-scientific)? What universal aspiration does it express? Today psychoanalysis provides us with a means of finding out. It relates that dream to the urge to recover the euphoria which characterizes the most archaic stage before individuation—the stage of "primitive narcissism" when, as we are told by those who investigate these obscure beginnings, human beings feel that they are at one with the surrounding universe and each individual feels himself to be organically the Whole as though he were god in a pantheistic sense.[2] Thus the childish paradise of total happiness is in the final analysis that of the preconscious life in the womb, before the "fall" into the world. One can extrapolate this view of the development of the human psyche to the psychic development of the human species; one can compare the emergence of consciousness in the individual with the process by which the human species itself emerged. And if we do so, do we not find, in mankind as a species, the same archaic longing for a great return to the beginnings, for a fusion with Mother Nature? Do not all mythologies bear witness to this longing?

* Cf. above, p. 151.

The Mosaic tradition alone, by separating man from nature and overthrowing the idols of wood or stone, proclaimed the everlasting dream to be something illusory and sacrilegious, and in doing so it aroused permanent hostility—a hatred and resistance which was extended to the Jews who, whatever they might do or say, were in the eyes of the world the bearers of the Old Testament message. We have explained elsewhere how abuse directed against this stupid and barbarous people, whose superstitions swamped the West, was once a stock technique of anti-religious propaganda.[3] After its beginnings in the infant science of the Enlightenment, the struggle against the old demythologizing books, by way of historical and social changes of every kind, and involving every aspect of life, finally led to a war of extermination against men. The same link exists between the elaboration of the Aryan myth at the beginning of the nineteenth century when it arraigned the truth of the Biblical genealogies and its murderous consequences in our own times.

NOTES

Introduction

1 *Mein Kampf*, London 1939, trans. by James Murphy, pp. 252-73.
2 *Ibid.*, pp. 243-8.
3 Paul Mercier, *Histoire de l'Anthropologie*, Paris 1966, p. 15.
4 "Delving into the mystery of our origins and the complex feelings upon which it rests, appeared no doubt with the first gleams of intelligence", André Leroi-Gourhan, *Le Geste et la Parole*, Paris 1964, p. 9.
5 A. Borst, *Der Turmbau von Babel, Geschichte der Meinungen über Ursprung und Vielfalt der Sprachen und Völker*, Stuttgart 1957-63, 6 vols. This work is a real encyclopaedia of the genealogical legends of western history.
6 "In the race relations field more than in many others, social science theory is little more than a weathercock shifting with ideological winds" (P. L. van den Berghe, *Race and Racism, A Comparative Perspective*, New York 1967, p. 8).
7 Sigmund Freud, *Totem and Taboo* (*Standard Ed.*, Vol. XIII), p. 32. See also p. 70: "where there is a prohibition there must be an underlying desire".
8 Cf. The French Press of 23 May 1968.
9 Cf. A. Borst, *op. cit.*, vol. I, p. 126.
10 Sanhedrin 59 b; cf. Hans Kohn, *The Idea of Nationalism*, New York 1951, p. 585.
11 "Évangile arabe de l'enfance", *Évangiles apocryphes*, trans. by Peeters, Paris 1914, Vol. II; cf. F. Lovsky, *L'antisémitisme chrétien, Textes choisis et présentés...*, Paris 1970, p. 351.

Chapter One

1 A. Borst, *op. cit.*, Vol. II/1, pp. 445-56, and Hans Messmer, *Hispania—Idee und Gotenmythos*, Zürich 1960, especially pp. 103 *et seq.*
2 Cf. E. F. Hertzberg, *Political Works*, Vol. I, pp. 9 *et seq.*, Berlin 1795.
3 Editorial Note in *Anthropological Review*, January 1868, p. 37 (in the article "Broca on Anthropology").
4 Cf. A. Castro, *La realidad histórica de España*, Mexico 1954, pp. 69-88.
5 On the subject of "purity of blood" in modern Spain see L. Poliakov, *Histoire de l'antisémitisme*, Vol. II: *De Mahomet aux Marranes*, Paris 1961, and A. Sicroff, *Les controverses des status de "pureté de sang" en Espagne du XVe au XVII siècle*, Paris 1960.
6 B. de Saint-Vincent, *L'homme, essai zoologique sur le genre humain*, Paris 1827, p. 161.

7 A. Morel-Fatio, *Études sur l'Espagne*, Paris 1923, p. 169.

8 This description is to be found in a sonnet, attributed to the knight of the Sun (*Caballero del Febo*), at the beginning of *Don Quixote*.

9 J. A. Maravall, *El concepto de España en la edad media*, Madrid 1954, pp. 320 and 354.

10 Cf. A. Borst, *op. cit.*, Vol. III/1, p. 985.

11 Cf. Hanno Helbing, *Goten und Wandalen*, Zürich 1954, pp. 3-52.

12 Cf. Samuel Kliger, *The Goths in England*, Harvard 1952, and John Haslag, "*Gothic*" *im 17 und 18 Jahrhundert*, Köln-Graz 1963.

13 Cf. Th. Bieder, *Geschichte der Germanenforschung*, Vol. I, Leipzig 1921, p. 61.

Chapter Two

1 *Des désordres actuels de la France et des moyens d'y remédier*, by M. le Comte de Montlosier, Paris 1815, p. 7.

2 Cf. the article under the heading "Esclave" in the *Dictionnaire historique de l'ancien langage français*, by La Curne de Sainte-Palaye, Vol. VI, Paris 1879.

3 Cf. G. Fournier, *Les Mérovingiens*, Paris 1966, p. 78.

4 Cf. O. Dippe, *Die frankischen Trojanersagen*, Wandsbeck 1896.

5 Marc Bloch, "Sur les grandes invasions. Quelques positions de problèmes", *Revue de synthèse*, 1940-45, p. 56.

6 Cf. Robert Folz, *Le souvenir et la légende de Charlemagne dans l'Empire germanique médiéval*, Paris 1950, p. 191.

7 *Ibid.*, p. 567.

8 *Die Nibelungen*. A universal history based on the legend. From Wagner's *Œuvres*, Paris, Vol. II, p. 44.

9 "I fashioned my *Franciade* without worrying too much whether it was true or not" (Preface to the 1587 ed.).

10 "Nothing is more widely known than the Trojan descent of which the Franks boasted. All the witness of the Ancients, all the memorials of the Germans, were at one in attributing their origin to those regions where a universal tradition has placed the cradle of the human family." A. F. Ozanam, *Les Germains avant le Christianisme*, Paris 1872, p. 41.

11 Cf. Don Cameron Allen, *The Legend of Noah, Renaissance Rationalism in Art, Science and Letters*, Urbana Ill., 1949.

12 Jean du Tillet (d. 1570), *Recueil des Roys de France, leur Couronne et Maison*, 1618.

13 François de Belleforest, *Les Grandes Annales et Histoires générales de France, de la venue des Francs en Gaule*, 1579, Vol. 1, fol. 364.

14 G. Postel, *La loy salique* (1552). I am indebted to Maurice de Gondillac for this information.

15 De Bello Gallico, VI, 24, 1.

16 J. Bodin, *Methodus ad facilem historiarum cognitionem*, 1556.

17 Audigier, *De l'origine des Français et de leur empire*, 1676, Vol. I, Preface.

18 Cf. Roland Mousnier, *Fureurs paysannes . . .*, Paris 1967, p. 32.

19 Fr. de Mézéray, *Histoire de France, depuis Faramond jusqu'à maintenant . . .*, 1646, Vol. I, p. 3.

20 Cf. Henri Martin, *Histoire de France*, Vol. I. Preface to the 1874 ed., p. vi.

21 Bossuet, *Discours sur l'histoire universelle;* Pascal, *Pensées* (No. 623).

22 *Antiquités de la nation et de la langue des Celtes, autrement appelés Gaulois*, by Dom P. Pezron, Doctor in Theology of the Faculty of Paris, 1703 ed., Preface and pp. 1-24.

23 Henri Martin, *Histoire de France*, Vol. I, p. 2, note.

24 *Histoire de la pairie de France et du Parlement de Paris*, by D. B., London 1740, pp. 88-90.

25 *Histoire de l'ancien gouvernement de la France . . .*, by M. le Comte de Boulain-villiers, Amsterdam 1727, Vol. I, pp. 26 *et seq.*; Vol. III, p. 84.

26 *Histoire critique de l'établissement de la monarchie française dans les Gaules* (1734), by Abbé Dubos.

27 *Esprit des Lois*, XIV 14, XXVIII 20, XXVIII 23, XXX 17, and *passim*.

28 Commentary on the *Esprit des Lois*.

29 Article in *Dictionnaire philosophique* on "Franc ou franq; France, François, Français".

30 "This book has another kind of interest for us: it depicts the customs of our ancestors" (Burnouf's introduction to the *Annals* of Tacitus. Pocket Ed., Paris 1965).

31 *Observations sur l'histoire de France*, by Abbé Mably, 1765, p. 398.

32 Fr. Furet and D. Richet, *La Révolution*, Paris 1965, Vol. I, p. 60.

33 *Op. cit.*, p. 151.

34 Cf. the article entitled "Noblesse".

35 *Des désordres actuels de la France*, etc., *op. cit.*, p. 9.

36 "*Observations, etc.*", 1972 ed., "Éloge historique de l'abbé de Mably", p. 23.

37 *Origines gauloises, celles des plus anciens peuples d'Europe*, by La Tour d'Auvergne-Corret 1792; 3rd ed., Hamburg 1801, Vol. IV, p. 221.

38 Quoted by Marc Bloch, *Sur les grandes invasions*, etc., in the article referred to above: see p. 322.

39 *Mémoire et plan de travail sur l'histoire des Celtes et des Gaulois*, by M. de Fortia d'Urban, Paris 1807, p. 10.

40 *Letters from the Empress Catherine II to Grimm*, St Petersburg 1878, p. 536 (letter of 13 April 1793).

41 Jules Michelet, "Journal de mes idées", 15 March 1826, from *Mon Journal*, Paris, 1888, p. 304.

42 Comte Fr. de Montlosier, *De la monarchie française*, Paris 1814, Vol. I, pp. 136 *et seq.*; *Des désordres de la France . . .*, *op. cit.*, pp. 6-7.

43 *Souvenirs d'Alexis de Toqueville*, Paris 1893, p. 235.

44 *Les Martyrs*, Books VI and VII, but see especially *Analyse raisonnée de l'histoire de France*, 1845, pp. 129 *et seq.*

45 *Sur l'histoire d'Écosse . . .* (1824); cf. "Dix ans d'études historiques", 1883 ed., p. 147.

46 *Sur l'antipathie de race qui divise la nation française*, 1820, pp. 261-2.

47 *Ibid.*, p. 258. Cf. also *Histoire véritable de Jacques Bonhomme* (1820). ". . . there was war and Jacques was the victor because a number of friends among his former masters embraced his cause . . .", *Ibid.*, p. 271.

48 *Du gouvernement de la France depuis la Restauration et du ministère actuel*, by F. Guizot, 2nd ed., Paris 1820, pp. 1-2.

49 C. Jullian, "L'ancienneté de l'idée de nation", *Revue bleue* LI (1913), p. 66.

50 *Le Cabinet des Antiques*, at the end.

51 "Catéchisme des Industriels", Ier Cahier; cf. *L'œuvre d'Henri Saint-Simon*, ed. C. Douglé, Paris 1925, pp. 171-2. My thanks are due to M. Roger Errera for having drawn my attention to this passage.

52 Thus Friedrich List about 1835 or 1840. Cf. *Gesammelte Schriften* 1850, Vol. II, p. 110. Immediately after the armistice of January 1871, Bismarck summarized this German view: "The Revolution of 1789 was the defeat of the Germanic by the Celtic element and see what has happened since?" Cf. P. Dehn, *Bismarck als Erzieher*, Munich 1903, p. 205.

53 *Introduction* of 1869.

54 *Histoire de France*, 2nd ed. of 1835, pp. vii, 133, 431.

55 *Ibid.*, pp. 111, 150, 170.

56 "Nothing served me better than Grimm's tremendous work (*Deutsche Reichsaltertümer*). I shall one day give an account of the incredible passion with which I set about to understand and to translate this book." (The *Introduction* of 1869.)

57 Camille Jullian, *op. cit.*

58 *Histoire de France depuis les temps les plus reculés jusqu'en 1789*, by Henri Martin, Vol. I (1837); 4th ed. 1874, *passim*.

59 *Histoire de France*, Vol. I, p. 2 (the italics are Martin's).

60 "I have always been struck by the superior intelligence and diligence of the Germans. It is scarcely surprising that in the art of war, which is after all an inferior though complicated art, they should have attained the superiority I have found in all their works which I have studied and about which I know something—Yes indeed, gentlemen, the Germans are a superior race." Cf. The *Journal* of the Goncourt brothers, 6 September 1870. As to the germanophil sentiments of Renan, particularly between 1855 and 1870, see the texts collected by Ernest Seillière, "L'impérialisme germaniste dans l'Œuvre de Renan", *Revue des deux Mondes* 135/5 and 135/6 (1906), pp. 836-58 and 323-52.

A number of texts could also be quoted from Taine such as: "This is the race, a last-comer, which at a time of decadence among its Greek and Latin Sisters, brings a new civilization, with a new character and spirit, to the world. . . . Moral and manly instincts have held sway and among these, the need for independence, the taste for serious and severe habits, feelings of devotion and reverence, the cult of heroism. These are elements of a late, albeit a healthier civilization; one which is less influenced by ease and elegance but more solidly established on truth and justice." *Histoire de la littérature anglaise*, Paris ed. 1905, p. 63.

Chapter Three

1 Cf. L. Poliakov, *Histoire de l'antisémitisme*, Vol. II, Part Three.

2 Kenneth Sisam, *Anglo-Saxon royal genealogies*. Proceedings of the British Academy, XXXIX (1953) pp. 287-348.

3 Cf. E. Wingfield-Stratford, *The History of English Patriotism*, London 1913, Vol. I, p. 9.

4 *Ibid.*, p. 49.

5 Cf. Gilbert Chinard, *Thomas Jefferson: The Apostle of Americanism*, Boston 1929, p. 86.

6 Cf. A. Borst, *op. cit.*, I, p. 473.

7 *De excidio et conquestu Britanniae*, Ch. XXVI.

8 Hosea, I, 9.

9 E. Faral, *La légende arthurienne, études et documents*, Paris 1929, Vol. I, p. 53.

10 Bede, *Historia ecclesiastica gentis Anglorum*, II, 2; I, 15; V, 9.

11 Cf. Christopher Hill, *Puritanism and Revolution, Studies in Interpretation of the English Revolution of the Seventeenth Century*, London 1958, p. 117.

12 Cf. Erna Hackenberg, *Die Stammtafeln der angelsächsischen Königsreiche*, Berlin 1918, pp. 49 *et seq.*

13 Cf. A. Borst, *op. cit.*, p. 910, and Hans Matter, *Englische Gründungssagen von Geoffrey bis zur Renaissance*, Heidelberg 1922, p. 530.

14 This view is held by Kenneth Sisam in *Anglo-Saxon Royal Genealogies*, Proceedings of the British Academy 1953, p. 316, and by Denys Hay in *Europe, the Emergence of an Idea*, Edinburgh 1957, pp. 47-8.

15 Quoted by E. Hackenberg, *Die Stammtafeln der angelsächsischen Königsreiche, op. cit.*, p. 59.

16 In the case of Egbert of Mercia (eighth century) and Henry II (twelfth century), cf. Marc Bloch, *Les rois thaumaturges*, Paris ed. 1961, pp. 464-7 and p. 41; and in the case of George VI (twentieth century), cf. *The Times*, 13 May 1937: "George VI, anointed, crowned and enthroned, is become a sacramental, even a sacrificial, man, in one sense set apart from his fellows, but in a far deeper and more ancient sense made one with them as never before . . . he has become the mortal vessel of an immortal idea and the idea is the life of his people . . . that is the truth upon which the Christian Faith is built; and in the Coronation, where the king becomes the Lord's Anointed, Christus Domini, its two expressions, religious and secular, are visibly fused into one."

It should be observed that etymologically, the Latin adjective *christus* means quite simply "the anointed, he who has been anointed"; but in this sacramental sense it went out of use during the Middle Ages, and it was only in England that this royal qualification of *christus domini* has been retained until our own days. (I am indebted to M. l'abbé Louis Grégoire for this information.)

17 For Chilperic, see H. Leclercq in the article "Sacre impérial et royal", *Dictionnaire d'archéologie chrétienne et de liturgie*, Vol. XV/1, Paris 1950, c. 319. For Charlemagne, cf. Marc Bloch, *op. cit.*, p. 69, note.

18 "Henry declares that within his kingdom he is king, emperor and pope", the imperial ambassador, Chapuys, reported to Charles V (cf. G. Constant, *La Réforme en Angleterre*, Paris 1930, Vol. I, p. 67). It seems probable also that after the Act of Supremacy Henry VIII considered having himself tonsured. Cf. Dixon, *History of the Church of England*, London 1878.

19 Quoted by Hans Kohn, *The Idea of Nationalism*, New York 1951, p. 176.

20 *Ibid.*, p. 173.

21 *Ibid.*, p. 635.

22 *Busy*: "In the way of comfort to the weak I will go and eat. I will eat exceedingly and prophesy; there may be good use made of it too, now I think on it: by the public eating of swine's flesh, to profess our hate and loathing of Judaism, whereof the brethren stand taxed. I will therefore eat, yea, I will eat exceedingly." *Bartholomew Fair* (1614), Act I, Scene 1.

23 John Sadler, *Rights of the Kingdom; or Customs of our Ancestors*, London 1649.

24 Cf. *Die Juden und das Wirtschaftsleben*, Leipzig 1911, p. 99. English transl. by M. Epstein, *The Jews and Modern Capitalism*, New York 1962.

25 Cf. Herbert Schöffler, *Wirkungen der Reformation, Religionssoziologische Folgerungen für England und Deutschland*, Frankfurt 1960, p. 69.

26 The Rev. E. L. Hebden Taylor, *The Crown and the Common Market*, reprinted from *The National Message*.

27 *An Harborewe for Faithfull and Trewe Subjects* . . ., quoted by Hans Kohn, *op. cit.*, p. 625.

28 *Coryat's Crudities*, Glasgow 1905, Vol. II, p. 70. There followed (p. 71 *et seq.*) the insertion of "An Oration made by Hermannus Kircherius in praise of Travell".

29 *Restitution of Decayed Intelligence*, 1605 ed., p. 187.

30 C. Hill, *Puritanism and Revolution*, p. 69.

31 *Ibid.*, p. 61.

32 *Ibid.*, p. 80.

33 *Ibid.*, p. 77.

34 *Ibid.*, p. 73.

35 *Ibid.*, Ch. III.

36 *An historical and political discourse of the laws and government of England*, 1649, London 1782, pp. 2, 70, 10, 8, 13, 11.

37 *An Abstract of the History of England*, from the prose works of Jonathan Swift, London 1879-1908, Vol. X, pp. 225-6.

38 *Remarks on the History of England*, "The works of Viscount Bolingbroke" London 1754, Vol. I, p. 314.

39 *The History of England from the invasion of Julius Caesar*, London 1762, Vol. I, pp. 141 *et seq.*, note on p. 9 and pp. 170 *et seq.*

40 Christopher Hill, *op. cit.*, p. 99, quoting "Common Sense" by Tom Paine.

41 *Ivanhoe*, Ch. XXVII.

42 Augustin Thierry, *Dix ans d'études historiques*, Paris 1883, p. 142, p. 131.

43 A. Pushkin, "On journalistic criticism", 1830; cf. *Complete Works*, Moscow 1962, VI, p. 37.

44 Cf. F. E. Faverty, *Mathew Arnold the Ethnologist*, Evanston 1951, Ch. II (The Teutomaniacs).

45 E. Freeman, *The History of the Norman Conquest of England*, Vol. V, Oxford 1876, p. 335.

46 C. Kingsley, *The Roman and the Teuton*, London 1889, p. 49.

47 J. Beddoe, *The Races of Britain, A Contribution to the Anthropology of Western Europe*, Bristol 1885, p. 269.

48 A. Keith, *Nationality and Race*, Robert Boyle Lectures, 1919, p. 10.

49 *The History of the Kings of Britain*, ed. Lewis Thorpe, London 1966, p. 54.

50 Cf. L. Poliakov, *Histoire de l'antisémitisme*, Vol. III: *De Voltaire à Wagner*, 1968, p. 363.

51 *Recessional* (1897).

52 André Siegfried, *L'âme des peuples*, Paris 1950, p. 83.

53 D. Douglas, *The Norman Conquest and British Historians*, Glasgow 1946, p. 9.

Chapter Four

1 Cf. O. Cullmann, *Saint Pierre, Disciple-Apôtre-Martyr*, Neuchâtel 1952, p. 116.

2 *Ibid.*, p. 116, note 1, and p. 118.

3 "Quae in numero gentium nequequam computatur." Letter from Stephen II to Charlemagne in 769. Cf. Ph. Jaffé *Monumenta Carolina*, Berlin 1867, pp. 158-64.

4 Cf. L. Musset, *Les invasions; les vagues germaniques*, Paris, 1965, p. 205.

5 The following account is based on L. Duchesne, *Les premiers temps de l'État pontifical*, Paris 1911, and H. Hubert, "Étude sur la formation des États de l'Église", *Revue historique*, LXIX (1899), pp. 1-38 and 241-72.

6 Letter from the Apostle Peter to Pepin and the Frankish people, February/March 756. Cf. Ph. Jaffé, *op. cit.*, pp. 55-60.

7 Article on Saint Peter in *Dictionnaire d'archéologie chrétienne et de liturgie*, Vol. XIV/1, Col. 906.

8 *Divina Commedia, Paradiso* XX, 56-7.

9 *Enciclopedia Italiana*, Vol. XIX, 1933, p. 805.

10 *Romanorum epistola de electionis senatoria*, 1261; cf. Nancy Lenkeith, *Dante and the Legend of Rome*, London 1954, p. 17.

11 Cf. P. E. Schramm, *Kaiser, Rom und Renovatio . . .*, Leipzig 1929, Vol. II, pp. 53 *et seq.*, 73 *et seq.*

12 Fazio degli Uberti, *Dittamento. . . .* Cf. A. Graf, *Roma nella memoria e nelle imnaginazioni del Medio Evo*, Vol. I, Turin 1882, p. 84.

13 G. Villani, *Istorie fiorentine*, Book I, Chs. V, VI and VIII. Cf. also Ernst Mehl, *Die Weltanschauung des Giovanni Villani*, Leipzig 1927, pp. 101-106.

14 Cf. the classic work of Comparetti, *Virgilio nel medioevo*, of which the second part is dedicated to Italian folklore.

15 Cf. *Il Messaggero* of 31 January 1972 (four columns on page 1 and five on page 3). I have to thank my pupil, Antonella Pieroni, for referring me to this article.

16 See Thomas Aquinas, *De Regimine Principum*, I, 14, and its continuation by Tolomeo da Lucca, III, *passim*.

17 *Inferno*, II, 20-24.

18 *Paradiso*, XXVII, 25-6.

19 According to a recent study of the Divine Comedy, the Donation of Constantine, in Dante's eyes, constituted the original sin of Christianity. Cf. B. Nardi, *La Donatio Costantini e Dante*, "Studi danteschi", XXVI (1940), pp. 47-95.

20 *Paradiso*, XIX, 13-15.

21 *De Monarchia*, Book II, and *Inferno*, Canto XXXIV.

22 *Purgatorio*, VI, 124-5.

23 *Purgatorio*, XXXII, 101-102.

24 *Divina Commedia, passim*, and *De Monarchia*, Book II, Ch. 3, in which Dante, basing himself now on Livy, deals at length with the nobility of the ancestors of Aeneas and his family.

25 *Purgatorio*, VI, 82-3.

26 Cf. Paul Piur, *Cola di Rienzo, Darstellung seines Lebens und seines Geistes*, Vienna 1931.

27 *Aeneae Sylvii Piccolominei* . . ., opera, Helmstedt 1707, *Historia Bohemica* . . ., Chap. II, p. 186; Arno Borst, *op. cit.*, III/1, p. 971; C. Paparelli, *Enea Silvio Piccolomini*, Bari 1950; C. Burck, *Selbstdarstellung und Personenbildnis bei Enea Silvio Piccolomini*, Basle 1956, pp. 29 *et seq.*

28 Cf. Henri Marc-Bonnet, *Les papes de la Renaissance*, Paris 1953, p. 5.

29 Machiavelli, *Discorsi sopra la prima deca di Tito Livio*, Book I, Ch. XII; Guicciardini, *Storia d'Italia*, Paris ed. 1837, Vol. II, p. 179.

30 Cf. A. Borst, *op. cit.*, Vol. III/1, pp. 975-7.

31 Cf. the anonymous study "Storia degli studi sulle origini italiche" in *Rivista Europea*, Milan 1846, pp. 731 *et seq.*

32 Borst, Vol. III/2, p. 1480, quoting *Geschichte der Teutschen*, by J. Mascov.

33 "Storia degli studi sulle origini italiche" in *Rivista Europea* (see above), p. 102.

34 V. Cuoco, *Platone in Italia*, Micolini, Bari 1916-1924; Vol. I, p. 3; Vol. II, p. 297.

35 A. Mazzoldi, *Delle origini italiche e della diffusione dell'incivilmento italiano all'Egitto, alla Fenicia, alla Grecia e a tutte le nazioni asiatiche poste sul Mediterraneo* (1840); G. Iannelli, *Tentamina Hieroglyphica, Tabulae rosettanae*, etc. (1840-1841): cf. B. Croce, *Storia della Storiografia italiana*, Vol. I, Bari 1921. pp. 55 *et seq.*

36 V. Gioberti, *Del Primato morale e civile degli italiani*, Milano 1938, Vol. II, pp. 251 and 214.

37 Cf. the texts of Mazzini quoted by Maurice Vaussard in *De Pétrarque à Mussolini, Évolution du sentiment nationaliste italien*, Paris 1961, p. 46.

38 G. Prezzolini, *Le legs de l'Italie*, Paris 1949, p. 9.

39 Manzoni developed this thesis in *Discorso sopra alcuni punti della storia longobardica in Italia*, (1822).

40 *Note autobiografiche*, by Giuseppe Mazzini, quoted in Vaussard, *op. cit.*, pp. 46-7.

41 *Ibid.*, p. 44, quoting the *Epistolario* of Mazzini.

42 *Primato*, . . ., Vol. II, p. 247.

43 Cf. B. Croce, *Storia della storiografia italiana*, Vol. II, p. 15; Vol. I, pp. 60-61.

44 Cesare Lombroso, *L'uomo bianco e l'uomo di colore, Lettere sull' origine e sulla varietà delle razze umane*, Turin 1892, *passim* and particularly p. 203 ("Le razze gialle, le camite e le semite si convertirono in arie").

45 G. Sergi, *Der Arier in Italien*, in *Ursprung und Verbreitung des mittelländischen Stammes*, Leipzig 1897, pp. 137-60.

46 E. de Michelis, *L'Origine degli Indo-Europei*, Turin 1903, pp. 84-8.

47 Cf. Renzo De Felice, *Storia degli ebrei sotto il fascismo*, Turin 1962, p. 278.

48 Renzo De Felice, *op. cit.*, p. 114.

49 *Ibid.*, p. 159.

50 *De Monarchia*, II, 3.

Chapter Five

1 "The German soul is above all manifold, varied in its source, aggregated and superimposed, rather than actually built: this is owing to its origin. A German who would embolden himself to assert: 'Two souls, alas, dwell in my breast,' would make a bad guess at the truth, or, more correctly, he would come far short of the truth about a number of souls. As a people made up of the most

extraordinary mixing and mingling of races, perhaps even with a preponderance of the pre-Aryan element, as a 'people of the centre' in every sense of the term, the Germans are more intangible, more ample, more contradictory, more unknown, more incalculable, more surprising, and even more terrifying than other peoples are to themselves:— they escape *definition*, and are thereby alone the despair of the French." Nietzsche, *Beyond Good and Evil*, trans. by Helen Zimmern, London 1967, p. 197.

2 "The word *Stamm*", writes Robert Minder, "has no equivalent here because the thing itself is lacking. *Stamm* means a more or less homogeneous, ethnic group settled in a fairly well-defined geographical environment and forming during the course of centuries a precise social and cultural entity. The origin of the different *Stämme* is as obscure as their survival is tenacious. The existing *Stämme* appear in the third and fourth centuries A.D. It is not known what their precise relations were with the old Germanic clans . . . ." R. Minder, *Allemagnes et Allemands*, Paris 1948, Vol. I, p. 29.

3 Relatio de legatione Constantinopolitana, c. 12; *Die Werke Liutprands*, Hanover 1915.

4 Thus Dr V. Steinecke, *Deutsche Erdkunde für höhere Anstalten*, Leipzig-Vienna 1910, p. 5: "Germany is the country of the Germans, namely, of the compatriots. It is therefore, properly speaking, the country in which our German language is spoken, our native country, as opposed to the lands of the *Welsche* (*Welschland*) or the lands of foreigners."

5 Leo Weisgerber, *Die geschichtliche Kraft der deutschen Sprache*, Düsseldorf 1959, pp. 35-79.

6 *Ibid.*, p. 77 ("die Anerkennung des Geistigen als Grundlage der Völkerordnung").

7 Cf. Kenneth Sisam, *Anglo-Saxon Royal Genealogies*, "Proceedings of the British Academy", 1953, p. 323.

8 "Nos vero, qui Teutonica sive Theustica lingua loquimur". Cf. M. Hessler, *Die Anfänge des deutschen Nationalgefühls in der östfränkischen Geschichtschreibung des neunten Jahrhunderts*, Berlin 1943, p. 110.

9 Cf. Borst, II/2, pp. 824-7, and III/1, 1,017-1,018.

10 Borst II/2, pp. 665 *et seq.*, also A. Daube, *Der Aufstieg der Muttersprache im deutschen Denken des 15. und 16. Jahrhunderts*, Frankfurt a/M 1940. Pp. 8-11 (for the Ascanian genealogy) and A. Grau, *Der Gedanke der Herkunft in der deutschen Geschichtschreibung des Mittelalters*, Leipzig 1938, p. 21 (for towns founded by Julius Caesar).

11 Borst II/2, p. 659.

12 Quoted by L. Weisgerber, *op. cit.*, p. 137.

13 N. Cohn, *The Pursuit of the Millennium*, 3rd ed., London and New York 1970, p. 125: "The result is almost uncannily similar to the phantasies which were the core of National-Socialist 'ideology'. One has only to turn back to the tracts—already almost forgotten—of such pundits as Rosenberg and Darré to be immediately struck by the resemblance. There is the same belief in a primitive German culture in which the divine will was once realized and which throughout history has been the source of all good—which was later undermined by a conspiracy of capitalists, inferior non-Germanic peoples and the Church of Rome—and which must now be restored by a

new aristocracy of humble birth, but truly German in soul, under a God-sent saviour who is at once a political leader and a new Christ. It is all there. . . ."

14 "Adam ist ein tuscher man gewesen." Cf. the analysis of *The Book of a Hundred Chapters* by Hermann Haupt, *Ein oberrheinischer Revolutionär aus dem Zeitalter Kaiser Maximilians I,* "Westdeutsche Zeitschrift für Geschichte und Kunst", Ergänzungsheft VIII, Trier 1893, p. 141.

15 Cf. Borst, Vol. III/1, p. 1,012.

16 "Ipsos Germanos indigenas crediderim minimeque aliarum gentium adventibus et hospitiis mixtos . . . . Ipse eorum opinio accedo, qui Germaniae populos nullis aliis aliarum nationum conubiis infectos propriam et sinceram et tantum sui similem gentem extitisse arbitrantur." *Germania,* II, 1, and IV, 1, Harmondsworth 1970, pp. 101, 104.

17 *Oratio ad regem Maximilianum de laudibus atque amplitudine Germaniae.* When this discourse was published, Bebel added another chapter with the characteristic title of *Germani sunt indigenae.* Cf. Paul Joachimsen, *Geschichtsauffassung und Geschichtsschreibung in Deutschland unter dem Einfluss des Humanismus,* Leipzig, 1910, pp. 97-98.

18 *Epithoma rerum germanicarum,* Strasbourg 1505. Cf. Joachimsen, *op. cit.,* pp. 64-79.

19 *Memorabilium omnis aetatis et omnium gentium chronici commentarii,* 1516. Cf. Borst, Vol. III/1, pp. 1,051-1,052.

20 Borst, III/1, pp. 1,058-1,059, and A. Daube, *Der Aufstieg der Muttersprache,* op. cit.

21 *Germaniae exegeseos* . . . Cf. Borst, III/1, p. 1,058 and Joachimsen, *op. cit.,* pp. 169-83.

22 "Nostri enim sunt Gotorum, Vandalorum, Francorum triumphi, nobis gloriam sunt illorum imperia in clarissimis Romanorum provinciis." Cf. Joachimsen, *op. cit.,* pp. 125-46.

23 Joachimsen, pp. 110-112, and Borst, pp. 1,053-1,054.

24 Sebastian Franck, *Chronica des gantzen Teutschen Lands* (1538).

25 Quoted by Hans Kohn, *The Idea of Nationalism,* New York, p. 621.

26 "Germanis meis natus sum, quibus et serviam." (Letter to Gerbel, 1521.)

27 Maurice Gravier, Introduction to Luther, *A la noblesse chrétienne de la nation allemande,* Paris 1945, p. 48.

28 *A la noblesse chrétienne,* etc., Gravier's edition already quoted, p. 203.

29 Ch. XXVI. Cf. the Introduction by M. Gravier, p. 42.

30 Werner Fritzemeyer, *Christenheit und Europa,* Munich 1931, p. 55.

31 Otto Scheel, "Der Volksglaube bei Luther", *Historische Zeitschrift,* 1940, pp. 477 et seq.

32 Borst, III/1, pp. 1,062-1,069, and L. Weisgerber, *op. cit.,* p. 151-2.

33 Borst, *ibid.*

34 The italics are Joachimsen's.

35 Paul Joachimsen, *Die Reformation als Epoche der deutschen Geschichte,* Munich 1951, p. 56.

36 Anna Daube, *Der Aufstieg der Muttersprache im deutschen Denken des 15. und 16. Jahrhunderts, op. cit.,* p. 15.

37 Alain Besançon, *Le Tsarévitch immolé,* Paris 1967.

38 Cf. P. Joachimsen, *Geschichtsauffassung*, etc., *op. cit.*, p. 64, and Émile Gabory, *Anne de Bretagne, duchesse et reine*, Paris 1841, pp. 85-6.

39 H. Heine, Zur *Geschichte der Religion und Philosophie in Deutschland*, Conclusion.

40 Cf. H. H. Ahrens, *Die nationalen religiösen, nationalen und sozialen Gedanken Johann Eberlin von Günzburgs*, Hamburg 1939, especially pp. 38 *et seq.*

41 Cf. Friedrich Gotthelf, *Das deutsche Altertum in den Anschauungen des sechszehnten und siebzehnten Jahrhunderts*, Berlin 1900.

42 1573, Mathias Holzwart, Cf. E. Picot, "Le pangermanisme au XVIᵉ siècle", *La Revue hebdomadaire*, Paris 1916, pp. 462-71.

43 *Johann Fischarts Geschichts-Klitterung*. Halle Ed., 1891, p. 54; Wolfgang Spangenberg, *Sämtliche Werke*, Berlin Ed., 1969 ("I. Singschul: Von der Musica").

44 Such as the well-known chronicler Tschudi. Cf. Fr. Gundolf, *Anfänge deutscher Geschichtschreibung*, Amsterdam 1938.

45 Cf. Borst, Vol. III/1, pp. 1,215-1,226.

46 Poem "Ad linguam germanicam", quoted in the *Teutsche Poemata* of Martin Opitz, Halle Edition 1902, p. 13.

47 Fr. Gotthelf, *Das deutsche Altertum* . . ., *op. cit.*, pp. 39-43, and Borst III/1, pp. 1,225-1,226.

48 The texts are collected by Th. Bieder, *Geschichte der Germanenforschung*, Leipzig 1921, Vol. I, pp. 53-55. Conring's book was called *De habitus corporum Germanicarum antiqui ac novi causis*, (*1645*).

49 Opitz, *Aristarchus sive de contemptu linguae Teutonicae*, "Dedicatio"; cf. "Teutsche Poemata"; *op. cit.*, pp. 150 *et seq.*

50 *Satyrische Geschichte Philanders von Sittewald*, 1644.

51 *Grossmütiger Feldherr Arminius oder Hermann*, 1689.

52 *Simplicius Simplicissimus*, London 1964, pp. 178, 181-2. (Ch. 13, Jupiter talks to Simplex of the German hero who will give peace to the world.)

53 Thus Paul Gutzwiller, *Der Narr bei Grimmelshausen*, Basle 1959.

54 Thus Josef Wilhelm Schafer, *Das Nationalgefühl Grimmelshausens*, Würzburg 1936.

55 *Teutscher Michel*, cf. Grimmelshausens Werke, ed. Bochardt, Vol. IV, p. 256.

56 Schottel, *Teutsche Sprachkunst*. . . . Brunswick 1651 ("Dritte Lobrede, p. 60).

57 *Ibid.* ("Achte Lobrede").

58 G. W. Leibniz, *New Essays concerning Human Understanding*, Bk. III, Ch. II, 1; trans. by A. G. Langley, Chicago and London 1916; cf. Y. Belaval, "Leibniz et la langue allemande" in *Études Germaniques*, Paris, II, 1947, and Borst, Vol. III/2, pp. 1,475-1,478.

59 *Brevis designatio meditationum de originibus gentium ductis potissimum ex judicio linguarum*, (1710).

60 *Beweis, dass die alten Deutschen und nordischen Völker weit vernünftigere Grundsätze in der Religion gehabt haben als die alten Griechen und Römer*, pp. 5-6.

61 *Beweiss, dass die alten Deutschen keine Kannibalen waren.*

62 Cf. J. Murat, *Klopstock, les thèmes principaux de son œuvre*, Paris 1959, p. 286.

63 Cf. Kommerell, *Der Dichter als Führer in der deutschen Klassik*, 1928, p. 59, and Strich, *Die Mythologie in der deutschen Literatur von Klopstock bis Wagner*, 1910, Vol. I, pp. 60 *et seq.*

M

64 Cf. J. Murat, *op. cit.* We have borrowed most of the quotations which follow from Murat's book. Also H. Kindermann, *Klopstocks Entdeckung der Nation*, Berlin 1935.

65 F. Strich, *Die Mythologie in der deutschen Literatur . . ., op. cit.*, Vol. I, pp. 173-81.

66 *Ibid.*, p. 180.

67 "Dissertation tendant à expliquer les causes de la superiorité des Germains sur les Romains et à prouver que le Nord de la Germanie ou Teutonie entre le Rhin et la Vistule, et principalement la présente monarchie prussienne, est la patrie originaire de ces nations héroïques qui . . . ont fondé et peuplé les principales monarchies de l'Europe." Cf. *Huit dissertations . . .*, par M. le Comte de Hertzberg, Berlin 1787, pp. 1-38.

68 Jean-Paul, "Sermon of Peace to Germany" (*Friedenspredigt an Deutschland 1808*). "Hertzberg showed in a learned treatise", wrote Jean-Paul, "that the Germans founded and peopled all the kingdoms of Europe. . . ." And he concluded that "in a higher sense, all the wars on mankind's earth are wars between fellow-citizens". Cf. Jean-Paul, *Weltgedanken und Gedankenwelt*, Stuttgart 1938, pp. 146 *et seq.*

69 *Outlines of a Philosophy of the History of Man*, trans. by T. Churchill, London 1803, Book XVI, pp. 361, 362.

70 Cf. The writings of Schiller quoted by L. Schemann, *Die Rasse in den Geisteswissenschaften*, Munich 1938, Vol. III, pp. 100-105, and L. Weisgerber, *Die geschichtliche Kraft der deutschen Sprache, op. cit.*, p. 208.

71 Cf. L. Schemann, *op. cit.*, Vol. II, p. 95 (*Von den Deutschen* by H. von Kleist).

72 Cf. Jacques Droz, *L'Allemagne et la Révolution française*, Paris 1949, pp. 469-73.

73 *Kleine Bücherschau, Reden an die deutsche Nation*, Cf. *Jean Pauls sämtliche Werke*, Weimar 1938, I, Vol. XVI, pp. 338-52.

74 *Mein Kampf, op. cit.*, p. 243.

75 Quoted by L. Weisgerber, *Die geschichtliche Kraft der deutschen Sprache, op. cit.*, p. 237.

76 Cf. E. Weymar, *Das Selbstverständnis der Deutschen*, Stuttgart 1961, p. 322.

77 Cf. L. Poliakov, *Histoire de l'antisémitisme, op. cit.*, Vol. III, where the reader will find, pp. 393-9, an analysis of the ideas of E. M. Arndt and F. L. Jahn.

78 E. Weymar, *Das Selbstverständnis der Deutschen*, p. 125.

79 *Reden an die deutsche Nation*, XIII Lecture.

80 Cf. Michael Freund, *Deutsche Geschichte*, Gütersloh 1960, p. 304.

81 *Novum Organum* of Francis Bacon, Oxford 1889, Bk. I, Ch. 84, p. 283. Cf. also Robert Lenoble, *Histoire de l'idée de nature*, Paris 1969, Ch. I (La révolution mécaniste du XVIIe siècle), especially pp. 322-3, which served as a starting point for the considerations outlined above.

82 Blaise Pascal, "Fragment d'un traité du vide 1647"; cf. *Œuvres . . .* ed. by H. Massis, Paris 1927, Vol. VI, pp. 14-15.

83 Pascal, *loc. cit.*

84 Th. Bieder, *Geschichte der Germanenforschung, op. cit.*, Leipzig 1925, Vol. III, p. 63.

85 Cf. L. Poliakov, *Histoire de l'antisémitisme, op. cit.*, Vol. III, pp. 440-67.

86 Cf. Th. Mommsen, "Ninive und Sedan" in *Die Nation*, 25 August 1900, and *Deutschland und England, ibid.*, 10 August 1903.

Chapter Six

1 Cf. A. Amalrik, *Will the Soviet Union survive until 1984?*, London 1970. Preface by H. Kamm, p. xv.
2 *Crime and Punishment*, VI, 8, "Go to the cross-roads, bow down to the people, kiss the earth for you have sinned against it, and proclaim in a loud voice to the whole world: I am a murderer." Trans. by David Magarshack, Harmondsworth, 1966, p. 536.
3 Cf. M. Gorlin, "Salomon et Ptolémée; la légende de Volot Volotovic", *Revue des Études Slaves*, XVIII (1938), pp. 41 *et seq*. The same idea occurs in the poem *Zadonschina* which celebrated the victory in 1380 of the Muscovite Dimitry Donskoy over the Tartars.
4 Cf. A. Kartashev, *Ocherk istorii russkoy tserkvi* (An Outline of the History of the Russian Church), Paris 1959, Vol. I, p. 460.
5 Cf. H. Pirenne, *The Medieval City*. Trans. by Frank D. Halsey, New York.
6 Cf. G. Vernadsky, *A History of Russia*, Vol. III (*The Mongols and Russia*), Yale 1953, pp. 153 *et seq*., and E. Voegelin "The Mongol Order", *Byzantion*, XV (1941).
7 See the Chinese chronicles and sources referred to by Vernadsky, *op. cit.*, pp. 87-8.
8 Cf. O. Jensen (R. Jakobson), "Sobaka Kalin Tsar" (Dog Tsar Kalin), *Slavia*, XVII, 1939, pp. 82-98.
9 Cf. D. Chyzhevsky, *History of Russian Literature from the Eleventh Century to the end of the Baroque*. The Hague 1960, p. 167.
10 Quoted by P. Kovalevsky, *Saint Serge et la spiritualité russe*, Paris 1958, p. 110.
11 Cf. G. P. Fedotov, *op. cit.*, p. 227.
12 *Le Domostroi*, trans. by E. Duchesne, Paris 1910, p. 47 (Ch. XVII: "How to educate one's children and save them by terror").
13 Quoted by Kartashev, *op. cit.*, Vol. I, p. 386.
14 Cf. D. Strémooukhov, "La tiare de Saint Sylvestre et le Klobuk blanc", *Revue des Études Slaves*, 34 (1957), pp. 123 *et seq*.
15 Cf. Chyzhevsky, *History of Russian Literature*, *op. cit.*, p. 202. It appears that the story was based on a Byzantine legend adapted to Russian needs.
16 Cf. D. Stremoyukhov, "Moscow the third Rome: sources . . .", *Speculum*, 28 (1953), p. 94.
17 Cf. The report of the voyage of Sigmund Herberstein (Moscovia"). Erlangen ed., 1926, p. 57.
18 Cf. *The Correspondence of Ivan IV and Kurbsky*, edited by J. C. Fennel, Cambridge, 1955, pp. 86-7.
19 Cf. R. P. Dimitrieva, *Skazanie o knyaziakh Vladimirskikh* (The Legend of the Princes of Vladimir) (in Russian), Moscow 1955. The author of this forgery appears to have been the former Metropolitan Savva-Spiridon who reproduced or imitated certain traditions of the southern Slavs.
20 Cf. *Nikonovskaya Letopis*, Moscow 1963, p. 9.
21 Cf. R. P. Dmitrieva, *op. cit.*, p. 155.

22 Cf. V. Ikonnikov, *Opyt russkoy istoriografii* (Essay on Russian Historiography), Kiev 1908, Vol. II, p. 1,402.

23 *Ibid.*, pp. 1,408–1,409.

24 Dmitrieva, *op. cit.*, p. 150.

25 Cf. Borst. *op. cit.*, pp. 1,043, 1,065, 1,129 and *passim*.

26 Cf. V. Ikonnikov, *op. cit.*, Vol. II, p. 1,403.

27 G. Krizhanich, *Politika* (Politics) (*c.* 1660), Moscow ed., pp. 497, 502, 630–633. The "devastation" of which Krizhanich speaks is the "time of troubles". For this Slav patriot see especially P. Milukov, *Ocherki po istorii russkoy kultury* (Essays on the History of Russian Culture), Paris 1930, Vol. III, pp. 135-55.

28 It is to be found, for instance, in the Marquis de Custine's work: "The Romanovs were of Prussian origin and since acquiring the throne by election they have mostly married German princesses contrary to the usage of the Muscovite sovereigns." *La Russie en 1839*, Paris 1843, Vol. IV, p. 13, note.

29 In 1887 the genealogist Barsukov declared: "Up to now we have continued to cultivate the age-old legend according to which the ancestor of the Romanovs, the 'man of worth' Andrew Kobyla (a russified form of the name Cabila) was of foreign origin or from 'German lands' as was said formerly". "Imperatorskaya Akademia Nauk" ("Imperial Academy of Sciences"), Vol. LIV, Saint Petersburg 1887, pp. 51-2.

30 See below p. 245. Gobineau also supported this view. Cf. *Essai sur l'inégalité des races humaines*, Bk. VI, Ch. V (Derniers migrations arianes-scandinaves).

31 Cf. Ikonnikov, *op. cit.*, Vol. I, p. 63.

32 Cf. Barsukov, *op. cit.*, pp. 75-7.

33 Ikonnikov, *loc. cit.*

34 Cf. *Prince Kurbsky's History of Ivan IV*, ed. by J. Fennel, Cambridge 1965, pp. 12, 214, 220.

35 This was Simon Bekbulatovich, former Prince of Kasimov. Cf. Vernadsky, *A History of Russia, op. cit.*, Vol. V/1, pp. 142 *et seq.*

36 Cf. Ikonnikov, *op. cit.*, p. 1,410, and Vernadsky, *op. cit.*, Vol. III, p. 370.

37 Cf. N. Trubetskoy, *Problemy russkoyo samosoznania* (Problems of Russian Self-awareness), Paris 1927, and P. Milukov, *op. cit.*, Vol. III, pp. 90–91.

38 Cf. *Eugene Onegin*, III, 26-27.

> *Tatyana read no Russian journal,*
> *She did not speak the language well*
> *And found it rather hard to spell;*
> *And so of course the girl decided*
> *To write in French. . . . What's to be done?*
> *For lady never, no, not one,*
> *Her love in Russian has confided;*
> *Our native tongue turns up its nose*
> *At mere epistolary prose.*

Trans. by Babette Deutsch, Harmondsworth 1964, p. 81.

Cf. also Dostoevsky's *Diary of a Writer*, July-August 1876. "At Ems, naturally, you recognize Russians above all by the manner in which they talk, that is, by that Russian-French dialect which is characteristic only of Russia and which is beginning to startle even foreigners. I say: 'is beginning to startle', since up to the present we have only been praised for it. . . .''

39 Cf. *Peter the Great*, ed. by L. J. Oliva, Englewood Cliffs 1970, pp. 78-80 ("The official view").

40 *Ibid.*, pp. 81-9 ("Panegyric to the Sovereign Emperor, Peter the Great").

41 Quoted in the *Great Soviet Encyclopaedia*, 2nd ed., Vol. XXXII, Moscow 1955, pp. 582-5 (article on Peter I).

42 Cf. above, p. 94.

43 Cf. W. Hinz, *Peters des Grossen Anteil an der wissenschaftlichen und künstlerischen Kultur seiner Zeit*, "Jahrbücher für Kultur und Geschichte der Slaven", VIII (1932), p. 397.

44 Quoted by Paul Milukov, *Glavnye techenia russkoy istoricheskoy mysli* (Main Currents of Russian Historical Thought), St Petersburg 1913, p. 122.

45 Quoted by Hans Rogger, *National Consciousness in Eighteenth-Century Russia*, Harvard 1960, p. 199.

46 Quoted by André Martel, *Michel Lomonossov et la langue littéraire russe*, Paris 1933, pp. 22-3.

47 Alexander Sumarokov, *O proiskhozhdenii rossyskogo naroda* (On the Origin of the Russian People), cf. *Complete Works*, Moscow 1787, Vol. X, pp. 105-121.

48 Mihkail Lomonosov, *Drevnyaya rossyskaya istoriya* (A History of Ancient Russia . . .); cf. *Complete Works*, Moscow 1952, Vol. VI, pp. 163 *et seq.*, and especially pp. 179-80.

49 *Oda Elisavete* (Ode to Elisabeth) (1750).

50 *Zamechaniya na dissertatsiyu G. F. Millera* (Observations on the dissertation by G. F. Müller on "The Origin of the name and of the people of Russia": a report to the Chancery of the Academy of Sciences) (1750). In his capacity of "a sworn official and a loyal subject of his country" Lomonosov requested that Müller's work should not be published. *Complete Works*, *op. cit.*, Vol. VI, pp. 79-80.

51 *Letters of the Empress Catherine II to Grimm*, St Petersburg 1878; see especially the letters of September to October 1784 and that of 13 April 1785.

52 *Memoir on Ancient and Modern Russia*, ed. R. Pipes, Harvard 1959, pp. 21-5.

53 *Histoire de l'Empire de Russie*, by M. Karamzin, French trans., Paris 1819, Vol. I, pp. 139-41.

54 Letter of 19 October 1836 (not despatched).

55 *Ode to the Slanderers of Russia*, August 1831.

56 Cf. G. Shpet, *Ocherk razvitia russkoy filosofii* (An Outline of the Development of Russian Philosophy), St Petersburg 1922, Vol. I, p. 206.

57 P. Chaadaev, *Lettres philosophiques*, Ed. François Rouleau, Paris 1970, pp. 48-55.

58 *Ibid.*, p. 208 ("Apologie d'un fou").

59 Cf. Marquis de Luppé, *Adolphe de Custine*, Monaco 1957, pp. 234-40.

60 *La Russie en 1839*, by Marquis de Custine, Paris 1843, Vol. II, p. 203.

61 A. Khomyakov, *Sobranic socheneniy* (Collected Works), Moscow 1882, Vol. III, pp. 91-2 and *passim*; cf. N. Ryazanovsky, *Russia and the West in the Teaching of the Slavophiles*, Harvard 1962, pp. 67-74.

62 Cf. Ryazanovsky, *op. cit.*, pp. 76-7.

63 Khomyakov, *Works* . . ., Vol. III, p. 107.

64 Dobrolyubov, *Sochenenia M. M. Dobrolubova* (Works by M. M. Dobrolyubov) St Petersburg 1893, Vol. II, p. 31 ("The organic development of man in relation to his intellectual and moral activities").

65 Chernyshevsky, *Izbrannye filosofskie sochenenia* (Selected Philosophical Writings), Moscow 1951, Vol. III, p. 569, p. 578 ("On races").

66 Cf. Thomas Masaryk, *The Spirit of Russia*, London 1919, Vol. II, p. 68.

67 D. Anuchin, "Begly vzglyed na proshloe antropologii i na eyo zadachi v Rossii" (A quick glance at the past of anthropology and its tasks in Russia) in *Russky antropologichesky journal*, 1/1902, pp. 25-42.

68 Cf. N. Trubetskoy, *Problemy russkogo samopoznania*, Paris 1927.

69 Roman Jakobson, "Les unions phonologiques de langues", *Le Monde Slave*, January 1931, pp. 371-78; P. Savickij "L'Eurasie révélée par la linguistique", *ibid.*, pp. 364-70.

70 N. Trubetskoy, *Evropa i chelovechestvo* (Europe and Mankind), Sofia 1920, p. 82.

71 D. Mirsky, *The Eurasian Movement*, "The Slavonic Review", VI (1927), p. 312.

72 In the second of his works quoted above, N. Trubetskoy defended the cause of the "inferior races" as follows: "The primitive man retains in his mind a vast quantity of knowledge of all kinds. He knows to perfection the ways of all nature around him and the habits of animals including the details which even the most observant European naturalist fails to notice. This knowledge is not retained without order. It is systematically organized under headings which may not be those of a European scientist but which are better adapted to the needs of a hunter. Moreover, the mind of the savage normally contains the complex mythology of his tribe; its code of morals and rules of behaviour, which are often very detailed, and, finally, a considerable heritage of the spoken literature of his people. Indeed the primitive man's brain is well filled even if what fills it is very different from the knowledge of a European. In view of the disparity of their respective intellectual endowments it is idle to ask which of the two is superior to the other" (*op. cit.*, p. 39).

73 *V poiskakh predkov*, Moscow 1972, p. 289.

74 *Ibid.*, pp. 264-8.

75 *Ibid.*, pp. 296-7.

76 *The Twelve, and Other Poems*, Transl. by Jon Stallworthy and Peter France, London 1970, p. 161.

PART TWO

Chapter Seven

1 The main references to these speculations are to be found in H. J. Schoeps, *Philosemitismus im Barock*, Tübingen 1952, p. 15.

2 Aristotle's *Politics*. The references are to be found in Hans Kohn, *The Idea of Nationalism*, New York 1951, pp. 51 *et seq.*

3 Cf. Borst, I, pp. 339 and 358.

4 Quoted by Menéndez y Pelayo, *Historia de los heterodoxos españoles*, Santander 1948, Vol. VII, p. 324.

5 Borst IV, p. 2,098.

6 *Ibid.*, III/1, p. 1,077.

7 *Spaccio della bestia trionfante*, published in London (with the incorrect indication "Paris") in 1584. See also Borst III/1, pp. 1,183-1,185.

8 Cf. Borst, III/1, p. 1,231, and Marcel Bataillon, "L'unité du genre humain du P. Acosta au P. Clavigero", *Mélanges à la mémoire de Jean Sarrailh*, Vol. I, 1966, p. 84.

9 Quoted by Don Cameron Allen, *The Legend of Noah*, Urbana, Ill., 1949, pp. 132-3.

10 On La Peyrère, see M. J. Schoeps, *Philosemitismus im Barock*, Tübingen 1952, pp. 3-18. With the exception of this penetrating study, the encyclopaedia articles and other works of erudition unanimously consider La Peyrère as a good Christian. His contemporaries knew better, as is shown by the epigram which was much quoted after his death. "La Peyrère is buried here, a good Israelite / Huguenot, Catholic and Pre-Adamite / Four religions pleased him equally / And his detachment was so rare / When he had to make up his mind at the end of eighty years / He departed without choosing any of them". Cited by Schoeps, p. 14.

11 Cf. Robert Lenoble, *Mersenne ou la naissance du mécanisme*, Paris 1943.

12 *Goethe's Conversations with Eckermann*, Everyman ed., London 1930, pp. 265-6 (in the talk with the naturalist, von Martius, on 7 October 1828).

13 Cf. Marcel Bataillon, *L'unité du genre humain . . .*, *op. cit.*, p. 93.

14 On Bernier's classification see p. 143.

15 It should be remembered that the curse on Ham in the ninth chapter of Genesis, verse 25, is directed against his fourth son, Canaan. In the Jewish exegesis of Rachi this verse is interpreted as follows: *Cursed be Canaan.—* "Because of you I shall not have a fourth son to serve me. Cursed be your fourth son therefore, he shall be enslaved to the descendants of his elder brothers on whom falls the duty of serving me." And what was Ham's reason for making him an eunuch? He said to his brothers: "Adam had two sons and one killed the other to inherit the earth, and our father has three sons and desires a fourth!" For Protestant exegesis, see Don Cameron Allen, *The Legend of Noah, op. cit.*, pp. 77-8.

16 Cf. Winthrop D. Jordan, *White over Black: American Attitudes Toward the Negro, 1550-1812*, University of North Carolina Press 1968, pp. 158-9 and p. 501.

17 See *Othello* (Old black ram . . . tupping your white ewe); *Moby Dick* (the cryptogram of the White Whale); *The Adventures of Arthur Gordon Pym* (an inversion of the theme, where the *poète maudit*, Edgar Allan Poe, displays a phobia against whiteness).

For the German literature see Erich Bierhahn, "Blondheit und Blondheitskult in der deutschen Literatur", *Archiv für Kulturgeschichte*, 46 (1964), pp. 309-33.

18 In *Discours sur l'origine et les fondements de l'inégalité parmi les hommes*.

19 In *Essai sur les moeurs et l'esprit des nations; Traité de métaphysique*, and other writings.

20 Cf. the second volume of our *Histoire de l'antisémitisme*, *op. cit.*

21 Borst III/1, p. 1,145.

22 *Ibid.*, p. 1,145 and p. 1,152.

23 Rabbi Manasseh ben Israel of Amsterdam put forward the theory in his book *The Hope of Israel* (1650) which he translated into Latin and dedicated to the English Parliament. He later went to England and negotiated with Cromwell for the return of the Jews to that country.

24 *Histoire naturelle et morale des Indes* . . ., written in Castilian by José de Acosta, Paris 1606, Ch. XVI, p. 30 a. Cf. also Borst III/1, pp. 1,157-8.

25 See the theories of the *Kulturkreis* inspired by Father Wilhelm Schmidt; cf. Marvin Harris, *The Rise of Anthropological Theory*, London 1968, pp. 382-92.

26 Acosta, *op. cit.*, p. 47 b.

27 Cf. M. Harris, *op. cit.*, pp. 16-18 and W. H. Mühlmann, *Geschichte der Anthropologie*, pp. 44-6.

28 Cf. *Lettres théologiques* . . ., posthumous work of M. l'abbé Gaultier, Paris 1756, Vol. II, p. 57.

29 Cf. The article "Uroffenbarung" in *Lexikon für Theologie und Kirche*.

30 Cf. Mircea Eliade, *La Nostalgie des Origines*, Paris 1971, pp. 85-90.

31 Cf. C. Gusdorf, *Les sciences humaines et la pensée occidentale, La révolution galiléenne*, Paris 1969, Vol. II, pp. 106-9.

32 As to Huet, see Borst III/1, pp. 1,290-1,292; A. Dupront, *P. D. Huet et l'exégèse comparatiste au XVIIème siècle*, Paris 1930; Abbé Flottes, *Étude sur Daniel Huet, évêque d'Avranches*, Montpellier 1857.

33 From a letter quoted in the work of Abbé Flottes, *op. cit.*, p. 91, from which we have also taken the other judgements on the *Démonstration évangélique* reproduced above.

34 Cf. Don Cameron Allen, *The Legend of Noah*, *op. cit.*, especially pp. 90-91 ("the attempts to fit the Bible to the yardstick of reason . . .").

35 *Ibid.*, p. 55.

36 *Ibid.*, p. 128.

37 Borst III/1, pp. 1,298-1,300.

38 Borst III/1, pp. 1,305-1,307; and Adalbert Klemm, *Die Säkularisierung der universal-historischen Auffassung; Zum Wandel des Geschichtsdenkens* . . ., Göttingen 1960, p. 113.

39 *Journal des Sçavans*, Paris, 24 April 1684, pp. 85-9.

40 *Otium Hanoveriana sive Miscellanea*, Leipzig 1718, p. 37 (quoted by Ashley Montagu in *Edward Tyson, M.D., F.R.S.*, Philadelphia 1943, p. 397).

41 Cf. Ch III, pp. 39-42.

42 Cf. Sir Charles Firth, "Sir Walter Raleigh's 'History of the World' ", *Essays Historical and Literary*, Oxford 1938, and E. Strathmann, *Sir Walter Raleigh*, New York 1951, pp. 255-6.

43 *The Historie of the World* . . ., London 1652, especially pp. 118-19. "But before I go on with Noah and his sons, I think it necessary to disprove the fiction . . . an invention indeed very ridiculous. . . . For which reasons we doubt not these personal plantations of Janus, Gomer, Tubal in Italy, Spain or France are merely fabulous. . . ." According to Borst III/2, p. 1,238 this criticism of Raleigh was prompted by the prudent scepticism of the Spanish Jesuit, Benito Pereyra.

44 Borst III/2, p. 1,399.

45 *Sidereus Nuncius* (1610), which could also be translated as the *Message of the Stars*. Cf. Alexandre Koyré, *Du monde clos à l'univers infini*, Paris 1962, p. 90, note.

46 Cf. François de Dainville, *La géographie des humanistes*, Paris 1960, pp. 210–12.

47 Cf. A. Koyré, *op. cit.*, p. 92.

48 "In the course of centuries the *naive* self-love of men has had to submit to two major blows at the hands of science. The first was when they learned that our earth was not the centre of the universe but only a tiny fragment of a cosmic system of scarcely imaginable vastness. . . . The second blow fell when biological research destroyed man's supposedly privileged place in creation. . . . But human megalomania will have suffered its third and most wounding blow from the psychological research of the present time which seeks to prove to the ego that it is not even master in its own house . . ." (*Introductory Lectures on Psycho-Analysis, Standard Ed.* Vol. XVI, pp. 284–5).

49 *An Essay concerning Human Understanding*, Bk. IV, Ch. VII.16 — Instance in Man.

50 "The child certainly knows that the nurse that feeds it is neither the cat it plays with, nor the Blackamoor it is afraid of . . ." (*An Essay . . . I, II, 25*).

51 *An Essay . . .* II, XXV, 1.

52 Leibniz, who was a better logician than Locke, rebutted the latter in his *New Essays concerning Human Understanding*, p. 236: ". . . there is no term so absolute and so loose as not to include relations and the perfect analysis of which does not lead to other things and even to all others; so that you can say that relative terms indicate expressly the relationships they contain". In this sense, if Caius the husband led to the idea of his wife, Caius the white man would lead to the black man even more clearly than the human species leads to the animal species. On this reasoning the setting up by Locke of the white man as an absolute is particularly revealing.

53 *New Essays concerning Human Understanding*, I, II, §9.

54 Preface by Leibniz to his *New Essays concerning Human Understanding*.

55 *New Essays concerning Human Understanding*, II, XXVIII, 4.

56 *Essays*, I, XXIII.

57 Article under the heading "Irréligieux" (by Diderot) in the big *Encyclopédie* of Diderot and d'Alembert.

58 See, for instance, the *Nouveau dictionnaire national* of Bescherelle (1893 edition) in the article entitled *Raison*, "1. . . . The faculty by which we acquire universal ideas, absolute truths, unalterable principles . . . . The body of enlightenment produced by the undeniable principles of truth and justice which alone can give the thoughts and actions of man a just, wise and lawful orientation. 2. Subject, cause, motive . . . . The strongest argument used to convince someone. The flames at the stake were for centuries the decisive reason of the inquisition, as artillery is the decisive reason of kings." (A. Martin.)

59 "Entretiens avec Burman." Cf. G. Gusdorf, *op. cit.*, Vol. IV (*La révolution galiléenne*, II, p. 132).

60 *An Essay concerning Human Understanding*, Bk. III, Ch. VI, 23.

61 Cf. J. Rostand, "Réaumur embryologiste . .".., *Revue d'histoire des sciences*, XI (1958), p. 49. Linnaeus drew attention to this sensational news in his *Metamorphosis Planetarium* (1755).

62 *Lettres sur le progrès des Sciences* by Maupertuis (1752), p. 103.

63 Cf. J. Rostand, *loc. cit.*, p. 47.

64 Cf. Jacques Roger, *Les sciences de la vie dans la pensée française du XVIIIe siècle*, Paris 1963, pp. 31-4, 44, 83 and *passim*.

65 The emergence of these ancient traditions or aspirations, banned by the Old Testament, has been detected in some of the talmudic commentaries by Richard L. Rubenstein, *The Religious Imagination, A Study in Psychoanalysis and Jewish Theology*, Indianapolis and New York 1968.

66 "Nature passes so gradually from inanimate to animate things, that from their continuity their boundary and the mean between them is indistinct. The race of plants succeeds immediately that of inanimate objects; and these differ from each other in the proportion in which they participate; for, compared with other bodies, plants appear to possess life, though when compared with animals, they appear inanimate.

The change from plants to animals, however, is gradual, as I observed. For a person might question to which of these classes some marine objects belong . . . the progress is always gradual by which one appears to have more life and motion than another." Aristotle's *History of Animals*, trans. by Richard Cresswell, London 1887, pp. 195-6.

67 Gusdorf, *op. cit.*, Vol. II ("Les origines des sciences humaines"), p. 137.

68 Frank Tinland, *L'homme sauvage, Homo ferus et homo sylvestris*, Paris 1968, pp. 40-45.

69 "Die Krisis der europäischen Wissenschaft und die transzendentale Phänomenologie", *Gesammelte Werke*, Vol. VI, The Hague 1954, pp. 216-19.

70 *Ibid.*, p. 64.

71 Cf. B. D. Lewin, "Conscience and Consciousness in Medical Psychology: a historical study" in *Psychoanalysis in America; historical perspectives*, edited by M. H. Sherman, Springfield 1966, pp. 431-37.

72 Letter to a disciple of Malebranche (1687); cf. Paul Hazard, *La crise de la conscience européenne*, Paris 1961, pp. 195-6.

73 *Ethics*, Part V, Proposition XVII, Corollary.

74 *Ibid.* (" non ridere, non lugere, neque detestari sed intelligere").

75 The most thoroughgoing indictment of this kind is contained in Chestov's *Athènes et Jérusalem*.

Chapter Eight

1 *La Fontaine's Fables*, trans. by Sir Edward Marsh, Everyman's ed., London 1952, Bk. 12, XXIII, p. 314.

2 Richard S. Westfall, *Science and Religion in Seventeenth-century England*, New Haven 1958, p. 46.

3 Charles E. Raven, *Natural Religion and Christian Theology*, Cambridge 1958, Vol. I, p. 107.

4 Preface by Ray to his *Synopsis stirpium Britannicarum* (1690).

5 Preface by Ray to Willoughby's *Ornithology* (1670).

6 Job xlii, 3.

7 R. S. Westfall, *op. cit.*, p. 37.

8 Cf. Raven, *op. cit.*, Vol. I, p. 120, quoting *Synopsis Quadrupedum* (1693) by Ray.

9 Conclusion of the *Wisdom of God* (1693) by Ray; cf. Raven, *John Ray, naturalist . . .*, p. 469.

10 *A discourse on the Specific Differences of Plants* (1674); cf. Th. Birch, *History of the Royal Society of London*, London 1756, Vol. III, pp. 162-73.

11 The anthropologist Ashley Montagu. Cf. *Edward Tyson, M.D., F.R.S.*, Philadelphia 1943, from which the above quotations are taken.

12 In *The Lay Monastery, Consisting of Essays, Discourses, etc.* Cf. Ashley Montagu, *op cit.*, pp. 402-3.

13 Quoted by John C. Greene, *The Death of Adam*, New York 1961, p. 361 and p. 219.

14 Quoted by Frank Tinland, *L'homme sauvage, op. cit.*, p. 128.

15 C. White, *An account of the Regular Gradation in Man, and in Different Animals and Vegetables . . .*, London 1799, pp. 134-5.

16 Cf. E. Guyénot, *Les sciences de la vie aux XVIIe et XVIIIe siècles*, Paris 1941, p 298.

17 Cf. J. Roger, *Les sciences de la vie dans la pensée française du XVIIIe siècle*, Paris 1963, pp. 367-8.

18 *Ibid.*, p. 712.

19 Cf. E. Guyénot, *op. cit.*, p. 299, and Herbert Wendt, *A la recherche d'Adam*, Paris 1953, p. 90.

20 For instance, Guyénot, *op. cit.*, p. 296, and Jean Rostand, *Esquisse d'une histoire de la biologie*, Paris 1968 (Coll. "Idées"), pp. 27-32.

21 H. Wendt, *op. cit.*, p. 90.

22 Cf. Knut Hagberg, *Carl Linné*, Paris 1944, p. 72.

23 *Système de la Nature* de Charles Linné, Brussels Ed. 1793, p. 32.

24 Cf. Frank Tinland, *op. cit.*, p. 117, quoting Linnaeus. *Amoenitates Academicae*, Erlangen 1789, Vol. VI, p. 65.

25 Cf. L. Poliakov, *Histoire de l'antisémitisme, op. cit.*, Vol. III, p. 153.

26 Cf. Franck Tinland, *op. cit.*, pp. 124-5.

27 Cf. John Greene, *The Death of Adam, op. cit.*, pp. 193-4, quoting *Dissertations sur les variétés naturelles qui caractérisent la physionomie des hommes de divers climats et des différents âges . . .* (1781) by Pieter Camper.

28 Cf. Preface by Jean Rostand to E. Callot's *Maupertuis, Le savant et le philosophe*, Paris 1964, pp. 7-9.

29 *Lettre sur le progrès des sciences par M. de Maupertuis*, 1752, pp. 105 et seq. ("Expériences sur les animaux").

30 *Ibid.*, p. 83 ("Utilités du supplice des criminels").

31 *Ibid.*, pp. 122-3 and p. 117.

32 *Dissertation physique à l'occasion du Nègre blanc*, 1777, Chap. III ("Production de nouvelles espèces").

33 We have not found among the published writings of Maupertuis any details of this project which is only known through its being mentioned in 1783 by Immanuel Kant. "The project of M. de Maupertuis to rear, in any designated province, a variety of men with a noble nature, amongst whom intelligence, energy and honesty would be hereditary, rests upon the possibility of at last creating a permanent variety of this sort of man thanks to

careful selection and the elimination of degenerate births. Such a selection, which would, I think, be desirable in itself, does not seem to me capable of achievement because of the superior wisdom of nature . . ." etc. *Von den verschiedenen Rassen der Menschen;* cf. Poliakov, *Histoire de l'antisémitisme,* Vol. III, p. 156, note 3.

34 *Dissertation . . . op. cit.,* Chap. VI ("Difficulté sur l'origine des nègres levée").

35 *Histoire naturelle générale et particulière . . .* ("L'âne").

36 *Histoire naturelle . . .* ("Le lion").

37 *Ibid.* ("Les abeilles").

38 *Ibid.,* ("Variétés de l'espèce humaine").

39 *Ibid.,* ("De l'âge viril.") Cf. Aristotle's description. "In man, the parts of the body are more naturally divided into upper and lower than in any other animal, for all the upper and lower parts of his body are arranged according to the order of nature above and below. . . . But in other animals some of these parts are not at all so placed, or they are much more confused than in man. The head is placed above the body in all animals, but in man alone, as we have said, is this part corresponding to the order of all things." Aristotle, *History of Animals,* trans. by Richard Cresswell, London 1887, Book I, p. 18.

40 Cf. *Histoire de l'antisémitisme,* Vol. III, p. 150.

41 *Histoire naturelle* ("De la dégénération des animaux").

42 In his old age Goethe summed up the influence of Buffon in Germany: "The Comte de Buffon published the first volume of his *Histoire naturelle* the year in which I was born. It aroused the liveliest interest among Germans who were, at that time, highly susceptible to French influence. The other volumes followed year after year and the interest in them of cultivated society coincided in this way with my growing-up . . ." (*Critique des principes de philosophie zoologique de Geoffroy de Saint-Hilaire,* 1830). The two last editions of Buffon's complete works in German date from 1836 and 1837.

As for France, the following note gives an indication of Buffon's influence. "The student who wants to evaluate the success of Buffon in the nineteenth century should consult the *Catalogue général* of the Bibliothèque Nationale. . . . Beginning with the *Morceaux choisis* in 10 volumes and going on to Benjamin Rabier's *Buffon* by way of the *Buffon des écoles, Buffon des familles, Buffon des demoiselles* and even the *Buffon du premier âge . . .* one finds more than 120 titles constituting a mass of more than 325 editions . . .." *Œuvres philosophiques de Buffon,* ed. Jean Piveteau, Paris 1954, pp. 527-8.

43 Cf. P. Charles, "Les Noirs, fils de Cham le maudit", *Nouvelle Revue théologique,* 1928, pp. 721-739.

44 *Histoire philosophique et politique des établissements et du commerce des Européens dans les Deux Indes* (1770), Bk. XI, chap. XXXI.

45 "Not only is their colour different but they are distinct from other men on account of all the features of their faces; the large flat noses, the big lips and the wool instead of hair seem to form a new species of men. If one moves from the Equator to the Antarctic pole, the darkness becomes lighter but the ugliness persists: there too one finds the same uncouth people who inhabit the southern tip of Africa. . . . If one may chance to meet some good people among the Negroes of Guinea (the bulk of them is always vicious)

they are for the most part given to lechery, to vengeance, to theft and to lying. They are so obstinate as never to admit a fault whatever chastisement is imposed upon them. Even the fear of death does not stir them."

46 In the "Supplément au voyage de Bougainville". Cf. Poliakov, *Histoire de l'antisémitisme*, Vol. III, p. 150.

47 In the "Rêve de d'Alembert", cf. Jean Rostand, "Diderot et la biologie", *Revue d'histoire des sciences*, V, (1952), i, p. 9.

48 Cf. Jean Rostand, "La conception de l'homme selon Helvétius et selon Diderot". *Revue d'histoire des sciences*, IV (1951), 3-4, pp. 213-22.

49 *Réflections sur l'esclavage des nègres* (published by Condorcet under the name of pastor Schwartz), Neufchâtel 1781, p. ili.

50 Cf. *Histoire de l'antisémitisme*, Vol. III, pp. 139-43.

51 Cf. The famous note (j) or note 10 in the *Discours sur l'origine de l'inégalité parmi les hommes* (1755).

52 Particularly in *Totemism*, Harmondsworth 1969, pp. 172-6, and in *The Savage Mind*, Harmondsworth 1966, pp. 38, 163, 247.

53 "It would be a solemn moment if the Orang-Outang, or some other apes, were shown to be of human species, and if the dullest observers could be convinced of this, even by some demonstration. But, apart from the fact that one generation would not suffice for this experiment, it must be considered impracticable because it would be necessary to prove that which is now only a supposition, before an experiment for obtaining this proof could be carried out without blame." *Discours sur l'origine de l'inégalité*, note (j) quoted above.

54 Wilhelm A. Mühlmann, *Geschichte der Anthropologie*, Frankfurt a/M 1968, p. 57.

55 I. Kant, *Anthropologie du point de vue pragmatique:* trans. by Michel Foucault, Paris 1964, p. 148.

56 *Ibid.*, p. 160.

57 *Ibid.*, pp. 157-8.

58 *Ibid.*, p. 160.

59 The first paragraph of this text, which is entitled *Worin bestekt das Fortschreiten zum besseren Menschengeschlecht*, reads as follows:

"The prospect may be that either there will be constantly improving people, or people (in their commissions and omissions) will act in a progressively better manner. With regard to the first sort of progress, in which nature would develop new and better races or produce them through the commingling of two races there is little ground for hope in as much as nature has long since exhausted the forms appropriate to soil and climate, whilst cross-breeding (for example of the American with the European or of these with the Negro) has debased the good without raising proportionately the level of the worse—hence the governor of Mexico wisely rejected the order of the Spanish Court to encourage interbreeding."

60 *Ibid.*

61 Cf. *Histoire de l'antisémitisme*, Vol. III, p. 196.

62 *Of the unity of the human race and of its varieties*, cf. *Histoire de l'antisémitisme*, Vol. III, p. 157.

63 *Decas quarta collectionis suae cranorum diversarum gentium illustrata* (cf. *ibid.*).

64 *Outlines of a Philosophy of the History of Mankind*, trans. by T. Churchill, London 1803, Vol. I, Book VII, Chap. I.

65 *Outlines of a Philosophy of the History of Mankind*, Book VI, p. 260.

66 *Ibid.*, p. 267.

67 *Ibid.*, pp. 270-271.

68 *Ibid.*, p. 259.

69 *Cosmos, A Sketch of a Physical Description of the Universe*, trans. by E. C. Otté, London 1848, Vol. I, p. 368.

70 Letter quoted by Manfred Steinkühler, *Gobineau au jugement de ses contemporains d'Outre Rhin*, from a typed university thesis, Paris 1961, p. 279.

71 A voyage to Guinea . . . (1723); quoted in W. D. Jordan, *White over Black*, *op. cit.*, p. 17.

72 *Ibid.*, pp. 31-2.

73 Cf. *Œuvres complètes de Voltaire*, Moland ed., Vol. XII, p. 192 and p. 210.

74 *Ibid.*, Vol. XI, p. 7.

75 *Ibid.*, Vol. XII, p. 380 ("Nature has subordinated to this principle its various degrees of genius and those characteristics of nations which are so rarely seen to change. It is for this reason that Negroes are the slaves of other men. One buys them like beasts on the coasts of Africa . . ." etc.)

76 *Ibid.*, Vol. XII, p. 367 *et seq.* ("De l'Inde en deçà et au delà du Gange").

77 *Ibid.*, p. 368.

78 "In these one hundred and eighteen articles, about thirty denounce the Jews —'our masters and our enemies whom we believe in and whom we hate' (article on Abraham); 'the most abominable people on earth' (article on Anthropophagists); a people 'whose laws say not a word about the spirituality and immortality of the soul' (article on the Soul) and so forth . . .." *Histoire de l'antisémitisme*, Vol. III, p. 105.

79 Moland ed., Vol. XXVI, pp. 402-4.

80 "Of National Characters." Cf. *Essays, Moral, Political and Literary*, London 1875, pp. 244-58.

81 *Ibid.*, p. 252, note.

82 *Sketches of the History of Man* . . ., Basle ed. 1796, Vol. I, pp. 58-9 and Vol. III, p. 106.

83 *Ibid.*, pp. 47-8.

84 Armand de Quatrefages, "Histoire naturelle de l'homme", *Revue des Deux Mondes*, March 1857, p. 162.

85 Cf. W. D. Jordan, *White over Black*, *op. cit.*, pp. 492-5.

86 E. von Eickstedt, *Geschichte und Methoden der Anthropologie*, Stuttgart 1940, p. 286.

87 Wilhelm E. Mühlmann, *Geschichte der Anthropologie*, Frankfurt a/M 1968, pp. 59-61.

88 As pointed out by Mühlmann, *ibid.*, p. 61 and p. 203.

89 Meiners, *Untersuchungen über die Verschiedenheiten der Menschenrassen* . . ., Tübingen 1811, Vol. III, pp. 312 *et seq.*; Vol. I, p. 1, p. 7, p. 166.

90 *Grundriss der Geschichte der Menschheit*, Lemgo 1793, pp. 123-4.

91 *Untersuchungen* . . ., Vol. III, chap. VI.

92 *Ibid.*, Vol. III, p. 129 and p. 306.

93 *Ibid.*, Vol. III, pp. 17 *et seq.*, especially pp. 74-77; Vol. I, pp. 469 *et seq.*

94 Joh. Christ. Fabricius, *Betrachtungen über die allgemeinen Einrichtungen der Natur*, Hamburg 1781, pp. 328-32.

95 Joh. Christ. Fabricius, *Systema antliatorum*, Brunswick 1805, p. 340; cf. also *Nouveau Dictionnaire d'histoire naturelle*, Vol. XXVIII, Paris 1819, article on "Pou".

96 *Histoire naturelle de genre humain*, pp. 145-6.

97 *Histoire naturelle . . .*, pp. 146-7 and p. 151.

98 *Nouveau Dictionnaire d'histoire naturelle*, Vol. XV, p. 152 (article on "Homme"). Does *pediculus nigritarum* exist in the view of modern science? We obtained information on this subject from the Institut Pasteur in Paris. The head of the entomological medical service, Professor P. Grenier, kindly furnished the following note on 19 December 1969. "The question of lice associated with different human races is an old problem since it began with Fabricius as you yourself have pointed out. But it is not only a question of the Negro louse. There is also a Chinese louse (P. *humanus chinensis*), a louse of the Peruvian mummies (P. h. *americanus*), a Japanese louse and finally the P. *pseudohumanus* (Ewing 1938) which is attached to the natives of the Marquesas Islands, of Tahiti and of Guatemala and also to monkeys. The problem is a very complex one and no definite conclusion has so far been formulated. . . ."
The question of race among lice seems to be as much disputed as that of the races of mankind. From the point of view of the history of racism, however, the essential point is that a number of authors have attempted to draw the conclusion that Negroes were subhuman from the supposed existence of *pediculus nigritarum*.

99 *The Descent of Man*, "Modern Library", New York, p. 532 and p. 536 (see references to Virey).

100 Philip D. Curtin, *The Image of Africa, British Ideas and Actions*, 1780-1850, London 1965, p. 371.

Chapter Nine

1 *Des époques de la nature*, "septième époque". Cf. *Œuvres philosophiques de Buffon*, Ed. by J. Piveteau, Paris 1954.

2 Cf. E. A. W. Zimmermann, *Geographische Geschichte des Menschen und der allgemein verbreiteten vierfüssigen Thiere*, Vol. III, Leipzig 1783, pp. 192-5.

3 T. Morgan, *A brief examination of the Rev. Mr. Warburton's Divine Legation of Moses*, London 1791. Cf. *Histoire de l'antisémitisme*, Vol. III, pp. 80-81.

4 See the articles "Adam" and "Génèse" in the *Dictionnaire philosophique* by Voltaire as well as Chap. CXLIII ("De l'Inde") in the *Essai sur les moeurs et l'esprit des nations*.

5 Cf. Raymond Schwab, *La Renaissance orientale*, Paris 1950, p. 26.

6 *Lettres sur l'origine des sciences et sur celle des peuples de l'Asie adressées à M. de Voltaire par M. Bailly et précédées de quelques lettres de M. de Voltaire à l'auteur*, Paris 1777, p. 3 (letter from Voltaire of 15 December 1775).

7 *Dissertation sur les moeurs et les usages de l'Inde*, translated by M. B. ★★★, pp. xiii-xiv.

8 Cf. Helmuth v. Glasenapp, *Das Indienbild deutscher Denker*, Stuttgart 1960, pp. 11-12.

9 Cf. René Gérard, *L'Orient et la pensée romantique allemande*, Paris 1963, p. 40.

10 *Ibid.*, p. 22.

11 J. G. Herder, *Outlines of a Philosophy of the History of Man*, trans. by T. Churchill, London 1803, Vol. II, p. 34.

12 *Ibid.*, Vol. I, pp. 517, 518.

13 The conclusion of "Älteste Urkunde des Menschengeschlechts" (*Sämmtliche Werke, Vol. VI*), Berlin 1883, p. 500.

14 *La Renaissance orientale, op. cit.*, p. 225.

15 Cf. Georges Mounin, *Histoire de la Linguistique des origines au XXe siècle*, Paris 1967, pp. 144 and 150.

16 On the ideas of Michaelis and his colleagues Gatterer and Schlözer, see A. Borst, *op. cit.*, Vol. III/2, pp. 1,499-1,502.

17 On the question of chronology, cf. A. Klempt, *Die Säkularisierung der universalhistorischen Auffassung . . ., op. cit.*, pp. 188 *et seq.*

18 Cf. Th. Benfey, *Geschichte der Sprachwissenschaft und orientalischen Philologie in Deutschland*, Munich 1869, pp. 333 *et seq.*

19 *Ibid.*, p. 348, quoting *Asiatic Researches* by Jones (3rd Anniversary discourse delivered to the Royal Asiatic Society on 2 February 1786).

20 Cf. *Ibid*, p. 355.

21 On Adelung's theory, see *Histoire de l'antisémitisme*, Vol. III, p. 325.

22 Cf. Paul Busch, *Friedrich Schlegel und das Judentum*, Munich 1939, especially p. 67.

23 "Vorlesungen über Universalgeschichte" (1805-1806); *Werke*, J.-J. Anstett ed., Vol. XIV, Munich 1960.

24 Letter to Ludwig Tieck of 15 December 1803; cf. *ibid.*, p. xxxi.

25 Schlegel referred expressly to Voltaire and was especially inspired by the *Essai sur les moeurs et l'esprit des nations;* cf. *ibid.*, p. xxviii.

26 The quotations given here are from *The Aesthetic and Miscellaneous Works of Friedrich von Schlegel*, trans. by E. J. Millington, London 1900, Bohn's Standard Library, pp. 505, 506-7.

27 Cf. *Metamorphoses*, XV, 75-142, where the eulogy of a primitive and vegetarian Golden Age is put in the mouth of Pythagoras.

28 Cf. *Histoire de l'antisémitisme*, Vol. III, pp. 440-67 ("Le cas de Richard Wagner").

29 Quoted by René Gérard, *L'Orient et la pensée romantique allemande, op. cit.*, p. 132.

30 Jakob-Joseph Görres, *Mythengeschichte der asiatischen Welt . . .*, cf. Gérard, *ibid.*, pp. 181-7.

31 Friedrich Creuzer, *Symbolik und Mythologie der alten Völker . . .*, cf. Gérard, *ibid.*, pp. 173-81.

32 Johann Arnold Kanne, *Erste Urkunden der Geschichte oder allgemeine Mythologie . . .* (1808) and *System der indischen Mythe oder Chronos . . .* (1815); cf. Gérard, *ibid.*, pp. 187-91.

33 For the descent of the term "Aryan" see Hans Siegert; "Zur Geschichte der Begriffe 'Arisch' und 'arisch' ", *Wörter und Sachen*, Heidelberg, 4/1941-1942, pp. 73-99. ". . . *Aire* in Irish law-texts means the free, ruling class of Irishmen; bö-aire means the freeman who has tenants under him" (Siegert in the article quoted, p. 85). This resembles the Russian *boyard* or more properly *boyarin*.

34 Cf. Gustav Meyer, "Von wem stammt die Bezeichnung Indogermanen?" *Indogermanische Forschungen*, II (1892), pp. 125-30.

35 Cf. Siegert, in the article quoted above.

36 "I am unable to approve the expression *Indo-German*", wrote Bopp, "for I cannot see why one should take the Germans as representing all the peoples of our continent" (*Vergleichende Grammatik*, Preface).

37 Boetticher-Lagarde's thesis for his degree, which he wrote in Latin, opened with the words, *Inter linguas japetiticas* . . ., Cf. Siegert in the article quoted, p. 74.

38 "Über das Studium der Theologie". Cf. *Schellings Sämmltliche Werke*, Vol. V, Stuttgart 1859, pp. 296 *et seq.*

39 Letter of 18 December 1806 to Windischmann, quoted by H. Gérard, *op. cit.*, p. 213.

40 *Einleitung in die Philosophie der Mythologie* (1841-1854).

41 *Noten und Abhandlungen zu besserem Verständnis des West-Östlichen Divans.*

42 Cf. *Die Vernunft in der Geschichte*, Hoffmeister ed., Hamburg 1955, pp. 158 *et seq.*

43 *Ibid.*, p. 163.

44 Cf. H. von Glasenapp, *Das Indienbild deutscher Denker*, *op. cit.*, pp. 38-60.

45 *Die Vernunft in der Geschichte*, p. 158.

46 See the cycle "Heimekehr" (which dates from 1823-1824): "I called up the Devil and he appeared . . .. He is an able diplomat and speaks eloquently of Church and State. He is somewhat pale but small's the wonder, for he is now studying Sanskrit and Hegel. . . ."

47 *Die Vorhalle des Europäischen Völkergeschichte* . . . by Carl Ritter, 1820 (in R. Gérard, *op. cit.*, pp. 192-4).

48 *Die heilige Sage und das gesamte Religionssystem der alten Baktrier, Meder und Perser* . . . by J. G. Rhode (1820). Cf. *Histoire de l'antisémitisme*, Vol. III, pp. 325-6.

49 Christian Lassen, *Indische Altertumskunde*, Vol. I, Bonn 1847, p. 414.

50 *Ibid.*, p. 513.

51 *Etymologische Forschungen* (1833-1836), Vol. I, p. xxi.

52 K. F. O. Westphal, *Philosophische Grammatik*. Cf. S. Reinach, "Le mirage oriental", *Anthropologie*, 5-6 (1893), p. 1.

53 *Geschichte der deutschen Sprache*, by Jakob Grimm, Leipzig 1868 (Third ed.), Vol. I, p. iv.

54 *Ibid.*, pp. 113-22 (chap. VIII, *Einwanderung*).

55 *Ibid.*, pp. iv-vi.

56 Cf. *Histoire de l'antisémitisme*, Vol. III, pp. 440-67 ("Le cas de Richard Wagner").

57 *Arisch als ein technischer Ausdruck;* M. Müller, *Essays*, Leipzig 1879, Vol. II, p. 333.

58 "Variétés de l'espèce humaine"; G. Cuvier, *Le règne animal*. . ., Paris 1817, p. 94.

59 *Introduction to the 1831 Edition; cf. Michelet*, A choice of texts by L. Fèbvre, Paris 1946, p. 154 and pp. 95-6. "The womb of the world" is in English in the original text.

60 *Parallèle des langues de l'Europe et de l'Asie*, by Frédéric-Gustave Eichhoff, Paris 1836, p. 12.

61 Cf. Gabriel Monod, *La vie et la pensée de Jules Michelet*, Paris 1923, Vol. II, p. 224.

62 Cf. Jean Richer, *Gérard de Nerval et les doctrines ésotériques*, Paris 1947, pp. 10-14. (Letter from Nerval to M. Cavé, a departmental head at the Ministry of Interior, 31 March 1841.)

63 *Louis Lambert*, "Livre de Poche" Edition, Paris 1968, pp. 100-101.

64 P. Leroux, "De l'influence des idées orientales", *Revue encyclopédique*, Paris, Vol. LIV, April-June 1832, pp. 69-80.

65 P. Proudhon, *De la justice dans la Révolution et dans l'Église*, 1930 edition, Vol. I, p. 445.

66 A. Viatte, *Claude-Julien Bredin (1776-1854), Correspondance philosophique et littéraire avec Ballanche*, Paris 1958. Introduction and *passim*.

67 Cf. P. M. Burtin, *Le Baron Eckstein, Un semeur d'idées au temps de la Restauration*, Paris 1931. Eckstein was the son of a Jewish convert.

68 *Ibid.*, p. 263.

69 Quoted by R. Schwab, *La Renaissance orientale, op. cit.*, p. 343.

70 "In cultured Catholic countries", wrote Hegel, "the government has ceased to stand aside any longer from the requirements of rational thought and has felt the need to make an alliance with science and philosophy." He then cited the names of Lamennais, Rémusat, Saint Martin and continued: "Baron d'Eckstein, for his part and in his own way, namely by arguments and methods of the philosophy of nature which are superficial and drawn from Germany in imitations of Fr. von Schlegel, though with more wit than the latter, has given his support, in his journal, *Le Catholique*, to this primitive Catholicism and has, in particular, controlled the government's subsidies...." *Die Vernunft in der Geschichte*, in the ed. quoted above, p. 159, note.

71 E. Vermeil, *L'Allemagne, Essai d'explication*, Paris 1940, p. 134.

72 Quoted by A. Albalat, *La vie de Jésus d'Ernest Renan*, Paris 1933, p. 60.

73 R. Schwab, *La Renaissance orientale, op. cit.*, p. 393 and pp. 397-8.

74 Letter from Tocqueville to Gobineau dated 20 December 1853. Cf. *Œuvres Complètes*, Vol. IX, Paris 1959, p. 205.

75 Thomas Mann, *Pariser Rechenschaft . . .*, pp. 59-60.

76 As to the change of view by Renan see Ernest Seillière, "L'Impérialisme germaniste dans l' œuvre de Renan", *Revue des deux Mondes*, 134/5 and 135/6 (1906) pp. 836-58 and 323-52. In a lecture in 1878 Renan declared peremptorily: "The phenomenon of the appearance of families of languages is, therefore, a phenomenon which has nothing in common with the problems of which anthropology seeks to find a solution. . . ." Cf. *Œuvres complètes*, 1947-1961 Ed., Vol. VIII, p. 1,224. See also Vol. I, pp. 935 *et seq.* "Le judaïsme comme race et comme religion", 1883. As to Müller's change of view, see further on.

77 Letter of Renan to Müller of 17 November 1855. *Œuvres . . ., op. cit.*, Vol. X, p. 178.

78 Cf. N. Burtin, *Le baron d'Eckstein . . ., op. cit.*, p. 183.

79 Letter of Renan to Gobineau, 26 June 1856. *Œuvres. . . .*, Vol. X, pp. 203-5.

80 See especially the end of *Histoire générale et système comparé des langues sémitiques* (1847-1855). *Œuvres*, Vol. VIII, pp. 580-9.

81 *Histoire . . . des langues sémitiques. Œuvres*, Vol. VIII, p. 586.

82 *L'Avenir religieux des sociétés modernes* (1860). *Œuvres*, I, 239, 242, 243.

83 *Histoire . . . des langues sémitiques, loc. cit.*

84 *De l'origine du langage* (1848-1858). *Œuvres*, VIII, 98.

85 "Discours d'ouverture au Collège de France" (1862). *Œuvres*, II, 333.

86 Review of the *Life of Jesus* in *Revue des Deux Mondes;* cf. S. Posener, *Adolphe Crémieux*, Paris 1933, Vol. II, p. 157.

87 Cf. A. Albalat, *La vie de Jésus d'Ernest Renan, op. cit.*, p. 62 and p. 73.

88 *Bible de l'humanité*, Paris 1864, pp. 6-8. Daniel Halévy pointed out how the success of the *Life of Jesus* by Renan had inspired Michelet to write his "Aryan Bible"; cf. R. Schwab, *op. cit.*, p. 417.

89 *La Bible dans l'Inde, Vie de Iezeus Christna*, by L. Jacolliot, Paris 1873 (4th Ed., pp. 7, 64, 141).

90 Cited by Thomas Huxley, *The Aryan Question and Prehistoric Man* (1890), "Collected Essays", Vol. VII, London 1906, pp. 281-2, note.

91 *Op. cit.*, pp. 207-19.

92 Cf. Max Müller, *Lectures on the Science of Language*, London 1862, pp. 163-4.

93 A. Ellegard, *Darwin and the General Reader*, Gothenburg 1958, pp. 96 *et seq.*

94 "The Miltonic hypothesis"; cf. Thomas Huxley, *Lectures on Evolution* in "Essays", Vol. IV, p. 65.

95 *Zanoni*, Book III, Ch. I.

96 *Coningsby* (1844) and *Tancred* (1847); cf. *Histoire de l'antisémitisme*, Vol. III, pp. 341-3.

97 "The Sacred Scriptures, whose testimony is received by all men of unclouded minds with implicit and reverential assent, declare that it pleased the Almighty Creator to make of one blood all the nations of the earth, and that all mankind are the offspring of common parents." *The Natural History of Man*, London 1855 ed., Vol. I, Ch. II, p. 5.

98 *Ibid.*, p. 134.

99 Cf. A. Ellegard, *Darwin and the General Reader, op. cit.*, p. 101.

100 "What is the question now placed before society with a glib assurance the most astounding? The question is this—Is man an ape or an angel? My Lord, I am on the side of the angels. . . ." (Speech by Disraeli at Oxford in 1864.)

101 Huxley, *The Aryan Question and Prehistoric Man* (1890), "Essays", Vol. VII, p. 275.

102 *Ibid.*, p. 282.

103 Cf. *Genesis versus Nature* (1885), "Essays", Vol. IV, pp. 161-2.

104 *Prologue, Controverted Questions* (1892), "Essays", Vol. V, pp. 55-7.

105 Letter of 29 June 1869 (*The Life and Letters of the Right Honourable Friedrich Max Müller*, London 1902, Vol. I, p. 367).

106 Letter of 9 July 1869 (*ibid.*, p. 368).

107 *Ibid.*

108 *Lectures on the Science of Language*, London 1862, p. 213.

109 Cf. The article under the heading "Aryan" in *The Imperial Dictionary of the English Language*, Vol. I, London 1883, p. 159.

110 Letter of 7 March 1871 (*The Life and Letters . . .*, Vol. I, p. 415).

111 Cf. *The Life and Letters . . ., op. cit.*, Vol. I, p. 420.

112 *Über die Resultate der Sprachwissenschaft, Vorlesung gehalten in der kaiserlichen Universität zu Strassburg am 23 mai 1872.*

113 John Fiske, *Evolution of language* (*North American Review*, Oct. 1863); *The genesis of language* (*ibid.*, Oct, 1869); *Our Aryan Forefathers* (*Excursions of an Evolutionist*, New York 1883); *What we learn from old Aryan words* (*ibid.*) and *The Destiny of Man* (Boston 1884).

Chapter Ten

1 Jean-Baptiste Lamarck, *Philosophie zoologique*, ed. J.-P. Aron, Paris 1968, pp. 295-7.

2 *Ibid.*, pp. 51-2.

3 *Œuvres de Claude-Henri de Saint-Simon*, Paris 1966, Vol. V, p. 55.

4 *Ibid.*, pp. 25-7.

5 *Ibid.*, pp. 52-3.

6 *Lettre d'un habitant de Genève à ses contemporains. Œuvres*, *op. cit.*, Vol. I, pp. 46 *et seq.*

7 See for example *Observations sur les hommes de couleur des colonies* by César de l'Escale de Vérone, Paris 1790; "O Frenchmen . . . you should be afraid lest that native populace whom you might consider French and call by the name of brothers, to whom you might think yourselves bound by ties of commerce and mutual interest, should come to infuse into the very heart of our country that thick, heavy, impure, black, crafty blood so unworthy of that which flows in your veins, the renown of which has covered the whole earth and eclipsed all that ever acquired by the Greeks and Romans" (p. 13).

8 *Rapports du physique et du moral chez l'homme*, Paris 1824, Vol. I, pp. 133-4.

9 *Ibid.*, Vol. II, p. 127.

10 *Ibid*, Vol. II, p. 452, and Vol. I, p. xvii.

11 *Ibid.*, Vol. I, pp. 410-11.

12 *Ibid.*, Vol. II, p. 327. On Draparnaud, who planned to establish "an ideological scale of the races" in a work to be called *Idéologie comparée*, see Fr. Picavet, *Les idéologues*, Paris 1891, pp. 445-50.

13 *Ibid.*, p. 411, in the note marked (E).

14 Cf. the typed thesis by Jean Boissel, *Victor Courtet de l'Isle*, Paris 1969, Vol. I, p. 38.

15 Cf. George W. Stocking, "French Anthropology in 1800", *Isis*, LV (1964), and *Le règne animal* by Cuvier, Paris 1817, p. 94.

16 *L'homme* (*homo*), *Essai zoologique sur le genre humain*, 2nd Edition, pp. 148, 102 *et seq.*, p. 318.

17 *Aperçu philosophique sur la possibilité de perfectionner l'homme par les modifications de son organisation*, by M. A. Desmoulins, Paris (undated, *c.* 1820) pp. 24-5.

18 According to V. Schoelcher the belief in racial inequality was a prejudice which was bound to disappear in time. *De l'abolition de l'esclavage*, 1840; cf. *Histoire de l'antisémitisme*, Vol. III, p. 353.

19 Cf. *Lettres sur la race noire et la race blanche* by Gustave d'Eichthal and Ismayl Urbain, Paris 1839, p. 14.

20 A. de Quatrefages, "La Floride", *Revue des deux Mondes*, March 1843, pp. 757 *et seq.*

21 Cf. William Stanton, *The Leopard's Spots, Scientific attitudes towards race in America*, Chicago 1961, p. 103.

22 Cf. C. G. Carus, *Über ungleiche Befähigung der verschiedenen Menschenrassen für höhere geistige Entwicklung*, 1849, p. 19, and Renan's letter to Max Müller of 10 June 1857.

23 *Lectures* . . ., pp. 475 *et seq.* (Chap. VIII, Differences in moral and intellectual qualities).

24 Cf. T. K. Penniman, *A Hundred years of Anthropology*, London 1952, pp. 58 *et seq.*, and E. Von Eickstedt, *Geschichte und Methoden der Anthropologie*, Stuttgart 1940, pp. 346 *et seq.*

25 Cf. Philip D. Curtin, *The Image of Africa, British Ideas and Action, 1780-1850*, London 1965, p. 236.

26 *Ibid.*, p. 242.

27 Cf. Marvin Harris, *The Rise of Anthropological Theory*, London 1969, pp. 76-8, and E. von Eickstedt, *op. cit.*, pp. 350-51.

28 J. Hunt, "On the Negro's place in Nature", *The Anthropological Review*, II (1864), section II, p. xv.

29 What follows is taken from *Cours de philosophie positive*, Vol. V, Paris 1841, pp. 4 *et seq.*, and from *Système de politique positive ou traité de sociologie*, Vol. II, Paris 1852, pp. 461-2 and *passim*.

30 "This puerile and untimely display of a sterile and ill-directed erudition, which in our day tends to trammel the study of our social evolution by a wanton mingling of the history of populations, like those of India and China etc., that cannot have exercised any real influence on our past, should be authoritatively exposed as an inextricable source of fundamental confusion in the search for the true laws governing human sociality," *Cours de philosophie positive, loc. cit.*

31 *Système de politique positive*, Vol. II, p. 461.

32 Cf. W. Mühlmann, *Geschichte der Anthropologie, op. cit.*, p. 48.

33 *Des caractères physiologiques des races humaines considérés dans leurs rapports avec l'histoire. Lettre à M. Amédée Thierry*, by F. W. Edwards (Paris 1829).

34 "I shall quote . . . an example which will leave no room for doubt. Jewish features are so clearly marked that there can scarcely be any mistake about them and as Jews are to be found in all European countries there is no national characteristic more generally known and recognizable. They might be considered as forming colonies of the same race in these countries . . . climate has not assimilated them to the nations among which they live."

35 Ch. Comte, *Traité de législation, ou exposition des lois générales suivants lesquelles les peuples prospèrent, dépérissent ou restent stationnaires*, Paris 1827-1835; see especially Vol. I, Preface; Vol. II, p. 57-8; Vol. III, pp. 360-61; Vol. IV, pp. 443-6.

36 Barthélemy Dunoyer, *Nouveau traité d'économie sociale*, 2 vols., Paris 1830. Cf. also E. von Eickstedt, *Geschichte und Methoden der Anthropologie, op. cit.*, p. 340.

37 De Courtet's philosophy of history is partially summarized, in what follows, from the thesis of M. Jean Boissel, *Victor Courtet de l'Isle (1813-1867)*, Paris 1969, as well as from his *Mémoire sur les races humaines (Extrait du Journal de l'Institut historique)*, Paris (1835?), which was the conclusion of *La science politique fondée sur la science de l'homme.*

38 *La science politique* . . ., pp. 262-3.

39 *Ibid.*, p. 233.

40 "The hand of some awful power, bearing down upon these aberrant peoples, deprives them of the two distinctive traits of our greatness, foresight and perfectibility. . . . Just as the most abject and revolting substances are nevertheless susceptible of some further degeneration, so the natural vices of humanity are further vitiated in the savage. He is a thief, he is cruel, he is dissolute, but he is so in another way than ourselves. To be criminals we have to go beyond our nature; the savage follows his; he has an appetite for crime and he feels no remorse." *Les soirées de Saint-Petersburg*, Deuxième entretien.

41 B. Constant, *Mélanges de littérature et de politique*, Paris 1829, pp. 149-50.

42 Quoted by E. J. Young, *Gobineau und des Rassismus, Eine Kritik der anthropologischen Theorie*, Meisenheim 1968, p. 207.

43 H. Taine, *Histoire de la littérature anglaise* Paris 1865, Vol. I, p. xxvi.

44 Thomas Arnold, *Introductory Lectures on Modern History*, New York 1842; *The Life and Correspondence of Thomas Arnold*, London, 6th ed., p. 488.

45 *Ibid.*, p. 240 (letter to the Archbishop of Dublin, 22 March 1835).

46 *Coningsby*, London 1844, pp. 182-3.

47 Cf. *Histoire de l'antisémitisme*, Vol. III, pp. 339-49.

48 Cf. *The Image of Africa*, op. cit., p. 377.

49 *The Races of Men: A philosophical enquiry into the influence of race over the destinies of nations*, by Robert Knox, M.D., London 1862 (2nd ed.). Preface, p. 1.

50 See Marvin Harris, *The Rise of Anthropological Theory*, op. cit., pp. 99-100; also Wilhelm Mühlmann, *Geschichte der Anthropologie*, op. cit., p. 99.

51 *The Races of Men . . .*, pp. 194 and 208. "But where are the Jewish farmers, Jewish mechanics, labourers? Can he not till the earth or settle anywhere? Why does he dislike handicraft labour? Has he no inventive power, no mechanical or scientific turn of mind? . . . And then I began to enquire into this and I saw . . . that the Jews who followed any calling were not really Hebrews, but sprung of a Jewish father and a Saxon or Celtic mother; that the real Jew had never altered since the earliest recorded period; . . . that the real Jew has no ear for music, no love of science or literature; that he invents nothing, pursues no enquiry, etc . . .", p. 194.

52 Cf. Karl Koehne, "Untersuchungen über Vorläufer und Quellen der Rassentheorie des Grafen Gobineau". *Archiv für Rassen-und Gesellschaftsbiologie*, XVIII (1926), pp. 369-96.

53 Letter to Baron von Prokesch-Osten. Cf. A. Cambris, *La philosophie des races du comte de Gobineau*, Paris 1937, pp. 158-9.

54 Cf. A. Tocqueville, *Œuvres*, Vol. IX (Correspondance d'Alexis de Tocqueville et d'Arthur de Gobineau), Paris 1959, p. 259.

55 *Essai sur l'inégalité des races humaines*, Paris 1967, p. 208.

56 *Ibid.*, p. 154.

57 *Ibid.*, pp. 57-66 (Chap. IV "De ce qu'on doit entendre par le mot dégénération . . .". It is in this chapter that Gobineau develops his principle of "historical chemistry").

58 *Ibid.*, p. 223.

59 *Ibid.*, p. 95.

60 *Ibid.*, p. 161.

61 *Ibid.*, pp. 317-18.

62 *Ibid.*, pp. 84-5.

63 *Ibid.*, p. 253.

64 *Ibid.*, pp. 477-8.

65 *Ibid.*, p. 817.

66 *Ibid.*, pp. 852-3.

67 *Ibid.*, pp. 870.

68 *Ibid.*, p. 872.

69 See p. 233 above and note 54 above.

70 Letter from de Tocqueville of 30 July 1856; *op. cit.*, p. 267.

71 Cf. E. Renan, *Œuvres*, Vol. X, Paris 1961, pp. 203-5. (Letter of 26 June 1856.)

72 "I can see only one way", wrote Fichte, "of protecting ourselves from them; to conquer their promised land and send them all there . . . to grant them civic rights would be possible on one condition only: to cut off all their heads during a single night and provide each of them with a new one which should not contain a single Jewish idea." Cf. *Histoire de l'antisémitisme*, Vol. III, pp. 198-200.

73 *Introduction to the Philosophy of Mythology*, Vol. I, "Fifth Lesson".

74 *Ibid.*, Vol. II, "Twenty-first lesson". This second part of the *Philosophy of Mythology* dates from the period when Schelling, in his later years, had been appointed to a chair of philosophy in the University of Berlin where he succeeded Hegel as Prussian State philosopher with the responsibility of struggling against the "scattering of dragon's teeth" by the young left-wing Hegelians.

75 *Ibid.*, Vol. I, "Seventh Lesson".

76 Oken, *Lehrbuch der Naturphilosophie*, Third Part, Jena 1811, pp. 353-5 and 373-4.

77 "Oken, the cleverest thinker and one of Germany's greatest citizens," wrote H. Heine. Cf. *Zur Geschichte der Religion und Philosophie in Deutschland*, "Third Book".

78 Cf. *Encyclopädie der philosophischen Wissenschaften*, §411 ("Die wirkliche Seele").

79 Cf. *Grundlinien der Philosophie des Rechtes*, § 270 (note on the grant of civic rights to Quakers and Jews).

80 *The Philosophy of History*, trans. by J. Sibree, New York 1956, pp. 93, 95, 98.

81 *Ibid.*, pp. 420-2.

82 Or mystico-revolutionary according to the interpretation of Georg Lukacs, *Der junge Hegel*, Zürich 1967, especially pp. 67 *et seq.*, and p. 110.

83 "The attempt of Jesus to give the Jewish crowd an awareness of the divine could only end in failure because faith in divinity cannot exist in the mire. The lion cannot find room inside a nut; the infinite spirit finds no place in the dungeon of a Jewish soul. . . . The great tragedy of the Jewish people is not a Greek tragedy; it cannot arouse either fear or pity since each of these derives from the destiny of inevitable aberration by a beautiful being; it can only arouse horror. The destiny of the Jewish people is the destiny of

Macbeth. . . . All the conditions of the Jewish people, including the condition of misery, meanness and baseness in which it still finds itself today, are but the consequences. . . ." Cf. *Histoire de l'antisémitisme*, Vol. III, pp. 200-203.

84 Cf. *Early Theological Writings*, trans. by T. M. Knox, Chicago 1948, pp. 146, 149. These works of Hegel were not published until the twentieth century.

85 Joseph Görres, *Deutschland und die Nationen*, "Politische Schriften", Vol. IV, pp. 371-2.

86 "Even the lower senses, the sense of smell or of taste, are raised up in man to the level of spiritual acts, of scientific acts. . . . Yes, even man's *stomach* which we look down on with lofty contempt, is not of animal essence but of human essence since, as it is not limited to certain kinds of nourishment, it is universal." *Grundsätze der Philosophie der Zukunft*, §53; "Sämmtliche Werke" Stuttgart edition 1904, Vol. II, pp. 315-16).

87 "The *heart*—the feminine principle, the sense of the finite, the seat of materialism—is *French*; the *head*—the masculine principle, the seat of idealism—is *German.*" *Thesen zur Reform der Philosophie;* cf. ed. quoted, Vol. II, pp. 235-6.

88 *The Ego and His Own*, London 1912, trans. by S. T. Byington, pp. 67-72.

89 *Dialectics of Nature*, trans. from the German by Clemens Dutt, Moscow 1964, p. 173 ("The Part played by Labour in the Transition from Ape to Man") and especially the section entitled "On the Prototypes of the Mathematical Infinite in the Real World", pp. 270 *et seq.*

90 *The Origin of the Family, Private Property and the State*, Chicago 1902.

91 Marx to Engels, 24 June 1865.

92 Marx to Engels, 7 August 1866.

93 Trémaux's book about which Marx was so enthusiastic was called *Origine et transformations de l'homme et des autres êtres* (Paris 1865). As we have not been able to consult the book itself the quotations are from a summary of his theory which Trémaux made under the title "L'homme blanc devient nègre et vice versa" in his *Voyage en Éthiopie, au Soudan oriental et dans la Nigritie*, Vol. II, Paris 1863, pp. 407 *et seq.*

94 *Ibid.*, 428.

95 Marx to Engels, 7 August 1866.

96 Engels to Marx, 2 October 1866, ". . . I have reached the conclusion that his theories are valueless because he has no understanding of geology and is incapable of exercising even the most rudimentary literary or historical criticism", etc.

97 Marx to Engels, 3 October 1866.

98 Marx to Engels, 30 July 1862.

99 On the subject of Marx's anti-semitism, see *Histoire de l'antisémitisme*, Vol. III, pp. 432-40.

100 Marx described Augustin Thierry as the "father of class warfare in French historiography" (Marx to Engels, 27 July 1854).

101 Marx to Engels, 13 April 1867.

102 Cf. Karl Marx, *Pages choisies pour une éthique socialiste*, ed. M. Rubel, Paris 1948, p. 339 (an extract from the *German Ideology*).

103 *Parerga und Paralipomena*, "Über Religion", § 179 ("Altes und Neues Testament").

104 *Ibid.*, "Zur Ethik", § 119, and *passim*.

105 *Ibid.*, "Über Religion", § 117 ("Über das Christentum").

106 "The Jews! Curse them! They are much worse than the Hegelians!" Cf. *Schopenhauers Gespräche*, Hübscher ed., Heidelberg 1933, pp. 322 *et seq.*

107 *Die Welt als Wille und Vorstellung*, § 68. Cf. Helmuth von Glasenapp, *Das Indienbild deutscher Denker*, Stuttgart 1960, p. 70.

108 Cf. E. J. Young, *Gobineau und der Rassismus* . . ., Meisenheim 1968, pp. 10-11.

109 *Parerga und Paralipomena*, "Zur Ethik", § 115 ("Spicilegia 103").

110 For Wagner cf. *Histoire de l'antisémitisme*, Vol. III, pp. 330, 440 *et seq.* and for Ascher cf. *ibid.* p. 413.

111 Cf. *ibid.*, pp. 410 *et seq.*

112 Börne, *Letters from Paris*, 74th Letter.

113 *Psyche*, L. Klages edition, Jena 1926, p. 90.

114 *Über ungleiche Befähigung der verschiedenen Menschheitsstämme für höhere geistige Entwicklung (1849); Symbolik der Menschlichen Gestalt (1853); Die Frage nach Entstehung und Gliederung der Menschheit vom Standpunkte gegenwärtiger Forschung* (undated but later than 1856); *Natur und Idee* (1861).

115 *Die Frage nach Entstehung und Gliederung* . . ., *op. cit.*, pp. 90-98.

116 *Symbolik der menschlichen Gestalt* . . ., *op. cit.*, pp. 366-9.

117 H. Heine, *Ludwig Börne*, Fourth Book.

118 The summary below is taken from Erwin Schuppe, *Der Burschenschaftler Wolfgang Menzel, Eine Quelle zum Verständnis des Nationalsozialismus*, Frankfurt a/M, 1952, pp. 101-12.

119 Together with the Germans, the Jews had "regenerated the West"; cf. *Geist der Geschichte*, p. 162.

120 "Litteraturblatt 1853, No. 55". Cf. W. Menzel, *Unsere Grenzen*, Leipzig 1868, pp. 262-4.

121 "Die Gelehrte Lüge, Wir Deutschen seien nur ein Volk von Denkern", *Unsere Grenzen*, pp. 251 *et seq.*

122 *Allgemeine Kultur-Geschichte der Menschheit*, Vol. I, Leipzig 1843, pp. 195-6.

123 *Ibid.*, pp. 203-4.

124 *Ibid.*, p. 200.

125 *Ibid.*, Vol. IV, p. 234.

126 *Ibid.*, Vol. IV, p. 230.

127 *Ibid.*, Vol. IV, p. 252.

128 *Ibid.*, Vol. IV, p. 232.

129 *Zur Geschichte der Religion und Philosophie in Deutschland*, Bk. I.

130 Cf. Julius Lippert, *Kulturgeschichte der Menschheit in ihrem organischen Aufbau*, 2 vols., Stuttgart 1886, Vol. I, pp. 43-4.

131 Cf. *Hitler's Table Talk*, London 1953, p. 141.

Chapter Eleven

1 ". . . Our science is dreaded, not because its deductions form the basis of all genuine political economy, but because it is supposed to threaten a system of government which has for its goal the high-sounding letter of universal equality, fraternity and brotherhood. May it be the lot of our society to show that such chimeras are not supported by the indications of science. . . ." Cf. *The Anthropological Review*, Vol. V, 1867, pp. lxiii *et seq.*

2 M. Berthelot, *La science idéale et la science positive*. Cf. E. Renan, *Œuvres* . . ., *op. cit.*, Vol. I, p. 667.

3 H. Taine, *Histoire de la littérature anglaise*, Paris 1905, Introduction, p. xxii.

4 I. Taylor, *The Origin of the Aryans, An account of prehistoric ethnology and civilisation of Europe*, London 1890, p. 332.

5 P. Broca, "La linguistique et l'anthropologie", *Mémoires d'anthropologie* Paris 1871, Vol. I, pp. 232 *et seq.*

6 E. B. Tylor, *Anthropology, An introduction to the study of man* . . ., London 1881, pp. 152, 112.

7 P. Topinard, *L'Anthropologie*, Paris 1876, pp. 453, 429.

8 T. Waitz, *Anthropologie der Naturvölker*, Leipzig 1859, Vol. I, pp. 281-3.

9 A. Bastian, *Das Beständige in den Menschenrassen und die Spielweite ihrer Veränderlichkeit*, Berlin 1868, pp. 23-4 and 156.

10 R. Virchow, *Die Urbevölkerung Europa's*, Berlin 1874, pp. 35-6.

11 F.-G. Bergmann, *Les peuples primitifs de la race de Japhète*, Colmar 1853, p. 6.

12 Honoré Chavée, *Les langues et les races*, Paris 1862, p. 60.

13 A.-F. Pott, *Die Ungleichheit menschlicher Rassen, hauptsächlich vom sprach-wissenschaftlichem Standpunkte, unter besonderen Berücksichtigung von des Grafen von Gobineau gleichnamigen Werkes*, Lemgo 1856. It was this work which inspired Wagner with such enthusiasm for Gobineau's theory. Cf. "Lettres de Cosima Wagner à Gobineau". *Revue hebdomadaire*, 23 July 1938, p. 287.

14 A. Schleicher, *Compendium der vergleichenden Grammatik* . . ., (1861), pp. 7-8.

15 Reinach was writing of historians and natural philosophers. Cf. "Le mirage oriental", in *L'Anthropologie*, Vol. IV (1893), p. 553.

16 Cf. M. Müller, *Lectures on the Science of Language*, London 1862, pp. 240 *et seq.*, especially p. 249, note 3 ("I state these views on the authority of M. Pictet").

17 A. Pictet, *Les origines indo-européennes ou les Aryas primitifs, Essai de palé-ontologie linguistique*, Paris 1859, p. 1, pp. 753-4.

18 Cf. *Marc Aurèle, et la fin du monde antique, Œuvres Complètes*, 1947-1961 ed., p. 1,142.

19 *On the Great Race-Elements in Christianity* by the Rev. Dunbar I. Heath, in "Journal of the Anthropological Society of London", V (1867), pp. xix-xxviii.

20 Cf. The lectures of Quatrefages in 1868: "I shall deal first of all with the Europeans whose ancestors were the Aryans . . . ." *Revue des cours scientifiques de la France et de l'étranger*, V, (1868), p. 727.

21 A. de Quatrefages, *La race prussienne*, Paris 1871. This work was first published in a more abbreviated form in the *Revue des Deux Mondes* of February 1871, pp. 687 *et seq.*

22 L. Figuier, *Tableau de la nature; Les races humaines*, Paris 1872 (4th ed., 1885), p. 59.

23 *Revue d'anthropologie*, I (1872), pp. 163-4 (*La race prussienne et M. Mantegazza*).

24 A. de Quatrefages, "Les origines européennes", *Revue scientifique de la France et de l'étranger*, 1872, 2nd semester, p. 28.

25 A. de Quatrefages, *Histoire générale des races humaines*, Paris 1889, pp. 454-5.

26 *Zeitschrift für Ethnologie*, IV (1872), pp. 45-64 (a review of *La race prussienne* by Quatrefages. It is signed B.)

27 Cf. above, pp. 213-14.

28 H. Grätz, "Mein letztes Wort an Professor von Treitschke", 28 December 1879. *Der Berliner Antisemitismusstreit,* published by W. Boehlich, Frankfurt a/M 1965, p. 52.

29 Cf. Erich Bierhahn, "Blondheit und Blondheitskult in der deutschen Literatur". *Archiv für Kulturgeschichte,* XLVI (1964), pp. 309-33. What emerges from this study is that, in common with a tradition that goes back to J.-J. Rousseau and to Goethe, blond hair and blue eyes, for the great majority of German authors, were the mark of an undecided, dreamy and sentimental temperament. It was only in the second half of the nineteenth century, and especially in the aftermath of the Franco-Prussian War, that they were generally considered the attributes of virile and conquering heroes.

30 A. Retzius, *Ethnologische Schriften,* Stockholm 1864.

31 "In the course of digging, the archaeologist must collect the maximum number of samples and not content himself with sending a few skulls to the laboratory of the École des Hautes Études with the question: tell me, are they Franks, Burgundians, Saracens or Romans?" P. Topinard, *L'Anthropologie,* Paris 1876, p. 235; cf. also p. 229.

32 Cf. R. Virchow, "Ueber die Methode der wissenschaftlichen Anthropologie, Eine Antwort an Herrn de Quatrefages", *Zeitschrift für Ethnologie,* IV, 1872, pp. 300-302. Also *Die Urbevölkerung Europa's,* Berlin 1874, especially p. 31.

33 *Correspondenzblatt der deutschen Gesellschaft für Anthropologie, Ethnologie und Urgeschichte,* June-October 1871, p. 53.

34 Virchow, "Gesammtbericht über die von der deutschen anthropologischen Gesellschaft veranlassten Erhebungen über die Farbe der Haut der Haare und der Augen der Schuhlkinder", *Archiv. für Anthropologie,* XVI (1886), pp. 275-475, and especially pp. 284-5.

35 *Ibid.,* p. 282.

36 R. Virchow, "Vortrag über die physische Anthropologie der Finnen", *Zeitschrift für Ethnologie,* VI (1874), pp. 169-89.

37 R. Virchow, *Die Verbreitung des blonden und des brünetten Typus in Mitteleuropa,* "Sitzungsberichte der königlich preussischen Akademie der Wissenschaften", 1885, Vol. I, pp. 39-47.

38 R. Virchow, "Die Anthropologie in den letzten 20 Jahren", *Correspondenzblatt der deutschen Gesellschaft für Anthropologie . . .* January 1889, p. 91.

39 Cf. R. Virchow, *Crania Ethnica Americana,* Berlin 1894, especially p. 32.

40 Virchow's comments at the anthropological conference at Danzig. Cf. *Correspondenzblatt der deutschen Gesellschaft für Anthropologie . . .,* September 1891, p. 79.

41 I. Taylor, *The Origin of the Aryans,* London 1890, pp. 226, *et seq.*

42 S. Reinach, *L'Origine des Aryens, Histoire d'une controverse,* Paris 1892, p. 90.

43 S. Feist, "Archäologie und Indogermanentum", *Correspondenzblatt der deutschen Gesellschaft für Anthropologie . . .,* 1916, p. 68.

44 R. Virchow, "Die Anthropologie in den letzten 20 Jahren", *Correspondenzblatt . . .,* 1889, p. 99; J. Kollmann, "Die Menschenrassen Europas und die Frage nach der Herkunft der Arier", *Correspondenzblatt . . .,* 1892, p. 105; F. von Luschan, "Die Anthropologische Stellung der Juden", *Correspondenzblatt . . .,* 1895, p. 95.

45 R. Virchow, *Correspondenzblatt . . .*, 1891, p. 77.

46 G. Heberer, *Rassengeschichtliche Forschung im indogermanischen Urheimats-gebiet*, Jena 1943. Cf. Karl Saller, *Die Rassenlehre des Nationalsozialismus*, Darmstadt 1961, pp. 57-9.

47 A circular of the "Aussenpolitisches Amt der NSDAP an die Beauftragten für Bevölkerungs-und Rassenpolitik bei den Gauleitungen" signed by Dr Gross and dated 24 October 1934. "Already a year ago I was obliged to make an energetic stand against the emphasis given to the physical characteristics of the Nordic race. This very clumsy propaganda, which is not supported by the facts, arouses feelings of inferiority and is a threat to the growing feeling of community among the people. I insisted that the different racial elements of the German people should be referred to as little as possible, or not at all, so as to avoid the undesirable results referred to above. . . ." Cf. L. Poliakov—J. Wulf, *Das Dritte Reich und seine Denker*, Berlin 1959, pp. 411-13.

48 P. Topinard in *L'Anthropologie*, IV (1893), p. 505.

49 G. Vacher de Lapouge, *L'Aryen, son rôle social*, Paris 1899, p. vii, pp. 22 and 464.

50 *Ibid.*, p. 238.

51 *Ibid.*, pp. 372-3.

52 *Ibid.*, p. vii and "l'Anthropologie et la science politique", *Revue d'anthropologie*, 15 May 1887, p. 15.

53 This opinion is reported by G. Montandon, "Georges Vacher de Lapouge", *L'Ethnie française*, May-June 1941, p. 5.

54 Cf. *L'Aryen, son rôle social*, especially pp. 413-61.

55 Cf. C. Bouglé, "Anthropologie et démocratie", *Revue de métaphysique et de morale*, V (1897).

56 A. Fouillée, "Dégénérescence? Le passé et le présent de notre race", *Revue des Deux-Mondes*, 1895 (5), p, 815. Cf. also *Psychologie du peuple français*, (1898) and *Esquisse psychologique des peuples européens* (1903) where Fouillée developed his ideas about the "racial mixture" of the French.

57 Cf. The thesis of Mme Capitan-Peter, *Une pensée de droite: l'Action française*, Paris 1970.

58 *Ibid.*

59 J. Bainville, *Histoire de France*, "Livre de Poche" ed. 1964, pp. 7 and 18.

60 Cf. G. Montandon, "L'aryanisme français", *L'Ethnie française*, April 1941, p. 5.

61 Th. Huxley, *Emancipation—black and white*, "Lay sermons . . .", London 1887, pp. 18 *et seq.*

62 É. Burnouf, *La science des religions*, Paris 1885, especially p. 229. ("The highest abstract speculations are not accessible to this race [the Chinese] who also lack that part of the brain in which they are rooted. This is also why they are unable to grasp metaphysics which is the essence of religion. . . .") and p. 99 ("Christianity, taken as a whole, is an Aryan doctrine", etc.).

63 E. Renan, *L'avenir de la science*, 1890 preface (*Œuvres . . ., op. cit.*, Vol. III, p. 724).

64 Büchner, *Conférences sur la théorie darwinienne*, Paris 1869, p. 132.

65 While the "inferior race" would advance at the rate of 1 : 16, the "white race" would advance at 2 : 32 so that the gap would widen. Büchner,

Volkstum und Geschichte; Fr. von Hellwald, *Kulturgeschichte*, Leipzig 1896, Vol. I, p. 105.

66 Quoted by Ch. Darwin, *The Descent of Man, op. cit.*, p. 875, note 26.

67 *Volkstum und Geschichte, op. cit.*, pp. 159-74.

68 *Ibid.*, p. 71.

69 *Ibid.*, p. 106.

70 *Ibid., Einleitung*, Vol. I, p. 20.

71 *Ibid.*, Vol. III, p. 600.

72 *Ibid.*, Vol. I, pp. 399 *et seq.*, especially pp. 475-8.

73 Cf. J. Lippert, *Kulturgeschichte der Menschheit in ihrem organischen Aufbau*, Stuttgart 1886, Vol. I, pp. 447 and 186. This work was for long considered authoritative. In 1931 it was translated by G. Murdock in the United States with the title, *The Evolution of Culture*.

74 A. E. Brehm, *Merveilles de la nature: Les races humaines*, trans. by Dr. R. Verneau with a preface by A. de Quatrefages, Paris 1890, p. 557.

75 "The Jews had neither arts, nor sciences, nor industries, nor anything which constitutes a civilization. They have never brought the least contribution to the development of human knowledge. . . . No people has left any book containing so many obscene stories as those which are to be found on every page of the Bible. One can examine all the writings of the world such as the Vedas, the Avesta, the Buddhist texts, the Koran, etc., without finding anything like them. . . . There is a real abyss between the feelings and ideas of Jews and of Aryans. . . ." G. Le Bon, "Du rôle des Juifs dans l'histoire de la civilisation", *Revue scientifique*, 1888, pp. 386, 493 *et seq.*

76 *Le Figaro*, 28 February 1882; cf. *La France Juive*, Paris 1943, Vol. I, pp. 398-401

77 "The big young men with the blue eyes had gone away to die in other countries. Their places were taken by pot-bellied individuals whose strictly military uniforms hinted at protuberances which were unmistakably civilian. These were the functionaries of the cultural and economic occupation. They were numerous, very numerous. They bore high-sounding titles each longer and more complicated than the other; Kriegsverwaltungschef, Oberkriegsverwaltungsrat, Sturmbannführer, without counting the small fry of the Sonderführer. . . ." Gérard Walter, *La Vie à Paris sous l'Occupation, 1940-1941*, Paris 1960, p. 39.

78 A. de Candolle, *Histoire de la science et des savants depuis deux siècles . . .*, Geneva 1873, pp. 400-408.

79 J. Finot, *Le préjugé des races*, Paris 1906, pp. 354-7.

80 J. C. Nott and G. R. Gliddon, *Types of mankind . . .*, London 1854, pp. 115 *et seq.*

81 "I have for long held the view that the different races of men must have had an independent origin because I saw the time coming when the origin of man and that of animals would become confounded . . ." etc. L. Agassiz, "Hommes et singes", *Revue scientifique de la France et de l'étranger*, 28 February 1874, p. 816.

82 Cf. The Historical Sketch at the beginning of the *Origin of the Species*. Schaafhausen was also one of the authors most often quoted by Darwin in the *Descent of Man*.

83 H. Schaafhausen, *Les questions anthropologiques de notre temps*. A speech to a congress of German naturalists and doctors; *Revue scientifique*, 1866, pp. 769-76.

84 In making the comparison between men and anthropoid apes, Vogt wrote as follows: "To establish this comparison we have chosen two types which are situated almost at the two extremities of the range of human types and who are, on the one hand, the Negro, and on the other, the German. . . ." C. Vogt, *Leçons sur l'homme* . . ., Paris 1865, p. 223.

85 *Ibid.*, pp. 623 *et seq.*

86 Cf. H.-V. Vallois, "Les preuves anatomiques de l'origine monophylétique de l'homme", *L'Anthropologie*, XXXIX (1929), p. 78.

87 Cf. H. Klaatsch, *Der Werdegang der Menschheit und die Entstehung der Kultur*, Bonn 1920, p. 90.

88 Cf. M. Grison, *Problèmes d'origines* . . ., Paris 1954, p. 278, note 57.

89 Cf. The report by W. de Fonvielle, *Revue Scientifique*, 1867, p. 120.

90 G. Harris, "The plurality of races and the distinctive character of the adamite species", *The Anthropological Review*, V (1867), pp. 175-85.

91 J.-Chr. Boudin, *Traité de géographie et de statistiques médicales* . . ., Vol. II, Paris, 1856.

92 C. Vogt, *Leçons sur l'homme* . . ., *op. cit.*, p. 565.

93 R. Virchow, "Über den Transformismus", *Archiv für Anthropologie*, XVIII (1889), p. 13.

94 Cf. *Histoire de l'antisémitisme*, Paris 1956, Vol. I, pp. 159 *et seq.*

95 L. Gumplowicz, *La lutte des races, Recherches sociologiques*, Paris ed., 1893, p. 331: "The Jews followed the example of the Phoenicians, they became traders and spread over the face of the whole world. The organization of their communities in Europe is certainly an imitation of the ancient establishments of the Phoenicians. There is only one point, but it is perhaps the most important, on which the Jews were unable to follow the example of the Phoenicians: the Jews displayed, and indeed they still display, an inability to disappear."

96 G. Vitoux, *L'agonie d'Israël*, Paris 1898.

97 E. Drumont, *La France juive*, Paris ed. 1943, Vol. I, p. 201.

98 "De certaines immunités physiologiques de la race juive", *La Revue scientifique de la France et de l'étranger*, 1881/1, pp. 530 *et seq.* and 618 *et seq.*

99 "Even relatively strong admixtures of foreign blood were overcome; these mixtures gave rise to the birth of no new type; no amalgam took place. Semitic blood achieved a decisive victory and the old and monumental Jewish body was preserved as well as the old Jewish spirit hereditarily transmitted by this body." R. Andree, *Zur Volkskunde der Juden*, Leipzig 1881, pp. 24-5.

100 "Similar cases have so frequently occurred, that careful breeders avoid putting a choice female of any animal to an inferior male, on account of the injury to her subsequent progeny which may be expected to follow." Charles Darwin, *The Variation of Animals and Plants under Domestication*, 2nd ed., London 1875, Vol. I, p. 437. For breeding of the human species, *ibid*, p. 21. As to Spencer's theory, cf. Y. Delage, *La structure du protoplasma et les théories de l'hérédité* . . ., Paris 1895, p. 365 ("Théories sur la télegonie").

101 The theory of telegony provided the main theme for Arthur Dinter's popular novel *Die Sünde wider das Blut*, the first edition of which appeared in 1914 and of which by 1933 nearly a million copies had been printed.

102 Cf. Broca, *Mémoires d'anthropologie*, Paris 1871, Vol. III, pp. 445 *et seq.*

103 "On the other hand, mules from the horse and ass are certainly not in the least wild, though notorious for obstinacy and vice", according to Darwin who added, when describing the cross-breeding of pigeons and ducks; "These latter facts remind us of the statements, so frequently made by travellers in all parts of the world, on the degraded state and savage disposition of crossed races of man" which he attributed in part to atavistic reversions due to cross-breeding. *The Variation* etc., Vol. II, pp. 20-21.

104 Cf. for example S. Weissenberg, "Die südrussischen Juden", *Archiv für Anthropologie*, XXXIII (1895), pp. 347-423 and 531-79; A. D. Elkind, *The Jews* (in Russian), St Petersburg 1903.

105 Anatole Leroy-Beaulieu, *Israël chez les nations*, Paris 1893, pp. 185-6.

106 Théodule Ribot, *L'hérédité psychologique*, 4th ed., Paris 1890, p. 410.

107 *Ibid.*, pp. 118-37 (Ch. VII, "L'hérédité et le caractère national").

108 E. Haeckel, *Der Monismus als Band zwischen Religion und Wissenschaft*, Bonn 1893. On Haeckel, see the recent work of Daniel Gasman, *The Scientific Origins of National Socialism; Social Darwinism in Ernst Haeckel and the German Monist League*, London, New York 1971. In particular, Professor Gasman states: "Nearly all . . . leading figures in the field of eugenics and racial science were deeply and consciously indebted to Haeckel for many, if not for most of their ideas" (p. 147).

109 *Revue scientifique de la France et de l'étranger*, 1889/2, pp. 19 *et seq.* and especially 1886/1, pp. 694-5.

110 Cf. Charcot, *Leçons du Mardi à la Salpêtrière*, Paris 1889, p. 348. "I introduce him to you as a true descendant of Ahasuerus or Cartaphilus" said Charcot to his hearers when presenting a Jewish patient (*loc. cit.*, cf. also pp. 11 and 353).

111 H. Meige, *Étude sur certains névropathes voyageurs: le Juif Errant à la Salpêtrière* (thesis for a doctorate in medicine), Paris 1893, pp. 6, 8, 43 and 61.

112 Le Bon, *La psychologie des foules*, Paris 1896, pp. 17-18. This work was translated into fifteen lnaguages and had reached its 21st edition by 1921. Freud used Le Bon and quoted him copiously in *Massenpsychologie und Ich-Analyse* (1919-1920) and C. J. Jung recommended the reading of his work soon after 1945. Cf. *Aufsätze zur Zeitgeschichte*, Zürich 1946, p. 140. English trans. by Elizabeth Welsh, Barbara Hannah and Mary Briner: *Essays on Contemporary Events*, London 1947.

113 *La France juive*, Paris 1943, Vol. I, pp. 107-110.

114 *Das Gesetz des Nomadentums und die heutige Judenherrschaft*, Karlsruhe 1887, p. 137 and *passim*.

115 Cf. G. L. Mosse, *The Crisis of German Ideology*, New York 1964, p. 18; and W. Mühlmann, *Geschichte der Anthropologie, op. cit.*, p. 122-6.

116 "Israel rises over Europe like the sun; at its coming new light bursts forth; at its going all falls into decay." *Die Juden und das Wirtschaftsleben*, Leipzig 1911. English trans. by M. Epstein, *The Jews and Modern Capitalism*, New York 1962, p. 36.

117 Cf. Werner Maser, *Hitlers Mein Kampf*, Munich 1966, pp. 80-81.

118 "During his stay, Jung had a dream: he was in a ghetto, and the place was narrowed and twisted, with low ceilings and staircases hanging down. He thought to himself: 'How in hell can people live in such a place.' This came rather as a shock. He could not identify the place with Vienna, and further, so far as he knew, he was happy to be there." (A dream related by E. A. Bennet, *C. J. Jung*, London 1961, p. 34.)

119 Cf. E. Jones, *Sigmund Freud*, London 1953-1957; Vol. I, p. 348, and II, p. 61.

120 Letter to Arnold Zweig, 30 September 1934. Cf. *The Letters of Sigmund Freud and Arnold Zweig*, London and New York 1970.

121 Cf. especially *Moses and Monotheism, The Standard Edition of the Complete Psychological Works of Sigmund Freud*, London 1964, Vol. XXIII.

122 Cf. "The infantile return of totemism", *in fine*.

123 *Moses and Monotheism*, p. 100.

124 Letters of 11 May and 11 October 1908 "Just because I get on most easily with you (and also with our colleague Ferenczi of Budapest), I feel it incumbent on me not to concede too much to racial preference and therefore neglect the more alien Aryan [C. G. Jung]". Cf. *A Psycho-Analytic Dialogue: The Letters of Sigmund Freud and Karl Abraham 1907-1926*, London 1965.

125 "And evidence of the presence of a peculiar psychical aptitude in the masses who had become the Jewish people is revealed by the fact that they were able to produce so many individuals prepared to take on the burdens of the religion of Moses in return for the reward of being the chosen people and perhaps for some other prizes of a similar degree." *Moses and Monotheism*, p. 111.

126 "My position, no doubt, is made more difficult by the present attitude of biological science, which refuses to hear of the inheritance of acquired characters by succeeding generations. I must, however, in all modesty confess that nevertheless I cannot do without this factor in biological evolution. . . . If it is not so, we shall not advance a step further along the path we entered on, either in analysis or in group psychology. The audacity cannot be avoided." *Moses and Monotheism*, p. 100.

127 I reproduce what I think is an accurate analysis by Frau L. Frey-Rohn: 'Freud regarded the Id as a sphere which, on the one hand, was open to the somatic or 'drew its energy thence' and, on the other hand, was the bearer of a secret which lost itself in the depths and inner recesses of the phylogenetic or primitive heritage of our ancestors." *Von Freud zu Jung, Studien aus dem C. G. Jung-Institut*, Zürich 1969, p. 151.

128 "But this sort of psycho-analytic argumentation reminds us here, as it so often does, of Dostoevsky's famous 'stick with two ends'. The opponents of those who argue in this way will on their side think it quite natural that the female sex should refuse to accept a view which appears to contradict their eagerly coveted equality with men. The use of analysis as a weapon of controversy can clearly lead to no decision." *Female Sexuality, Standard Ed.*, London 1961, Vol. XXI, p. 230.

129 Cf. for example with reference to the constancy of desires driven back into the Id: "This seems to offer an approach to the most profound discoveries. Nor, unfortunately, have I myself made any progress here. . . . We would

give much to understand more about these things!" *New Introductory Lectures, Standard Ed.*, London 1964, Vol. XXII, p. 74.

130 "Address to the Society of B'nai B'rith", 6 May 1926, *Standard Ed.*, Vol. XX, p. 274.

131 "Freud has not penetrated into that deeper layer which is common to all men. He could not have done so without being untrue to his historical task. And this task he has fulfilled—a task enough for a whole life's work, and fully deserving the fame it has won." "Sigmund Freud als kulturhistorische Erscheinung", 1932, *Wirklichkeit der Seele*, Zürich 1939, p. 131. English trans. by R. F. C. Hull, *The Collected Works of Jung*, Vol. XV, London and Princeton 1966, p. 40.

132 "Das Allgemeinverbreitete, das nicht nur die Individuen unter sich zum Volke, sondern auch rückwärts mit den Menschen der Vergangenheit und ihrer Psychologie verbindet." *Wandlungen und Symbole der Libido*, Leipzig 1912, p. 171; cf. L. Frey-Rohn, *op. cit.*, p. 171. English trans. by R. F. C. Hull, *The Collected Works of Jung*, Vol. V, London and Princeton 1967, 2nd ed., p. 177.

133 "Das kollektive Unbewusste ist der Niederschlag aller Welterfahrung aller Zeiten, daher also ein Bild der Welt, das seit Eonen sich gebildet hat" (*Die Psychologie der unbewussten Prozesse*, Zürich 1917, p. 117). There is a similar definition in *Analytische Psychologie und Weltanschauung*, 1927-1932; cf. Jung, *Complete Works*, Zürich 1964, pp. 428 *et seq.* English trans. by R. F. C. Hull, *The Collected Works of Jung*, Vol. VII (rev. ed.), London and New York 1966. See Frey-Rohn, pp. 171-5.

134 C. G. Jung, *L'homme à la découverte de son âme* (with a preface and adaptation by Dr Roland Cahen), Paris 1962, p. 298. Dr Cahen, who assigns this text to the year 1934, explains that it is based on notes (taken down by a member of the audience) which Jung revised before they were published.

135 *Der Gegensatz Freud und Jung*, Collected Works, Vol. IV, Zürich 1969, p. 387 and pp. 391-2. English trans. by R. F. C. Hull: *The Collected Works of Jung*, Vol. IV, London and Princeton, 1961, pp. 335 and 339.

136 *Geleitwort des Herausgebers*, "Zentralblatt für Psychotherapie", VI (1933). Jung became co-editor of this journal in 1933 when Ernst Kretschmer resigned.

137 ". . . The Jews have this peculiarity in common with women: Being physically the weaker they have to aim at the chinks in their opponent's armor, and since this technique has been enforced upon them during a history of many centuries, the Jews themselves are best covered at the spots where others are most vulnerable. In consequence of their more than twice as ancient culture they are vastly more conscious of human weaknesses and inferiorities and therefore much less vulnerable in this respect than we are ourselves. They also owe to the experience of ancient culture the ability to live consciously in benevolent, friendly and tolerant neighborhood with their own defects (*Untugenden*), while we are still too young to have no illusions about ourselves. Moreover we have been called upon by fate still to create culture (for we are in need of it), to which end so-called illusions in the shape of one-sided ideals, convictions, plans, etc., are essential. The Jew as a member of a race whose culture is about 3,000 years old, like the educated Chinese, is psychologically conscious in wider areas than we are. Consequently it is

N

less dangerous, generally speaking, for the Jew to devaluate his unconscious. The Aryan unconscious, on the other hand, contains tensions and creative germs of an as yet unfulfilled future which one may not devaluate as nursery romanticism without endangering the soul. The still young Germanic peoples are entirely able to produce new forms of culture, and this future still lies in the darkness of the unconscious of each individual, as a germ laden with energy, capable of a mighty blaze. The Jew, as relatively a nomad, never has produced and presumably never will produce a culture of his own, since all his instincts and gifts require a more or less civilized host-people for their development. Therefore the Jewish race as a whole has, according to my experience, an unconscious which can only conditionally be compared to the Aryan. Aside from certain creative individuals, the average Jew is already much too conscious and differentiated to be pregnant with the tensions of the unborn future. The Aryan unconscious has a higher potential than the Jewish; that is the advantage and the disadvantage of a youthfulness not yet fully estranged from barbarism. In my opinion, it has been a great mistake of all previous medical psychology to apply Jewish categories, which are not even binding for all Jews, indiscriminately to Christian Germans or Slavs. In doing so, medical psychology has declared the most precious secret of the Germanic peoples—the creatively prophetic depths of soul—to be a childishly banal morass, while for decades my warning voice has been suspected of anti-Semitism. The source of this suspicion is Freud. He did not know the Germanic soul any better than did all his Germanic imitators. Has the mighty apparition of National Socialism, which the whole world watches with astonished eyes, taught them something better? Where was the unheard-of tension and energy when there was yet no National Socialism? It lay hidden in the Germanic soul, in that profound depth which is every thing else except the garbage bin of unreliable childish wishes and unresolved family resentments. A movement which seizes a whole people has ripened in every individual, too . . ." *Zur gegenwärtigen Lage der Psychotherapie*, "Zentralblatt für Psychotherapie", VII, 1934. The translation is from *Origins of Modern Psychiatry* by Ernest Harms, Springfield, Ill., 1967, pp. 222-3.

138 Cf. The study entitled *Wotan* published in Switzerland in 1936, in which Jung showed his interest in the Nazi phenomenon in a manner less marked by mental reservations of a political or tactical nature. *Aufsätze zur Zeitgeschichte*, Zürich 1946, pp. 1-23. English trans.: *Essays on Contemporary Events*, London 1947.

139 Preface by Dr Cahen to C. G. Jung, *Aspects du drame contemporain*, Geneva 1948, p. 62.

140 Cf. E. A. Bennett, *C. G. Jung*, London 1961, pp. 95-102 (in a correspondence between Jung and Bennett).

141 Letter of 13 May 1913, in *A Psycho-Analytic Dialogue: The Letters of Sigmund Freud and Karl Abraham*, London 1965.

142 Jones recalled the incident in the following terms: "He came to me afterwards, observing that I was one of the dissidents, and said: 'I thought you were a Christian' (i.e. non-Jew). It sounded an irrelevant remark, but presumably it had some meaning." *Sigmund Freud . . ., op. cit.*, Vol. II, p. 115.

143 Under the sub-title "Phylogenetische Erbschaft und historische Verdran-

gung", Frau Frey-Rohn writes: "The quoted passages (from *Moses and Mono-theism*) are sufficient to show the unbridgeable abyss between his opinions and Jung's. It was not merely by individual categories that the latter explained historical and mythical events but generally also through collective memories of historic happenings as a basis of the phylogenetic heritage. *At the decisive moment Freud always tended to see things in individual and concrete terms whereas Jung concentrated on the impersonal and the general.*" (*Von Freud zu Jung, op. cit.*, pp. 182-3).

144 "First Principles"; cf. R. Hofstadter, *Social Darwinism in American thought*, 1955 ed., p. 37. See also Spencer's *Social Statics*, London 1851, p. 34.

145 Letter from Spencer to a Japanese admirer; cf. Th. Gosset, *Race: The History of an Idea in America*, 1965 ed., p. 151.

146 "The variability or diversity of the mental faculties in men of the same race, not to mention the greater differences between men of distinct races, is so notorious that not a word need here to be said. . . ." *The Descent of Man, op. cit.*, p. 414.

147 *Ibid.*, p. 508.

148 *Ibid.*, pp. 542-50 ("On the Extinction of the Races of Man").

149 Cf. A. R. Wallace, "The Origin of Human Races and the Antiquity of Man deduced from the theory of 'Natural Selection'." *The Anthropological Review*, II (1862), pp. clviii *et seq.*, and V (1867), pp. 103-104.

150 *The Descent of Man*, pp. 501-9 ("Natural selection as affecting civilised Nations").

151 *Ibid.*, p. 507, where the article by Greg is quoted.

152 *Hereditary Genius*, London 1869, pp. 336-50 ("The comparative worth of different races").

153 *Ibid.*, pp. 1 *et seq.*

154 *Ibid.*, pp. 351-62.

155 "Eugenics and the Jew", *The Jewish Chronicle*, 30 July 1910.

156 *Probability, the Foundation of Eugenics*, Oxford 1907, pp. 11 and 30.

157 *The Principles of Sociology* (1876), Ch. XXII.

158 A. R. Wallace, *Human Progress: Past and Future* (1892); cf. *Studies Scientific and Social*, London 1900, Vol. II, pp. 493-508.

159 Richard Hofstadter, *Social Darwinism in American thought, op. cit.*, p. 58, quoting *The Challenge of Facts* by W. G. Sumner.

160 Cf. *Ibid.*, p. 186 (a quotation from *National Life and Character*, by K. Pearson).

161 Cf. *Dialectics of Nature, op. cit., passim.*

162 Cf. Haeckel, *Freie Wissenschaft und freie Lehre*, quoted by K. Pearson, *The chances of death . . .*, London 1897, pp. 106-7.

163 O. Beta, *Darwin, Deutschland und die Juden oder der Juda-Jesuitismus*, Berlin, 1876, especially pp. 11 and 32.

164 "The 'Emancipation of the Jews', as the setting apart of those evil social influences has been called for short, is for that reason a big social problem and above all one which in the present condition of society remains practically insoluble. Socialism is the only force which can prevent a situation in which the population will have a higher admixture of Jews. . . ." E. Dühring, *Cursus der Philosophie als streng wissenschaftlicher Weltanschauung und Lebensgestaltung*, Leipzig 1875, pp. 392-3.

165 Dr Alfred Ploetz, *Die Tüchtigkeit unsrer Rasse und der Schutz der Schwachen*, Berlin 1895, pp. 5, 8, and 130-42 ("Die besten Rassen—Westarier—Juden").

166 Karl Saller, *Die Rassenlehre des Nationalsozialismus in Wissenschaft und Propaganda*, Darmstadt 1961, pp. 74 and 117. (The secret society was called *Ring der Norda* or *Nordischer Ring*.)

167 Cf. *Natur und Staat, Beiträge zur naturwissenschaftlicher Gesellschaftslehre, Eine Sammlung von Preisschriften*, Jena 1903, pp. 1-24.

168 *Ibid.*, p. 380 (Dr Schallmayer, "Vererbung und Auslese im Lebenslauf der Völker").

169 *Die Germanen und die Renaissance in Italien*, Leipzig 1905, and *Die Germanen in Frankreich*, Jena 1907. It was Woltmann's view that Napoleon was a "descendant of the Germanic vandals".

170 Dr S. R. Steinmetz, "La guerre, moyen de sélection collective", in A. Constantin, *Le rôle sociologique de la guerre*, Paris 1907, pp. 268 *et seq.*

171 L. Woltmann, *Politische Anthropologie, Eine Untersuchung über den Einfluss der Descendenztheorie auf die Lehre von der politischen Entwicklung der Völker*, Leipzig 1903, *passim*, and especially pp. 298 *et seq.*

172 Cf. K. Saller, *Die Rassenlehre des Nationalsozialismus*, op. cit., pp. 17-18.

173 "If we were to allow culture, in so far as its selective influence is concerned, to dominate our lives as hitherto, it is absolutely certain that all European peoples will perish at a constantly increasing rate." The article entitled "Sozialanthropologie" in *Handwörterbuch der Sozialwissenschaften*, Jena 1913, Vol. IX, pp. 172-88.

174 Cf. Saller, *op. cit.*, pp. 74-5.

175 Cf. *Archiv für Rassen-und Gesellschaftsbiologie*, I (1904), pp. 885 *et seq.*, and XI (1914), p. 125.

176 The philosopher Heinrich Rickert wrote in 1910 of a "biologistische Modephilosophie" (cf. his article "Lebenswerte und Kulturwerte" in *Logos*, II (1911-1912), pp. 141-68).

177 Cf. W. Mühlmann, *Geschichte der Anthropologie*, op. cit., p. 196.

178 Dr A. Forel, "Gelbe Rasse und weisse Rasse, Ein praktischer Verschlag", *Archiv für Rassen-und Gesellschaftsbiologie*, V (1908), pp. 249-51.

179 Chr. von Ehrenfels, "Leitziele zur Rassenbewertung" (*Archiv* . . ., IX (1912), pp. 730-761) and "Biologische Friedensrüstungen" (*Archiv* . . ., XI (1914), pp. 580, 613).

180 Cf. Max Hirsch, "Ehe und Eugenetik", *Archiv für Frauenkunde und Eugenetik*, II (1916), pp. 115-18.

181 *Archiv* . . ., VI (1909), pp. 577 *et seq.*, and X (1913), pp. 403 *et seq.*

182 G. K. Chesterton, *Eugenics and Other Evils*, London 1922, pp. 182 *et seq.*

183 O. von Verschuer, *Manuel d'eugénique et d'hérédité humaine*, trans. by Montandon, Paris 1943, p. 5.

184 Quoted by R. Hofstadter, *op. cit.*, p. 171.

185 *Ibid.*, p.p 175-89.

186 See the speeches reported by Arrens, *Guillaume II, ce qu'il dit, ce qu'il pense*, Paris 1911, p. 33 and *passim*.

187 Cf. E. McNall Burns, *Ideas in Conflict* . . ., London 1966, pp. 474-5.

188 T. F. Gossett, *Race: The History of an Idea in America*, New York 1965, pp. 109-10.

189 Cf. *Ibid.*, pp. 377-78 and 415.

190 Speech in Birmingham (1898) and especially a speech at Leicester (1903).

191 Cf. Charles Andler, *Nietzsche, sa vie et sa pensée*, Paris 1958, especially Vol. III, pp. 458 *et seq.* ("La sélection humaine"); Walter Kaufmann, *Nietzsche: Philosopher, Psychologist, Antichrist*, Princeton 1950; and Richard Lonsbach, *Nietzsche und die Juden*, Stockholm 1939.

192 Cf. "Lebenswerte und Kulturwerte", *Logos*, II (1911-1912), pp. 141-68.

193 *Thoughts out of Season*. Trans. by Adrian Collins, T. M. Foulis Edinburgh and London 1909, Vol. II, pp. 83-4.

194 "Unveroffentliches aus der Umwertungszeit", in Nachgelassene Werke, Vol. XIII, Leipzig 1903, paras. 818, 856, 858, 880, and *passim*. ("Cultur"); cf. Charles Andler, *Nietzsche, sa vie et sa pensée*, Vol. IV, Paris 1958, p. 462. See also *The Will to Power* (an Essay towards the Transvaluation of all Values), trans. by Walter Kaufmann, London 1965.

195 Cf. Duhring, *Die Judenfrage . . .*, 6th ed., p. 93, and Fritsch, *Nietzsche und die Jugend*, "Der Hammer", III, 1911, p. 115.

196 Cf. Lonsbach, *op. cit.*, pp. 72, 15-16, 27 and 55.

197 *Historische und politische Aufsätze*. Cf. Schemann, *Die Rasse in den Geisteswissenschaften, op. cit.*, Vol. III, p. 355.

198 *Politik . . .* (cf. Ch. Andler, *Les origines du pangermanisme*, Paris 1915, pp. 196 *et seq.*).

199 *Ibid.*, pp. 224-5.

200 *Deutschland und der nächste Krieg*, 1911. Cf. *Germany and the Next War*, London 1915, p. 18 and *passim*.

201 Klaus Wagner, *Krieg*, Jena 1906, especially pp. 179 *et seq.* and p. 230 *et seq.*

202 Cf. L. Poliakov, *Le bréviaire de la haine*, Paris 1951, pp. 311 *et seq.*

203 *Ein pangermanistisches Deutschland, Versuch über die Konsequenzen der gegenwärtigen wissenschaftlichen Rassenbetrachtung für unsere politische und religiöse Probleme*, Berlin 1905.

204 On the eve of the First World War, German colonial expansion was the subject of much discussion among the leaders of German Social Democracy. Kautsky expressed himself in favour of it in his pamphlet *Sozialismus und Kolonialpolitik*, and Bebel, in 1906 at the Congress of Jena, declared: "To conduct a colonial policy can be a cultural activity in some circumstances." Credits for the colonies were regularly voted in the Reichstag by the Social Democrat Party. Some of its militants envisaged the founding of a great colony of settlers in Mesopotamia, as part of a scheme for the Berlin-Bagdad railway, and another in Mongolia. Cf. Ch. Andler, *Le socialisme impérialiste dans l'Allemagne contemporaine*, Paris 1912.

205 *Wenn ich der Kaiser wär*, Leipzig 1912 (Class published this work under the pen-name of Daniel Frymann).

206 *Ibid.*, 5th ed., Leipzig 1914, pp. 104-5.

207 *Warrant for Genocide, The Myth of the Jewish World-Conspiracy and the Protocols of the Elders of Zion*, Harmondsworth, 1970.

208 Cf. Alfred Krieck, *Geschichte des alldeutschen Verbandes* (1890-1939), Wiesbaden 1954, pp. 130 *et seq.*

209 In 1870, during the First Vatican Council, 68 bishops presented a petition "begging the Pope to speed the hour when, thanks to missionary zeal, the

anathema would be removed from the descendants of Ham". This petition achieved no result. Cardinal Lavigerie thought that the progress of Christian missions in Africa was part of the plan of "divine providence to put an end to the malediction on the unfortunate race of Ham". Cf. Pierre Charles, S.J., "Les Noirs, fils de Cham le maudit", *Nouvelle Revue théologique*, 1928, pp. 721-39.

210 See the article "Was ist deutsch?" *Gesammelte Schriften*, Vol. I, Leipzig 1883, p. 73.

211 Cf. Louis Sauzin, "The political thought of Constantin Frantz", *The Third Reich*, London 1955, p. 115.

212 *Die preussische Intelligenz und ihr Grenzen*, Munich 1874, p. 68.

213 *Die Weltpolitik, unter besonderer Bezugnahme auf Deutschland*, Chemnitz 1882, Vol. II, pp. 128 *et seq.*

214 *Die preussische Intelligenz* . . ., pp. 63 *et seq.*

215 *Der Nationalliberalismus und die Judenherrschaft*, Munich 1874, p. 10.

216 *Die Weltpolitik* . . ., Vol. III, pp. 175-7.

217 From *Die Weltpolitik* . . ., Vol. III, pp. 108-122, and *Der Nationalliberalismus*, etc.

218 *Abfertigung der nationalliberalen Presse nebst einer höchst nötigen Belehrung über den Ultramontanismus*, Leipzig 1873, p. 35.

219 *Ibid.*, pp. 26-34.

220 Cf. The remarkable book by Professor Fritz Stern, *The Politics of Cultural Despair, A Study in the Rise of the Germanic Ideology*, Berkeley 1961, p. 11.

221 Cf. *Ibid.*, p. 18 (letter written by de Lagarde on 2 January 1871).

222 "Über die gegenwärtige Lage des deutschen Reichs" (1875), *Deutsche Schriften*, 1934.

223 "Über die gegenwärtigen Aufgaben der deutschen Politik" (1853), *ibid.*

224 *Ibid.*, p. 20. De Lagarde stated that Renan had been the only person in whom he confided his ambitions and his political plans.

225 Die Religion der Zukunft" (1878), *ibid.*, p. 262; "Die graue Internationale" (1881), *ibid.*, p. 367.

226 "Verhältnis des deutschen Staates zu Theologie, Kirche und Religion" (1873), *ibid.*, p. 65.

227 "Über die gegenwärtigen Aufgaben", *ibid.*, p. 30.

228 "Verhältnis des deutschen Staates . . .", *ibid.*, pp. 62-3.

229 "Only a single man's great, strong and pure will can help us; a King's will, not Parliament, not laws, not the efforts of powerless individuals. . . ." *Ibid.*, p. 286; cf. also p. 41: "I was afraid that the stage-manager would be missing . . .", etc.

230 "Verhältnis . . .", *ibid.*, pp. 79 *et seq.*

231 "Die Religion der Zukunft", *ibid.*, p. 285.

232 "Programme für die konservative Partei Preussens" (1884), *ibid.*, p. 425.

233 "Über die gegenwärtigen Aufgaben . . .", *ibid.*, p. 30.

234 "Die nächsten Aufgaben der deutschen Politik", *ibid.*, p. 449. The plan to banish all European Jews to Madagascar was the subject of prolonged study from 1938 to 1941 by Hitler's government. Cf. L. Poliakov, *Le bréviaire de la haine*, pp. 50-54.

235 Cf. *Ausgewählte Schriften*, Munich 1934, p. 239.

236 *Hitler's Table-Talk*, trans. by N. Cameron and R. H. Stevens, London 1953, p. 332.

237 *Deutsche Schriften*, p. 130.

238 Cf. Stern, *op. cit.*, pp. 84-5.

239 *Selbstzersetzung des Christentums und die Religion der Zukunft (1874)*: *Die Religion als Selbst-Bewusstsein Gottes (1906)*: *Der Ersatz der Religion durch Vollkommeneres und die Ausscheidung alles Judäertums durch den modernen Völkergeist* (1885).

240 Helmut Groos, *Der deutsche Idealismus und das Christentum*, Munich 1927, pp. 488 *et seq.*

241 Cf. especially *Histoire de l'antisémitisme*, Vol. III (De Voltaire à Wagner), pp. 203 *et seq.*

242 *Die grosse Täuschung* (1921), also *Babel und Babel* (1903). Cf. A. Borst, *Der Turmbau von Babel* . . ., *op. cit.*, Vol. III/2, pp. 1,697 *et seq.*, 1,728 *et seq.* and 1,837 *et seq.*

243 Cf. Chr. von Bunsen, *Gott in der Geschichte*, 3 vols., Leipzig 1857-1858.

244 Cf. E. von Bunsen, *Die Überlieferung, ihre Entstehung und Entwicklung*, Leipzig 1889.

245 Cf. Hans-Joachim Kraus, "Die Evangelische Kirche" in *Entscheidungsjahr 1932, Zur Judenfrage in der Endphase der Weimarer Republik*, Tübingen 1965, p. 254.

246 Through List's disciple Lanz von Liebenfeld. Cf. George L. Mosse, *The crisis of German ideology* . . ., *op. cit.*, pp. 73-8 and 181, and "The Mystical Origins of National-Socialism", *Journal of the History of Ideas*, XXII/1 (1961), pp. 81-96.

247 *Das entdecke Geheimnis der Heiligen Schrift und des deutschen Volkes Rettung; Das Geheimnis der Runen; Die Entdeckung des Paradieses*, etc. Cf. on this subject Raoul Patry, *La religion dans l'Allemagne d'aujourd'hui*, Paris 1926, pp. 154-78 ("Le Christianisme païen"). This work by a far-sighted journalist has the merit of not being a prophecy *post eventu*.

248 One of Guido von List's cronies who was known as "Tarnhari" passed himself off as the resurrected chief of the Germanic tribe of the Völsungen. Cf. G. L. Mosse . . ., *op. cit.*

249 In his book *Baldur und Bibel*, F. Döllinger published a letter from the procurator of Judaea, Publius Lentulius, to the Emperor Tiberius, in which Jesus was described as having the features of a blond hero. William II hastened to acquaint H. S. Chamberlain with this sensational discovery. Cf. Houston S. Chamberlain, *Briefe 1882-1924 und Briefwechsel mit Kaiser Wilhelm II*, Vol. II, Munich 1928, pp. 273-4.

250 "The supreme God of the Germans, Wotan, need not necessarily have given way to the God of the Christians; he could have been absolutely identified with him . . . for in him there was found this decisive analogy with Christ the Son of God that he too was killed and was then mourned and avenged as we ourselves still avenge the death of Christ on the Jews". R. Wagner, *Die Nibelungen, Œuvres*, Paris, Vol. II, p. 90.

251 Cf. *Leiden und Grösse Richard Wagners* (1932) and later *Wagner und unsere Zeit* (1940). In 1940 Th. Mann wrote: "I feel deeply moved when the sound of this music reaches my ear. . . . This must not make us forget that this

work, created and directed "against civilization", against the culture and the society which we have had since the Renaissance, was brought forth by the humanist-bourgeois period which was likewise the begetter of Hitlerism. ... From a spiritual point of view Wagner's work was a clear proclamation of that 'metapolitical' movement which today terrorizes the world". *Wagner und unsere Zeit*, Frankfurt 1963, p. 158.

252 Cf. A. Coeuroy, *Wagner et l'esprit romantique*, Paris 1965, in the "Idées" series, pp. 197-200.

253 In *Le cru et le cuit* (Paris 1964). C. Lévi-Strauss recalls "the service dedicated since childhood at the altars of the god Richard Wagner" (p. 23).

254 Cf. *Le regard sur la prairie:* "The prophet of Bayreuth came in his time to discipline those who no longer understood either dogmas or codes. Let us go to Wahnfried and on Wagner's tomb render homage to the intuitions of a universal ethic."

255 C. Mendès, "Notes sur la théorie et l'œuvre wagnériennes", *Revue wagnérienne*, I (1885), p. 33.

256 Von Wolzogen, "L'art aryen", *Revue . . .*, II (1886), pp. 70-80.

257 E. Dujardin, "Théories wagnériennes", *Revue . . .*, I (1885), p. 208.

258 Michel Domenach Espagnol, *L'apothéose musicale de la religion catholique, Parsifal de Wagner*, Barcelona 1902, p. 245. Cf. also pp. 1-3: "Wagner's Parsifal is a new and brilliant argument, in addition to the old ones, in favour of Religion . . .", etc.

259 "Discours sur l'antisémitisme"; cf. *Journal officiel*, report of the session of 27 May 1895.

260 Wagner's ideas are mostly to be found in the following writings: *Die Nibelungen, Das Judentum in der Musik, Religion und Kunst, Christentum und Heroismus*. Cf. his *Complete Works* and *Histoire de l'antisémitisme, op. cit.*, Vol. III.

261 Cf. *Histoire de l'antisémitisme*, III, pp. 440-67 ("Le cas de Richard Wagner").

262 *Die Vollendung des arischen Mysteriums in Bayreuth*, Munich 1911; *Die arische Religion*, Leipzig 1914.

263 *Die Vollendung . . .*, p. 211.

264 Cf. H. S. Chamberlain, *Briefe*, Munich 1928, Vol. I, pp. 169-70; letter of 26 December 1907.

265 *Ibid.*, p. 60; letter of 15 November 1897 to Hans von Wolzogen. Also the biography by L. von Schröder, *Houston Stewart Chamberlain, ein Abriss seines Lebens*, Munich 1919, p. 61.

266 *The Foundations of the Nineteenth Century*, London 1911, Vol. II, pp. 289-90.

267 *Ibid.*, Vol. II, pp. 20-25.

268 *Ibid.*, Vol. II, p. 291.

269 On the subject of these polemics, in which the Nobel prize-winners P. Lenard and J. Stark featured prominently, see L. Poliakov—J. Wulf, *Das Dritte Reich und seine Denker*, Berlin 1960, pp. 289-322.

270 Cf. *Briefe . . .*, I. p. 77. Cf. also the letter to L. von Schröder quoted above.

271 *La Génèse du XIXe siècle* (Preface to the 4th French ed.).

272 *The Foundations of the Nineteenth Century, op. cit.*, especially Vol. I, p. 204, 214, 467; Vol. II, p. 123.

273 *Ibid.*, Vol. I, p. 290. Immediately after a journey to Africa, Forel wrote: "It is in the interests of the Blacks themselves to take them for what they are and to treat them as an inferior race of mediocre value and, of itself, without culture. That is what needed saying, once and for all."

274 *Ibid.*, Vol. I, p. 569. Chamberlain was writing in this passage of the "fearful power of the Physis over Psyche" and quoted in support "the essays of Dr. Sigmund Freud" ("The Aetiology of Hysteria" and "Sexuality in the Aetiology of the Neuroses"), which "are the most interesting summaries of late years".

275 *Ibid.*, Vol. I, pp. 564-74, especially p. 571. (It was in this context that Freud was quoted.)

276 *Ibid.*, Vol. I, pp. 391-2.

277 *Ibid.*, Vol. I, p. 457.

278 *Ibid.*, Vol. I, p. 352.

279 *Ibid.*, Vol. I, pp. 330-31.

280 *Ibid.*, Vol. I, pp. 174-251 (Chap. III, "The Revelation of Christ").

281 *La Génèse du XIXe siècle*, trans. by R. Godet, Paris 1913 (Preface, p. xlii).

282 Cf. *Briefe . . .*, I, pp. 115-17 (Letter to J. F. Lehmann of 16 February 1903).

283 Letter from William II of 31 December 1901 (*Briefe . . .*, II, pp. 141-4).

284 Cf. R. Patry, *La religion dans l'Allemagne d'aujourd'hui, op. cit.*, p. 165.

285 Cf. Colin Holmes, "Houston Stewart Chamberlain in Great Britain", *The Wiener Library Bulletin*, XXIV, No. 2, 1970, pp. 31-6.

286 Quoted by R. Godet, *La Génèse au XIXe siècle*, Preface to the French ed., p. lxv.

287 Cf. Th. F. Gosset, *Race: The History of an Idea in America, op. cit.*, p. 352, p. 492.

288 M. Kufferath, "Les déments du pangermanisme, M. H. S. Chamberlain", *Revue bleue*, pp. 342-4.

289 "La faillite du Christianisme en Allemagne", *Revue bleue*, 1915, pp. 423-5.

290 H. Cohen, *Ein Bekenntnis in der Judenfrage*. Cf. *Der Berliner Antisemitismusstreit*, Walter Boehlich, Frankfurt a/M 1965, pp. 126 *et seq.*

291 Hermann Cohen, *Deutschtum und Judentum*, Giessen 1916, pp. 37-8.

292 Otto Weininger, *Geschlecht und Charakter*, Vienna 1905 (6th ed.), p. 411: "The most genuine Aryans, those who are most Aryan and most sure of their Aryanism are not anti-Semites . . . on the other hand, in the *aggressive* anti-Semite one can always detect certain Jewish traits even when his blood is free from any Semitic strain. . . . That is why the most violent anti-Semites are Jews. . . ."

293 *Ibid.*, p. 410.

294 *Ibid.*, p. 452.

295 *Ibid.*, p. 412.

296 *Höre Israel!* (under the pseudonym of W. Hartenau), "Die Zukunft", 6 March 1897.

297 *Von Schwachheit, Furcht und Zweck*. Cf. *Gesammelte Schriften*, Vol. IV, Berlin 1925, pp. 9-33.

298 *Kritik der Zeit*. Cf. Walther Rathenau, *Schriften*, Berlin 1965, pp. 144-54.

299 *Ibid.*, p. 151.

300 Quoted by H. Kessler, *Walther Rathenau*, Paris 1933, pp. 31-2. Cf. also the *Ungeschriebene Schriften*, "Assuming its Nordic origin, the Aryan race must be the most rigorous example of natural selection which exists." *Collected Works*, Vol. IV, pp. 222-3.

301 Rathenau, *Briefe*, Dresden 1927, Vol. I, pp. 202-203.

302 Vielen ist eine Seele geboren, alle können sie erringen. Die Seele wird jedem zuteil der *bonae voluntatis* ist. *Breviarium mysticum*, "Gesammelte Schriften", Vol. VIII, p. 171.

303 Cf. especially as to the psychology and motivation of Rathenau's murderers, Norman Cohn, *Warrant for Genocide, op. cit.*, pp. 159-61.

Conclusion

1 The relevant passage from Linnaeus which we have not quoted so far runs as follows: "It is said that Réaumur has fertilized a chicken with a rabbit. The eggs produced chicks which were like ordinary fowl except that instead of having feathers they were covered by white fur. The experiment is conclusive up to a point but we cannot draw general conclusions from such cases. Indeed the most appalling consequences might result from doing so. With regard to the human race one might be induced to think that Negroes have a rather peculiar origin but for my part I refuse to believe this." *Metamorphosis Plantarum*, 1755; cf. W. D. Jordan, *White over Black, op. cit.*, p. 236.

2 Cf. S. Freud, "*On Narcissism: an Introduction*" (1914) etc., and B. Grundberger, *Le narcissisme. Une étude psychoanalytique*, Paris 1971.

3 With reference to this aspect of the anti-religious polemic see Vol. III (*De Voltaire à Wagner*) of *Histoire de l'antisémitisme*.

INDEX